CATALOGUE OF CANADIAN COMPOSERS

Catalogue

of

Canadian Composers

EDITED BY

HELMUT KALLMANN, *Mus. Bac.*

Revised and Enlarged Edition

CENTRAL

CANADIAN BROADCASTING CORPORATION

Republished 1972
Scholarly Press, Inc., 22929 Industrial Drive East
St. Clair Shores, Michigan 48080

Library of Congress Catalog Card Number: 75-166240
ISBN 0-403-01375-5

Preface

IN 1947 *the CBC distributed a Catalogue of Canadian Composers. It had been compiled over a period of nearly five years under the guidance of the late Captain J. J. Gagnier and the then supervisor of music for the Corporation, Jean Beaudet. The catalogue contained the biographies and lists of compositions of 238 composers living at the time of inquiry and supplied much information not available from any other source. The catalogue met with enthusiastic response but the stock was limited and not all requests for copies could be met.*

Since 1947, composition in Canada has seen a most encouraging upward surge. New names have appeared and older composers have added important works to their lists. Performances of Canadian works have become more frequent not only in Canada but in many parts of the world. With the awakened interest in Canadian composition the need for a reference book on the subject has become more urgent; the CBC recognizes the great value of such a publication not only in Canada but increasingly so abroad. While realizing that the preparation of such a volume lay somewhat outside its usual field of activity, such a publication was considered so important at this time that the CBC has undertaken the responsibility. It is hoped that something of value will not only be available for the present, but for the future when others may be in a position to undertake the necessary revisions. The CBC is by far the greatest single performer and user of music in this country, and acutely aware of its responsibilities to Canadian composers; it was also recognized how valuable such a compilation would be in broadcasting operations.

For all these reasons it was felt that a revision of the catalogue was needed, and in June 1950 a new survey was begun under the supervision of Geoffrey Waddington, CBC Music Adviser. This made use of material already collected in the old catalogue, and extended the scope and framework in several directions. The final result is now offered to those interested.

The work could not have been accomplished without the foundation laid by Captain Gagnier and by Jean Beaudet, and the co-operation of various libraries in Canada; of organizations like the Composers, Authors and Publishers Association of Canada Limited, and BMI Canada Limited (Broadcast Music Incorporated), and the Canadian Music Council. There has been help from various CBC departments, and from the composers themselves, who have generally responded splendidly to inquiries.

Above all others in connection with this work, credit must be accorded to Helmut Kallmann, of the staff of the CBC's Music Library in Toronto, who added to his expert skill at this task an unflagging enthusiasm.

CHARLES JENNINGS
Assistant Director General of Programs, CBC

CONTENTS

INTRODUCTION

As IN THE CASE of other books of reference the raw material of the Catalogue of Canadian Composers determines the plan of arrangement of the book. The reader who would get full value is therefore advised to glance through the table of contents and to acquaint himself with the various new features in this revised edition. For instance, those with an historical interest in Canadian music will find the Historical Guide a useful key; those wishing to buy published works by Canadians will find the list of addresses of the principal Canadian music publishers of value; concert planners in search of, let us say, a ballet or a concerto will find the cross-index of large-scale works of help; those who must lecture or write about some phase of Canadian composition will welcome the Bibliography. It is wise also to keep in mind the various additional lists of composers. If the name of a given composer is not found in the Biographical Section which forms the main part of the book, it is quite possible that the name will appear in one of the added lists.

As in the first edition of the Catalogue, the selection of composers for the Biographical Section has been on generous principles for at least two reasons: the general lack of reference material on Canadian music and the impossibility of judging the worth of a composer by the mere titles or quantity of his or her works, especially when most of these works are in manuscript. *The Catalogue attempts to be as complete as possible a record of musical composition of serious aspiration in Canada, from the earliest-known examples up until the present time.* No doubt, musicians are included in the Biographical Section whose reputation as teachers or performers will far outlive their compositions, but their efforts should at least be recorded.

On the other hand, over one hundred musicians about whom little information could be gathered or whose output has been very small, or who are still in the student stage, have been merely mentioned in brief. Brief mention also had to do in the case of those who were born in Canada but left the country at an early age, those who resided here temporarily and those whose efforts lie entirely in the popular field.

To distinguish among these groups is not always easy. Thus some émigrés are listed in the Biographical Section because they have kept close ties with Canada. A few composers who are best known as popular song writers have nevertheless been included in the Biographical Section for their serious works.

Newcomers, even of fairly recent arrival in Canada, have been included as it is hoped they will make Canada their permanent home.

Altogether then one should keep in mind that the 356 names in the Biographical Section must remain a somewhat arbitrary total of the composers that Canada has produced or absorbed.

In compiling the lists of works by each individual composer listed in the Biographical Section we have not attempted to select from the information given to us by the living composers, but have reproduced their lists in full. Only in the case of smaller works in manuscript has summary treatment usually been adopted. Some composers have given us very complete information on their works while others have chosen only the most representative works. Some arrangements are also listed.

Knowledge of music written in Canada before 1900 is far from complete. Very few libraries or archives hold any deposits of old manuscripts and even music published in Canada in bygone days is almost unobtainable in our music libraries. The basic facts about early composition in Canada have been recorded here but further research may lead to many more discoveries.

Among the many sources consulted, the Dictionnaire biographique des musiciens canadiens and Thompson's International Cyclopedia of Music and Musicians take a front place. Sources have been carefully compared and discrepancies, which often were discovered, have been eliminated or noted. In spite of careful preparation, inaccuracies may be found; and in spite of careful search some names of Canadian composers may not have come to our attention. The CBC Toronto Music Library will be only too grateful to receive criticism and suggestions.

HELMUT KALLMANN

Toronto, January, 1952.

MUSIC IN CANADA

A Short Historical Guide

RECORDS of musical interest date back to the time of Canada's discovery and colonization by the French—to the travels of Cartier, to the colony of Port Royal with its "Order of Good Cheer" and to the foundation of Quebec as a centre of missionary and trading activity. In three and a half centuries Canada has passed through many phases of exploration and settlement, of political and industrial development. A powerful modern nation has emerged, through the efforts of people of greatly varied national origins and cultural traditions. Our musical history—from spontaneous singing to elaborate concerts—bears the stamp of this development. As in all newly-settled countries, there was at first little possibility for a musical life with distinctive local characteristics. The settlers continued, as it were, to breathe the musical atmosphere of their mother country, to reconstruct and adapt the musical patterns and customs that were habitual with them. The influence of the musically more advanced countries, constantly reinforced by the stream of immigrants, for a long time stifled any musical effort genuinely characteristic of the country. This explains, perhaps, why music in a newly-settled country, in reproductive, technical and organizational aspects, is ahead of the development of creative expression and of taste. It is only in recent years that composition has become a definite factor in our musical life, and that appreciation of fine music has become widespread.

One of the principal objects of the missionaries, who were among the first European settlers in Canada, was to befriend and convert the Indians. Music was found to be a most excellent means to this end. Many of the Fathers had musical training. The chants of the church were translated into native dialects and, on occasion, the Fathers would invent new tunes. The missionaries did not always manage to establish harmonious relations with the Indians, but their musical diplomacy had good results. To this day certain Indian tribes in Eastern Canada have preserved the chants taught to them three hundred years ago.

One composition written in Canada in the 17th century has been preserved—a setting of the "Sainte Famille" written by the Abbé

MARTIN*, and said to be a beautiful specimen of plain chant. But without doubt the greatest musical treasures that have been handed down to us from the earliest times of European settlement in Canada are the countless French folk songs which the immigrants brought with them. While many of the songs were modified by the new environment, many others have been preserved in a purer form than in the mother country.

Very little information exists about music in 18th-century Canada. For Canada the period was one of exploration, unrest, commercial rivalries, frequent warfare and even the uprooting of whole sections of the population. In 1760 the country finally passed under British rule and there started a constant stream of new immigrants of Anglo-Saxon origin, with their own traditions, settling in the Maritimes and in Ontario and gradually spreading westwards to the Pacific coast. Despite this, the French Canadians retained and continued to develop their own social, cultural and religious traditions.

The contrasts in temperament and the similarities in environment between the French and English Canadians have become a characteristic feature of our musical life. The French Canadians lived a more gregarious life; they had an innate love of song and dancing, and in later times their taste has favored opera. Isolated settlements, a shifting population and hostility to secular music among some religious sects discouraged art in early times among English-speaking Canadians. Yet the traditional British love of choral music took firm root and in certain parts of the country, (the Maritimes and Newfoundland, for example) a great fund of folk song has been kept alive.

As far as organization was concerned, music developed along much the same lines in the towns of both sections of the country. At first, musical activity centred around folk-singing and dancing, church service and the regimental band. From the resources of church choirs and military bands were formed our first musical societies. These performed choral and instrumental works, interspersed with solos by the best local talent. Visiting artists, orchestras and opera troupes followed, conservatories were established and native musicians with creative talent started to gain recognition. This, very briefly, was the pattern of musical development during the 19th century.

Instrumental music in the early period of the British regime in Canada was, in the main, provided by regimental bands stationed

---

*See Biographical Section (beginning on page 27) for further information about persons whose names appear in capitals.

in the garrison towns. Some officers took great pride in their bands which were used for many occasions; apart from military functions, they sometimes played on public squares, provided music for church services and social events of high society, and assisted in the rare theatrical and concert performances—which were usually of dubious quality. The beginnings of the theatre in Canada are associated with the name of QUESNEL. Quesnel's stage works with music, his poems and his musical compositions, had little to do with the Canadian scene. Society at that time was not sufficiently developed to provide an appreciative audience and, as a composer, Quesnel had no successor for several decades.

Many of the musicians of the early 19th century were German immigrants associated with the bands. GLACKEMEYER, BRAUNEIS Sr., and MOLT were among out first music teachers and importers of printed music and instruments.

As we approach the middle of the 19th century we find in the towns the beginnings of musical life as we know it in the modern city, with its musical organizations, its subscription concerts, its music teachers, critics, dealers and instrument manufacturers. These beginnings were stimulated by a rapid increase in population, improved transportation facilities and the growth of commercial life. Musical societies were formed in Quebec in 1820, in Montreal in 1837, in Halifax in 1842 and in Toronto in 1845. These bodies consisted of instrumental and, more frequently, of vocal forces which were built around the nucleus of a band or a church choir. They would meet for weekly practice during the winter season and give a number of concerts each year. However, these early musical societies never flourished very long and often were reorganized from season to season.

Undoubtedly the standard of performance was poor and public taste still little developed. Yet the concert programs of 90 and 100 years ago contain a good share of Handel, Haydn, Mozart and Weber, apart from the more fashionable Rossini, Bellini and Donizetti.

In the 1850's famous artists like Jenny Lind, Sigismund Thalberg and Henri Vieuxtemps performed in Canada and by 1870 all the larger towns had been visited by opera troupes. At the same time oratorios and even operas were presented with local talent.

Pianos were rare in those days and music lessons were considered fit only for young ladies. Professional careers were discouraged and the artist was looked upon with suspicion. Yet older native musicians like the pioneer of instrumental music SAUVAGEAU and the teacher BRAUNEIS, Jr., had achieved distinction and during the 1840's a number of musicians were born in Canada who gained great reputations in Canada or abroad, such as Gustave GAGNON, R. O. PELLETIER, VEZINA, LAVALLEE and Mme Albani (Emma LAJEUNESSE), one of the world's great prima donnas. It is noteworthy that French Canada with its older traditions produced musicians long before English Canada—which was not far behind in its concert life. In general, however, musical life in all Canada was dominated by the immigrant or foreign visitor whose superior training and musical heritage were eagerly welcomed. But, sometimes, unfortunately, this occurred at the expense of recognition for the native musician. Among the immigrants, SABATIER and DESSANE in French Canada and J. P. CLARKE in Toronto did much to help the cause of music.

The period from Confederation (1867) to the First Great War was one of gradual strengthening of musical life in Canada, a period not without its hard struggles and temporary setbacks. These were the great days of musical organizing, of "first in Canada" performances, of brave acts of musical faith on the part of musicians with initiative, vision and salesmanship. DESSANE, VEZINA and Arthur Lavigne in Quebec, Charles Porter in Halifax, COUTURE, R. O. PELLETIER and E. LAVIGNE in Montreal, Torrington, Edward Fisher and VOGT in Toronto—these men and many others were the pioneers in this period. With tireless energy they worked to create a taste for the great in music, to raise the standards of instrumental and choral performance and to establish a solid system of musical education. They persuaded artists like Hans von Buelow, Anton Rubinstein or Henri Wieniawski to perform for Canadian audiences (all before 1880) and invited the best American orchestras. The Union Musicale of Quebec and the philharmonic societies of Toronto and Montreal established high standards of performance. The Montreal society introduced to Canadians works like Beethoven's Ninth Symphony and Wagner's Tannhaeuser (in concert performance)—both performed with the assistance of American artists.

Canada shared the 19th-century love of big-scale enterprises. Music festivals with massed choirs of hundreds of singers and combined bands and orchestras were not rare. In 1878, 19 bands from many cities and towns participated in a competition-festival in Montreal; in western Ontario the German singing societies met for their *Saengerfeste* and memorable festivals were held in Quebec in 1883 and in Toronto in 1886.

However, musical enterprises, though launched with great enthusiasm, did not always meet with success. Amateur societies, musical magazines and conservatories mushroomed in the 80's and

90's only to disappear as fast as they had come, almost always due to weak finances and lack of public support. Music had to grow up in Canada without a sponsoring social class or official state support.

Regrettably, though perhaps naturally in a newly-opened country, musical taste tended to follow traditional European lines and composition was imitative of the sophisticated music of Europe. The folk music brought by the early settlers and still alive at that time, on which a national art might have been based, was ignored. Only in French Canada did music have an intimate link with patriotism, and folk song was not entirely forgotten there. In 1865, Ernest Gagnon published some of these tunes in his *Chansons populaires*, still the classic in its field. A number of musicians, starting with MOLT and SAUVAGEAU, contributed patriotic songs among which SABATIER's *Le Drapeau de Carillon*, J. B. LABELLE's *O Canada, mon pays, mes amours* and LAVIGUEUR's *La Huronne* have enjoyed great popularity. With Confederation, the need for a national Canadian song arose. Of many songs written to answer this need, two have won lasting favor: Alexander Muir's *The Maple Leaf Forever*, limited in its appeal to English Canadians, and LAVALLEE's *O Canada*. VEZINA's *Mosaïque* gives a summary of the French-Canadian songs which were most popular during the late 19th century.

Our knowledge of music written in Canada during the 19th century is still incomplete. There was little encouragement for composition, apart from band, dance and church music. LAVALLEE, like many of his Canadian contemporaries, studied in Paris. He was the first of our composers with an impressive (even though not fully known) list of works. Indeed, no Canadian has yet surpassed Lavallée in the variety of musical media and branches of composition. Other well-known composers in French Canada before the First Great War were CONTANT, COUTURE, FORTIER and A. TREMBLAY; the first Anglo-Canadians to be primarily interested in composition were FORSYTH, LUCAS and BRANSCOMBE. Most of the works of these composers were in the smaller forms, but there was a fair share of oratorio and operetta. It is surprising what a large proportion of Canadian compositions of that time succeeded in getting published.

Impetus to our musical life was also given by many immigrants. From Belgium came JEHIN-PRUME, J. J. Goulet and J. B. Dubois who pioneered in chamber and orchestral music in Montreal; and from England (between 1882 and 1913): HARRISS, BROOME, HAM, HORNER, H. C. Perrin, HEINS—and (still living) O'NEILL, ANDERSON, WHITEHEAD, SMITH and WILLAN. Most of these musicians came with a thorough background in church music and all of them have contributed to our musical life as organists, composers, teachers or conductors. Ties with Britain were also strengthened by visits of outstanding musicians such as Sir Alexander MacKenzie who conducted a series of festivals of British music across the country in 1903. These festivals brought music for the first time to many of the towns that had sprung up in the West. When we read of the hardships of the early pioneers on the Prairies, in the Rockies and on the West Coast, we do not think of cultural activities. Yet Winnipeg had its town band and Victoria its amateur orchestra before 1880, and most of the Western towns had some form of organized music within a very few years after they were founded.

The trend of musical expansion culminated in the decade before the outbreak of war in 1914. The amateur artist was disappearing from the concert stage and concert life began to assume a more cosmopolitan character. All the famous artists who toured on this continent could be heard in Canadian cities. In place of the old musical societies new ones appeared and choral and orchestral groups became separate units. Some of these bodies or their successors are still active today. After many unsuccessful attempts during the 90's, professional and amateur orchestras began to have a regular existence. In the choral field, Toronto held a leading position on the entire continent with its three or four large concert-giving groups, foremost among them the Mendelssohn Choir, while Montreal had an opera company that gave many weeks of performances for a number of years but depended heavily on foreign talent. Altogether, music prospered. The relative number of amateurs involved in music-making was undoubtedly greater than it is to-day. Canada had become a music-minded country. But, by and large, the musical life still lacked distinctive national characteristics.

With the end of the First Great War, these days of "musical prosperity" did not return; but several new forces emerged: the mechanical reproduction and transmission of music; the festival movement; immigration from a greater variety of countries bringing musicians of diverse background; the influx of American popular music; improved standards of musical training and performance; a revival of folk songs; and, most important, greater activity among composers at home.

Radio and the phonograph record helped tremendously to popularize music in a country where great distances and the sparse population discouraged visiting artists and put those outside the large centres at a great disadvantage, musically. Radio in particular has created a vast new audience of music lovers and it is an important binding force in Canada.

While the mechanical methods of reproducing music have led to a decline in amateur music-making, the musical programs of our schools and, above all, the competitive music festivals acted as a counterbalance. These festivals started in the West, in Alberta (1908) and Saskatchewan (1909) and have become great community forces in all the English-speaking parts of Canada.

At the same time the quality of performance has improved and the best of our orchestras and choirs can compete with those of any country. In the face of the ever-increasing variety of diversions, choral singing has somewhat declined in popularity but now appears to be experiencing a revival. Many of our large cities now have permanent orchestras although much more could be achieved with greater financial support. Among the countless musicians who held or hold leading positions in their own cities, there are (to mention only a few): J. J. GAGNIER, D. CLARKE and Wilfred Pelletier in Montreal; Edwin Bélanger and H. GAGNON in Quebec; Harry Dean in Halifax; von KUNITS, FRICKER, Ettore Mazzoleni and Sir Ernest MACMILLAN in Toronto; Gregory Garbovitski in Calgary; Vernon Barford in Edmonton; COLLINGWOOD in Saskatoon; and DE RIDDER in Vancouver; and the radio conductors Geoffrey Waddington and Jean Beaudet. Many Canadians have achieved fame chiefly outside Canada: Edward Johnson, Rodolphe Plamondon, Eva Gauthier as singers; Kathleen Parlow as a violinist; Ellen Ballon as a pianist; Lynwood Farnam as an organist; Percival PRICE as a carilloneur. On the other hand, a number of artists of international reputation have settled in Canada.

A great force in our recent musical life has been a revival of interest in the folk song, coming at a time when folk singing was on the verge of extinction. An Arctic expedition collected Eskimo songs in 1914-16 and thousands of songs—French, Indian and others— were collected in the following years by various scholars, foremost among them Marius Barbeau. Thus one of Canada's richest possessions has been preserved for future generations. Some of the songs are published in books, others are on non-commercial phonograph records or in notation in the National Museum of Canada at Ottawa and in other archives. In the villages of Quebec, on the coast of Nova Scotia and of Newfoundland and in the lumber camps across the country, many of the songs can still be heard. Among the men who popularized Canadian folk songs in the 1920's were James Murray

Gibbon and Charles Marchand; among the events were the folk song festivals in Quebec City.

Our musicians were not slow to take an interest in this movement. Many of the best of the period harmonized French or Indian folk songs: MACMILLAN, WILLAN, O'HARA, O'BRIEN, LALIBERTE, ROY, Pierre Gauthier and others. Prizes were awarded for compositions based on Canadian folk songs. CHAMPAGNE's *Suite Canadienne* is the best known of them.

But the influence extended further. Up to the 1920's most of our composers were trained abroad; and they were composers who happened to live in Canada, rather than "Canadian composers" by style or conviction. Partly through the revival of our folklore, partly through the growing national consciousness, composers began to strive for a specifically Canadian content in composition, or at least to ponder the possibility of doing so. Musical nationalism has not up to now developed into a great force, and our composers continue to be influenced by a variety of international currents. It is therefore hardly possible to observe distinct schools although there certainly are some composers whose works bear unique characteristics of style and expression—sometimes distinctly Canadian, and often drawing inspiration from Indian, Eskimo and French-Canadian themes, or from our landscape.

We have already mentioned the composers of British origin of the older generation. Among the first of our native composers to express themselves in a contemporary idiom were a number of French-Canadians (born between 1880 and 1900) who were often strongly influenced by French impressionism: CHAMPAGNE, J. J. GAGNIER, GRATTON, LALIBERTE, LAPIERRE, R. MATHIEU, MORIN, ROY, TANGUAY and others.

A generation with even more modernistic tendencies matured in the 1930's. Unlike that of most of the earlier composers, their background is usually secular and their training chiefly American or Canadian. Among those whose work is most often heard are ARCHER, BLACKBURN, BROTT, COULTHARD, DELA, GEORGE, PAPINEAU-COUTURE, PENTLAND, RIDOUT, VALLERAND and WEINZWEIG.

The 1940's yielded a very rich crop of composers but possibly it is too early to single out any of them by name. Our young composers have the advantage of advice from native composers versed in modern techniques, and of a vastly improved educational system on the school, conservatory and university levels. Nevertheless not a few of the young composers take advantage of scholarships and prizes that have been awarded more generously during the last decade to broaden their experience by study in the United States or in France.

Among the composers listed in this catalogue will also be found many who have specialized in writing for church services, for bands, for children and students. It is encouraging to notice a good number of amateur composers among our business men, farmers, housewives and the clergy. There are also composers of great gifts who have come to Canada in more recent years.

In the last decade Canada has become more self-sufficient in all musical matters but a great deal of pioneering remains to be done. It may, however, be said that later than painting and literature, musical composition in Canada has finally come of age. This development is obvious even from a glance at the statistical section of this catalogue or from a comparison with the first edition. But what is more encouraging than the mere quantity of our composers is the fact that so much of their music is good. At last the Canadian public is becoming aware of the existence of the Canadian composer and audiences in other American and in European countries are demanding to hear our music. Still, the situation for our composers is not ideal. Radio and film as well as certain other functional types of music provide an outlet for a number of them (see list on p. 248), but commissions and publications are not very frequent and few of our composers are able to devote sufficient time to composition. Performances and publications of Canadian works need to be multiplied and public curiosity stimulated. Perhaps this catalogue can in its way help to make Canadian music better known and understood. Its purpose will be fulfilled only when the music listed here in silent print—or at least the best of it—is transformed into living sound.

—H.K.

COMPOSITION IN CANADA

A Bibliography

BMI CANADA LIMITED, biographies and lists of works of many Canadian composers available on request.

BRIDLE, Augustus, Composers Among Us. (Year Book of the Arts in Canada, 1928-29)

BRIDLE, Augustus, Who Writes Our Music? a survey of Canadian composers. (Maclean's Magazine, vol. 42, Dec. 15, 1929)

CANADIAN MUSIC, a list of, published for The Canadian Federation of Music Teachers Associations by the Oxford University Press, 1946.

THE CANADIAN REVIEW OF MUSIC AND ART, 1942-48.

CATALOGUE OF CANADIAN COMPOSERS, Canadian Broadcasting Corporation, (first edition, 1947)

HOULE, Léopold, *Nos compositeurs de musique.* (Royal Society of Canada, Transactions, 1946)

LEVASSEUR, Nazaire, *Histoire de la musique et des musiciens à Québec.* (La Musique, 1919-23)

LOGAN, John Daniel, *Canadian Creative Composers.* (Canadian Magazine, September, 1913)

LOGAN, John Daniel, *Musical Composition in Canada.* (The Year Book of Canadian Art, 1913)

MACMILLAN, Sir Ernest, *Musical Composition in Canada.* (Culture, 1942)

MORIN, Léo-Pol, *Papiers de musique.* (Published in Montreal, 1930)

MUSICAL CANADA, 1906-33.

PAPINEAU-COUTURE, Jean, *Que sera la musique canadienne?* (Amerique Française, 1942)

PENTLAND, Barbara, *Canadian Music, 1950.* (Northern Review, 1950)

ROY, Leo, *Quebec Composers.* (Musical Canada, 1930)

SAMINSKY, Lazarre, *Canadian Youth.* (Modern Music, November-December 1941)

SAMINSKY, Lazarre, *Living Music of the Americas.* (Published in New York, 1949)

SOEURS DE SAINTE-ANNE, *Dictionnaire biographique des musiciens canadiens.* (Published in Lachine, P.Q., 1935)

WALTER, Arnold, *Canadian Composition.* (Music Teachers National Association, Proceedings, U.S.A., 1946)

FOLK SONG IN CANADA

A Bibliography

BARBEAU, Marius, *Alouette!*, Montreal, 1946.

BARBEAU, Marius, *Come A'Singing!*, Ottawa, 1947 (with Arthur Lismer and Arthur Bourinot).

BARBEAU, Marius, *Folk-Songs of Old Quebec*, Ottawa, 1936.

BARBEAU, Marius, *Romancero du Canada*, Montreal, 1937.

BARBEAU, Marius, and SAPIR, Edward, *Folk-Songs of French Canada*, New Haven, 1925.

CREIGHTON, Helen, *Songs and Ballads from Nova Scotia*, Toronto, 1932.

CREIGHTON, Helen and SENIOR, Doreen H., *Traditional Songs from Nova Scotia*, Toronto, 1950.

DOYLE, Gerald S., *Old-Time Songs and Poetry of Newfoundland*, St. John's, Nfld., 1940.

GAGNON, Ernest, *Chansons populaires du Canada*, Montreal, 1865, 1947.

GIBBON, Murray, *Canadian Folk Songs (Old and New)*, Toronto, 1927, 1949 (with Geoffrey O'Hara and Oscar O'Brien).

GREENLEAF, Elizabeth Bristol, and MANSFIELD, Grace Yarrow, *Ballads and Sea Songs of Newfoundland*, Cambridge, Mass., 1933.

KARPELES, Maud, *Folk Songs from Newfoundland*, Oxford University Press, 1934.

MACKENZIE, William Roy, *Ballads and Sea Songs from Nova Scotia*, Cambridge, Mass., 1928.

ROBERTS, Helen and JENNESS, D., *Eskimo Songs*, Song of the Copper Eskimos, Ottawa, 1925.

PRINCIPAL CANADIAN MUSIC PUBLISHERS

referred to in the Biographical Section

ANGLO CANADIAN MUSIC CO., 1261 Bay Street, Toronto, Ont.

ED. ARCHAMBAULT, INC., 500 St. Catherine Street East, Montreal, P.Q.

LA BONNE CHANSON, St. Hyacinthe, P.Q.

BOOSEY & HAWKES, 209 Victoria Street, Toronto, Ont.

A. J. BOUCHER, 1769 Amherst Street, Montreal, P.Q.

BMI CANADA LIMITED, 229 Yonge Street, Toronto, Ont., and 1500 St. Catherine Street West, Montreal, P.Q.

CANADIAN MUSIC SALES, 1261 Bay Street, Toronto, Ont.

CHAPPELL & CO., 1263 Bay Street, Toronto, Ont.

EDITIONS CANADIENNES (See A. J. BOUCHER, above)

A. FASSIO PUBLICATIONS, Lachute, P.Q.

FREDERICK HARRIS CO., Oakville, Ont.

JARMAN PUBLICATIONS LIMITED, 80 Richmond Street East, Toronto, Ont.

MELLO-MUSIC PUBLISHING CO., 507-314 Broadway Avenue, Winnipeg, Man.

MUSICA ENR., Blvd. Jarry, St. Martin, Laval Co., P.Q.

MUSIQUE CANADIENNE, 4519 Berri, Montreal, P.Q.

OXFORD UNIVERSITY PRESS, 480 University Avenue, Toronto, Ont.

LE PARNASSE MUSICAL (A. Fassio), Lachute, P.Q.

PASSE-TEMPS, INC., Les Editions du, 218 Notre Dame Street West, Montreal, P.Q.

PROCURE GENERALE DE MUSIQUE, ENR., 9 rue d'Aiguillon, Quebec, P.Q.

SOUTHERN MUSIC PUBLISHING CO., 1231 St. Catherine Street West, Montreal, P.Q.

GORDON V. THOMPSON, 902 Yonge Street, Toronto, Ont.

WATERLOO MUSIC CO., Waterloo, Ont.

WESTERN MUSIC CO., 570 Seymour Street, Vancouver, B.C., and 229 Yonge Street, Toronto, Ont.

WHALEY ROYCE & CO., 310 Yonge Street, Toronto, Ont.

CANADIAN COMPOSERS' ORGANIZATIONS

BMI CANADA LIMITED (Broadcast Music Incorporated)
229 Yonge Street, Toronto, Ont.
1500 St. Catherine Street West, Montreal, P.Q.

BMI Canada Limited is a music publishing and performing rights organization. It was activated in 1947 in affilation with Broadcast Music Incorporated in the United States and is under joint direction of the Canadian Broadcasting Corporation and the Canadian Association of Broadcasters. Its purpose is to publish Canadian music and to help make Canada's own composers and their music more widely known both on this continent and abroad. BMI Canada Limited has so far published about one hundred serious compositions by over thirty Canadians, and about three hundred popular compositions. Several Canadian publishing houses have become affiliated with BMI Canada Limited.

THE CANADIAN LEAGUE OF COMPOSERS
  c–o John Weinzweig, 101 Belgravia Road, Toronto, Ont.

This organization was formed in 1951 by a number of composers across Canada. Its object is to stimulate by all possible means the performance of Canadian music both at home and abroad and to act as a central administrative organization for information and education research. It aims at giving composers closer contact with each other and their writing and promoting creative effort. It also wants to see that Canada is adequately represented in international festivals.

COMPOSERS, AUTHORS AND PUBLISHERS ASSOCIATION OF CANADA
  LIMITED (CAPAC)
  132 St. George Street, Toronto, Ont.

The Composers, Authors and Publishers Association of Canada (CAPAC) was established in 1925, to collect fees for the public performance of the copyright musical works of its members and to restrain unauthorized performances. All fees collected are distributed among the composers, authors and publishers concerned, in proportion to the relative use of their works. No expenses are deducted from the fees collected beyond the cost of administration. The Association has its counterpart in almost every civilized country and, by virtue of affiliation agreements, it controls in Canada the performing rights in the compositions of the members of other such national societies. Similarly, the fees due Canadian composers and authors, who are members of CAPAC, for performance of their works abroad, are collected by the foreign societies and remitted to CAPAC for distribution to the Canadian members.

RECORDINGS

Commercially available records are listed under the individual composer's name. In addition, the CBC International Service has recordings that are available to embassies and radio stations through its transcription service. These recordings include works by Adaskin, Bales, Betts, Blackburn, Brott, Champagne, Coulthard, Freedman, J. J. Gagnier, H. Gagnon, Gratton, McMullin, Mercure, Morawetz, Morel, Papineau-Couture, Pentland, Pepin, Perrault, Rathburn, Somers, Weinzweig and Willan.

The CBC Canadian Album No. 3 is still in preparation at the time this book goes to press.

STATISTICAL SUMMARY OF CANADIAN COMPOSERS

OF THE 356 composers listed in the Biographical Section, 229 were born in Canada, 127 outside Canada. Five were born before 1800, approximately 186 were born during the 19th century and approximately 165 during the 20th century. Of 356, approximately 290 are alive.

Of those born in Anglo-Saxon countries, 68 were born in England, 7 in Scotland, 2 in Wales and 1 on Guernsey. Of those born in continental Europe, 6 were born in Belgium, 6 in France (counting Sabatier as a Frenchman), 5 in Russia, 3 in Italy, 3 in Germany (all 3 before 1800), 3 in what is now Czechoslovakia, 2 each in Hungary, Austria and Holland, 1 each in Poland, Latvia and Spain.

Of 229 Canadian-born composers the following have done part of their musical studies outside Canada (figures are approximate and overlap where a student has studied in two or more countries): 50 in the United States, 45 in France, 12 in England, 11 in Germany, 6 in Belgium, 3 in Italy, 2 each in Austria and Switzerland, 1 in Hungary.

Of 356 composers, 52 are women.

Of 356 composers, 54 have a doctor of music degree (earned or honorary), 1 has a doctor of philosophy degree in music.

Some of the earliest composers in Canada, in order of date of birth are:

Martin; Quesnel; Glackemeyer; Brauneis, Sr.; Molt; J. P. Clarke; Sauvageau; Brauneis, Jr.; Sabatier; Dessane; Perreault; J. B. Labelle.

The earliest composers from each province:

Quebec	Martin
Ontario	Vogt
New Brunswick	Sheppard
Nova Scotia	Burchell and MacIntosh
Prince Edward Island	Poirier
Manitoba	Standing
British Columbia	Coulthard
Alberta	McLeod and Strang (Now in U.S.A.)
Saskatchewan	Harmer
Newfoundland	None

Of the approximate number of 290 living composers, 259 resided in Canada late in 1950. Seventy-one lived in Montreal and vicinity; 57 in Toronto; 13 in Ottawa; 11 in Quebec City; 9 in Winnipeg and 9 in Vancouver. One hundred and six lived in the Province of Quebec; 95 in Ontario; 16 in British Columbia; 13 in Alberta; 11 in Manitoba; 8 in New Brunswick; 5 in Nova Scotia; 4 in Saskatchewan and 1 on Prince Edward Island. Of 31 residing outside Canada late in 1950, 19 lived in the United States; 8 in Paris (mostly students who will return to Canada) and 4 in various European countries.

A Statistical Table of Canadian Composers According to Place and Time of Birth

(based on the Biographical Section of the Catalogue of Canadian Composers)

Place of Birth	–1700	1700 1799	1800 1819	1820 1829	1830 1839	1840 1849	1850 1859	1860 1869	1870 1879	1880 1889	1890 1899	1900 1909	1910 1919	1920 1929	Since 1930	Total
Greater Montreal				1		1	4	3	4	2	7	9	13	8		52
Quebec City	1		2		2	1				2	3	1	2	1		15
All Prov. of Quebec (Lower Canada till 1867)	1		2	1	2	6	5	4	8	11	25	22	20	14	1	122
Toronto										2	1	7	9	4	1	24
All Ontario (Upper Canada till 1867)								4	2	13	8	15	15	7	2	66
Nova Scotia (after 1867)										2	2			1		5
Prince Edward Island (after 1873)										1			2	1		4
Newfoundland																0
New Brunswick (after 1867)								1		1			3			5
Manitoba (after 1870)											2		2	1		5
Saskatchewan (after 1905)													3	5		8
Alberta (after 1905)												1	5			6
British Columbia (after 1871)												1	3	4		8
All Canada	1		2	1	2	6	5	9	10	28	37	39	53	33	3	229
Great Britain*		4	1			1	2		15	17	17	11	7	3		78
Continental Europe				2	2			5	4	4	6	7	4	1		35
United States				1		1			1	1	6	3	1			14
All Immigrants		4	1	3	2	2	2	5	20	22	29	21	12	4		127
All Composers	1	4	3	4	4	8	7	14	30	50	66	60	65	37	3	356

*Including Channel Islands.

Note: In those few cases where the birth-date of a composer is not known, an approximate decade has been assumed.

CANADIAN COMPOSERS AND THEIR WORKS

THE ARRANGEMENT of compositions under each composer in the following Biographical Section is according to type and scoring of composition. Large scale and instrumental works are usually listed first, choral and vocal works at the end. Sub-headings according to type and scoring of composition are used in the case of long lists.

In describing the scoring of a work no distinction is made between the terms *strings* and *string orchestra*. By *vocal* are understood works for solo voice. Works described simply as *vocal* or *choral* may or may not have accompaniment.

The letters *MS.* mean manuscript. In the case of deceased composers *MS.* merely refers to the fact that, so far as is known, the work was never published but does not necessarily imply that the manuscript is still preserved. Likewise, the name of a publisher does not imply that the composition is still in print or that the publisher is still in business.

Dates given with the name of the publisher refer to the year of publication.

A blank space in any column indicates that the information is either unknown or unavailable.

The Toronto Conservatory of Music changed its name in 1946 to Royal Conservatory of Music of Toronto. Throughout this catalogue the conservatory is referred to as *Royal Conservatory, Toronto*.

Likewise, the Canadian Performing Rights Society is always referred to under its present name *CAPAC* (Composers, Authors and Publishers Association of Canada Limited.)

The Conservatoire de Musique et d'Art Dramatique de la Province de Québec is referred to as *Quebec Provincial Conservatory*. Most French-Canadian institutions are referred to under the French name.

Although the degrees of bachelor of music and doctor of music are given different abbreviations by various universities, the standard abbreviations *Mus.Bac.* and *Mus.Doc.* are used throughout.

Under *Affiliation* is indicated the membership of a composer in one of the performing rights societies: BMI, CAPAC (see p. 22) and ASCAP (American Society of Composers, Authors and Publishers).

Abbreviations for Diplomas

A.C.C.O.	Associate Canadian College of Organists
A.R.A.M.	Associate Royal Academy of Music
A.R.C.M.	Associate Royal College of Music
A.R.C.O.	Associate Royal College of Organists
A.R.C.T.	Associate Royal Conservatory of Music, Toronto
A.T.C.L.	Associate Trinity College of Music, London
A.T.C.M.	Associate Toronto Conservatory of Music (now A.R.C.T.)
F.C.C.O.	Fellow Canadian College of Organists
F.R.C.M.	Fellow Royal College of Music
F.R.C.O.	Fellow Royal College of Organists
F.T.C.L.	Fellow Trinity College of Music, London
G.R.S.M.	Graduate of the Royal Schools of Music
L.A.B.	Licentiate of the Associated Board (now L.R.S.M.)
L.L.C.M.	Licentiate London College of Music
L.R.A.M.	Licentiate Royal Academy of Music
L.R.C.T.	Licentiate Royal Conservatory of Music, Toronto
L.R.S.M.	Licentiate Royal Schools of Music
L.T.C.L.	Licentiate Trinity College of Music, London
L.T.C.M.	Licentiate Toronto Conservatory of Music (now L.R.C.T.)

Ackland, Jeanne Isabel Dorothy

Pianist, Hammond organist, violinist and composer. Born in Calgary, Alta.

Studied at Columbia University, N.Y. Private teachers: Gregori Garbovitski and Jessie Ackland. Member of the Calgary Junior Symphony Orchestra for seven years. Composed and played background music for radio plays for Canadian Cancer Society and other documentary plays since 1948. Winner of the Song of the Week Contest, in connection with a commercial radio program.

Address: 819 17th Avenue West, Calgary, Alta.

COMPOSITIONS

TITLE	DATE	TYPE	TIME (MIN.)	PUBLISHER
Lavender, Lace and Love	1950	*musical comedy*		MS.
Tut	1951	*operetta*		MS.
Sonata in C minor	1935	*orchestra or piano*	20	MS.
Sonata in G minor	1935–36	*orchestra or piano*	20	MS.
Valse Grace	1945	*piano and organ*	3	MS.
Valse Barbara	1948	*piano and organ*	3	MS.
Tango d'Amour	1945	*piano and organ*	2½	MS.
Camille	1948	*piano and organ*	3	MS.
Danza Cubana	1938	*2 or 1 piano*	5	M.S.
Tango Tzigane	1940	*2 or 1 piano*	3	MS.

Piano pieces in manuscript:

Concerto in C minor (1st mvmt); *Flight; Country Dance; Reminiscing; Sleigh Ride; Valse Triste; The Chimes; In Sunny Spain;* Minuet; *Humoresque;* Chinese Suite; *California; Morocco; Song My Fiddle Plays; Berceuse; Trois Petites Valses; Dedication; Buster Brown; Nautical Sketches.*

Songs in manuscript:

Dawn in Vienna; A Fairy Ship; Scottish Love Song; Two Lullabies; Sister O'Mine; A Prayer; A Tribute; Evensong; Come Along Canadians; University of Alberta Song; Salute to Australia; Our Empire; Defenders of the Air.

Many popular songs.

Ackland, Jessie Agnes

Pianist, music teacher and composer. Born in Ontario.

Musical education with Annie Glen Broder in Calgary, with Ernest Hutcheson and Rossiter G. Cole in New York. Specializes in music teaching (piano, harmony and history). Diploma: L.R.S.M.

Address: 819 17th Avenue West, Calgary, Alta.

COMPOSITIONS

TITLE	DATE	TYPE	TIME (MIN.)	PUBLISHER
Cottage of Dreams		*vocal*	2½	Musart Co., Chicago
By Night, By Day		*vocal*		MS.
Bluebirds		*vocal*		MS.
Lullaby of Flowers		*vocal*		MS.
Theme Song		*vocal*		MS.

Many other pieces for violin, piano, 'cello, voice and two-piano arrangements:

Berceuse; Rose of the Desert; Sea Song; Maid of Spain; My Dream Ship; Ballet; Irish Melody; Lilacs; Coquette; Canadian March, etc.

Adaskin, Murray

Composer and violinist. Born in Toronto, March 28th, 1906.

Musical education at Royal Conservatory, Toronto, Ecole Normale, Paris, and Music Academy of the West, California. Studied composition with John Weinzweig, Charles Jones and Darius Milhaud.

In radio since 1920. Musical director, Royal York Hotel, Toronto. Member of American Musicological Society.

Address: 27 Winchester Street, Toronto, Ont.

Affiliation: CAPAC.

COMPOSITIONS

TITLE	DATE	TYPE	TIME (MIN.)	PUBLISHER
Ballet Symphony	1951	orchestra	24	MS.
Suite for Orchestra	1947	orchestra	15	MS.
Suite for Strings	1948	string orchestra	14	MS.
Sonata	1946	vln and piano	15	MS.
Canzona and Rondo	1949	vln and piano	8	MS.
Sonata	1950	piano	9	MS.
Epitaph	1947	vocal		MS.

Addison, Laidlaw Fletcher

Double-bass player, bandmaster and composer. Born in Hamilton, July 4th, 1878. Died in Toronto, August 1949.

Musical education with Arthur W. Hughes (theory), with own father and W. Anderson (violin). Toured with the Kilties Band of Canada as musical director in 1906. Was director of music with the Canadian Machine Gun Corps in World War I and continued to be active in band work. For about 15 years was director of Toronto Symphony Band, besides playing double-bass in Toronto Symphony and Philharmonic Orchestras.

COMPOSITIONS

TITLE	DATE	TYPE	TIME (MIN.)	PUBLISHER
Sunshine (waltz)		orchestra		MS.
Love (waltz)		orchestra		MS.

Marches for band (all in manuscript, about 3 minutes each):
Echo Park; Elwood; Fort York; Grandeur of the Rockies; Acting Rank; Spark Plug; The Grenadiers; Sunnyside; Muskoka; Rossmoyne; Good Old Ontario.

Adeney, Marcus

Violoncellist, poet and composer. Born in London, England, July 1st, 1900.

Studied 'cello with Leo Smith, Boris Hambourg and others. Came to Canada in 1904. Has done literary and critical work for Canadian Forum, Canadian Bookman, Saturday Night, Canadian Review of Music and Art. Poetry is published in periodicals and n *The Book of Canadian Poetry.* Was 'cellist with the Detroit Symphony, 1923-24, with Toronto Symphony Orchestra, 1926-48. For several years was member of Hambourg Trio and now is member of Solway String Quartet. Is program annotator for Toronto Symphony Orchestra.

Address: 18 Fallingbrook Road, Toronto, Ont.

COMPOSITIONS

TITLE	DATE	TYPE	TIME (MIN.)	PUBLISHER
Three Irish Tunes (from Joyce Collection)	1933	'cello and piano	9	MS.
Elegie	1933	'cello and piano	4	MS.
From the Lake of Bays	1948	'cello solo	5	MS.
Three Children's Songs (Joan Easdale)	1931	vocal	8	MS.
The Gallant's Song (Thomas Hardy)	1932	vocal	3	MS.

Agostini, Giuseppe

Conductor, clarinetist, oboist and composer. Bcrn in Fano, Italy, May 20th, 1890.

Musical education at Rossini Conservatory of Music, Pesaro, Italy under Calestani (oboe and theory). Came to Canada in 1915. Was conductor in principal theatres in Montreal for ten years. Conductor of bands in and around Montreal. Conductor and arranger cf feature radio programs since 1933.

Address: 6831 Drolet Street, Montreal, P.Q.

COMPOSITIONS

TITLE	DATE	TYPE	TIME (MIN.)	PUBLISHER
Le Venredi Saint		orchestra	3½	MS.
Lost Forever (tone poem)		orchestra	5	MS.
Le Rêve de Noël (waltz)		orchestra	6	MS.
Melody		Eng. hn and orchestra	4	MS.
Ave Maria		voice and orch.	3	MS.
		or piano	3	Parnasse Musical
Buio		voice and orch.	3	MS.
Let Me Dream		voice and orch.	3	MS.
The Three Trumpeters		band	3	Boosey & Hawkes
The Three Clarinets		band	4	MS.
Four Festival Overtures	1937–41	band	ea. 9	MS.
Viola (suite)		band	9	MS.
Marcia funebre		organ		Passe-Temps
Eternamente (tango)		4 vlns, piano		Parnasse Musical
Griserie		vocal		Parnasse Musical
Reviens, reviens		vocal		Parnasse Musical

Agostini, Lucio

Conductor, composer, violoncellist, pianist, clarinetist and saxophonist. Born in Fano, Italy, December 30th, 1913.

Musical education with Giuseppe Agostini, Louis Michaels, Enrique Miro (harmony, composition etc.) Peter van der Meerschen ('cello). Came to Canada in 1915. Has been active as arranger, composer and conductor of radio programs since the age of 15 and on the CBC networks for the last 13 years. Composed and conducted all music for *Canada at War* and *World in Action* pictures produced by the National Film Board and for CBC drama series from Toronto, *Stage 44* to *Stage 51*. Musical director of Associated Screen News, Montreal. Son of Giuseppe Agostini.

Address: 176 Morningside, Swansea, Ont.

Affiliation: CAPAC.

COMPOSITIONS

TITLE	DATE	TYPE	TIME (MIN.)	PUBLISHER
Concerto	1948	piano, voices, orchestra	30	MS.
Pickwick Papers (tone-poem)	1948	orchestra	15	MS.
Elegie		orchestra	3	MS.
Subway		orchestra	4	MS.
The Ghost Speaks		orchestra	4	MS.
Scherzo		orchestra	6½	MS.
Pizzicato Rhumba	1951	orchestra	4	MS.
Full Speed Ahead	1951	orchestra	4	MS.
An Eye for an Eye	1951	orchestra	4	MS.
Caramba	1951	orchestra	4	MS.
Shakespearean String Suite	1948	string orchestra	18	MS.

About 200 half-hour scores of incidental music for radio plays such as: *Dear Mr. Axis; My Own, My Native Land; The Fir Tree; The Lion and the Mouse; Tommy Tucker; Mrs. Arcularis; The Rhyme of the Ancient Mariner; Willie the Squowse; Romeo and Juliet*, etc.

About 300 short descriptive numbers for radio such as machines, engines, orientals, weirds and others.

Albani, Emma

(see: Lajeunesse, Emma)

Aldous, John Edmund Paul

Organist, conductor and composer. Born in Sheffield, England, 1853. Died in Hamilton, January 23rd, 1934.

Degree: B.A. (Cambridge). Came to Canada in 1877, settling in Hamilton as organist. Conducted the Hamilton Philharmonic Society for two years and started an orchestral club in the 1880's. Examiner for University of Toronto. Member of board of governors, Hamilton Conservatory of Music, 1914-18.

COMPOSITIONS

TITLE	DATE	TYPE	TIME (MIN.)	PUBLISHER
Four Light Operas		light opera		MS.
String Quartet		string quartet		MS.
Trio		vln, vc, piano		MS.
Prelude and Fugue		organ		published
Minuet		organ		Ashdown
Magnificat and Nunc Dimittis		choral		Vincent

Anthems, songs, pieces for piano and harp.

Allard, Emilien

Pianist, clarinetist and composer. Born in Montreal, June 12th, 1915.

Musical education in Three Rivers with Antonio Thompson (piano and theory). Degree: Lauréat (Laval Univ.). Diploma: L.Mus. (Conservatoire National, Montreal).

Address: 732 5th Avenue, Grand'Mère, P.Q.

COMPOSITIONS

TITLE	DATE	TYPE	TIME (MIN.)	PUBLISHER
Légende		orchestra	4	MS.
Scherzo, Op. 5		strings	6½	MS.
Marche du commandant		band	4	MS.
Fugue		fl, vln, clar		MS.
Allegro		vln and piano	6	MS.
Vieux Conte		vln and piano	6	MS.
Adagio; Moderato; Andante; Andantino; Variations, Op. 3		piano		MS.
Ave Maria; O Salutaris; De Profundis		vocal		MS.

No recent information obtained.

Ambrose, Paul

Organist and composer. Born in Hamilton, October 11th, 1869. Died in Hamilton, June 1st, 1941.

Musical education with own father, Robert Ambrose and others. When 18 went to United States but returned to Canada in his later years. Was organist in New York and Trenton, N.J. Was director of music at State Normal School, Trenton and since 1939 president of Canadian College of Organists.

COMPOSITIONS

TITLE	DATE	TYPE	TIME (MIN.)	PUBLISHER
To-morrow Comes the Song		vocal		Arthur P. Schmidt
In Heavenly Love		vocal		Arthur P. Schmidt
Master, I Would Follow Thee		vocal		Theodore Presser
O Master, Let Me Walk With Thee		vocal		Theodore Presser
If Any Little Word		vocal		Theodore Presser

Many other songs, anthems, piano and organ pieces. Altogether over 200 works.

Anderson, William Henry

Vocalist, conductor and composer. Born in London, England, April 21st, 1882.

Musical education with private teachers (voice and composition) and on scholarship at Guildhall School of Music. Came to Canada in 1910, settling in Winnipeg where he has since been active as conductor, examiner, teacher, lecturer and composer. Has conducted *The Choristers* for the CBC for the last thirteen years.

Address: 257½ Young Street, Winnipeg, Man.

Affiliation: CAPAC.

COMPOSITIONS AND ARRANGEMENTS

TITLE	PUBLISHER

Choral works for mixed voices:

Five Christmas Carols (in book "Gallilee"); The Christmas Rose; The World's Desire — H. W. Gray & Co.

The Mother and Child; O for a Closer Walk; Easter Joy; At the Manger — G. Schirmer

In Praise of Christmas; Greensleeves (English folk song); The Holy Child — C. C. Birchard & Co.

Come I Pray Thee; Born of Marie; Carol O Ye Angels; A Quiet Corner; Wassail Song; Cradle Hymn; Give Ear to My Prayer; Come O Thou Fount (Gluck); Prayer of Thanksgiving (Dutch); With Songs of Joy We Welcome (Besançon); This Is the Day (Besançon); O Little Children, Lead Us Now; Hark All Around; Ane Song of the Birth of Christ; Joy Fills Our Inmost Heart; Christmas Questionings; Send Her on Along (French Canadian folk song); O Lord of All (Handel's Largo); The Sleep of the Holy Child; Liberty — Western Music

O Brother Man; In the Silence of the Winter Night (Ippolitoff-Ivanoff) — Th. Presser

If Thou but Suffer God to Guide Thee; Bread of the World; Come Holy Ghost, Our Souls Inspire — Carl Fischer

Everyman (incidental music); Christmas in Heaven; Maranoa Cradle Song (Australian Aboriginal) — MS.

Choral works for men's voices:

A Prayer for these Days — C. C. Birchard & Co.

Whence O Shepherd Maiden (French Canadian folk song); I Have Culled a Lovely Rosebud (ditto) — Galaxy Music Corp.

Send Her on Along (French Canadian folk song); Soldiers' Song — Western Music and W. Paxton & Co.

Choral works for two sopranos and alto:

Fairest Isle (arranged from Purcell); Praise the Lord (ditto); The White Dove; All Through the Night (Welsh); Twilight; Evening Prayer (arranged from Humperdinck); Scarlet Sarafan (Russian); Katarina (Ukrainian); Long, Long Ago; Liberty; Berceuse (Rebikoff); Gaelic Croon (Scottish); A Memory; The Children's Friend; Golden Slumbers (old English); Wind in the Lilacs; Piper Wind; Bird in the Nest; Good Night Beloved (Czechoslovakian); Once a Cuckoo Bird (Ukrainian); The Bird's Song (Swedish); Mary; As Mary Sings; Christmas Gifts; Lullay My Likin'; O Little Children, Lead Us — Western Music

The Loveliest Picture; Swallow Song; Our Master Hath a Garden; Sing Loud, Sing Low — Carl Fischer

Whence O Shepherd Maiden — Galaxy Music Corp.

To Immortality; Christmas Blessings — Arnolds, London

The Sea-Blue Gardens — Oxford Univ. Press

Fairyland — Boosey & Hawkes

To a Bluebell — Stainer & Bell

Madonna's Cradle Song — C. C. Birchard & Co.

Sleep Little Jesus — Western Music and W. Paxton & Co.

Maranoa Cradle Song (Australian Aboriginal); Lullaby of the Little Angels — MS.

Choral works for soprano and alto:

Sweet and Low; Spring Is Here; Cuckoo Song (Ukrainian); Come O Thou Fount (Gluck); In the Fall of the Year; The Birth Night; Sweet Afton; Carol, O Ye Angels; Steal Away, Little Birds — Western Music

Fairy Ring — Western Music and W. Paxton & Co.

Pease-porridge Tawny — Oxford Univ. Press

Choral works in unison:

Sleep Little Jesus; Fire Bird; Sweet Afton; Lady May; Meadows and Maidens; In the Garden Flowers Are Growing; Cradle Song (Icelandic); Liberty; 'Twas in the Silent Night He Came; Song for a Baby Sister; Sweet Nightingale; Margery Maketh the Tea; The Spider Hunter; Sing Ivy; A Child's Prayer; Alone (Ukrainian); Fairies in the Moonlight (Icelandic); The Ivy Green; Long, Long Ago; Popping Corn; To a Baby Brother; Torchbearers; several French Canadian, English and Irish songs — Western Music

Mary — Arnolds, London

Skipping Song — Stainer & Bell

The Moon Baby — Boosey & Hawkes

Fairy Cobbler — W. Paxton & Co.

A Load of Turnips — Western Music and W. Paxton & Co.

Songs:

Sweet Afton; Spring Magic; The Old Shepherd's Prayer; A Litany; Fairy Cobbler; A Memory; Last Year; The Little Jesus Came to Town; Sleep Little Jesus; Hospitality; Song of Mary; The Two Nests; Indian Lullaby; To a Girl on Her Birthday — Western Music Co.

Eight Icelandic folk songs; Eight Czechoslovakian folk songs; Eight Ukrainian folk songs; Eight French Canadian folk songs — MS.

Angus, Roy Alexander

Pianist, composer and arranger. Born in Toronto, July 1st, 1902.

Musical education in Toronto with Frank Welsman (piano) and Sir Ernest MacMillan (theory and composition). Degree: Mus.Bac. (Toronto, 1926). Diplomas: L.T.C.M., Fellow, Royal Society of Arts (London, 1929). Winner of the Governor General Willingdon Award for serious songs, 1929.

On staff of Canadian Academy of Music, 1920-25, of Royal Conservatory, Toronto, 1926-36. In 1936 established own music publishing business. Since 1940 engaged in bee-keeping, small farming, composing and arranging popular and serious music.

Address: R.R. No. 1, Downsview, Ont.

COMPOSITIONS

TITLE	DATE	TYPE	TIME (MIN.)	PUBLISHER
Ode to the Brave	1925	*choir, orchestra*	30	MS.
Piano Concerto in E flat	1951	*piano, orchestra*		MS.
Phantasie Suite	1927	*string quartet*	20	MS.
Horn Trio	1931	*Fr. hn, vln, piano*	15	MS.
Sonata	1929	*vln and piano*	20	MS.
Serious Songs	1920-1942	*vocal*	ea. 3-5	MS.
including: A Red, Red Rose		*vocal*		Waterloo Music

Anhalt, István

Composer, conductor and music teacher. Born in Budapest, April 12th, 1919.

Musical education in Hungary and France with Zoltan Kodály, Louis Fourestier and Nadia Boulanger. Won first prize in composition at Budapest Academy of Music. In 1945 was made assistant conductor, Opera of Budapest. Came to Canada in 1949. Is Lady Davis Fellow, assistant professor at McGill Conservatorium, Montreal (composition and score-reading).

Address: 5309 Park Avenue, Montreal, P.Q.

COMPOSITIONS

TITLE	DATE	TYPE	TIME (MIN.)	PUBLISHER
Ballet Music	1950	2 pianos	18	MS.
Concerto in stilo di Handel	1946	strgs, 2 ob, 2 hn	20	MS.
Interludium	1949	strgs, piano, tymp.	5	MS.
Sen scheorim	1951	choir and organ	2	MS.
Six Songs from Na-Conxi-Pan	1948	vocal	14	MS.
Two Songs (W. Whitman)	1949	vocal	10	MS.
Songs of Love	1951	vocal	7	MS.

Several other works written prior to arrival in Canada.

Applebaum, Louis

Conductor and composer. Born in Toronto, April 30th, 1918.

Musical education in Toronto with Boris Berlin, Healey Willan, Leo Smith and Sir Ernest MacMillan, in New York with Bernard Wagenaar and Roy Harris. Winner of CAPAC award.

From 1942-46 was in charge of music department of the National Film Board in Ottawa. In 1946 became music director of World Today, Inc., N.Y. and of several N.Y. independent motion picture producers. In 1949 returned to Canada to continue work in motion picture and radio field. Is now music consultant to National Film Board.

Has worked primarily in film. In Hollywood composed the score for *Tomorrow the World* (won special award from Hollywood Writer's Mobilization, 1945) and *Story of G.I. Joe* (nominated for Academy Award, 1946). In N.Y. wrote score for *Lost Boundaries* (won citation from National Board of Review, N.Y., 1950).

Address: 5 Wellwood Avenue, Toronto, Ont.

Affiliation: CAPAC.

COMPOSITIONS

TITLE	DATE	TYPE	TIME (MIN.)	PUBLISHER
East by North	1949	orchestra	15	MS.
Piece for Orchestra		orchestra	10	MS.
Rondo		small orchestra	3	MS.
Variations on a theme from a film score	1948	vln, va, vc, ob, piano	15	MS.
String Quartet No. 1		string quartet	11	MS.
String Quartet No. 2		string quartet	12	MS.
Piano Sonata		piano	9	MS.
Donkey and Dream		piano	4	MS.
Suite of piano duets for children		piano duet	15	MS.
Eight Songs		vocal	ea. 5	MS.
Five Newfoundland Songs	1950	vocal	12	MS.

Feature Film Scores:
Tomorrow the World; Story of G.I. Joe; Lost Boundaries; Teresa; The Whistle at Eton Falls.
About 120 scores for documentary films for various sponsors and governments. Scores for radio (CBC and United Nations).

Archer, Violet Balestreri

Composer and pianist. Born in Montreal.

Musical education at McGill Conservatorium with Claude Champagne and Douglas Clarke. Also studied with J. J. Weatherseed, Miss D. Shearwood-Stubington, Bela Bartok (1942 in New York) and with Paul Hindemith (1949 at Yale School of Music). Degrees: Mus.Bac. (McGill), Master of Music (Yale, 1949, high honors). Diplomas: Licentiate in piano (McGill), A.C.C.O.

Won four scholarships for composition at McGill University. 1947-49 was awarded special grants by the Quebec Government for further studies in composition at Yale School of Music. Won two scholarships at Yale. In 1949 the Ladies Morning Musical Club of Montreal awarded special bursary for travels in England and Europe. Won composition prize of Quebec Music Festival and in 1949 Woods-Chandler prize in composition.

Compositions have been performed in Canada, England, France, Switzerland and Italy. Has given radio recitals in Canada, U.S., England and Switzerland. Composer-in-residence, North Texas State College, since 1950.

Address: Box 6813, North Texas State College, Denton, Texas, U.S.A.

Affiliation: CAPAC.

COMPOSITIONS

TITLE	DATE	TYPE	TIME (MIN.)	PUBLISHER
Orchestral works:				
Symphony No. 1		*orchestra*		MS.
Symphonic Suite		*orchestra*		MS.
Britannia—A joyful overture		*orchestra (or 2 pianos)*		MS.
Ballade		*orchestra*		MS.
The Nun (H. Wolfe; tone poem)		*orchestra*		MS.
Variations on "A la claire fontaine"		*orchestra*		MS.
Fantasy on a Ground		*orchestra*		MS.
Concertino for clarinet and orchestra		*orchestra*		MS.
Capriccio for hand tympani and orchestra		*orchestra*		MS.
Fanfare and Passacaglia		*orchestra*		MS.
Intermezzo		*small orchestra*		MS.
Miniature Suite		*small orchestra*		MS.
Fantasia Concertante		*fl, ob, cl, strings*		MS.
Fantasy		*clarinet and strings*		MS.
Scherzo and Andante		*string orchestra*		MS.
Variations on an original theme		*string orchestra*		MS.
Chamber works:				
String Quartet No. 1		*string quartet*		MS.
String Quartet No. 2		*string quartet*		MS.
Variations on an original theme		*string quartet*		MS.
Fugue-fantasy		*string quartet*		MS.
Quartet		*fl, ob, cl, bn*		MS.
Divertimento		*ob, cl, bn*		MS.
Sonata		*fl, cl, and piano*		MS.

COMPOSITIONS

TITLE	DATE	TYPE	TIME (MIN.)	PUBLISHER
Fantasy		*fl, cl, and piano*		MS.
Sonata		*vln and piano*		MS.
Two Pieces for flute		*flute*		MS.
Little Prelude		*harp*		MS.
Six Pieces		*tympani and piano*		MS.

Keyboard works:

Habitant Sketches (Jig; Church Scene; Christmas at Quebec)		*piano*		Mercury Music
Sonatina No. 1 (4 mvmts)		*piano*		MS.
Sonatina No. 2 (3 mvmts)		*piano*		Boosey & Hawkes
Little Prelude		*piano*		MS.
Two easy arrangements of Can. folk songs		*piano*		MS.
Variations on Isabeau s'y promène		*piano*		MS.
Capriccio Fantastic		*piano*		MS.
Sonata (3 mvmts)		*piano*		MS.
Fantasy (for Rose Goldblatt)		*piano*		MS.
Three Preludes		*piano*		MS.
Three Preludes		*piano*		MS.
Four Two-part Inventions		*piano*		MS.
Three Sketches		*two pianos*		MS.
Birthday Fugue à la Weinberger		*two pianos*		MS.
Improvisation		*organ*		MS.
Dominus Regit Me (chorale prelude)		*organ*		MS.
Henlein (chorale prelude)		*organ*		MS.
Aeterna Christi munera (choral prelude)		*organ*		MS.
Sonatina (3 mvmts)		*organ*		MS.
Five Chorale Preludes		*organ*		MS.

Choral and vocal works:

Lamentations of Jeremy		*choir and orchestra*		MS.
Suite from "Leaves of Grass" (Whitman)		*choir and orchestra*		MS.
Choruses from "The Bacchae" (Euripides)		*choir and orchestra*		MS.
The Bell (John Donne; cantata)		*choir and orchestra*		MS.
O Praise God in His Holiness		*choir and organ*		MS.
Death Be Not Proud (John Donne)		*choral*		MS.
Mass		*choral*		MS.
Landscapes (T. S. Eliot)		*choral*		MS.
Silver (De la Mare)		*vocal*		MS.
The Ship of Rio (De la Mare)		*vocal*		MS.
Someone (De la Mare)		*vocal*		MS.
Moon Songs (V. Lindsay)		*vocal*		MS.
Under the Sun (song cycle; A. Bourinot)		*vocal*		MS.
Snow Shadows		*vocal*		MS.
Two Songs for Children		*vocal*		MS.
Three Biblical Songs		*vocal*		MS.

Assaly, Edmund Phillip

Pianist and composer. Born in Rosetown, Sask., January 4th, 1920.

Musical education in Rosetown with private teachers and in Saskatoon with Lyell Gustin (piano and composition). Diplomas: A.T.C.M., L.R.S.M. After a year with CBC Winnipeg moved to Montreal for further study with Michel Hirvy and also writes and plays for CBC.

Address: 1446 St. Marc, Montreal, P.Q.

Affiliation: BMI.

		Compositions		
Title	Date	Type	Time (Min.)	Publisher
Ballet Suite	1950	*orchestra*	11	MS.
Mount Royal Fantasy	1948	*piano and orchestra*	5½	MS.
Two Piano Suite		*two pianos*	15	MS.
Sonata		*piano*	5	MS.
Humoresque		*piano*	3	MS.
Two Preludes		*piano*	4	MS.
Requiem		*vocal*		MS.

— Audoire, John Norman

Conductor and composer. Born in St. Albans, England, December 6th, 1897.

Musical education at Trinity College of Music, London. Has been bandmaster of Salvation Army in Montreal for the last 26 years. Diploma: L.T.C.L.

Address: 5618 Coolbrook Avenue, Montreal, P.Q.

		Compositions		
Title	Date	Type	Time (Min.)	Publisher
Call to Service		*vocal*	6	MS.

Band works in manuscript: ea. 4-8

Earlscourt; Montreal; Certitude; Halifax Bicentennial	*marches*
An Irish Melody; Coming Thru' the Rye	*sop cornet solo and band*
Glory of His Name	*cornet duet and band*
Glory	*cornet trio and band*
Priceless Gift	*trombone and band*
We'll All Shout; Old Black Joe	*euphonium and band*
Omnipotence; Impetus; Blue Bells of Scotland; When Our Band Plays	*band*

Baker, Dalton

Organist, choirmaster and composer. Born in London, England, 1879.

Started musical career as chorister in 1890. Won singing scholarship, Royal Academy, London, 1901. Career included concert appearances as baritone principal in British and American festivals. Came to Canada in 1914, settling in Toronto as choirmaster and voice teacher (Royal Conservatory). Since 1934 lives in Vancouver. Conductor for ten years of *Vesper Hour* and *Eventide* programs on CBC.

Address: 1325 Moody Avenue, North Vancouver, B.C.

Affiliation: CAPAC.

COMPOSITIONS

TITLE	DATE	TYPE	TIME (MIN.)	PUBLISHER
Shadows of Evening (anthem)		*choral*	3	Western Music

Anthems in manuscript (2-3 minutes each):

From Glory unto Glory; O God of Earth and Altar; Kyrie and Sanctus; Praise the Lord; God Is Working; Lord of the Universe; Faith of Our Father; Father Eternal; O Worship the Lord; Ave Verum; Sanctus; Lead Us; Heavenly Father.

Bales, Gerald Albert

Pianist, organist, composer and conductor. Born in Toronto, May 12th, 1919.

Musical education at Royal Conservatory, Toronto with Healey Willan and Albert Procter. Began musical studies at the age of five.

Toured Canada as piano and organ recitalist. Is organist and choirmaster, St. Andrew's Presbyterian Church, Toronto. Has appeared as soloist with symphony orchestras, including Chicago Philharmonic in a performance of his *Fantasy for Piano and Orchestra*. Has composed background music for film and radio and has given numerous organ recitals over CBC.

Address: 86 Meadowvale Avenue, Scarborough Bluffs, Ont.

Affiliation: BMI.

COMPOSITIONS

TITLE	DATE	TYPE	TIME (MIN.)	PUBLISHER
Lazarus	1940	*solo, choir, organ*	40	MS.
Suite for Orchestra	1938	*orchestra*	25	MS.
Nocturne	1937	*orchestra*	10	MS.
Summer Idyll	1940	*orchestra*	5	MS.
Fantasy	1939	*piano and orch.*	13	MS.
Concerto for Organ	1950	*organ and strgs*	20	MS.
Essay	1947	*strings*	9	MS.
Reverie		*piano*	5	MS.
Suite		*piano*	10	MS.
Toccata	1946	*piano*	2	BMI Canada
Invention	1946	*piano*	2	MS.
Two Preludes		*organ*	10	MS.
Two Improvisations		*organ*	8	MS.
Prelude in E minor	1936	*organ*	4½	BMI Canada
Thou Art So Like a Flower		*choral*	4	MS.
Your Tears	1945	*vocal*	1½	MS.
My Debt	1946	*vocal*	2	MS.

Barclay, Robert

(original name: Leonard Edwin Basham)

Composer, conductor and writer. Born in Penticton, B.C., February 2nd, 1918.

Musical education in Vancouver, Toronto and New York. Studied composition with Arthur Benjamin and Bernard Wagenaar. Awarded three-year Juilliard fellowship in 1944, graduated in 1947. Diploma: A.T.C.M. (composition).

Won two composition prizes from CAPAC, 1938-39. First composition performed in public in 1941. Works performed over CBC and BBC, in Canada, U.S. and Europe.

Appeared as conductor with CBC and Vancouver Symphony orchestras. Now lives in New York as composer, editor, dance and music critic.

Address: 30 Old Field Lane, Lake Success, N.Y., U.S.A.

Affiliation: CAPAC.

COMPOSITIONS

TITLE	DATE	TYPE	TIME (MIN.)	PUBLISHER
Symphony	1950	*orchestra*	15	Boosey & Hawkes, N.Y. (rental)
Legend	1940	*orchestra*	5¼	MS.
Alaskan Overture	1942	*orchestra*	8½	MS.
Ballade	1946	*orchestra*	9	Am. Music Centre (rental)
Rhapsody	1947	*orchestra*	8½	Am. Music Centre (rental)
Seaport Town Overture	1950	*orchestra*	6¼	Chappell & Co.
Music for a Film	1950	*orchestra*	7½	MS.
Ballet Suite	1950	*small or full orch.*	20	MS.
Nocturne and Scherzo	1947	*small orchestra*	10	Am. Music Centre (rental)
Elegy	1941	*strings*	3½	MS.
Caprice	1950	*strings*	5	MS.
Quartet	1945	*clar, vln, va, vc*	20	Am. Music Centre (rental)
Prelude and Capriccio	1947	*vln and piano*	8½	MS.
Rumba	1950	*clar and piano*	1½	MS.
Allegro	1950	*piano*	3	MS.

Bartley, Ewart Andrew

Organist, choirmaster and composer. Born in Toronto, January 4th, 1909.

Musical education with A. D. Jordan (organ) and at Royal Conservatory, Toronto with Ernest Seitz (piano) and Healey Willan (composition). Became church organist in Ingersoll, Ont. at the age of 17. Since 1943 is organist and choir director of Knox's Presbyterian Church, Galt. Is supervisor of music for Preston Public Schools.

Address: 28 Chisholm Street, Galt, Ont.

COMPOSITIONS

TITLE	DATE	TYPE	TIME (MIN.)	PUBLISHER
Sketch	1950	*strings*	14	MS.
Adagio	1950	*string quartet*		MS.
Rhapsodie	1950	*string quartet*		MS.
Rhapsodie	1949	*piano*	8	MS.
Two Dances	1950	*piano*	4	BMI Canada
Suite for Children	1950	*piano*	4	MS.
Beauty (John Masefield)	1949	*vocal*	3	MS.

Short piano pieces in manuscript:
Two Impressions; *A Dance; Nocturne; Scherzino.*

Basham, Leonard
(see: Barclay, Robert)

Battle, Rex

Pianist and composer. Born in London, England, January 4th, 1895.

Musical education with Dr. E. H. Thorne (organ), V. Budmani (piano, theory and composition), Mrs. Hedwig Rosenthal, Moriz Rosenthal (piano). As a boy, played before Queen Alexandra at Buckingham Palace many times. Concertized in the United States and Canada.

Address: 1250 Avenue Road, Toronto, Ont.

COMPOSITIONS

TITLE	DATE	TYPE	TIME (MIN.)	PUBLISHER
Simon says "Thumbs Up"		orchestra or band	2½	G. V. Thompson
Meditation		violin	5	MS.
St. Andrews by the Sea		vocal	3	R. A. Irving
The Quest		vocal	4	MS.
A Romany Tale		vocal	3	MS.
Five transcriptions		piano	12	MS.

Bayley, Robert Charlton

Organist, choirmaster, school music supervisor and composer. Born in Buctouche, N.B., April 4th, 1913.

Musical education with William J. Smith, Dr. Ernest Bullock, Dr. Sydney Nicholson and summer sessions with Finley Williamson, Father Finn and Olaf Christiansen. Degree: B.Sc. in Arts (Univ. of N.B.). Diplomas: L.Mus. (McGill), L.T.C.L.

Has been organist and music director at various churches; now at First Baptist Church, Moncton, N.B. Supervisor of school music, Moncton, since 1946. Has conducted the Cecilian Singers, Fredericton, the CNR Glee Club, Moncton. Has appeared in many broadcasts. Published poetry. Editor, music section of Educational Review (New Brunswick).

Address: 75 Elm Street, Moncton, N.B.

Affiliation: BMI.

COMPOSITIONS

TITLE	DATE	TYPE	TIME (MIN.)	PUBLISHER
Into This World of Sorrow	1949	choral	2¾	Frederick Harris
Blessed Are the Pure in Heart	1950	choral	3	BMI Canada
Child Jesus	1950	choral	2½	BMI Canada
Five-fold Amen	1950	choral	1	to be published
My Love Is Fair (with S. B. Hains)	1949	vocal	3	Frederick Harris
Three Songs (Requiem; Desire; Golden Slumber)	1949	vocal	ea. 2	MS.

Bearder, Dr. John William

Organist, choirmaster and composer. Born in Yorkshire, England, December 26th, 1873.

Came to Canada in 1907 and resided in Ottawa from 1913-50. Was choirmaster and organist in England and at St. Matthew's Church, Ottawa. Founder in 1915 and past director of Ottawa Collegiate Institute orchestras. Past president, Canadian College of Organists. Now retired after 64 years of service as organist. Degree: Mus.Doc. (Bishop's). Diploma: F.R.C.O.

Address: 68 Pacific Avenue, Toronto 9, Ont.

COMPOSITIONS

TITLE	DATE	TYPE	TIME (MIN.)	PUBLISHER
Communion Service in B flat		*choral*		Woodward
Festival Te Deum in B flat		*choral*		published
Festival Magnificat and Nunc Dimittis in B flat		*choral*		published
Five Anthems		*choral*		MS.
Four Songs (Angus Mackay)		*vocal*		published
Canadian Born (monologue; Pauline Johnson)		*vocal*		MS.
Canadian Song Cycle (Mrs. M. H. Bowen)		*vocal*		MS.
Two Sacred Songs		*vocal*		MS.

Violin and piano pieces; arrangements.

Beckwith, John

Pianist, composer and writer. Born in Victoria, B.C., March 9th, 1927.

Musical education at Royal Conservatory, Toronto with Alberto Guerrero (piano) and at University of Toronto. Degree: Mus.Bac. (Toronto, 1947). Winner of many scholarships (piano) and prizes (composition).

Was art, music and drama editor, The Varsity (University of Toronto student daily) during 1947-48. Has written musical and theatrical articles for Victoria and Toronto newspapers. From 1948-50 was publicity director, Royal Conservatory, Toronto. In 1950 received Canadian Amateur Hockey Association award to continue musical studies in France. At present studies composition with Mlle Nadia Boulanger.

Has performed as soloist, accompanist and on radio. Most compositions listed have received public performances.

Address: c-o Royal Conservatory of Music, 135 College Street, Toronto, Ont. (at present in Paris, France).

Affiliation: BMI.

COMPOSITIONS

TITLE	DATE	TYPE	TIME (MIN.)	PUBLISHER
Music for Dancing (suite of 7 pieces)	1948	*piano duet*	17	MS.
Four Conceits	1948	*piano*	6	MS.
Rhapsody	1951	*piano*	4	MS.
Five Pieces for Brass Trio	1951	*tpt, Fr. hn, tb.*	12	MS.
Four Pieces	1951	*bassoon duet*	11	MS.
Five Pieces	1951	*flute duet*	12	MS.

Title	Date	Compositions Type	Time (Min.)	Publisher
The Great Lakes Suite (6 poems by J. Reaney)	1949	sop, bar, clar, vc, piano	15	MS.
Five Lyrics of the T'ang Dynasty	1947	vocal	7	BMI Canada
Four Songs (Edith Sitwell)	1949	vocal	10	MS.
Two Songs (Colleen Thibaudeau)	1950	vocal	4	MS.
Four Songs (E. E. Cummings)	1950	vocal	8	MS.

Bédard, Louis

Pianist, organist and composer. Born in Montreal, January 14th, 1906.

Musical education with Mrs. F. Héraly, Alfred Laliberté (piano), Sara Campbell (piano and organ) and Oscar O'Brien (harmony). Is teacher and organist in Mont-Laurier, P.Q. Associated with the late Charles Marchand, the celebrated folklorist, as accompanist on tour throughout Canada, United States and France.

Address: 8575 Drolet Street, Montreal, P.Q.

Title	Date	Compositions Type	Time (Min.)	Publisher
Messe Solennelle		choral	20	MS.
Messe Solennelle in D		choral	20	MS.
Rhapsodie sur des airs de Noël		choral	10	MS.
Dernier Adieu		choral	2	Parnasse Musical
Idylle		choral	3	MS.
Cantate		choral	7	MS.
Le Chant du Souvenir		choral	2½	MS.
Ave Maria		vocal	2½	MS.
Ma Peine est semblable à ta peine		vocal	3	MS.
Le Printemps		vocal	3	Parnasse Musical
Le Père Noël		vocal	4	MS.
Les Cloches		vocal	3	MS.
La Discipline		vocal	4	MS.

About 17 French Canadian folk songs arranged for small ensemble, ea. 2-3 min. Several popular songs.

Book:

L'éducation musicale du subconscient. Montreal, 1950.

Bell, Hugh Poynter

Journalist and composer. Born in Kew, England, 1872.

Education in Cambridge and Germany. Came to Canada in 1912. Was music editor for Montreal Daily Star, 1923-50. Amateur composer.

Address: 4147 Dorchester Street West, Westmount, P.Q.

COMPOSITIONS

TITLE	DATE	TYPE	TIME (MIN.)	PUBLISHER
Love's Philosophy	1945	*vocal*		BMI Canada
Sonata	1946	*vln and piano*	15	MS.
Eight Interludes	1950	*piano*		MS.
15 Songs		*vocal*		MS.

Bell, Dr. Leslie R.

Choral conductor, lecturer, arranger, composer and writer. Born in Toronto, 1906.

Education at University of Toronto and Royal Conservatory, Toronto. Teachers included W. Dudley, Dr. Frederick Horwood, Louis Waizman. Majored in clarinet, harmony etc. Degrees: M.A. in English (Toronto), Mus.Doc. (Montreal).

Early musical career in orchestral and band work, arranging and choral work. From 1932-39 taught secondary school (English, history, dramatics, music); was lecturer in music (Ont. Dept. of Education summer school for teachers); did research on Newfoundland folk song. From 1939-48 was director of music, Ontario College of Education; lecturer in history of music, Queen's University; director of University of Toronto Band and Kingston Symphony Orchestra. At present is professor of choral technique, University of Toronto; director Leslie Bell Singers; musical editor and columnist Toronto Daily Star; writes textbooks for Ont. Dept. of Education; adjudicates; arranges for CBC programs, Fred Waring, Canadian Music Sales etc.

Address: 83 Bloor Street West, Toronto, Ont.

Affiliation: CAPAC.

COMPOSITIONS

TITLE	DATE	TYPE	TIME (MIN.)	PUBLISHER
Variations on a French Noël		*string quartet*		MS.
In Winter Cold (original carol)		*choral (S.S.A. or S.A.T.B.*		Can. Music Sales
Folk Song Suite		*choral (S.S.A.A.)*		Mills Music
Hebridean Suite		*choral (S.S.A.A.)*		MS.
Pavane (transcr. from Byrd)		*choral (S.S.A.)*		Can. Music Sales
This Is the Day Which the Lord Hath Made (original anthem)		*choral (S.A.T.B.)*		Can. Music Sales
Fantasy of Christmas Carols		*choral (S.S.A.A.)*		MS.

A large number of arrangements of folk songs for S.A., S.S.A., S.A.T.B., T.T.B.B. published by Canadian Music Sales, Mills Music, Gordon V. Thompson, Waring Shawnee Press, N.Y., Summy, Chicago.

Song Books:
The Chorister, 2nd., Gage, Toronto.

Belleau, Dantès

Pianist and composer. Born in Plessisville, P.Q., March 9th, 1897.

Musical education with Henri Gagnon and Alfred Laliberté (piano), at Paris Conservatory with George Darimont (piano) and in San Francisco with Ed. Lamarre (organ). Taught piano at Alberta College, Edmonton. Was organist at French Church in San Francisco. Was pianist at Rideau Hall, Ottawa; played for Lady Tweedsmuir, Princess Alice and Red Cross Organization. Teacher of piano at Conservatoire National, Montreal. Has made concert tours throughout Canada.

Address: 1929 Tupper Street, Montreal, P.Q.

COMPOSITIONS

TITLE	DATE	TYPE	TIME (MIN.)	PUBLISHER
Piano Concerto in E minor		orchestra		to be published, 1951
Sonata		piano		to be published, 1951
Cadence Espagnole	1945	piano	3	Fassio, Lachute
Nostalgie d'automne	1947	piano	5	Fassio, Lachute
Rêverie	1945	piano	3	Passe-Temps
Divertissements des muses	1947	piano	3	Passe-Temps
La Vieille Eglise	1945	piano	5	Passe-Temps

Benoist, Marius

Pianist, organist, singer, choirmaster, conductor and composer. Born in Ste. Anne des Chênes, Man., October 1st, 1896.

Musical education with R. Pepin (piano and organ), S. Hélie (singing) and at the Schola Cantorum in Montreal. Choirmaster of St. Boniface Cathedral.

Address: 234 La Verendrye Street, St. Boniface, Man.

COMPOSITIONS

TITLE	DATE	TYPE	TIME (MIN.)	PUBLISHER
Secret des Amati		opéra-comique	90	MS.
L'Escalier		opéra-comique	90	MS.
Great Bear		ballet	150	MS.
including: Overture		orchestra	5	MS.
Prelude 2nd act & dance		orchestra	9	MS.
Folk Dance 1 and 2		orchestra	4 & 10	MS.
Grain		ballet	4	MS.
Kilowatt Magic		ballet	4	MS.
Fantasia on Icelandic Themes		orchestra	4	MS.
Intermezzo		orchestra	4	MS.
Par un beau dimanche (suite)		orchestra	10	MS.
Légende	1948	orchestra	8	MS.
Vie de Mère Youville (stage music)		orchestra	11	MS.
O Crux Ave (tableaux)		orchestra	13	MS.
La Verendrye (Overture, tableux)		choir and orchestra	16	MS.
La Fin du maître-chantre		choir and orchestra	15	MS.
Erivadnus		voice and orchestra	25	MS.
An Ode to Spring	1949	voice, choir, orch.	30	MS.
Condoléances	1950	small orcheštra	9	MS.
Sérénade	1933	small orchestra	10	MS.
In Memoriam		strings	3	MS.

Berlin, Boris

Pianist and composer. Born in Kharkov, Russia, May 27th, 1907.

Musical education in Germany with Mark Hambourg and Leonid Kreutzer and in Russia and Switzerland. Came to Canada in 1925. In 1929 joined the faculty of the

Royal Conservatory, Toronto; is on board of examiners, board of studies. Teaches piano, lectures on piano technique and pedagogy and adjudicates at music festivals.

Address: 21 Ferndale Avenue, Toronto, Ont.

Affiliation: CAPAC.

COMPOSITIONS

TITLE	PUBLISHER
Our Animal Friends; Russian Cradle Song; Monkeys on the Tree; Pianos on Parade (2 volumes); Master Composers on Parade (arrangements); Modern Russian Music (arranged)	G. V. Thompson
The Merry-go-Round; Yanina; Squirrels at Play; March of the Goblins; The Marching Trumpets; Oranges and Lemons; Voyager's Farewell; Jets on Parade; Golden Album of Piano Solos; From the Golden Treasury of Music	F. Harris
Indian Chief Dance; Moonlight Waltz; Hop-Scotch	Jarman, Toronto
Pink Rabbit	MS.

Educational publications:

Guide for Teachers; The Very First Piano Work Book (2 parts; co-author with Norman Wilks and Muriel Boyle); *Complete Scale Book; Practical Hanon and Schmitt; Essential Daily Exercises*, G. V. Thompson. *Modern Piano Student* (co-author with Sir Ernest MacMillan); *Our Piano Class* (ditto); *For Little Piano Students* (with E. Magee); *Four Star Sight Reading Book; 20 Lessons in Ear Training* (with Sir Ernest MacMillan); *The A.B.C. of Piano Playing* (2 parts); *Lessons in Music Writing*, F. Harris.

Bernier, Rev. Dr. Alfred, S.J.

Composer of sacred music and lecturer. Born in Montreal, October 26th, 1896.

Musical education in Montreal with Arthur Laurendeau (vocal culture), Louis Michiels (harmony), in Italy with professors Refice, Casimiri, Vignanelli, Dobici, Ferretti and Dagnino at Pontifical Institute of Sacred Music. Degree: Doctor of Music from Institute of Rome. Founder and director of the Petite Maitrise de Montréal. Professor at the Gregorian Institute of America (Toledo). Dean of the faculty of music, Montreal University.

Address: 1855 Rachel East, Montreal, P.Q.

COMPOSITIONS

TITLE	DATE	TYPE	TIME (MIN.)	PUBLISHER
Ode à Marie de Montréal		*cantata*	8	Messager Canadien
Cor Jesu		*choral*	3	Messager Canadien
Ecce Fidelis Servus		*choral*	2	Messager Canadien
Cantique aux martyrs canadiens		*choral*	4	Messager Canadien
Suavi Iugo Tuo		*choral*	3	Messager Canadien
Hymne en l'honneur de Kateri-Tekakwitha		*choral*	6	Messager Canadien
Noël Huron		*choral*	5	Messager Canadien
Regnum Mundi		*choral*	3	Messager Canadien
J'ai perdu ma tourterelle		*choral*	3	MS.
Les Roses de Saadi		*choral*	4	MS.

20 folk songs.

Bernier, Conrad

Pianist, organist and composer. Born in Quebec, May 9th, 1904.

Musical education in Montreal with J. A. Bernier, in Paris at Conservatoire National with Georges Caussade (theory), Joseph Bonnet (organ), Isidor Philipp, Simone Plé and Silva Hérard (piano). Winner of Quebec Province *Prix d'Europe*, 1923. Teaches in Washington, D.C. and at Quebec Provincial Conservatory.

Address: c–o Quebec Provincial Conservatory, 1700 St. Denis, Montreal, P.Q.

COMPOSITIONS

TITLE	DATE	TYPE	TIME (MIN.)	PUBLISHER
Symphony in D minor		orchestra and organ	26	MS.
Laurentian Vacation		orchestra	18	MS.
Soir (tone poem)		orchestra	5	MS.
Croquis Petit-Capiens (suite)		2 pianos	18	Belgo-Canadienne
Variations and Fugue in A minor		2 pianos		MS.
Nursery Poem		piano		MS.
Silhouette		piano		Passe-Temps
Prière		organ		MS.
Esquisse in B minor		organ		MS.
Prélude in F minor		organ		MS.
Chant sans paroles		organ		MS.
Eglogues		organ		MS.
Feuille d'album		'cello		MS.
Cyngham (Welsh)		'cello		MS.
Mass in B flat major		choral		MS.
Motet		choral		MS.
L'Oiseau bleu		vocal		MS.
Les Colombes		vocal		MS.
Les deux ombres		vocal		MS.
Le Berceau		vocal		MS.

Manuals:

Accompagnement du 'Liber Usualis'	MS.
Notes et études sur l'improvisation à l'orgue	MS.
La Technique de l'orgue	MS.

No recent information obtained.

Bernier, Dr. Joseph-Arthur

Pianist, organist and composer. Born in Lévis, P.Q., March 19th, 1877. Died in May 1944.

Musical education in Paris at Conservatoire National with Alexandre Guilmant (organ) and Félix Fourdrain (harmony). Degree: Mus.Doc. (Washington College). Member, Société des Auteurs et Compositeurs de Paris. Was active as music teacher and organist in churches of Quebec city.

COMPOSITIONS

TITLE	DATE	TYPE	TIME (MIN.)	PUBLISHER
Berceuse	1903	vln and piano		A. Debert, Paris
Pastorale	1903	oboe and piano		A. Debert, Paris

		COMPOSITIONS		
TITLE	DATE	TYPE	TIME (MIN.)	PUBLISHER
Cantilène	1903	'cello and piano		A. Debert, Paris
Toccate et Allegro		organ		MS.
Prière	1903	organ		A. Debert
Méditation	1903	organ		A. Debert
Mazurka	1906	piano		Lavigueur et Hutchison
O Salutaris	1903	voice, vln, organ		A. Debert
Four Masses		choral		MS.
Si vous voulez des miracles		choral		MS.
Cor Dulce (motet)		choral		MS.
Ave Verum (motet)		choral		MS.
Tu Es Petrus (motet)		choral		MS.
In Manus Tuas (motet)	1940	choral		J. A. Bernier
Miseremini Mei (motet)	1933	choral		Le S leil, Quebec
Sub Tuum	1910	vocal		A. Lachance
Les Larmes	1916	vocal		Le Nationaliste, Montreal
Les Chaînes		vocal		MS.
Marie, o mon secours		vocal		MS.
Huit Nouveaux Cantiques	1928	vocal		J. A. Bernier
Les Blancs Moutons		vocal		Cons. National
Cantique à Sainte Agnès		vocal		MS.
Louanges		vocal		MS.
Notre Père	1942	vocal		Procure générale
Je vous salue, Marie	1942	vocal		Procure générale

Bertrand, Dr. Felix R.

Pianist, organist, choirmaster, music teacher and composer. Born in Montreal, October 12th, 1909.

Degrees: B.A., Mus.Doc. (Montreal, 1948). Is piano-accompanist, choral conductor, concert and church organist. Teaches piano, organ, harmony and Hammond organ; coaches.

Address: 64 Mozart West, Montreal, P.Q.

		COMPOSITIONS		
TITLE	DATE	TYPE	TIME (MIN.)	PUBLISHER
Peace (cantata)	1944	choir, organ, orchestra	20	MS.
String Quartet	1940	string quartet	20	MS.
12 Pieces		organ		MS.
Motets au St. Sacrement	1936	voice and organ	30	Parnasse Musical
Tristis Est Anima Mea	1935	vocal	3	Parnasse Musical
A Toi	1940	vocal	2½	Parnasse Musical
Five Bach Chorales (Christmas; arranged)	1940	vocal	15	Parnasse Musical

Arrangements and transcriptions for voice, piano and organ; some published.

Book:
La Musique à la Radio, published by Montreal Editions.

Bett, Dr. Sydney George

Music teacher and composer. Born in England, 1896.

Musical education at Royal College of Music, London. Was Signor Foli scholar in composition under Gustav Holst and R. Vaughan Williams. Degree: Mus.Doc. (Toronto, 1933). Came to Canada in 1923. Has been music master at Ridley College, St. Catharines, Ont. since 1923.

Address: 44 Monck Street, St. Catharines, Ont.

COMPOSITIONS

TITLE	DATE	TYPE	TIME (MIN.)	PUBLISHER
Two Lincolnshire Pieces	1921	*small orchestra*	10	MS.
Psalm 96	1933	*choir and orchestra*	30	MS.
Nothing Is Here for Tears (anthem)	1930	*choir and organ*	5	Oxford U.P.
Three Anthems	1936	*choir and organ*	2-5	Carl Fischer
God Is Gone Up	1933	*choir and organ*	5	MS.
Kyrie in Phrygian Mode	1920	*choral*	5	MS.
Two Short Pieces	1929	*piano*	4	Oxford U.P.

Betts, Lorne M.

Composer, organist and choirmaster. Born in Winnipeg, August 2nd, 1918.

Musical education in Winnipeg and Toronto. Teachers include Hunter Johnson and John Weinzweig. Diplomas: A.C.C.O., L.R.S.M. Is organist and choirmaster at St. Paul's Presbyterian Church, Hamilton and staff member of Hamilton Conservatory of Music.

Address: Apt. 3, 125 Bold Street, Hamilton, Ont.

Affiliation: CAPAC.

COMPOSITIONS

TITLE	DATE	TYPE	TIME (MIN.)	PUBLISHER
David	1949	*narrator, choir, orchestra*	16	MS.
Joe Harris 1913-1942	1951	*narrator, male choir, wd, perc.*	15	MS.
Sonata	1949	*orchestra*	18	MS.
Two Dances	1950	*orchestra*	8	MS.
Suite for Strings	1948	*string orchestra*	10	MS.
Music for the Theatre	1950	*5 winds, piano, cb*	8	MS.
Elegy	1949	*Eng. hn and strgs*	5	MS.
String Quartet	1948	*string quartet*	18	MS.
String Quartet	1951	*string quartet*	18	MS.
Sonata	1948	*vln and piano*	5	MS.
Sonata	1949	*clar and piano*	12	MS.
Suite	1950	*flute and clar*	7	MS.
Miniature Suite	1948	*piano*	5	MS.

COMPOSITIONS

TITLE	DATE	TYPE	TIME (MIN.)	PUBLISHER
Suite	1950	*piano*	9	MS.
Sonata	1950	*piano*	9	MS.
Five Songs	1949	*high voice, strgs*	12	MS.
Three Songs (J. Joyce)	1948	*vocal*	4	MS.
Five Songs (J. Joyce)	1950	*vocal*	7	MS.
Six Songs (J. Joyce)	1951	*vocal*	10	MS.

Bevan, Richard T.

Organist and composer. Born in England, 1894.

Musical education as chorister in Lichfield Cathedral (England). Studied with Dr. W. H. Harris (organ, piano, composition). Diplomas: A.R.C.O., L.R.A.M. Came to Canada in 1932. Was organist at cathedral in Victoria, B.C. and is now organist in Quebec.

Address: 25 St. Ursule Street, Quebec, P.Q.

COMPOSITIONS

TITLE	DATE	TYPE	TIME (MIN.)	PUBLISHER
Concerto in A minor	1950	*piano, strgs and tymp*	25	MS.
Three Contrasts	1947	*strgs (No. 2 with hp, fl, celeste)*	15	MS.
Blessed Are They (anthem)	1914	*choral*	5	Stainer & Bell
Thee We Adore (motet)	1947	*choral*	6	Western Music
Songs for Young Canadians		*children's voices*		Nelson, Toronto

Biltcliffe, Florence

Pianist, teacher of general musicianship and composer. Born in Yorkshire, England.

Musical education in Bristol with Blanche Smith (piano). Attended summer school of Queen's Univ., Kingston, 1944-45, summer school at Chautauqua, N.Y., 1946, 47 and 49. Diploma: L.R.A.M. Has been active as music mistress in private schools both in England and in Canada (for 20 years at Ovenden College, Barrie, Ont.)

Address: 8 Ridgway Avenue, Rhyl, North Wales, British Isles.

COMPOSITIONS

TITLE	DATE	TYPE	TIME (MIN.)	PUBLISHER
Berceuse		*vln and piano*	2½-3	MS.
Variations on "O! Dear, What Can the Matter Be"		*vln and piano*	6	MS.
Andante and Rondo		*vln and piano*	3-4	MS.
Prelude in G minor		*piano*	3	MS.
Prelude in D flat major		*piano*	4	F. Harris
Miniature Suite		*piano*	4	Patersons, Glasgow
Three Impromptus		*piano*	10	MS.
Sonata		*piano*		MS.
To Arm! To Arm!		*choral*	3	MS.
God Is Our Hope		*choral*	4	MS.
The Lord's Prayer (choral setting)		*choral*	3-4	MS.
Sweet Was the Song the Virgin Sang		*choral*		Can. Music Sales

Several smaller piano pieces, carols, choral works and songs.

Binet, Jocelyne

Composer. Born in East-Angus, P.Q., September 27th, 1923.

Musical education at Ecole Supérieure de Musique d'Outremont with Claude Champagne (theory and composition), Jean Dansereau and Jean Beaudet (piano). At present studies in Paris at Conservatoire National with Noël Gallon (counterpoint and fugue), Tony Aubin (composition) and Olivier Messiaen (analysis). Degree: Mus.Bac. Diploma: Licence en composition.

In 1946 won a CAPAC composition award; in 1948-49 was awarded bursary by French government; 1949-50, 1950-51 bursary by Quebec government. Works have been performed in Canada, Brazil and France on radio or in concert.

Address: 132 rue du Chateau, Paris 14e, France.

COMPOSITIONS

TITLE	DATE	TYPE	TIME (MIN.)	PUBLISHER
Evocation (symphonic poem)	1948	*orchestra*	7	MS.
Danse	1949	*orchestra*	5	MS.
Un Canadien à Paris	1951	*orchestra*		MS.
Suite	1946	*strings, fl, piano*	11	MS.
Trio	1945	*vln, vc, piano*	10	MS.
Poème oriental	1946	*vln and piano*	2½	MS.
Nocturne	1946	*female choir, piano*	3¼	MS.
Petite Suite (4 mvmts)	1946	*female choir, piano*	9	MS.

Songs in manuscript (1949-50):
La Captive (V. Hugo); Chinoise au Temple; Les Roses de Saadi; Poème; Mon Père me veut marier; La Bohème; Les Oiseaux de mer; L'Adieu (Apollinaire).

Bissell, Keith Warren

Composer, teacher, organist and choirmaster. Born in Ontario, February 12th 1912.

Musical education at Royal Conservatory, Toronto with Leo Smith and others. Degree: Mus.Bac. (Toronto, 1942). Taught music in schools around Toronto for 14 years and in Nelson, B.C. Since 1949 is supervisor of music for Edmonton schools.

Is conductor of Woodward Choral Society, organist and choirmaster at Christ Church, Edmonton.

Address: 11340-79th Avenue, Edmonton, Alta.

Affiliation: BMI.

COMPOSITIONS

TITLE	DATE	TYPE	TIME (MIN.)	PUBLISHER
Rumpelstiltzkin	1947	*operetta (school voices)*	60	MS.
Christmas Cantata	1949	*solo, choir, organ*	30	MS.
Sonata	1948	*vln and piano*	16	MS.
Ballad	1949	*vln and piano*	5	BMI Canada
Etude	1949	*piano*	4	MS.
Sonata	1947	*piano*	15	MS.
O Starry Night (carol)	1948	*choral (S.S.A.)*		Western Music
Now That the Morning	1950	*choral (S.A.T.B.)*	4	MS.
Wabanaki song	1950	*soprano, fl, str. quartet*	7	MS.
Three Songs (Blake)	1948	*mezzo soprano*	10	MS.

Numerous songs and operettas for school.

Blachford, Frank Edward

Violinist and composer. Born in Toronto in 1880.

Musical education at Leipzig Royal Conservatorium with Sitt, Beving, Reinecke and Quasdorf and at Geneva Music Conservatorium (post-graduate studies) with Henri Marteau. Toured Canada and the U.S. in recitals. On faculty of Royal Conservatory, Toronto since 1901. Organized Toronto String Quartet; played violin with Toronto Symphony Orchestra (concertmaster for first 12 years); has done much radio work.

Address: 588 Avenue Road, Toronto, Ont.

Affiliation: CAPAC.

COMPOSITIONS

TITLE	TYPE	PUBLISHER
Serenade	*male choir and piano*	Th. Presser
Minuet; Doll's Dance; Three Miniatures; Rhythmical Tunes; Two Pieces	*violin*	F. Harris
Indian River; Sur le lac; Eagle's Nest; Idylle; Romance; Serenade	*violin*	MS.
Your Gift; Thou Art So Like a Flower; Where Is Another; Sleepy-time Song; None but Thou; I Have Cull'd that Lovely Rosebud; So Sweet Is She	*vocal*	MS.

Transcriptions for orchestra of works by Bach, Corelli, Nardini.

Instruction books:
First 20 Lessons (violin instruction manual), F. Harris.
Blachford Violin Class Book, G. V. Thompson, 1949.

— Blackburn, Maurice

Composer, arranger and pianist. Born in Quebec, May 22nd, 1914.

Musical education in Quebec with Robert Talbot, J. M. Beaudet, Henri Gagnon, Arthur Bernier and G. E. Tanguay. Won a composer's scholarship from Quebec Provincial Government and spent two years at the New England Conservatory, Boston, studying with Francis Findlay and Quincy Porter. From 1946-48 studied with Nadia Boulanger in France. Is on the staff of the National Film Board, Ottawa.

Address: 62 Springfield Road, Ottawa, Ont.

Affiliation: CAPAC.

COMPOSITIONS

TITLE	DATE	TYPE	TIME (MIN.)	PUBLISHER
Les Filles du roi	1950	*operetta*	60	MS.
Symphonie en un mouvement		*orchestra*	15	MS.
Les Petites Rues du Vieux Québec		*orchestra*	8	MS.
Fantaisie en Mocassins (folklore)		*orchestra*	7	MS.
Petite Suite		*small orchestra*	6	MS.
Rigaudon	1948	*small orchestra*	6	MS.
Overture for a Puppet Show	1951	*small orchestra*	4	MS.
Piano Concerto in C major	1948	*piano and winds*	20	MS.

COMPOSITIONS

TITLE	DATE	TYPE	TIME (MIN.)	PUBLISHER
Nocturne		*flute and strings*	8	MS.
Bal à l'huile (folklore)		*strings*	6	MS.
Sonatine		*piano*	12	MS.
Etude		*piano*	5	MS.
Digitales (suite)		*piano*	5	MS.
Trois danses	1949	*piano*	6	MS.
Polka		*piano duet*	5	MS.
Messe	1949	*children's voices*	8	MS.
Notre Père		*choral*	5	MS.
Cloches du soir		*vocal*	4	MS.
Le Petit Zoo (suite of 3 pieces)		*vocal*	8	MS.
Tant mieux		*vocal*	3	MS.
Chant de mariage		*vocal*	3	MS.
Epithalame		*vocal*	2	MS
Trois poèmes d'Emile Nelligan		*vocal*	12	MS.

Several religious works and folk songs.

Blomfield, Patricia

Pianist and composer. Born in Lindsay, Ont., September 15th, 1910. Musical education with Norah de Kresz (piano) and Healey Willan (composition). In 1938 won Vogt Society award for best Canadian composition with her Violin Suite. Till 1939 was on faculty of Royal Conservatory, Toronto.

Address: 221 Stibbard Avenue, Toronto, Ont.

Affiliation: BMI.

COMPOSITIONS

TITLE	DATE	TYPE	TIME (MIN.)	PUBLISHER
Pastorale	1940	*orchestra*	11	MS.
String Quartet		*string quartet*		MS.
Suite No. 1		*violin and piano*		F. Harris
Suite No. 2		*vln or va and piano*		BMI Canada
Impromptu	1948	*piano*	4	BMI Canada
Three Songs for Baritone (The Winter Lakes; The Canadian Herd-Boy; Quiet)	1949	*bar, strings, harp, Fr. hn*	8	MS.
The Lost Cause	1948	*vocal*	3	MS.
Diedre	1948	*vocal*	3	MS.

Solos for 'cello and piano and violin and piano.

Boese, Helen

Pianist and composer. Born in Toronto in 1896.

Musical education with Frank Wrigley, John M. Williams and Doris MacLean. Has accompanied many renowned singers. Chairman of composition committee for Canadian Federation of Music Teachers (Alberta). Was official pianist and now is on board of directors, Calgary Symphony Orchestra.

Address: 1129-19th Avenue West, Calgary, Alta.

		COMPOSITIONS		
TITLE	DATE	TYPE	TIME (MIN.)	PUBLISHER
Two Sketches:				
1. The Family Breakfast		*choral*		MS.
2. A Quick Rubber		*choral*		MS.
Affinity		*vocal*	1½	MS.
Song of the Weaver		*vocal*	3	MS.

Boivin, Maurice F.

Composer. Born in Ottawa, October 11th, 1920.

Musical education at Ecole de Musique, Univ. of Ottawa, and at Univ. of Toronto. Degree: Mus.Bac. (Toronto, 1949).

Address: 3595 Ruskin Ville, St. Michel, Montreal, P.Q.

		COMPOSITIONS		
TITLE	DATE	TYPE	TIME (MIN.)	PUBLISHER
Cantate	1950	*soli, choir, orch.*	30	MS.
Messe in C	1950	*soli, choir, organ*		MS.
Poème pour orchestre	1950	*orchestra*	20	MS.
String Quartet	1949	*string quartet*	20	MS.
12 Preludes	1950	*piano*	ea. 5	MS.
Ainsi parla le hasard	1948	*vocal (female)*	10-12	MS.
Three Sacred Songs (Latin)	1950	*vocal (female)*	14	MS.
2 Sacred Songs (French)				
Notre Père	1947	*vocal (female)*	3	Parnasse Musical
Je vous salue Marie	1949	*vocal (female)*	4	Archambault
12 Concert Songs (French)	1949	*vocal (female)*		MS.

Borek, Minuetta

Pianist, teacher and composer. Born in Calgary, Alta.

Musical education with J. M. Williams, G. M. Egbert, Ernest Hutcheson, Helen Augustin, Ania Dorfman and Ivan Langstroth. Diplomas: L.A.B., Juilliard Certificate and Post Graduate Diploma. Won CAPAC awards 1945-46.

Performed own compositions in public at the age of five and was regular contributor to Composer's Day, arranged by Mrs. H. H. Sharples of Calgary. Made New York debut in 1945 playing own New York Suite. In 1946 played Ballet Sonatina in Town Hall program. In 1947 CBC sponsored premiere of Alberta Concerto with Montreal CBC orchestra.

Address: 134 Haven Avenue, New York 32, N.Y., U.S.A.

Affiliation: CAPAC.

		COMPOSITIONS		
TITLE	DATE	TYPE	TIME (MIN.)	PUBLISHER
Alberta Concerto	1947	*piano and orchestra*	22	photostat (parts)
Lake O'Hara	1947	*string and orchestra*	13	MS.
Sonata	1949	*violin and piano*	16	MS.

COMPOSITIONS

TITLE	DATE	TYPE	TIME (MIN.)	PUBLISHER
New York Suite (5 mvmts)	1942	*piano*	16	photostat
		also: *piano and orchestra*	16	MS.
Ballet Sonatina	1943	*piano*	6½	photostat
Sharples Sonata	1946	*piano*	14½	photostat
Etude Brilliante	1948	*piano*	2	photostat
Prelude	1941	*piano*	1	photostat
Early in the Morning	1948	*piano*	1½	photostat
Watching a Sunset	1948	*piano*	2	photostat
Rustic Dance	1948	*piano*	1	photostat
Fantasette	1943	*piano*	2	MS.
Three Songs of Western Canada	1946	*vocal*	6	photostat

Children's music:

TITLE	DATE	TYPE	TIME (MIN.)	PUBLISHER
A Day in the Park (suite)	1946	*piano*	2½	MS.
Baby's Music Box	1944-5	*vocal*	11	photostat
Baby Ballads of To-day	1946	*vocal*	14	photostat

Borré, César

Conductor and composer. Born in Belgium c. 1880. Died in Toronto, April 12th, 1950.

Education in Belgium. Was opera conductor in Belgium and guest conductor throughout Europe, specializing in Wagner operas. Came to Canada in 1920, settling in London, Ont. Founded London Ladies' Choir, London Philharmonic Union. In 1937 moved to Toronto. In 1938 founded Toronto Opera Company. Had charge of music at St. Michael's College. Authority on Gregorian Chant.

COMPOSITIONS

TITLE	DATE	TYPE	TIME (MIN.)	PUBLISHER
L'Amour d'Apache (words: Borre)	1905	*opera in one act*		MS.
Loneliness (meditation)		*organ*		J. Fischer & Bro.
O Salutaris		*vocal*		J. Fischer & Bro.
Tantum Ergo		*vocal*		J. Fischer & Bro.

Also composed a symphony, another opera, a symphonic poem, choral and organ pieces etc.

Bouchard, Victor

Pianist and composer, notary. Born in Ste. Claire, Dorchester, P.Q., April 11th, 1926.

Musical education at Quebec Provincial Conservatory with Mme Hélène L. Labelle (piano), A. Tardif and Mme F. Aubut-Pratte (theory). Degrees: B.A., L.LL. (Laval) Diploma: Lauréat (piano), Académie de Musique de Québec. Rotary piano prize winner, 1949; first piano prize winner, Quebec Provincial Conservatory, 1950. Has given recitals on radio and in concert. At present studies in Paris.

Address: Ste. Claire, Dorchester, P.Q.

COMPOSITIONS

TITLE	DATE	TYPE	TIME (MIN.)	PUBLISHER
Danse Canadienne	1945	*piano*	3	Th. Presser
Deux études	1948	*piano*	3	MS.

COMPOSITIONS

TITLE	DATE	TYPE	TIME (MIN.)	PUBLISHER
Danse rustique	1949	*vln and piano*	3	MS.
Three Folk Songs (harmon.)	1949	*choral*	6	MS.
Seven Folk Songs (harmon.)	1949	*vocal*	15	Tremblay & Dion, Quebec
Five Folk Songs (harmon.)	1950	*vocal*	10	MS.

Boucher, Lydia
(Soeur Marie Thérèse, S.S.A.)

Music teacher, instrumentalist, singer and composer. Born in St. Ambroise de Kildare, P.Q., February 28th, 1890.

Musical education with Auguste Descarries (piano), Raoul Pâquet (organ), J. Dalcourt (violin), Louis Michiels, Rodolphe Mathieu, Auguste Descarries, Claude Champagne (composition) and Fleurette Contant (singing). Degrees: Bachelor (Montreal), Mus.Bac. (Conservatoire National, Montreal, 1931). Diploma: Licentiate (Académie de Musique de Québec).

Has taught music in the various convents of the Soeurs de Sainte-Anne for 41 years.

Address: Académie Sainte Anastasie, 155 St. Joseph Boulevard East, Montreal, P.Q.

COMPOSITIONS

TITLE	DATE	TYPE	TIME (MIN.)	PUBLISHER
L'Oeuvre d'Esther Blondin		*oratorio*	60	MS.
La Ronde des aiguilles		*piano*	5	Editions Canadiennes
Prélude		*piano*	5	MS.
Pastorale		*piano*	5	MS.
Eglogue		*piano*	5	MS.
Prélude, D minor		*piano*		MS.
Cent Ans!	1948	*choir, piano, str. quartet*	10	MS.
Chant de triomphe et de victoire	1948	*choir, piano, str. quartet*	10	MS.
Anges gardiens de nos tombeaux	1949	*choir and organ*	5	MS.
Heureux ceux qui sont morts dans la paix du Seigneur	1949	*choir and organ*	5	MS.
Offertoire	1948	*choir and piano*	5	MS.
Sur le Mont des Béatitudes	1950	*soli, choir, piano*	10	MS.
A Marie par Sainte-Anne		*vocal*	5	Belgo-Canadienne
Nos heures d'aujourd'hui		*vocal*	5	Belgo-Canadienne
Ave Maria		*vocal*	5	Belgo-Canadienne
Dans l'urne d'une fleur		*vocal*	5	Musica Enr.
Noël (chansonette)		*vocal*	5	Editions Canadiennes

Vocal works in manuscript (each 5 min.):

O Marie conçue sans péché; Petite Thérèse; La Messe en Cantiques; Papa; Maman; Ecoute; Sourire de l'an qui s'achève; Salut petit Jésus; Notre-Dame de Montréal; Et je t'apporterais des fleurs; Louange à Sainte-Anne.

Bourdon, Dr. Rosario

Violoncellist, conductor and composer. Born in Longueuil, P.Q., March 6th, 1885.

Musical education in Montreal, Brussels and at Ghent Royal Conservatory in Belgium ('cello, chamber music, harmony etc.). Degree: Mus.Doc. (Montreal, 1944). Member of Cincinnati, Philadelphia and St. Paul orchestras. For 20 years worked for Victor Talking Machines. Recording artist for Victor, Brunswick, NBC, Thesaurus Musack, Electrical Research, Radio work since 1923.

Address: 121 Madison Avenue, Apt. 10E, New York 16, N.Y., U.S.A.

Affiliation: ASCAP.

	COMPOSITIONS			
TITLE	DATE	TYPE	TIME (MIN.)	PUBLISHER
Ginger Snaps		orchestra	2½	T. B. Harms
Danse Bagatelle		orchestra	2½	L. Feist
Poème Elégiaque		'cello solo and orchestra	3	MS.

Orchestral works published by E. Ascher (1½-3 minutes each):
Cities Service March; Through the Line; Sixty Wall Tower; Marche Automatique; Pepita; Step Ahead March; Lucille (romance with solo 'cello); *Blue Grass; Dreams; Flying Ace; Love's Lullaby; Nina; Dixie Airs; Russian Airs.*

Chinese Lament		vocal	3	Sam Fox
Is There a Santa Claus?		vocal	12	MS.

Vocal works in manuscript (2-3 minutes each):
If My Verse Had Wings; Darling; Clarion Song.

No recent information obtained.

Brabant, Pierre

Pianist and composer. Born in Montreal, August 26th, 1925.

Musical education with J. E. Savaria and others (piano) and in Paris. Musical activities are divided between concert work and composition.

Address: 7810 Casgrain, Montreal, P.Q.

	COMPOSITIONS			
TITLE	DATE	TYPE	TIME (MIN.)	PUBLISHER
La Gaspésienne (ballet)	1949	piano	22	MS.
Berceuse	1947	piano	3½	Editions de l'Aube (Pierre Brabant)
Souvenir d'un Musicien Polonais (Hommage à Chopin)	1947	piano	1	Editions de l'Aube (Pierre Brabant)
Sonatine in C	1947	piano	9	MS.
Suite (Etude, Cantilène, Scherzo)	1946	piano	7	MS.
Two Fantasies	1944, 48	piano	5, 4	MS.

		COMPOSITIONS		
TITLE	DATE	TYPE	TIME (MIN.)	PUBLISHER
Caprice Laurentien	1945	*piano*	3	MS.
Five Cantilènes	1948	*piano*	12	MS.
Five Eglogues	1948	*piano*	16	MS.
Six Danses Canadiennes	1948	*piano*	15	MS.
Pastorale	1949	*piano*	4	MS.
Bagatelle	1950	*piano*	3	MS.
Caprice Chinois	1948	*piano*	2½	MS.

Branscombe, Gena

Composer, conductor and pianist. Born in Picton, Ont., November 4th, 1881.

Musical education at Chicago Musical College (graduated in 1900), in Berlin and New York. Degrees: B.A. (Chicago Mus. College), hon. M.A. (Whitman College). Has held teaching positions in U.S. and conducted choirs (Branscombe Choral Society since 1934). First vice-president, National Association for American Composers and Conductors (1950) and member and functionary of many musical organizations. *Pilgrims of Destiny* won prize offered by National League of Pen Women in 1928. Has lived in U.S. for over 50 years except for frequent visits to Canada.

Address: 611 West 114th Street, New York City 25, N.Y., U.S.A.

Affiliation: ASCAP.

		COMPOSITIONS		
TITLE	DATE	TYPE	TIME (MIN.)	PUBLISHER
Choral drama:				
Pilgrims of Destiny (G. Branscombe)	1929	*soli, choir, orch.*	75	O. Ditson
Instrumental works:				
Quebec (symphonic suite)	1928	*orchestra*	17	MS.
Procession	1935	*orchestra*	14	MS.
Elegie; Pavane; Galliard; Rigaudon		*orchestra*	ea. 4-6	MS.
Baladine	1935	*small orchestra*	3	MS.
String Quartet		*string quartet*		
Violin Sonata	1920	*vln and piano*	12	MS.
Carnival Fantasy	1932	*vln and piano*	4	A. P. Schmidt
An Old Love Tale		*vln and piano*	2½	A. P. Schmidt
A Memory		*vln, vc, piano*	2½	A. P. Schmidt
When Joan of Arc Was a Little Girl		*piano*	8	A. P. Schmidt
A Woodsy Nymph Came Dancing		*piano*	2	A. P. Schmidt
Three Piano Pieces		*piano*	ea. 2	G. Schirmer
Works for voice:				
The Phantom Caravan (cantata)	1926	*male choir, orch.*	12	John Church
Youth of the World (cycle)	1932	*female choir, orch.*	9	M. Witmark & Sons
Maples (G. Branscombe)	1928	*female choir, orch.*	3	M. Witmark & Sons

COMPOSITIONS

TITLE	DATE	TYPE	TIME (MIN.)	PUBLISHER
Sun, and the Warm Brown Earth	1934	female choir, orch. (or piano)	2½	C. C. Birchard & Co.
Coventry's Choir	1944	female choir, piano, organ and per.	5¼	G. Schirmer
The Dancer of Fjaard (cantata)	1926	choral	15	A. P. Schmidt
The Morning Wind		solo or choral	2	A. P. Schmidt
I Bring You Heart's-ease		solo or choral	2¾	A. P. Schmidt
At the Postern Gate; Dear Lad O' Mine; A Wind from the Sea; Spirit of Motherhood; Roses in Madrid; In Arcady by Moonlight; Ol' Marse Winter; Hail Ye Tyme of Holidayes		solo or choral	ea. 2-4	A. P. Schmidt
Mary at Bethlehem (G. Branscombe)		choral	3	G. Ricordi
Prayer for Song		choral	3	G. Ricordi
Afar on the Purple Moor (G. Branscombe)	1945	choral (male or female)	2¾	G. Schirmer
Wood Winds	1949	choral (female)	3	Fitzsimons
The Lord Is Our Fortress (after Brahms)	1948	choral (mixed or female)	5½	J. Fischer & Bro.
O Maidens Run Quickly		choral (female)	2½	Elkan-Vogel
Our Canada, from Sea to Sea (hymn, A. Stringer)	1939	choral or vocal		G. V. Thompson
Wreathe the Holly, Twine the Bay (carol)	1938	choral (mixed or female)	2½	J. Fischer & Bro.
Into the Light (G. Branscombe)		choral		Carl Fischer
Across the Blue Aegean Sea	1939	voice and chamber group	2½	Galaxy Music Corp.
A Lute of Jade (4 songs)	1937	voice and wwds	9	A. P. Schmidt
By St. Lawrence Water (G. Branscombe)		vocal	3	A. P. Schmidt
Blow Softly Maple Leaves	1945	vocal	3	H. W. Gray & Co.

Many other songs published by Galaxy Music Corp., Arthur P. Schmidt, Boosey & Hawkes, O. Ditson and G. Schirmer.

About 50 choral arrangements published by Elkan-Vogel, Galaxy Music Corp., Gordon V. Thompson, Arthur P. Schmidt, Fischer, Sprague-Coleman, G. Ricordi and G. Schirmer.

See:
Reis, *Composers in America.*

Brassard, François

Organist, folklorist and composer. Born in St. Jérôme (Lac St. Jean), P.Q., October 6th, 1908.

Studied composition with Robert Talbot in Quebec, Claude Champagne in Montreal, Albert Bertelin and Guy de Lioncourt in Paris and R. Vaughan Williams in London.

Is assistant professor, Laval University. Member of editorial committee of Archives de Folklore (Quebec) and of International Council for Folk Music (London). Canadian delegate in 1949 to the International Congress of Folkmusic at Venice.

Address: 176 rue Saint-Charles, Jonquière, P.Q.

COMPOSITIONS

TITLE	DATE	TYPE	TIME (MIN.)	PUBLISHER
Marche Fantasque et Festival	1949	*orchestra*	7	MS.
Suite villageoise	1948	*vln and piano*	8	MS.
Trois Préludes	1945	*piano*	7	MS.
La Vierge dorée				
Air de Psalterion				
Ramage				
Orléanaises	1946	*piano*	12	to be published
Aubade				
Les Noisettes				
Le Moulin de Lirec				
Oratoire à la croisée des chemins				
Fête nautique				
Collines	1947	*choral*	2	Archambault
Jonglerie esquimaude aux bouches du Mackenzie	1947	*choral*	3	MS.
Pie Jesu	1938	*voice and organ*	2	publ. in "Chants et Motets pour les défunts", Quebec
Panis Angelicus	1942	*voice and organ*		Procure Générale

Folk song harmonizations:

C'est en passant par Varennes	1947	*choral*	3	MS.
Seven French Canadian songs		*vocal*		MS.

Brauneis, Jean-Chrysostome, Sr.

Bandmaster and music teacher. Born in Darmstadt, Germany, 1785. Died in Quebec, September 15th, 1832.

Came to Canada in or before 1814. Was musician in the band of the 70th Regiment at Quebec. After c. 1818 taught music (piano) and in 1823 opened a music store in Quebec. Imported and tuned pianos. In 1831 became bandmaster of the first purely local music corps of Quebec with which he gave a concert February 20th, 1832. He died in the same year of cholera.

Composition:

Instrumental Preface (dedicated to Lady Mary Lennox) 1819.

Brauneis, Jean-Chrysostome, Jr.

Organist, music teacher and composer. Born in Quebec, January 26th, 1814. Died in Montreal, August 11th, 1871.

Musical education at first in Quebec and from 1830-33 in Europe. From 1833-45 organist at Notre Dame Church, Montreal and later at St. Jacques, Montreal. In 1837 founded Société de Musique, probably the first musical society in Montreal. Importer of instruments and piano tuner. A teacher of great reputation in his day; taught instruments, voice, composition, orchestration and theory.

Son of J-Ch. Brauneis, Sr.

Compositions:
Mass (dedicated to Rev. M. Quiblier) 1835 choir, organ vln, fl, cb, bn
March (dedicated to the Société St.-Jean Baptiste) 1848

Brewer, George MacKenzie

Pianist, organist, lecturer, playwright and composer. Born in London, Ont.'
May 30th, 1889. Died in Montreal, March 18th, 1947.

Musical education with Dr. P. J. Illsley. Diploma: Fellow American Guild of
Organists (1911). Was organist and choir director of many churches in and around
Montreal. Travelled extensively (1913-1935) collecting native music of various countries.

COMPOSITIONS

TITLE	DATE	TYPE	TIME (MIN.)	PUBLISHER
Trois Préludes		piano	1½	Belgo-Canadienne
All Laud and Praise (Cantata 167-Bach)		piano	3½	Boston Music Co.
Susanni (unison carol)		choral		MS.
When Christ Was Born (unison carol)		choral		MS.
Je ne veux pas autre chose		vocal	3½	La Lyre
If She But Knew		vocal	3	Belgo-Canadienne

Songs in manuscript:

Brocade (3 songs with Japanese texts); *Dawn* (Japanese text); *Illusion*; *A Medley of Perfume* (2 songs);
Lines From the Tomb of an Unknown Woman; *Aghmat* (2 songs, words by Mutamid, King of Seville); *Night-long*; *Ora Nam Buadh* (2 songs); *Song of St. Bride*; *O Where are Thy White Hands*; *A Word From the Wind*;
Ave Maria; *Norwegian Lullaby*; *Icelandic Lullaby*; *O Man, Bewail Thy Sin*; *My Soul Doth Magnify*; *A Cradle Song of Smyrna.*

Various arrangements of music for dramatic productions.

Broome, Dr. Edward

Organist, choirmaster and composer. Born in Manchester, England, 1868. Died
in Toronto, May 10th, 1932.

Musical education in Wales where he started career as organist and choirmaster.
Came to Canada in 1894. Organist in Montreal, 1894-1905. After 1907 was organist
and choirmaster in Toronto. Founded Toronto Oratorio Society in 1910. Taught voice
and organ at Royal Conservatory, Toronto. Won eight medals and prizes at Welsh
national festivals for his compositions: *The Siege of Cardiff Castle* won £50 in 1908.
Degree: Mus.Doc. (Toronto, 1908).

COMPOSITIONS

TITLE	DATE	TYPE	TIME (MIN.)	PUBLISHER
The Siege of Cardiff Castle	1908	opera		
A Hymn of Trust (cantata)		solo, choir, orch.		G. Schirmer
Sea-Song (dramatic chorus)		choir, orchestra		O. Ditson
Over 40 opening sentences from the Psalms		choral		G. Schirmer

About 100 published works, including many anthems, part songs and songs. Publishers include Boston
Music Co., G. Schirmer, Arthur P. Schmidt, B. F. Wood Music Co., John Church Co. and O. Ditson & Co.

Brott, Alexander

Violinist, conductor and composer. Born in Montreal, March 14th, 1915.

Musical education at McGill Conservatorium (Licentiate Diploma in violin) and at Juilliard School of Music (post-graduate work with honors in violin, composition and conducting).

Founder and 1st violinist of McGill String Quartet, concert master and associate conductor of Les Concerts Symphoniques and of The Little Symphony. Professor and head of string department of McGill Conservatorium.

Twice awarded Elizabeth Sprague Coolidge Prize for chamber-music composition and four CAPAC awards for serious composition. Twice awarded Loeb Memorial Prize for chamber-music performance. Twice toured England and six European countries, conducting works by Canadian composers.

One of the five Canadian composers selected to represent Canada at the Prague festival in 1946. *From Sea to Sea* was commissioned by CBC International Service; Violin Concerto by The Little Symphony etc.

Address: 5459 Earnscliffe Ave., Montreal, P.Q.

Affiliation: CAPAC.

COMPOSITIONS

TITLE	DATE	TYPE	TIME (MIN.)	PUBLISHER
Oracle (symphonic poem)	1939	*orchestra*	10	MS.
War and Peace (symphonic poem)	1944	*orchestra*	22	MS.
Concordia (symphonic poem)	1946	*orchestra*	24	MS.
Fancy and Folly	1947	*orchestra*	8	MS.
From Sea to Sea (symph. suite) (5 mvmts)	1947	*orchestra*	38	MS.
Prelude to Oblivion	1951	*small orchestra*	4	M.S.
Violin Concerto	1950	*chamber orchestra*	20	MS.
Laurentian Idyll	1940	*concert band*	9	MS.
Lullaby and Procession of the Toys	1943	*string orchestra*	8	MS.
Five Miniatures for eight players	1950	*cl, hn, bn, strgs*	10	MS.
Quintet	1950	*strgs, percussion*	15	MS.
String Quartet	1943	*string quartet*	27	MS.
Quartet for recorders and strings	1948	*4 recorders, v, va, vc*	6	MS.
Characteristic Dance	1940	*vln and piano also: vln and cham. orch.*	5	MS.
Piano Suite	1941	*piano*	12	MS.
Songs of Contemplation (Four)	1945	*voice, str. quint.*	12	MS.

Recordings:

Concordia (CBC Canadian Album No. 3)

Cradle Song (CBC Canadian Album No. 3)

Brown, Allanson G. Y.

Organist, music teacher, accompanist and composer. Born in York, England, May 31st, 1902.

Musical education mostly self-taught and with Sir Edward Bairstow. Diploma: F.R.C.O. Organist since the age of 13. Came to Canada in 1932. Has conducted both choral and instrumental societies in British Isles and Canada. Has also done some theatre organ work.

Address: 177 Powell Avenue, Ottawa, Ont.

Affiliation: BMI

COMPOSITIONS

TITLE	DATE	TYPE	TIME (MIN.)	PUBLISHER
Legend of Grand Pré	1949	opera (one act)	80	MS.
Fantasy-Prelude	1948	piano and orch.	15	MS.
Fantasy on Irish Tunes	1949	orchestra	12	MS.
Christmas Suite	1950	strings	15	MS.
Chant Religieux		organ		H. W. Gray & Co.
A Festive Alleluia		organ		A. P. Schmidt
Fragrance (prelude)		organ		A. P. Schmidt
Three Religious Pieces		organ		McLaughlin & Reilly
Prelude on Austria Tune		organ		A. P. Schmidt
Two Meditations on Palestrina themes		organ		A. P. Schmidt
The Lee Shore		choral	5-7	BMI Canada
The Beatitudes		vocal		O. Ditson
Sabbath Morn		vocal		A. Fassio

Collection of arrangements for strings (folk songs, old masters) in manuscript. Anthems, sacred songs and other music published by Arthur P. Schmidt, Paterson's, H. W. Gray & Co., R. D. Row and Mello-Music Publishing Co.

Buck, Era Marguerite

Pianist, violinist, organist and composer. Born in Manitoulin Island, Ont.

Musical education at Regina Conservatory of Music with George Coutts, Edna Marie Hawkin and Lyell Gustin; in Toronto with Peter Kennedy; in New York with Howard Brockway (piano). Many other teachers.

Is teacher of piano and organ at Regina Conservatory. Winner of many prizes in composition contests at the Saskatchewan Music Festival.

Address: Regina College, Regina, Sask.

COMPOSITIONS

TITLE	DATE	TYPE	TIME (MIN.)	PUBLISHER
Good Night		choral	1	F. Harris

Songs in manuscript (1-3 minutes each):
The Forsaken Merman; Slumber Song; A Lament; The Plowman; O Can Ye Sew Cushions; The Three Fishers; Where No Land Lies; Where Dreams Are Sold; The Three Poplars (duet).

Buckley, Beatrice Barron

Singer, pianist, composer and author. Born in Sarnia, Ont.

Musical education with Louise Higgimbotham, Carl Koelling (Chicago, piano and composition), Isabelle MacArthur, Joseph O'Donnell (singing). Won highest award in song competition at Saskatchewan Music Festival. Advanced-member Story-crafters Guild, Hollywood, Calif.

Address: 219 College Street, Apt. 331, Toronto, Ont.

Affiliation: CAPAC.

COMPOSITIONS

TITLE	DATE	TYPE	TIME (MIN.)	PUBLISHER
Songs of Weeny Gopher (lyrics B. Buckley)—(25 songs for boys and girls. The cycle of the year on the Western Prairies)		*vocal*		MacMillan
My Sanctuary		*vocal*		Boosey & Hawkes

About 25 songs with piano accompaniment in manuscript, 3-4 minutes each.

Buckley, William Henry

Pianist, organist conductor, and composer. Born in Paris, Ont.

Musical education at Brantford Conservatory of Music, leading to award of gold medal and fellowship, Toronto College of Music. Post-graduate work with J. E. Hutcheson and A. Sclarewski (piano) and A. Riemenschneider (organ).

Address: 219 College Street, Apt. 331, Toronto, Ont.

COMPOSITIONS

TITLE	DATE	TYPE	TIME (MIN.)	PUBLISHER
March		*band*	3½	MS.
Canzonetta in A		*piano*	3	Th. Presser
Fascination Waltz		*piano*	4	Th. Presser
Away in a Manger		*choral*	4	Th. Presser
Blow, Golden Trumpets		*choral*	3-4	O. Ditson
That Glorious Song of Old		*choral*	3-4	O. Ditson
Jesus, the Weary Wanderer's Rest		*choral*	4	H. W. Gray & Co.
O Jesus, Full of Pardoning Grace		*vocal*	3	Th. Presser
Lord, Give Me Faith		*vocal*	3	Th. Presser

Choral works published by Lorenz (3-4 minutes each):
None Other Lamb; I Lay My Sins; Master Let Me Walk; O Lord, How Manifold; God Is Love; Bread of World; Lead On; Infant Holy; Ye Servants of God.

Burchell, H. Louise

Organist, choirmaster, music teacher and composer. Born in Sydney, N.S.

Education in St. John's, Nfld., London, England and Cambridge, Mass. Degrees: Mus.Bac. (Oxford), M.A., Radcliffe (Harvard). Held teaching positions in Mount Allison Univ., N.B., Dakota Wesleyan Univ., Milwaukee-Downer College, Halifax Conservatory of Music and other places. At present is organist and choir director at Trinity United Church, Windsor, N.S. *Lament, Acquiescence, Animation, A Christmas Folk-Song* were all performed over CBC (Harold Sumberg, Thelma Johannes, Anna Macdonald, Ernesto Vinci).

Address: Windsor, N.S.

COMPOSITIONS

TITLE	DATE	TYPE	TIME (MIN.)	PUBLISHER
Lament "S-4"		*strings*	4	MS.
Couperinesque		*strings, wood, horns*	2½	MS.
		arr. for strings	2½	MS.

TITLE	DATE	COMPOSITIONS TYPE	TIME (MIN.)	PUBLISHER
Variations on "St. Anne"		organ	6½	MS.
Acquiescence		piano	2	MS.
Animation		piano	1½	MS.
A Christmas Folk-Song		vocal	2	MS.
Griefs		vocal	1	MS.

Butler, Adrian Roderick

Organist, pianist, choirmaster and composer. Born in New Westminster, B.C., 1929.

Musical education with R. T. Bevan, Kenneth Ross (piano and organ), and Herald Keefer (organ). Is assistant church organist in Vancouver, teaches school in New Westminster and directs a choir.

Address: 3651 Smith Avenue, Burnaby, B.C.

TITLE	DATE	COMPOSITIONS TYPE	TIME (MIN.)	PUBLISHER
Symphony No. 1	1947	orchestra	31	MS.
Paul Pero	1948	orchestra	31	MS.
Piano Concerto No. 1	1945	piano and strings	30	MS.
Piano Concerto No. 2	1950	piano and orchestra		MS.
String Quartet	1948	string quartet	12	MS.
Prelude	1950	organ	4	MS.
Variations on Hymn Tune	1948	organ	9	MS.
Two Piano Sonatas	1947	piano	10 & 9	MS.
Suite	1950	piano	12	MS.
Eight Meditations	1947-50	piano	15	MS.
Mass	1946	choral	7	MS.
Songs	1950	vocal		MS.

Cable, Howard Reid

Arranger, conductor and composer. Born in Toronto, December 15th, 1920.

Musical education at Royal Conservatory, Toronto with Dr. Ettore Mazzoleni and John Weinzweig. Diploma: A.T.C.M. in conducting and bandmastership. Has arranged and composed incidental music for CBC since 1942, conducted since 1943. Has scored and conducted music for many films for the National Film Board. Chief composing activity is to write incidental music for radio and films.

Address: 7 L'Estrange Place, Toronto, Ont.

Affiliation: CAPAC.

TITLE	DATE	COMPOSITIONS TYPE	TIME (MIN.)	PUBLISHER
Newfoundland Sketches	1948	string orchestra	12	Can. Music Sales (rental)

Many popular works, light songs and marches.

Cadoret, Charlotte
(Soeur St-Jean-du-Sacré-Coeur)

Pianist and composer. Born in Newark, N.J., February 29th, 1908.

Musical education in Montreal at Conservatoire National, Institut Pédagogique and Schola Cantorum. Studied with E. Robert Schmitz (piano), Rodolphe Mathieu and Claude Champagne (theory and composition), Eugène Lapierre (accompaniment of Gregorian Chant). Degrees: Bachelor and Licentiate of Music (Ecole Normale de Musique de l'Institut Pédagogique, Univ. de Montréal). Since 1934 teacher at, and since 1942 director of, Ecole Normale de Musique de l'Institut Pédagogique.

Address: Congrégation Notre-Dame, 4873 Westmount Avenue, Montreal, P.Q.

Affiliation: BMI.

COMPOSITIONS

TITLE	DATE	TYPE	TIME (MIN.)	PUBLISHER
Messe à Notre-Dame		*2 equal voices, organ*		BMI Canada
Messe		*3 equal voices, organ*		MS.
Cantata in Honor of Blessed Marguerite Bourgeoys		*choral*		MS.
Tu Verras		*choral*	4	MS.
Parce Domine		*choral*	2½	MS.
Bone Pastor		*choral*	1½	MS.
Ecce Fidelis		*choral*	1	MS.
Cradle Song (P. Colum)		*vocal*	3	G. Schirmer
Les Communiantes		*vocal*	3-4	MS.
Lorsque je mourrai (R. Lasnier)		*vocal*		BMI Canada

Cadzow, Dorothy Forrest

Composer, arranger and teacher. Born in Edmonton, August 9th, 1916.

Graduated in music from University of Washington (B.A. degree and teacher's diploma). In 1942 received a three-year fellowship in composition at Juilliard Graduate School and studied with Frederick Jacobi and Bernard Wagenaar.

In 1943 began work for Robert Russell Bennett, composer and arranger, and became member of his Ford show chorus, also arranged for Ford and other radio shows. From 1945-49 did free-lance arranging and teaching. Was staff writer for International Musician. In 1949 orchestrated and arranged music for three children's records for MGM. Since fall of 1949 is on staff of music department of University of Washington, teaching theory, orchestration and composition.

Address: 4725 15th Avenue N.E., Seattle, Washington, U.S.A.

COMPOSITIONS

TITLE	DATE	TYPE	TIME (MIN.)	PUBLISHER
Northwestern Sketches	1945	*orchestra*	12	MS.
Prelude	1950	*string orchestra*	6	MS.
Quartet No. 1	1944	*string quartet*	12	MS.
Little Ben	1944	*piano*	2	Mercury Music
Prairie Lullaby	1944	*piano*	2½	Mercury Music
Who Told You So?	1948	*piano*	1½	Elkan-Vogel Co.
Heard Next Door	1948	*piano*	1½	Elkan-Vogel Co.

COMPOSITIONS

TITLE	DATE	TYPE	TIME (MIN.)	PUBLISHER
The Lord's Prayer	1949	*vocal*	3	Century Music Co.
A Blackbird Suddenly	1949	*vocal*	2½	Ass. Music Publishers
Golden Dawn	1949	*vocal*	2½	BMI Canada
Around a Toadstool Table	1946	*song cycle*	8	MS.
Br'er Rabbit Medley	1948	*song cycle*	6	MS.
Song to Poems (M. W. Brown)	1947	*song cycle*	8	MS.

Campbell, Edith Mary

Organist, choirmaster and composer. Born in St. Luc, St. Johns Co., P.Q., September 1st, 1912.

Musical education with Dr. Alfred Whitehead, Diploma: F.C.C.O. Is organist and choir director of St. James Church, St. Johns, P.Q. since 1932.

Address: 182 De Salaberry Street, St. Johns, P.Q.

COMPOSITIONS

TITLE	DATE	TYPE	TIME (MIN.)	PUBLISHER
Scherzo		*string orchestra*	4	MS.
Theme and Variations	1943	*string orchestra*	15	MS.
I Have Cull'd That Lovely Rosebud (arr.)		*string quartet*	3	MS.
Prelude and Fugue	1947	*organ*	8	MS.
Paraphrase on "Jesus Christ Is Risen"	1944	*organ*	5	H. W. Gray & Co.
The Victor's Triumph (arr.)	1947	*choir and organ*	3	O. Ditson
The Babe in Bethlehem's Manger (arr.)	1945	*choir and organ*	4	A. P. Schmidt
Christ Has Arisen (arr.)		*choral*	3	O. Ditson
Kings Shall Come from Saba		*choral*	2	Boston Music Co.

Caron, Allan

Pianist, organist, composer and music publisher. Born in L'Orignal, Ont., May 28th, 1898.

Musical education with own sisters (piano) and Dantès Belleau (organ). Has been active as pianist with theatre orchestras and on radio.

Address: 507-314 Broadway Avenue, Winnipeg, Man.

COMPOSITIONS

TITLE	DATE	TYPE	TIME (MIN.)	PUBLISHER
Jesu Sleep (carol)		*choral*		Mello-Music Publ. Co.
The Angelus		*choral*		Mello-Music Publ. Co.
Regina Coeli (Easter anthem)		*choral*		Mello-Music Publ. Co.
Prayer for Peace		*choral*		Mello-Music Publ. Co.
Rejoice and Sing (Easter)		*choral*		Mello-Music Publ. Co.

COMPOSITIONS

TITLE	DATE	TYPE	TIME (MIN.)	PUBLISHER
Panis Angelicus		*voice and violin*		Mello-Music Publ. Co.
Invocation		*violin*		Mello-Music Publ. Co.
Ave Maria		*vocal*		Mello-Music Publ. Co.
O Lord Most Holy		*vocal*		Mello-Music Publ. Co.
Slumber Song		*vocal*		Mello-Music Publ. Co.
The Lord's Prayer		*vocal*		Mello-Music Publ. Co.
Suite Nuptiale		*vocal*		Mello-Music Publ. Co.
Park Avenue Polka		*piano*		Mello-Music Publ. Co.

Many popular songs, ballads etc. published by the same publisher.

Caron, Joseph Charles Eugène

Organist, music teacher and composer. Born in Sherbrooke, P.Q., November 16th, 1900.

Musical education at Conservatoire National de Musique, Montreal, with Eugène Lapierre, and with Henri Gagnon (organ), R.O. Pelletier II (harmony), Mrs. M. C. Shea, Oscar Cartier and James Whitehead (piano). Degree: Licentiate in Music (Montreal University).

Has been organist for 33 years and teacher of piano, organ, solfeggio and theory for 28 years, residing in Sherbrooke, Montreal and now in Ottawa. Is organist and choirmaster at Ste-Anne Church, Ottawa and teaches music.

Address: 17 Myrand, Ottawa, Ont.

COMPOSITIONS

TITLE	DATE	TYPE	TIME (MIN.)	PUBLISHER
Symphony (3 mvmts)	1949	*orchestra*	18	MS.
Jubilé d'argent (cantata)	1933	*choir and piano*	10	MS.
Messe des morts	1947	*choir and organ*		MS.
Ave Maria	1941	*choir and organ*	3	MS.
Cor Jesu	1942	*choir, organ or piano*	2	A. J. Boucher
Jour de vacance	1934	*piano*	3	Parnasse Musical
Ronde sous les bois	1944	*piano*	2	Eugène Caron
La Jeune Fille	1925	*vocal*	2	La Bonne Chanson
As-tu vu le printemps?	1925	*vocal*	2	La Bonne Chanson
Chanson de Fileuse	1934	*vocal*	3	La Bonne Chanson
Mia	1942	*vocal*	3	Parnasse Musical

Songs in manuscript (2-3 minutes each):
Le Rouet de la vie; Les Nids; Chanson; L'Eglise du village; Notre rivière; Petit Bateau; Chanson de berger; Les Arbres; Le Soir.

Caron-Legris, Albertine

Pianist and composer. Born in Louiseville, Que.

Musical education with Sisters of the Assumption, R. Octave Pelletier and Michel Hirvy (piano), Rodolphe Plamondon (singing), Chanoine Elysée Panneton and Eugène

Lapierre (harmony). Degree: Mus.Bac. (Montreal). Won second prize in Abbé Gadbois competition. Has appeared on radio and as accompanist.

Address: 319 St. Joseph Boulevard East, Apt. 7, Montreal, P.Q.

Affiliation: BMI.

COMPOSITIONS

TITLE	DATE	TYPE	TIME (MIN.)	PUBLISHER
Poème pastorale	1948	piano	5	BMI Canada
Danse rustique	1947	piano	4	MS.
Soir d'hiver	1948	vocal	3	BMI Canada
La Chanson du Ber		vocal	4	MS.
Anne, Ma Soeur Anne		vocal		MS.
Chanson pour Don Quichote		vocal		MS.
La Berceuse de Donalda	1947	vocal	5	Musica Enr.
ᶜCantique à St. Joseph		vocal	2	MS.
C'est le mois de Marie		vocal	2	MS.
Cor Jesu		vocal		MS.
Six popular songs		vocal		MS.
11 French Canadian songs harmonized, including:		vocal		MS.
Ceux qui s'aiment		vocal		Passe-Temps, 1947
Four Fr. Can. songs (Gagnon collection) harmonized		vocal		MS.
Six Fr. Can. songs harmonized		vocal		MS.

Cayouette, Marius

Pianist, organist and composer. Born in Ste. Justine, P.Q., November 3rd, 1904.

Musical education with Rev. Père Alphonse Tardif and Henri Gagnon (organ and piano) and with Robert Talbot (harmony and allied subjects). Organist at St. Grégoire-le-Grand Church, Montmorency, P.Q. Secretary of Ecole de Musique de l'Université Laval, Quebec. Professor of music history at Quebec Provincial Conservatory. Diploma: Lauréat, Académie de Musique (organ).

Address: 9 rue Ste.Famille, Quebec, P.Q.

COMPOSITIONS

TITLE	DATE	TYPE	TIME (MIN.)	PUBLISHER
Prélude pour les Matines de Pâques		organ	5	MS.
Fantaisie sur un Noël		organ	5½	MS.
Petite Suite (Noël)		organ	10	MS.
Cinq interludes (Noël)		organ	6	MS.
Encensement		organ	3	MS.
J'ai chanté comme Chérubin		vocal	2	MS.
Kissing's No Sin		vocal	2	MS.
Tanka (Japanese)		vocal	1½	MS.
Le Tisserand		vocal	3	MS.
Ave Maria		vocal	4	MS.

Chamberlain, Sydney George

Bandmaster and composer. Born in England, April 3rd, 1884.

Musical education in Toronto under John Slatter, Richard Raven and W. Gourlay· Bandmaster of the 198th Canadian Buffs, 1916. Bandmaster of Collingwood Kiltie Band, 1919. Bandmaster of Chatham Kiltie Band for past 20 years.

Address: 159 Raleigh Street, Chatham, Ont.

COMPOSITIONS

TITLE	DATE	TYPE	TIME (MIN.)	PUBLISHER
Maple City March		band	4	Waterloo Music
Young Canada (overture)		band	8	MS.
Friendship Border (overture)		band	9	Waterloo Music
Return of the Rehabs (overture)		band	3½	MS.
Overture		band		MS.

Chamberland, Albert

Violinist, conductor and composer. Born in Montreal, October 12th, 1886.

Musical education at McGill Conservatorium of Music with Alfred De Sève (violin). Concert violinist. From 1910-20 member of the late Dubois String Quartet. From 1920-25 led own quartet. From 1935-41 was assistant concert-master with Montreal Symphony Orchestra and concertmaster with the Société des Concerts Symphoniques de Montréal. Senior Music Producer, CBC, Montreal.

Address: c/o Canadian Broadcasting Corporation, Montreal, P.Q.

COMPOSITIONS

TITLE	DATE	TYPE	TIME (MIN.)	PUBLISHER
Allegro Militaire		band	3	MS.
Serenade		vln and piano	3½	Belgo-Canadienne
Etude de Concert		vln and piano	2½	Belgo-Canadienne

Champagne, Dr. Claude

Composer, pianist, violinist, conductor and pedagogue. Born in Montreal, May 27th, 1891.

Musical education in Canada with R. O. Pelletier (piano) and Albert Chamberland (violin), in Paris (1920-28) with Jules Conus (violin), André Gedalge (counterpoint and fugue), Raoul Laparra (composition and orchestration). Degree: Mus.Doc. (Montreal). Diplomas from Dominion College of Music and Conservatoire National de Musique (Montreal).

Member of teaching staff of various colleges, of Ecole Normale de Musique, Ecole Supérieure de Musique d'Outremont, McGill Conservatorium of Music; past director of provincial solfeggio classes, assistant-director of Quebec Provincial Conservatory of Music, lecturer of *Radio-Collège* of CBC French network.

Winner of Beatty International Award for *Suite Canadienne*. Honorary member, Académie de Musique de Québec, Music editor of BMI Canada.

Address: 3425 Ridgewood Avenue, Ridgecrest Apt. 201, Montreal, P.Q.

Affiliation: BMI.

COMPOSITIONS

TITLE	DATE	TYPE	TIME (MIN.)	PUBLISHER
Suite Canadienne	1928	*choir and orchestra*	8	Durand, Paris
Images du Canada Français	1943	*choir and orchestra*	15	MS.
Symphonie Gaspésienne	1945	*orchestra*	20	MS.
Symphony No. 2		*orchestra*		under preparation
Hercule et Omphale	1918	*orchestra*	12	MS.
Ils sont un peuple sans histoire (background music)		*orchestra*	40	MS.
Berceuse (Lullaby)		*orchestra*	2½	MS.
Evocation		*orchestra*	2½	MS.
J'ai du bon tabac (folk song)		*orchestra*	1½	MS.
Concerto in D minor	1948	*piano and small orchestra*	14	MS.
La Ballade des Lutins		*band*	3	MS.
Danse Villageoise		*violin*	4	Parnasse Musical
Habanera		*violin*	2	MS.
Prélude et Filigrane		*piano*	3	MS.
Quadrilha Brasileira		*piano*	2½	BMI Canada
Ave Maria (motet)		*voice and 'cello*	2	BMI Canada
Scoutisme		*vocal*	2	Archambault
Laurentienne		*vocal*	2	Archambault

Folklore arrangements in manuscript:

Instrumental: *Vielle Chanson sur Thème de Richard Coeur de Lion* (str. qua. & hpchd); *Chanson de Croisade du Châtelain du Coucy* (quartet); *Henry IV; Par derrière chez ma tante* (small orchestra).

Mixed chorus: *Tableaux Canadiens* (with orch.); *Quand j'étais chez mon père; Une Perdriole; Cadet Roussel; Marianne s'en va* (with 1 or 2 pianos); *Noël Huron* (with 1 or 2 pianos or orchestra); *Ma Normandie; Vive la Canadienne; En roulant ma boule; Au clair de la lune; La Petite Galiote* (with piano).

Mixed chorus and solo voices: *V'là l'bon vent; Ah! qui marierons-nous?; J'ai cueilli la belle rose.*

Male chorus: *Isabeau s'y promène; Gai lon la, gai le rosier; C'est la belle Françoise; A St. Malo beau port; Vive Napoléon; Rondel.*

Voice and piano: *Au bois du rossignolet; C'est une belle tourterelle; Petit Jean* (also arr. for str. qua., Fr. hn & wwd); *Monsieur le Curé.*

Instruction manuals:
Initiation au Solfège, Archambault.
Solfège Pratique, Archambault.
Solfège Pédagogique, Archambault.
Solfège Scolaire, Archambault.
Leçons à Radio-Collège, MS.

Recordings:
Suite Canadienne (RCA Victor)
Symphonie Gaspésienne (Polydor)

See:
Léo-Pol Morin, *Papiers de Musique*, 1930.

▬Chatillon, Octave Hardy

Violinist, pianist, organist and composer. Born in Quebec, April 12th, 1831. Died in Nicolet, P.Q., 1906.

Teacher at Collège Ste-Thérèse and at Séminaire de Nicolet.

COMPOSITIONS

Six Masses for the Séminaire de Nicolet
Five Cantatas
Choral pieces
Works for band
Instrumental pieces
Quadrilles

Several stage plays, incl. *La Prise de Québec*, published by Beauchemin.

Chotem, Neil

Pianist, conductor and composer. Born in Saskatoon, Sask,. 1921.

Has composed since the age of six and gave first recital when seven. When thirteen appeared with Regina Symphony Orchestra and played over air. During World War II served in RCAF entertainment unit, giving 250 performances. Lives in Montreal since 1945 and has studied piano with Michel Hirvy. Has played on BBC and CBC and appeared as soloist with major Canadian orchestras.

Address: 38 Victoria, Pte. Claire, P.Q.

COMPOSITIONS

TITLE	DATE	TYPE	TIME (MIN.)	PUBLISHER
The Song of Solomon	1951	*radio oratorio*	60	MS.
Prairie Suite		*orchestra*		MS.
Three Symphonic Settings (arr.)		*orchestra*		MS.
Dances Out of the West	1951	*orchestra*		MS.
Scherzo Tarantelle	1936	*piano and orch.*		MS.
Prelude in C sharp minor		*piano*		MS.
Prelude in E flat minor		*piano*		MS.
Fuguey Wooguey		*piano*		MS.

Incidental music for *Canada to Britain* and CBC drama performance of *The Dybbuk*. Other scores for radio. No complete list of compositions available.

Christin, Leopold

Draughtsman, singer, writer, composer and sculptor. Born in Montreal, June 27th, 1877.

Started music as high boy soprano and later sang as tenor soloist in churches in Chicago, New York, Paris, Ottawa, Chicoutimi and Quebec. Professional draughtsman, musical amateur. Co-founder of Chicago Opera Club in 1905. President of Chess Federation of Canada (1947-48), now president emeritus. Is assistant-secretary of the Quebec Geographic Board. Has written several unpublished novels and poems in French and done clay modeling.

Address: 29 Artillerie Street, Quebec, P.Q.

COMPOSITIONS

TITLE	DATE	TYPE	TIME (MIN.)	PUBLISHER
Prière du soir à Marie		*choral*		MS. (photostat)
Sanctus Benedictus		*choral*		MS. (photostat)

Songs in manuscript (photostat):
Le P'tit Pont de bouleau; Si j'étais Botticelli; Rondel du petit Noël; Chanson triste; Chanson d'automne; En train le soir (R. Choquette). *Reste petite; Ballade à ma petite fille; Petit Pays; Jasette d'une vieille devant la*

crèche de Jésus (A. Desilets). *Les Parfums; Les Ombres; Les Fées* (P. Fréchette). *La chanson du passant; Je songe à la vieille maison* (J. Doucet). *Restez avec moi; Aveu* (M. Boissonnault). *Les Etrennes* (A. Bernier). *Nuit* (J. Francoeur). *Berceuse Atoena* (A. Ferland). *La Romance du vin* (E. Nelligan). *Le Miroir* (Y. Lauzière). *Claire; La Grammaire des oiseaux; Berceuse au premier né* (L. Christin). *Next Time* (P. L. Woodbridge). *My Mother* (J. Martin). *Prière du soir à Marie* (anon.)

Publication:

L'Art vocal, publ. by Contact (Quebec Civil Service Assn.)

Chuhaldin-Lind, Alexander

Violinist, conductor and composer. Born in Crimea, South Russia, August 27th, 1892. Died in Toronto, January 20th, 1951.

Musical education at Imperial Conservatory of Moscow under J. Conus (violin). First public appearance aged nine. In 1913 became member of Imperial Grand Opera orchestra, later its concertmaster. In 1924 undertook concert-tour through Asia and ᐯAustralia and in 1927 settled in Canada (Toronto). Was on faculty, Royal Conservatory, Toronto and conducted *Melodic Strings* on CBC.

Affiliation (estate): CAPAC.

COMPOSITIONS

TITLE	DATE	TYPE	TIME (MIN.)	PUBLISHER
Overture		*string orchestra*		MS.
Theme and Variations		*string orchestra*		MS.
Rondino		*string orchestra*		MS.
Scherzo		*string orchestra*		MS.
Troublesome Mosquito		*string orchestra*		MS.
The Mill		*string orchestra*		MS.
Alesha Popovich		*string orchestra*		MS.
Moto Perpetuo		*violin solo*		G. V. Thompson
Love Song of the Hero; Cradle Song; Fairy and the Gnome; A Dream; Reverie		*violin solo*		Paling & Co., Australia

Many arrangements and transcriptions for strings or violin.

Claman, Dolores Olga

Pianist and composer. Born in Vancouver, B.C., July 6th, 1927.

Musical education at Juilliard Graduate School, New York with Rosina Lhevinne (piano fellowship), Bernard Wagenaar and Vittorio Giannini (orchestration and composition) and Edward Steuermann (piano and composition). Has appeared as pianist on radio and concert stage. *Rêve Fantasque* was performed in Montreal at the Canadian Ballet Festival, 1950.

Address: 225 East 60th Street, New York City, U.S.A.

COMPOSITIONS

TITLE	DATE	TYPE	TIME (MIN.)	PUBLISHER
Prelude	1951	*orchestra*	8	MS.
Le Rêve Fantasque (ballet)	1950	*small orchestra*	21	MS.
Primitive Dance	1945	*piano*	5	MS.
Three Songs (James Joyce)	1948-50	*vocal*	5	MS.

Clark, Florence Durell

Pianist, violinist, violist, organist and composer. Born in Rochester, N.Y., April 29th, 1891.

Musical education at Royal Conservatory, Toronto with Sir Ernest MacMillan (organ and composition), Ella Howard, Luigi von Kunits (violin). Degree: Mus.Bac. (Toronto). Diplomas: L.T.C.M., F.C.C.O. Won prizes for numerous songs and branches of music study. Third woman in Canada to be made a Fellow of Canadian College of Organists. Was violist with Hamilton (Ont.) Symphony Orchestra for several years.

Address: 16 Blyth Street, Hamilton, Ont.

COMPOSITIONS

TITLE	DATE	TYPE	TIME (MIN.)	PUBLISHER
Ode for St. Cecilia's Day		choir and strings	20	MS.
Sarabande; Minuet (sketches)		string orchestra	5	MS.
Fantasy on a French-Canadian Tune		string quartet	5	MS.
Placid Lake; Aeolian Harp (sketches)		string trio	8	MS.
Prelude		organ		MS.
Pastorale in A		organ		Oxford U.P.
Carillon		organ	5-6	Elkan-Vogel Co.
Prelude on a Second Mode Melody		organ	3-4	Novello & Co.
Preludes (Picardy; This Endris Night; On Old 124th; Angelus ad Virginem)		organ	15	MS.
Now The Joyful Bells		unison or solo voice	3	MS.
Transcriptions from Bach		organ or piano duo		MS.

Numerous songs.

Clarke, Douglas

Pianist, organist, conductor and composer. Born in Reading, England, April 4th, 1893.

Musical education at Reading University College under Sir Hugh Allen and privately with Gustav Holst, R. Vaughan Williams and Charles Wood. Degrees: M.A., Mus.Bac. (Cambridge). Diploma: F.R.C.O., 1920 (Turpin Prize).

Scholar in composition at Reading University College, 1909-12 (Turbutt Memorial Prize, College Prize). Organist at Christ's College, Cambridge, 1923-27. Came to Canada in 1927. Conducted Winnipeg Male Voice Choir and Philharmonic Society and was organist at Holy Trinity Church, Winnipeg, 1927-29. Director of McGill Conservatorium of Music, Montreal since 1929; dean of faculty of music, McGill Univ. since 1930. Conductor of Montreal Symphony Orchestra for many years since 1930.

Address: c/o McGill Conservatorium of Music, Montreal, P.Q.

COMPOSITIONS

TITLE	DATE	TYPE	TIME (MIN.)	PUBLISHER
Piece for full orchestra		orchestra		MS.
Hunter's Moon		orchestra		MS.
Three Pieces		small orchestra		MS.
Handel in the Pram		strings and piano		MS.

COMPOSITIONS

TITLE	DATE	TYPE	TIME (MIN.)	PUBLISHER
Fantasia on "Lo, He Comes"		*organ*		MS.
Buffoon		*vln and piano*		MS.
O Domine Deus		*choral*		Stainer & Bell
A Late Lark		*choral*		Stainer & Bell
The Passion (in collaboration with D. Jones)		*choral*		Stainer & Bell
Magnificat and Nunc Dimittis		*choral*		Stainer & Bell
Various liturgical works, introits etc.		*choral*		Stainer & Bell
I Saw Three Ships		*choral*		MS.
Communion Service in D		*choral*		MS.
Epiphany		*choral*		MS.
The Song of Shadows		*choral*		MS.
Here's a Health unto His Majesty (arranged)		*choral*		MS.
Tom Bowling (arranged)		*choral*		MS.
Countess Cathleen (Yeats)		*incidental music*		MS.
A Late Lark (arranged)		*narrator, strings*		MS.

Many orchestral arrangements of hymns and carols.

No recent information obtained.

Clarke, Dr. James Peyton

Conductor, organist, music teacher and composer. Born in Scotland, 1808. Died in Toronto, August 27th, 1877.

In 1829 was leader of the psalmody in St. George's Church, Edinburgh. Came to Canada in 1835, at first settling as a farmer. In 1845 he was organist at Christ Church, Hamilton and went to Toronto that year to lead the choir in the first concerts given there. Said to have been appointed music instructor at King's College (Univ. of Toronto) 1845. The first to receive musical degrees in Canada: Mus.Bac., 1846 and Mus.Doc., 1856 (Toronto). Was organist and choral conductor at St. James and later St. Michael's Cathedral, Toronto. Conductor of various musical organizations in Toronto between 1845 and 1872. The first outstanding musician of Anglo-saxon origin in Canada.

COMPOSITIONS

TITLE	DATE	TYPE	TIME (MIN.)	PUBLISHER
Arise, O Lord God, Forget Not the Poor	1846	*anthem (8 parts)*		
The Lays of the Maple Leaf, A Song of Canada (4 songs, opening chorus, duet, chorus)		*choral and vocal*		Nordheimer, 1852 or 53
Airy Spirits (glee)		*choral*		
At Gloamin I'll Be There, Love		*vocal*		Anglo-American periodical, 1852
Sing Old Bard!		*vocal*		Anglo-American periodical, 1852
The Trapper's Song		*vocal*		Anglo-American periodical, 1852

	COMPOSITIONS			
TITLE	DATE	TYPE	TIME (MIN.)	PUBLISHER
A Forest Home		*vocal*		Anglo-American periodical, 1852
Dear England		*vocal*		Anglo-American periodical, 1852
A Canadian Christmas Carol		*vocal*		Anglo-American periodical, 1852
Jeanie, Love, Say!		*vocal*		Anglo-American periodical, 1853
Summer and Winter		*vocal*		Anglo-American periodical, 1853
Mary O'Lammerlaw		*vocal*		Anglo-American periodical, 1853
My Ain Fireside		*vocal*		Anglo-American periodical, 1853
Emblem of Canada		*vocal*		A. J. Boucher
Favorite Toronto Air		*vocal*		A. J. Boucher

In his later life Dr. Clarke composed a number of chamber trios and quartets.

The Canadian Church Psalmody, collected and edited by J. P. Clarke, publ. Roswell, Toronto, 1845, contains 8 anthems, hymns etc. by Clarke.

Waltzes, galops and quadrilles by one J. P. Clarke were published by Hopwood, Augener, Francis, Cramer and Williams.

Collingwood, Arthur

Pianist, organist and composer. Born in Halifax, England, November 24th, 1880.

Musical education with C. Pollard, Tobias Matthay (piano), W. H. Garland, Dr. K. Pyne (organ), Dr. Charles Pearce and Dr. Ebenezer Prout (theory). Musical director of different musical organizations in Aberdeen. Adjudicator at British and Canadian music festivals. Guest conductor with the BBC Orchestra. In 1931 was appointed dean of the faculty of music, University of Saskatchewan. Retired in 1947 as dean emeritus.

Address: c/o Dr. Thomson, 3521 University Street, Montreal, P.Q.

Affiliation: CAPAC.

	COMPOSITIONS			
TITLE	DATE	TYPE	TIME (MIN.)	PUBLISHER
Song of Hope		*choral (male) or vocal*	3	Paterson
O Mistress Mine		*choral or vocal*	4	J. Curwen & Sons
Requiem		*choral (mixed)*	4	Paterson
Requiem		*choral (male)*	4	Paterson
Song Cycle		*vocal*	14	J. Curwen & Sons
House Blessing		*vocal*		· Paterson
Three Christmas Carols		*vocal*		G. V. Thompson
Minuet and Trio in G		*piano*	5	Paterson
Valse in B flat		*piano*		MS.
Minuet No. 2		*piano*		MS.

Choral works (3-5 minutes each):   Paterson

My Love Is Like a Red, Red Rose; Who Is Sylvia; Under the Greenwood Tree; Gather Ye Rosebuds; God Be Merciful; I Will Magnify Thee; I Know a Bank; Ye Spotted Snakes; Dainty Little Maiden.

Collins, Edwin Alec

Organist, choirmaster and composer. Born in Debenham, Suffolk, England, April 25th, 1893.

Musical education with Sir Charles Villiers Stanford, Charles Wood and Dr. Cyril B. Rootham. Organist of Aspall Church, Suffolk, 1903-11. Organist and choirmaster of Littleport Parish Church, senior assistant organist and choirmaster of Ely Cathedral, 1911-15. Military service, 1915-20. Orgainst in Suffolk and London, 1920-26. Came to Canada in 1926. Has been dean of the faculty of music, Acadia University, Wolfville, N.S. since 1927.

Address: P.O. Box 471, Wolfville, N.S.

Affiliation: CAPAC.

COMPOSITIONS

TITLE	DATE	TYPE	TIME (MIN.)	PUBLISHER
Song of the Indian Maid		*choir and orch.*	13	MS.
Memorial Ode		*choir and orch.*	15	MS.
Psalm 90		*tenor, choir, orch.*	14	MS.
Graduation Anthem (W. Kirkconnell)	1949	*solo, choir, orch.*	3	MS.
Concertino in B minor	1949	*vln and orch.*	15½	MS.
Quintet "Grand Pré"		*piano and strgs*	35	MS.
Night Rhapsody		*vln and piano*	6	MS.
A Dance Fantasy	1947	*vln and piano*	3½	MS.
Suffolk Sketch		*vln and piano*	5½	MS.
Motet		*choral*		MS.
Almighty and Everlasting God		*choral*	3	MS.
Sea Dream		*voice and orch.*	5	MS.
Daffodils		*vocal*	4	MS.
Nova Scotia Suite (W. Kirkconnell)	1949	*vocal*	16	MS.

Contant, Alexis

Organist, pianist, composer and music teacher. Born in Montreal, November 12th, 1858. Died in Montreal, November 28th, 1918.

Musical education in Montreal with J. A. Fowler and G. Couture and in Boston with Calixa Lavallée. One of the first Canadian composers not to go to Europe for study. Taught piano at Collège Mount Saint-Louis for 28 years, also at Collège de Montréal and at convent of the Soeurs Jesus-Marie at Hochelaga. Was organist at St.-Jean-Baptiste Church in Montreal for 31 years.

Inquiries: Jean Contant, c/o CBC Montreal.

COMPOSITIONS

TITLE	DATE	TYPE	TIME (MIN.)	PUBLISHER
Cain (3 parts: La Haine; Le Sang; La Promesse)	1905	*oratorio*		MS. performed in Montreal 1905 under J. J. Goulet
Les Deux Ames (poème symphonique)	1909	*narrator, choir and orch.*		MS. performed in Montreal 1913

COMPOSITIONS

TITLE	DATE	TYPE	TIME (MIN.)	PUBLISHER
Mass		*soli, choir, orch.*		MS. perf. 1897
Mass		*soli, choir, orch.*		MS. perf. 1903
Missa Brevis		*choir and organ*		MS. perf. 1910
Fête du Christ-Roi à Ville Marie		*choir and organ*		Passe-Temps
Angelus	1898	*choir and orch.*		MS. perf. 1903
Patrie (patriotic song)		*choir and orch.*		MS. perf. 1903
Le Canada (patriotic song)		*choir and orch.*		MS. perf. 1906
Veronica (overture to unfinished opera)		*orchestra*		MS.
Marche du Sacre de Pie X		*orchestra*		MS. perf. 1903
L'Aurore		*orchestra*		MS. perf. 1913
Marche Heroïque	1914	*orchestra*		Archambault
Trio		*vln, vc, piano*		MS. perf. 1907
La Lyre enchantée (first composition)		*piano*		Archambault
Variations on "God Save the King"		*piano*		MS.
Variations on "Un Canadien Errant"		*piano*		MS.
Ballade		*piano*		MS.
Yvonne		*piano*		Archambault
Alice		*piano*		Archambault
Vive Laurier! (marche brilliante)	1897	*piano*		J. G. Yon
Romance sans paroles		*'cello and piano*		Belgo-Canadienne
Meditation	1913	*'cello and piano*		Belgo-Canadienne
Tarantelle	1903	*'cello and piano*		MS. perf. 1903
Seul sur la route	1911	*barit., choir*		MS.
Domine Jesu Christe		*male quartet*		MS. perf. 1918
Salut O Canada	1907	*vocal*		MS. perf. 1907
Vision		*vocal*		MS.
Vision de Jeanne d'Arc		*vocal*		MS. perf. 1906
Désespérance		*vocal*		MS. perf. 1922
Musique	1908	*vocal*		J. Hamelle, Paris
Six Melodies		*vocal*		Archambault
Cinq Cantiques Réligieux		*vocal*		Archambault
Quatre Cantiques de Noël (harmonized)	1904	*vocal*		Beauchemin

Cooper, Dr. Irvin

Pianist, conductor and composer. Born in Nelson, England, August 16th, 1900.

Musical education at Royal Manchester College of Music (1919-23) with Max Meyer (piano), Dr. Carroll (composition), Marie Brema (opera), Sir Hamilton Harty (conducting), at University of Manchester (1920-23) with Dr. Keighley and Dr. Wilcox. Degrees: Mus.Bac. (McGill, 1925), Mus.Doc. (Montreal, 1945). Diploma: Associate Royal Manchester College of Music, 1922.

Came to Canada in 1923. Held the following posts: director of music, West Hill High School, 1923-38; lecturer in music education, McGill University, 1926; supervisor of music, Montreal Protestant Schools, 1938; vice-chairman, International Cultural

Affairs Committee, 1944; director, Eastern Townships Conservatory of Music, Stanstead, P.Q., 1947-48; president, International Festival of School Music, 1947; educational director, G. V. Thompson Ltd., 1948-50; guest speaker at festivals and conferences in U.S., 1948-50. Appointed professor of music education, Florida State University in 1950.

In 1945 was awarded Order of Merit, P.Q. for outstanding services to education.

Address: 811 West Jefferson, Tallahassee, Florida, U.S.A.

Affiliation: BMI.

COMPOSITIONS

TITLE	DATE	TYPE	TIME (MIN.)	PUBLISHER
Full o' the Moon		light opera	150	MS.
Festival March		band	4	MS.
Exhibition March		band	3½	Remick Music Corp.
Coronation Overture		symphonic band	5	MS.
The Old Love		choral	25	MS.
Day of Early Autumn		choral (male)	4	Boston Music Co.
In the Glow of the Candles		choral	3	Boston Music Co.
Song for Canada		choral	3	G. V. Thompson
Pioneer Songs of Canada (24)		choral		G. V. Thompson
If All the World Could Sing		choral	2	MS.
Christmas Carol		choral	3½	MS.
Petals		choral (female)	3	Carl Fischer
Lullaby		choral (female)	3	Carl Fischer
Serenade for Spring		choral (female)	3	Carl Fischer
A la claire fontaine		choral	4	Boston Music Co.
Gai le rosier		choral	3	Boston Music Co.
Marianne		choral	3	Boston Music Co.
Dans tous les cantons		choral	3½	Boston Music Co.
Passing By		choral	2½	Boston Music Co.
Drink to Me Only		choral	3	Boston Music Co.
I Have Done		choral (female)	2	Carl Fischer
God Gave Us Song		choral and orch. or band		Carl Fischer
Panis Angelicus		choral	3	McLaughlin & Reilly Co.
Singing Teens (album of 22 songs)		choral		G. V. Thompson
Unison Songs for Teen Age (album)		choral		G. V. Thompson
Fair Canada		vocal	3	J. Curwen & Sons
He Will Give You Rest		vocal	4	Parnasse Musical
Play Up		vocal	3	G. V. Thompson
Canada Calls		vocal	3	G. V. Thompson
Supplication		vocal	3	G. V. Thompson
Litany for the Nations		vocal	4	G. V. Thompson

COMPOSITIONS

TITLE	DATE	TYPE	TIME (MIN.)	PUBLISHER
Look for the Rainbow		vocal	3	G. V. Thompson
There's an Empire		vocal	3	G. V. Thompson
Festival Song		vocal	3	MS.

Côte, Dr. Hélène

(Soeur Marie-Stéphane)

Pianist and composer. Born in St. Barthelemi, P.Q., January 9th, 1888.

Musical education in Montreal with R. O. Pelletier, Alfred Lamoureux, Alfred Laliberté, Claude Champagne and Raoul Pâquet, in Paris with Guy de Lioncourt. Degree: Mus.Doc. (Montreal, 1936). Diploma: Licentiate (Conservatoire National de Musique, Montreal).

Director of musical studies at Institut des Soeurs des Saints Noms de Jésus et de Marie for 30 years and director of Ecole Supérieure de Musique d'Outremont for the last 18 years. Author of musical textbooks.

Address: 1410 Boulevard Mount-Royal, Outremont, P.Q.

COMPOSITIONS

TITLE	DATE	TYPE	TIME (MIN.)	PUBLISHER
Andante		string quartet	10	MS.
Fugue		organ	8	MS.
Je n'ai qu'un seul Ami		choral	12	MS.

Coulthard, Jean

Pianist and composer. Born in Vancouver.

Musical education at Royal Conservatory, Toronto and at Royal College of Music, London. Teachers: Jan Cherniavsky, Kathleen Long (piano), Arthur Benjamin and Bernard Wagenaar (composition). Diplomas: A.T.C.M., L.R.S.M. Winner of CAPAC awards 1946-47; Olympiad award (honorable mention) for Oboe Sonata, 1948; North American Prize (second place), 1948; Pacific Coast Committee for the Humanities $750 grant, 1949; McGill University Chamber Music award, 1949; Clements Memorial Prize (London), 1949; CBC International Service song contest winner, 1950 with *Quebec May.*

Has appeared in piano recitals and as soloist with Vancouver Symphony Orchestra. In 1935 was appointed head of music department of St. Anthony's College, Vancouver and later to same position at Queen's Hall School. Since 1947 has been instructor in music at the University of British Columbia.

Address: 5726 Sperling Street, Vancouver, B.C.

Affiliation: BMI.

COMPOSITIONS

TITLE	DATE	TYPE	TIME (MIN.)	PUBLISHER
Excursion (ballet suite)	1941	orchestra	15	MS.
Symphony (3 mvmts)	1951	orchestra	30	MS.
Ballade		string orchestra	11	MS.
Music on a Quiet Song		flute and strgs	15	MS.
String Quartet	1948	string quartet		MS.

COMPOSITIONS

TITLE	DATE	TYPE	TIME (MIN.)	PUBLISHER
Sonata	1946	*oboe and piano*	11	MS.
Sonata		*'cello and piano*	12	MS.
Poem		*vln and piano*	12	BMI Canada (to be published)
Two Sonatinas		*vln and piano*		MS.
Four Etudes	1945	*piano*	10	No. 1 and 2: BMI Canada
Sonata	1947	*piano*		MS.
Three Sonnets (Shakespeare)		*voice and str. qua. or: sop, vln, piano*		MS.
Quebec May		*choir, 2 pianos*	12	MS.
Two Songs from the Haidas		*vocal*		MS.
Three Songs (J. Joyce)		*vocal*		MS.
Three Songs (L. A. McKay)	1948	*vocal*		MS.
October (D. LePan)	1951	*song cycle*		MS.

Recording:
Ballade (CBC Canadian Album No. 2)

Couture, Guillaume

Conductor, organist, choirmaster, music teacher and composer. Born in Montreal, October 23rd, 1851. Died in Montreal, January 15th, 1915.

Musical education in Paris, 1873-75 and 1876-78 with Th. Dubois and R. Bussine, graduating from Paris Conservatoire with first-class honors. In Paris associated with Saint-Saëns and was choirmaster at Ste-Clothilde while César Franck was organist.

At the age of 13 was choirmaster at Ste-Brigide, Montreal. Conducted Montreal Philharmonic Society from 1880-99, founded and conducted Société des Symphonistes and Montreal Amateur Operatic Club in 1880's, conducted many other concerts. Was choirmaster at various churches in Montreal, after 1893 at St. James Cathedral. Taught voice and harmony.

Member of Société Nationale de Musique in Paris, which performed some of his works under Edouard Colonne. Honored with title *Officier de l'Instruction Publique* of France. One of the great pioneers of music in Canada.

COMPOSITIONS

TITLE	DATE	TYPE	TIME (MIN.)	PUBLISHER
Jean le Précurseur (Poème lyrique réligieux, A. Lozeau and A. Lebel)	1912-14	*oratorio*		C. Joubert, Paris 1st perf. 1923, Montr.
Requiem Mass		*choral*		
Rêverie	1875	*orchestra*		Girod, Paris, perf. 1875
String Quartet	c. 1875	*string quartet*		
Memorare (Prière à la très sainte Vierge)	c. 1875	*soli and choir*		Girod, Paris, perf. 1875
Trois Chorales (Salut pour les double majeur et mineur)		*choral*		Girod, Paris, perf. 1875
Salut de la Fête-Dieu (3 plain-chants in florid cp.)		*choral*		Girod, Paris, perf. 1875
O Salutaris		*choral*		Breitkopf & Härtel
Berceuse		*vocal*		MS.

Church cantatas, hymns and other works.

See:

Léo-Pol Morin, *Papiers de Musique*, 1930.
Arthur Laurendeau, *Guillaume Couture*, L'Action Nationale, Sept. and Oct. 1950.

Crawford, Thomas James

Organist, lecturer and choral conductor. Born in Barrhead, Scotland, June 11th, 1877.

Musical education in Glasgow at Scottish National Academy of Music with Sandiford Turner and Otto Schweitzer, 1891-94, at Leipzig Conservatorium with Reinecke, Jadassohn and Homeyer, 1894-98. Degree: Mus.Bac. Diplomas: F.R.C.O., F.T.C.L.

Private assistant to Sir Frederick Bridge at Westminster Abbey, London, 1898-1905. Came to Canada in 1923 as organist of St. Paul's Church, Toronto. For 14 years was organist at Eaton Memorial Church, Toronto and for 28 years has been teacher, lecturer and examiner at the Royal Conservatory, Toronto. Was director of the Eaton Operatic Society for 22 years.

Address: 77 Poplar Plains Crescent, Toronto, Ont.

Affiliation: CAPAC.

COMPOSITIONS

TITLE	DATE	TYPE	TIME (MIN.)	PUBLISHER
Canadian Tone Poem				
Low Tide at Grand Pré		*string orchestra*	14	MS.
Rhapsody		*trpt and orch.*	10	MS.
Court Cards (ballet suite)		*string orchestra*	13	MS.
Marche Heroique		*orchestra*	6	F. Harris
Introduction and Toccata		*organ and strgs*	12	MS.
Prelude, Intermezzo and				
Fugue on B-B-B flat-F		*organ*	14	MS.
Seven Organ Pieces		*organ*		Bosworth & Co.
				Western Music
Prelude, Carol and Fugue		*organ*		MS.
Sonata (CAPAC prize work)		*vln and piano*		MS.
Communion Service in F		*choral*		Bosworth & Co.
Songs		*vocal*		MS.

Many other works.

Crépault, Napoléon

Organist, pianist, choirmaster and composer. Born in Kamouraska, P.Q., December 17th, 1849. Died in Quebec, September 28th, 1906.

Musical education in Quebec with A. Dessane and E. Gagnon. After 1876 taught in Quebec. Organist at St. Roch Church, Quebec, 1881-83.

COMPOSITIONS

TITLE	DATE	TYPE	TIME (MIN.)	PUBLISHER
La Communion des Saints		*oratorio*		perf. at St. Roch
Mass in G for St. Roch Church		*choir and organ*		performed 1882
Cantata for return of Abbé				
Bélanger		*choir and organ*		
Les Voix du soir (rêverie)	1900	*vocal*		

La Ruche harmonieuse: approx. 40 vocal works, some with organ or orchestra, published.
Les Joies du foyer: approx. 30 piano pieces, published.

Cusson, Gabriel

Singer, violoncellist and composer. Born in Roxton Pond, P.Q., April 2nd, 1903.

Musical education in Montreal at Nazareth Institute for the Blind with Achille Fortier, Arthur Letondal, R. O. Pelletier and Alfred Lamoureux (piano, organ, 'cello, singing and theory), in Paris at Ecole Normale with Nadia Boulanger, Alexanian and Panzera ('cello, voice and theory). Winner of Quebec Province *Prix d'Europe*, 1924.

Member, Académie de Musique de Québec. Teacher at Quebec Provincial Conservatory and Institut Nazareth; private practice.

Address: 3229 Maplewood Avenue, Apt. 5, Montreal, P.Q.

COMPOSITIONS

TITLE	DATE	TYPE	TIME (MIN.)	PUBLISHER
Jonathas (Biblical drama)		*choir, orchestra*		MS.
Tobie (Biblical lyrical mystery)		*choir, orchestra*		MS.
Antigone		*choir, orchestra*		MS.
To the Glory of Jeanne-Mance		*cantata*	11	MS.
Suite No. 1		*orchestra*	12	MS.
Suite No. 2		*orchestra*	11	MS.
Sirvente à Notre-Dame (Congrès marial)		*voices, orchestra*		MS.
Pieces for mixed choir (French and English)		*choral*		MS.
Motets (Latin)		*choral*		MS.
Arrangements of French Canadian folk songs				La Bonne Chanson

Dainty, Ernest Herbert

Pianist, organist, conductor and composer. Born in London, England, September 30th, 1891. Died in Toronto, October 30th, 1947.

Musical education in Toronto with Dr. Torrington (piano), Dr. Eggett (violin), and Luigi von Kunits (harmony), in Buffalo with Count Zielinski, in Vienna at Imperial Academy of Music in Godowski's piano classes (1913).

Came to Canada in 1901. After serving in Imperial Army for five years returned to Canada in 1921. After working in the U.S. for some years became active in Canada as teacher, conductor, pianist and organist, doing much radio work.

Affiliation (estate): BMI.

COMPOSITIONS

TITLE	DATE	TYPE	TIME (MIN.)	PUBLISHER
Romanza in D flat		*piano and orchestra*	7	MS.
Nocturne (Larghetto)	1936	*string orchestra*	10½	MS.
Giga all 'antica		*string orchestra (wds ad lib)*	8	MS.
Gavotte		*string orchestra*		MS.
Minuetto for strings		*string orchestra*		MS.
La Gazelle		*string orchestra*	4½	MS.
Deep River		*piano, hp, tymp, chimes*		MS.

COMPOSITIONS

TITLE	DATE	TYPE	TIME (MIN.)	PUBLISHER
Trio in D minor		*vln, vc, piano*		MS.
Serenade		*vln, vc, piano*		MS.
Sonata in C minor		*'cello and piano*	20	MS.
Indian Legend		*violin and piano*		MS.
Toccata in A flat major		*piano*		MS.
L'Espiègle		*piano*		Waterloo Music
To Gwendolyn (prelude)		*piano*		BMI Canada
Evangeline's Spinning Song		*piano*	5	MS.
Air		*piano*		MS.
Chinese Wind Glasses		*piano*	3½	MS.
Hungry Heart (O. Down)		*voice and chamber orch.*		MS.
Rose Tokens (O. Down)		*voice and orchestra*		MS.
The Brook (Tennyson)		*vocal*		Waterloo Music
My Ladye's Glove (John Hole)		*vocal*		BMI Canada
Northern Pioneers		*vocal*		G. V. Thompson
Carry On		*vocal*		G. V. Thompson

Many unpublished songs and arrangements for orchestra, piano, and piano and violin.

D'Aragon, Dr. Alexandre

Pianist, organist and composer. Born in St. Denis, Richelieu Co. P.Q., April 26th, 1889.

Musical education with Victoria Cartier (harmony), Charles Hopkins Ould, Dunham (organ). Has held the post of organist in many churches around Montreal since 1901. Teacher of organ and harmony at Montreal University and Conservatoire National de Musique, Montreal. Degree: Mus.Doc. (Montreal, 1943).

Address: 6426 Girouard Avenue, Montreal, P.Q.

COMPOSITIONS

TITLE	DATE	TYPE	TIME (MIN.)	PUBLISHER
Missa de Assumptione		*choral*	60	MS.
Missa da Requiem		*choral*	60	MS.
Messe de Noël		*choral*	45	MS.
O Salutaris (motet)		*choral*		Parnasse Musical
Regina Pacis (motet)		*choral*		Parnasse Musical
Ecce Fidelis		*choral*		Parnasse Musical
Tantum Ergo		*choral*		Parnasse Musical
Laudate Dominum		*choral*		Parnasse Musical
Ave Maria		*choral*		MS.
Four Pieces		*organ*		MS.

Gregorian Chant accompaniments.
About 50 settings of folk songs.
Publications bear the pseudonym Pierre Lefrancq.

Daunais, Lionel

Singer and composer. Born in Montreal.

Musical education with Célinie Mercier (voice) and Oscar O'Brien (harmony). Winner of Quebec Province *Prix d'Europe* in 1926. Made his debut as opera singer in Algiers. Has done considerable operatic work in Canada. Founder of the Trio Lyrique and co-director of the Variétés Lyriques (Montreal).

Address: 370 Outremont Avenue, Outremont, P.Q.

Affiliation: CAPAC.

COMPOSITIONS

TITLE	DATE	TYPE	TIME (MIN.)	PUBLISHER
A quoi bon rêver		*vocal*		Archambault
'Chanson de ma mie		*vocal*		Archambault
Chansons de notre âme		*vocal*		Archambault

About 100 vocal works and one number for string orchestra, all in manuscript.
No recent information obtained.

Davenport Goertz, Gladys

Violinist and composer. Born in Croydon, England, October 11th, 1895.

Musical education at Croydon Conservatory of Music with W. Sutcliff and L. Fowels (violin and composition). Private tuition in composition with C. W. G. Goodworth. For three years conducted St. Leonard's String Player's Club in England.

Address: 1887 West 45th Avenue, Vancouver, B.C.

COMPOSITIONS

TITLE	DATE	TYPE	TIME (MIN.)	PUBLISHER
Will 'o the Wisp		*vln and piano*		Bosworth & Co. (under maiden name Gladys Reeve)
Short Suite		*vln and piano*		Bosworth & Co.
England Awake		*vocal*		Western Music (in E. Arnold's Song Books)
Cool and Silent Is the Lake		*vocal*		Western Music

Songs in manuscript:

Cherry Time in Chilliwack; Above the Timber Line; Ladner Ferry; Precious Freight; Ships; Fraser River; The Storm; The Dogwood Tree; Sea Rapture; The Sunken Isle; London; Black Bess; Comes Now My Sweeting; Sweetly Sings the Thrush; Song of the Mad Prince; When Music Sounds; Gather ye Rosebuds; Down by the Water Willows.

Davis, Morris C.

Arranger, composer and conductor. Born in Ottawa, March 1st, 1904.

Studied piano with Nicholas Eichorn, A. E. J. MacCreary and Alfred Laliberté. Theory, arranging, composition and orchestration self-taught. Degree: B.A. (McGill). Wrote revues in school and college days. Played piano and conducted orchestra on radio since 1929. Joined CBC as producer in 1937, left in 1947. Now operates free-lance production office, conducts, arranges, orchestrates for commercial broadcasts.

Address: 1440 Ste-Catherine Street West, Montreal, P.Q.

Affiliation: CAPAC.

| | | COMPOSITIONS | | |
TITLE	DATE	TYPE	TIME (MIN.)	PUBLISHER
Blues and Finales in G (jazz concerto)	1942	*orchestra*	15	MS.
Canadiana (nine sketches, narrative background)	1950	*orchestra*	ea. 3-11	MS.
Le Violon magique (dramatic narrative)	1948	*orchestra*	14	MS.
Concerto for Radio in E major	1947	*strgs and piano*	6	MS.

Scores for movies:

While Safari, The Whispering City (including 2nd mvmt of *Quebec Concerto*, see A. Mathieu), *Sins of the Fathers, Le Curé de Village, La Pêche à la Cabane.*

Many scores for musical broadcasts, variety shows, comedies, popular "symphonic" arrangements etc.

Deacon, Mary Conner

Pianist, organist and composer. Born in Johnson City, Tennessee, February 22nd, 1907.

Musical education with S. Schroetter, E. Berumen, H. Deering (piano), at State Teacher's College, Johnson City (history, harmony etc.), in New York City with Wm. Stickles, Frank LaForge and S. Ross (singing and opera repertoire).

Address: 221 John Street, Belleville, Ont.

| | | COMPOSITIONS | | |
TITLE	DATE	TYPE	TIME (MIN.)	PUBLISHER
I Will Lift Up Mine Eyes		*choral*	3	G. Schirmer
Teach Me, Oh Lord, Thy Statutes		*choral*	3	G. Schirmer
Whistle While You Whittle	1944	*vocal*	3	G. Schirmer
Gavotte	1948	*piano*		MS.
Piano Playtime (beginner's piano book)	1950	*piano*		MS.

Songs in manuscript:

Infant's Prayer; Winter Rain; When Spring Comes Dancing; My Lady Autumn; A New Day; Sharing; Beautiful Canada; Gentle Angels Guard You; Where the Duby Lies; The Call of the Highroad

Décarie, Reine

(Soeur Johane d'Arcie)

Voice teacher and composer. Born in Montreal, January 4th, 1912.

Studied at Ecole Supérieure de Musique d'Outremont. Teachers include Claude Champagne (composition), Rodolphe Plamondon and Roger Filiatreult (voice). Received diplomas of Harmonization of Gregorian Chant, of Teacher of Gregorian Chant. of Teacher of Phonetics and Diction. Degree: Mus.Bac. Teaches voice at Ecole Supérieure de Musique d'Outremont.

Address: 1410 Mount-Royal Boulevard, Montreal, P.Q.

COMPOSITIONS

TITLE	DATE	TYPE	TIME (MIN.)	PUBLISHER
Poème symphonique	1950	*orchestra*		MS.
Prélude et Fugue	1946	*string orchestra*	12	MS.
Hindu-Shur	1949	*voice, clar, vc (soli)*		
		and 2 va, 3 vc,		
		celesta	5	MS.
La Jeu de ma subconscience				
(4 enigmes)	1948	*voice, hp, fl*	8	MS.
Sonatine	1948	*piano*	10	MS.
12 motets	1940-50	*choral*		MS.
Messe	1943	*choral*	20	MS.
Messe (a capella)	1947	*choral*	30	MS.
Quatre cantiques français	1943-48	*choral*		MS.
Palinods (poème lyrique)	1945	*choral*	21	MS.
L'Etang—le soir	1946	*solo and choir*	2	MS.
Cantate à Ste Cécile	1943	*solo and choir*	8	MS.

Songs in manuscript (1941-49):

Beauté, toi seule vraie; Le Parfum; Vieille chanson; Cimetière; Frou frou (folklore).

DeCelles, Maurice D.

Clarinetist, oboist, conductor and composer. Born in Trois Rivières, P.Q., October 11th, 1905.

Has held many posts as clarinetist and conductor. Teacher at the Quebec Provincial Conservatory. Member and Quebec representative of the Canadian Bandmasters Association.

Address: 66 St. Cyrille, Quebec. P.Q.

Compositions for band (3-7 minutes each):

Nos Héros Canadiens	Waterloo	Mon Alma Mater	MS.
Marguerite (valse-caprice)	Waterloo	Charmant séjour	MS.
En avant Laval!	MS.	Souvenir de la Jeune Lorette	MS.
Salut à Loretteville	MS.	Les Tisserands de Montmorency	MS.
Hommage à Jésus Hostie	MS.	Le Collègien de Lévis	MS.
Patro-Patrie	MS.	Citizens of Tomorrow	MS.

Dela, Maurice

Organist, composer, pianist, lecturer and critic. Born in Montreal, September 10th, 1919.

Musical education with Raoul Pâquet (organ), Claude Champagne (composition). Graduate in arts and music of Montreal University. Has taught literature, history and music at Holy Cross Normal School in Montreal. Is now organist of Notre-Dame-des-Sept-Douleurs in Verdun, P.Q., lecturer in music, contributor to *Le Passe-Temps* magazine and orchestral arranger.

Address: 448 Hickson Street, Verdun, P.Q.

Affiliation: BMI.

COMPOSITIONS

TITLE	DATE	TYPE	TIME (MIN.)	PUBLISHER
America (suite)		orchestra	15	MS.
Trois Danses		orchestra	13	MS.
Le Chat, la belette et le petit lapin		orchestra and commentator	7½	MS.
Piano Concerto		piano and orch.	30	MS.
Ballade		piano and orch.	12	MS.
Petite Suite Maritime		fl, ob, cl, bn, hn	8	MS.
Stringtime		strings, guitar, piano	4	MS.
Deux Danses		strings	6	MS.
Dans tous les cantons		strings	3½	MS.
Lullaby		strings	3	MS.
String Quartet		string quartet	10	MS.
Sonatine romantique		vln and piano	9	MS.
Pastorale		organ	4	MS.
Hommage		piano	4	BMI Canada, 1950
Prelude		piano	4	MS.
Polichinelle		piano	2	MS.
Messe Brève		choir and organ		MS.
Berceuse Béarnaise		vocal	2	Passe-Temps, 1947
Xami		vocal	3	Archambault, 1945
Ballade		vocal	3	M. Dela, 1946
Spleen		vocal	3	BMI Canada, 1950
Ronde		vocal	3½	BMI Canada, 1951
La Lettre		vocal	3	MS.
Berceuse à Christian		vocal	2	MS.

Delaquerrière, José Mario Louis

Singer, actor and composer. Born in Paris, France.

Musical education at Schola Cantorum in Paris with de la Tombelle, Charles Bordes, Vincent d'Indy (Gregorian chant), Dressen ('cello), St. Réquier (organ), at Conservatoire National de Paris with Pessart and Schwartz. Has toured extensively throughout France, Germany, Switzerland, Belgium, Africa, U.S. and Canada. Came to Canada in 1936. Member, S.A.C.E.M.

Address: 1251 St. Mark, Montreal, P.Q.

COMPOSITIONS

TITLE	DATE	TYPE	TIME (MIN.)	PUBLISHER
Angeline (opéra-comique in 1 act)		choir and piano	50	MS.
Le Chant du Soutier (dramatic sketch)		choir and piano	50	MS.
Les deux clochards (fantastic sketch)		choir and piano	35	MS.
Mon Ami Pierrot (lyrical scene)		choir and piano	40	MS.
Romani (lyrical scene)		choir and piano	45	MS.
Assoumah (lyrical scene)		choir and piano	30	MS.
Yael et Mitzi (lyrical scene)		choir and piano	30	MS.

COMPOSITIONS

TITLE	DATE	TYPE	TIME (MIN.)	PUBLISHER
L'Idiot		choir and piano	7	MS.
Etude genre Chopin		piano and saxophone	2¾	MS.
Polka de concert		piano and trombone	3	MS.
Au Bord du Nil		piano and violin	2½	MS.
Pourpre (valse)		piano	3¼	Chapsal, Paris
Pendant la valse		piano	11	MS.
Quasimodo		piano	14	MS.
En nous promenant		piano	2	MS.
Berceuse orientale		piano	2	MS.
Three Pieces		piano	6½	MS.
Masques		piano	2½	MS.
Petit Nègre		piano	1¾	MS.
Romance sans paroles		piano	2½	MS.
Soir au bord de la mer		piano	3	MS.
Coin d'Orient		piano	1¾	MS.
Rag-time on the deck		piano	2¾	MS.
Etude en forme de valse		piano	3¼	MS.
Clair de lune sur la mer		'cello	2¾	MS.
Fleur d'Espagne		guitar (mandoline)	2¾	MS.
Le Kifou-Kifou (ballet)		vocal	12	MS.
Le Miroir		vocal	2	Ricordi, Paris
A Montmartre, là-haut		vocal	3	Salabert, Paris
Djailé		vocal	3½	Salabert, Paris
Pavaravis		vocal	2½	Salabert, Paris
Ciel d'Algérie		vocal	3¼	Chapsal, Paris
Oh! les jolis yeux!		vocal	3	Chapsal, Paris
A Paris, parbleu!		vocal	2¾	Chapsal, Paris
Vive la France		vocal	2½	Parnasse Musical
Can.-Fran. du 21ème congrès de la Langue Française		vocal	3	Morency, Quebec

Many unpublished songs, 2-3 minutes each.

Delcellier, Joseph Henri

Clarinetist, conductor and composer. Born in Béziers, France, September 21st, 1872.

Musical education with own father (clarinet), A. Lafont (violin), and Vernazobres (harmony and allied subjects). Laureat diploma of Ecole de Musique Niedermeyer. Played violin in French and English orchestras. Acted as conductor in principal music centres in France. Came to Canada in 1911 as choral conductor of the Montreal Opera Company.

Address: 1763 North Avenue, Outremont, P.Q.

COMPOSITIONS

TITLE	DATE	TYPE	TIME (MIN.)	PUBLISHER
La Fête de Pierrette (mimodrame)		orchestra	10	MS.
Valse-caprice		orchestra or band	5	MS.
Fighting French (march)		band	4	MS.
Menuet des mandores		quintet	2½	MS.

Short orchestral works in manuscript:

Pastorale; Sérénade-barcarolle; Ronde des Hallebardiers; Nocturne in E major; Menuet; Tarantelle; Souvenir de Margate (waltz); *Elsa; Country Life; Gloire à Blériot* (march); *Kuroki* (galop); *J'ai du bon tabac.*

Delorme, Isabelle

Pianist, violinist, music teacher and composer. Born in Montreal, November 14th, 1900.

Musical education with Sister Madeleine-Marie and Arthur Letondal (piano), Albert Chamberland and Agostino Salvetti (violin), Claude Champagne (theory). Degree: Licentiate, Académie de Québec. Specializes in teaching theoretical subjects. Teacher at Quebec Provincial Conservatory in Montreal.

Address: 326 St. Joseph Boulevard, Montreal, P.Q.

COMPOSITIONS

TITLE	DATE	TYPE	TIME (MIN.)	PUBLISHER
Fantasy, Choral, Fugue		*string quartet*	12	MS.
Prelude and Fugue		*string quartet*	10	MS.
Andante		*string quartet*	5	MS.
Suite		*string quartet*	7½	MS.
Chorale in A minor on a Bach theme		*organ*	1	MS.
Chorale in G major on a Bach theme		*organ*	5	MS.
Chorale varié sur un thème de Bach		*organ*	3	MS.
Prélude		*organ*	4	MS.
Berceuse dans le style ancien		*piano*	2½	MS.
		also: string orchestra		
Cor Jesu		*motet*	1½	MS.
Ave Maria		*motet (a capella)*	2	MS.
O Salutaris		*motet*	2	MS.
Tantum Ergo		*motet*	2	MS.
Prière du soir		*choral*	12	MS.
Gloire à toi Maisonneuve (Montreal tercentenary)		*choral*	6	MS.
Prière à la Vierge		*vocal*	1½	MS.

De Marky, Paul Alexander

Pianist and composer. Born in Gyula, Hungary.

Musical education in Budapest with Stephen Thoman (a Liszt pupil, piano and composition). Career commenced at the age of 15. Has appeared in recitals and as guest soloist with orchestras in most of the music centres of the world. Naturalized Canadian (1931). Devotes his time to performing, composing and teaching.

Address: 2043 Metcalfe Street, Montreal, P.Q.

Affiliation: CAPAC.

COMPOSITIONS

TITLE	DATE	TYPE	TIME (MIN.)	PUBLISHER
Piano Concerto in B major	1948	*piano and orch.*	24	MS.
After a Farewell (song for piano)	1949	*piano*	2	MS.
Nightingale (song for piano)	1949	*piano*	2	MS.

COMPOSITIONS

TITLE	DATE	TYPE	TIME (MIN.)	PUBLISHER
Amber Mountain (song for piano)	1949	*piano*	2	MS.
Echo Island (song for piano)	1949	*piano*	2	MS.
Valse-Etude	1944	*piano*	2	Parnasse Musical
Tales from Vienna Woods (arr. concert version)	1944	*piano*	4	Parnasse Musical
Spring Voices (arr. concert version)	1944	*piano*	4½	MS.

De Ridder, Dr. Allard

Violinist, violist, conductor and composer. Born in Dordrecht, Holland, May 3rd, 1887.

Musical education with Erdelman, Carl Bayer (violin), Johan Wagenaar (composition) and at Conservatory of Cologne with Bram Eldering (violin), Ewald Straesser (composition), Fritz Steinbach and Hermann Abendroth (conducting). Post-graduate studies with Willem Mengelberg (conducting). Diploma for violin and conducting of Cologne Conservatory. Degree: Mus.Doc. (Toronto, 1946).

Was conductor of Amsterdam National Opera. Guest conductor with many orchestras in Holland, Canada and U.S.A. Founder of present Vancouver Symphony Orchestra and conductor, 1930-41. Violist with Hart House Quartet, 1941-1944. Founder and conductor of the Ottawa Philharmonic Orchestra, 1944-50. Guest conductor of Vancouver Summer Symphonies in 1945, 46, 48, 49, 50.

Address: 1727 West 36th Avenue, Vancouver, B.C.

COMPOSITIONS

TITLE	DATE	TYPE	TIME (MIN.)	PUBLISHER
Symphony in E minor		*orchestra*		MS.
The Ballad of Dowsabel		*soli, chorus, orchestra*	21	MS.
Violin Concerto		*vln and orchestra*	25	MS.
Sketch for solo flute and violin		*fl, vln, orchestra*	9	MS.
In the Woods (symphonic poem)		*orchestra*	15	MS.
On the Ocean (symphonic poem)		*orchestra*	12	MS.
Titania (symphonic poem)		*orchestra*	10	MS.
The Song of Lamia (symphonic poem)		*orchestra*	18	MS.
Overture in D		*orchestra*	11	MS.
Intermezzo		*orchestra*	5	MS.
Variations on a folk song		*orchestra*	12	MS.
At Night		*soprano and orchestra*	5	MS.
Impromptu		*string quartet*	3	MS.
Beware of Love		*choral*	4	MS.
Five Songs (Lilian Found)		*vocal*		MS.

Descarries, Dr. Auguste

Pianist, organist and composer. Born in Lachine, P.Q., November 26th, 1896.

Musical education at Ecole Normale de Paris with L. Conus (piano), Cellier, Dandelot, Pelliot, Catoire (harmony and composition). Winner of Quebec Province

Prix d'Europe in 1921. Degree: Mus.Doc. (Montreal). Diploma: Laureat (Académie de Musique, Quebec). Appointed vice-dean of faculty of music, Montreal University in 1951.

Address: 232 Querbes Avenue, Outremont, P.Q.

COMPOSITIONS

TITLE	DATE	TYPE	TIME (MIN.)	PUBLISHER
Rhapsody on Canadian Themes		*piano, orchestra*	17	MS.
Trio		*vln, vc, piano*	28	MS.
Conte		*vln, vc, piano*	5	MS.
Messe de Requiem		*choral*	35	MS.
Messe Brève des dimanches		*choral*	24	MS.
Messe Brève, D minor		*choral*		MS.
Messe poir voix mixte dite de St. Jean Baptiste		*choral*		MS.
Ave Maria		*3 equal voices*	4	MS.
Magnificat		*choral*	6	MS.
Le Vol du silence		*choral*	4	MS.
Le Temps perdu		*choral*	5	MS.
Série de Graduels et d'Allé-luias en faux bourdon		*choral*		MS.
Five Motets		*vocal*		MS.
En Sourdine		*vocal*		MS.
Crois-moi		*vocal*	3	MS.
Images dans l'eau		*vocal*	3	MS.
Fontaine, fontaine		*vocal*	3	MS.
Elle n'est plus		*vocal*	7	MS.
Je bénis le hasard		*vocal*	3	MS.

Piano works in manuscript:

Three Etudes; Valses; *Mauresque; Serenitas; Caprice;* Preludes; *Souvenir; Aubade* and others.
Mozart Sonata for two pianos arranged for octet.
Folk song settings for instrumental trio.

De Sève, Alfred

Violinist and composer. Born in Montreal, 1860. Died in Montreal, 1928.

Musical education in Canada and in Europe with Sarasate, Vieuxtemps and others. Lived in Boston for 19 years; was solo-violinist with Boston Symphony Orchestra and concertmaster with Boston Philharmonic Orchestra; teacher at New England Conservatory. Later taught music in Montreal.

COMPOSITIONS

TITLE	DATE	TYPE	TIME (MIN.)	PUBLISHER
Le Rêve de la Danseuse		*orchestra*		O. Ditson
Caprice fantastique, Op. 9		*vln and piano*		O. Ditson
Dancer's Dream, Op. 10		*vln and piano*		O. Ditson
Nearer My God to Thee		*vln and piano*		O. Ditson
Old Folks at Home		*vln and piano*		O. Ditson
Slumber Song, Op. 6		*piano*		Arthur P. Schmidt
Angel's Lullaby, Op. 7		*piano*		Arthur P. Schmidt

Many other works for violin and for church service.

See:

Arthur Laurendeau, Alfred De Sève, L'Action Nationale, March 1950.

Deslauriers, Jean

Violinist, conductor and composer. Born in Montreal, June 24th, 1909.

Musical education with Emile Taranto, Camille Couture (violin), Auguste Descarries, R. Pelletier and Claude Champagne (harmony and allied subjects). Toured Canada and the U.S. as violin virtuoso with the Canadian singers Paul Dufault and Joseph Saucier. For a time conducted Constant Spring Hotel orchestra of Jamaica. Conducted radio program *Serenade for Strings* on CBC network for several years.

Address: 2551 Fullum Street, Apt. 1, Montreal, P.Q.

COMPOSITIONS

TITLE	DATE	TYPE	TIME (MIN.)	PUBLISHER
Prelude		strings, harp, celeste	7½	MS.
La Musique des yeux		vocal	5½	MS.

Many arrangements and accompaniments for string orchestra.
No recent information obtained.

Dessane, Antoine (Antonin)

Organist, music teacher and composer. Born in Folcarquier, France, December 14th, 1826. Died in Quebec, June 8th, 1873.

Musical education from the age of seven to 16 at Paris Conservatoire, graduating with first prize in organ and 'cello. Associated with César Franck and Georges Onslow. Came to Canada in July 1849 as organist of Quebec Cathedral. From 1865-69 was organist in New York, then returned to Quebec. A pioneer of good music in Quebec; organized concerts and opera performances. One of the planners of a national conservatory.

COMPOSITIONS

TITLE	DATE	TYPE	TIME (MIN.)	PUBLISHER
Messe solennelle in D minor		choir and orchestra		
Messe solennelle in E flat major		choir and orchestra		
Messe solennelle in G major	1849	children's and men's voices		
Messe in C major		children's and men's voices		
Marche Cantata in honor of the Prince of Wales, later Edward VII	1860	choir and orchestra		
Suite for Grand Orchestra	1863	orchestra		
Les Gardes-nobles	1871	orchestra		
Polka	1867	orchestra		
Le Galop de Pégase		orchestra		
Quadrille sur des airs canadiens	1854	orchestra		
Fantaisie-Sonate (quintet)	1858	strings and flute		
Te Deum in F major		solo and choir		
Four Regina Coeli	1852, 60 etc.	choral		
Three Tantum Ergo	1867 etc.	choral		
Two Ave Maria No. 1:	1851	choral		
Venite, exultemus Domino	1868	choral		
Laudate in D major	1857	choral		
Hommage à la France	1860	vocal		

Other religious works, pieces for piano, 'cello, violin and flute.

Pieces by A. Dessane, possibly identical with the above, have been published by Heugel, Durdilly, Benoit and others.

A theory of orchestration was written in 1869.

For further details see *Bulletin des Recherches Historiques*, Lévis, 1933. Some of the information given there conflicts with that in the *Dictionnaire biographique des Musiciens canadiens*.

Destroismaisons, Abbé Léon

Pianist, organist, specialist in Gregorian chant and composer. Born in Sainte-Louise, P.Q., March 2nd, 1890.

Musical education in Quebec with Henri Gagnon (piano, organ and harmony), in Paris with M. Sergent, Marcel Dupré, Simone Plé, Georges Caussade, Vincent d'Indy and Henry Potiron (organ, piano, counterpoint, Gregorian chant and composition). Diploma of Gregorian Institute in Paris.

Teaches harmony, piano and organ at Ste. Anne de la Pocatière College. Member of Diocesan Commission on Sacred Chant and professor at Ecole de Musique, Laval University.

Address: c/o College de Ste. Anne de la Pocatière, P.Q.

COMPOSITIONS

TITLE	DATE	TYPE	TIME (MIN.)	PUBLISHER
Chorale varié sur un thème collégial	1929	*organ*	7	MS.
Chant à Ste. Cécile "O Saintes Harmonies"	1931	*choral*	1	MS.
Ave Maria	1940	*vocal*	2½	publ. in Boston
Panis Angelicus	1940	*vocal*	2½	Procure Générale
Caritas urget nos	1941	*vocal*	1½	MS.
Cantique à St.-Joseph	1941	*vocal*	1	MS.
Cantique de fin d'année "Adieu, Marie"	1948	*vocal*	1½	MS.

Note: all pieces for voice have organ accompaniment.

Dichmont, William

Pianist, organist, violinist, conductor and composer. Born in Accrington, England, February 3rd, 1882. Died in Vancouver, July 17th, 1943.

Musical education with Gerhard Kuhnel (piano and violin) and later at the Manchester School of Music. Assistant conductor of Princess and Royal Theatre orchestras, Manchester. Came to Canada in 1903. For a time was a member of faculty, teacher and examiner, College of Music, Winnipeg. Served with C.E.F., 1915-17. Was organist at Second Science Church Vancouver.

Affiliation (estate): CAPAC.

COMPOSITIONS

TITLE	DATE	TYPE	TIME (MIN.)	PUBLISHER
Prelude Improvisatore		*piano*		John Church Co.
Thinking of You		*voice, piano, vln, vc*		O. Ditson
Berceuse		*voice and vln*		Th. Presser
The Spirit of Life		*vocal*		Wm. Dichmont
The Magic Air		*vocal*		G. Ricordi
The Wind that Shakes the Barley		*vocal*		G. Ricordi
Garden Song		*vocal*		John Church Co.
If You Ain't There		*vocal*		Western Music

Songs published by Theodore Presser:

The Night Has a Thousand Eyes; Give Us the Tools; God Heareth Me; I Will Lift Up Mine Eyes.

Songs published by O. Ditson:

A Wish; Could I Forget; Together; The Heart o' Ye; My Day; To You; Where Violets Grow; In Sympathy; One Little Hour; Such a Lil'l Fellow; Dinna Forget; Peace I Leave With You; A Woman's Last Word; Four Arabian Songs.

Songs published by G. Schirmer:

Were I the Rose; My Little Banjo; South Wind; Consolation; The Angelus; Red Rose; That Holy Thing.

Songs published by B. F. Wood Music Co.:

Softly Now the Light of Day; Supplication; The Good Shepherds; In the Wilderness; The King of Love.
Many other works in manuscript.
Note: Some works bear the pseudonyms Francis Lowell and Arthur Rutherford.

Dolin, Samuel Joseph

Pianist and composer. Born in Montreal, August 22nd, 1917.

Musical studies with Weldon Kilburn, E. R. Schmitz and John Weinzweig. Degree: Mus.Bac. (Toronto, 1942). Diploma: A.T.C.M. From 1942-45 was music supervisor in Port Hope, Cobourg, Ont. district. Now teaches piano and theory at Royal Conservatory, Toronto.

Address: 378 Markham Street, Apt. 4a, Toronto, Ont.

COMPOSITIONS

TITLE	DATE	TYPE	TIME (MIN.)	PUBLISHER
Sinfonietta	1950	*orchestra*	12-14	MS.
Serenade (3 mvmts)	1951	*strings*	12-14	MS.
Sonatina	1951	*vln and piano*	6-7	MS.
Three Piano Preludes	1949	*piano*	6	MS.
Four Miniatures	1949	*piano*	3	MS.
Sonata (3 mvmts)	1949-50	*piano*	14	MS.
Three Songs	1951	*vocal*	8	MS.

Duchow, Marvin

Composer and music teacher. Born in Montreal, June 10th, 1914.

Musical education at McGill Conservatorium with Claude Champagne (composition). Awarded scholarship to study at Curtis Institute of Music, Philadelphia, with Rosario Scalero and Samuel Chotzinoff. Degrees: Mus.Bac. (McGill), B.A. (New York). Diploma in composition (Curtis). At present working for M.A. in musicology (Eastman School of Music).

Was on staff of Chatham Square and Greenwich House Music Schools in New York. Now teaches at Quebec Provincial Conservatory and McGill Conservatorium, Montreal.

Address: 4720 Queen Mary Road, Apt. 4, Montreal, P.Q.

Affiliation: BMI.

COMPOSITIONS

TITLE	DATE	TYPE	TIME (MIN.)	PUBLISHER
Variations on a Chorale		*orchestra*	15	MS.
Badinerie	1947	*small orchestra, piano*	2½	MS.
Quartet in C minor		*string quartet*	22	MS.
Scherzo		*string quartet*	5	MS.

COMPOSITIONS

TITLE	DATE	TYPE	TIME (MIN.)	PUBLISHER
Andante		*string quartet*	5½	MS.
Motet		*choral*	15	MS.
Benedictus		*choral*	2	Parnasse Musical
A Carol Choir	1948	*choral*		Boston Music Co.
Chant Intime	1947	*piano*	2	BMI Canada
Sonata	1950	*piano*		MS.

Songs in manuscript:
I Laved My Hands; Song from the Chinese; Song from the Gardener; Music; I Would That We Were.

Dugal, Madeleine

Pianist and composer. Born in Chicoutimi, P.Q., June 3rd, 1926.

Student at Quebec Provincial Conservatory. Teachers: Auguste Descarries and in Chicoutimi Eliane Saucier (piano). In 1944 won CAPAC composition prize, in 1950 2nd medal in solfeggio, Quebec Provincial Conservatory. Has played in concert in Montreal and on Chicoutimi radio.

Address: 67 rue Jacques Cartier, Chicoutimi, P.Q.

COMPOSITIONS

TITLE	DATE	TYPE	TIME (MIN.)	PUBLISHER
Sonata No. 1 in G major	1947	*piano*	18	MS.
Sonata No. 2 in C major	1948	*piano*	12	MS.
La Grenouille	1944	*vocal*	2	MS.
Souvenez-vous	1946	*vocal*	2	MS.
Pour être un vrai marin	1946	*vocal*	1	MS.

Short piano works (2-5 minutes each, all in manuscript):
Three Sonatinas; Fête Champêtre; Après l'orage; Sports d'hiver; Etude en double tierces; Etude en doubles notes; Nocturne; Au petit galop; Les Arbres; Souvenir de voyage; Petite Valse; Mazurka; Menuet et trio.

Duncan, Chester

Pianist, lecturer and composer. Born in Strasbourg, Sask., May 4th, 1913.

Musical education with private teachers. From 1936-42 taught music. Since 1942 lecturer and since 1947 assistant professor, English Department, University of Manitoba.

Address: 295 Ashland Avenue, Winnipeg, Man.

COMPOSITIONS

TITLE	DATE	TYPE	TIME (MIN.)	PUBLISHER
Suite for Piano, "Entertainment"		*piano*	15	MS.
Piano Piece One		*piano*	2	MS.
Three Songs (A. E. Housman) (With Rue My Heart Is Laden; The Land of Lost Content; O When I Was in Love with You)		*vocal*	4	MS.
Forget Not Yet (Wyatt)		*vocal*	2½	MS.

COMPOSITIONS

TITLE	DATE	TYPE	TIME (MIN.)	PUBLISHER
Thou Didst Delight My Eyes (R. Bridges)		*vocal*	2	MS.
Carol		*vocal*	2	MS.
Two Songs (L. Macneice)	1950	*vocal*	4	MS.
Four Songs (W. H. Auden) (The One; The Silly Fool; For What as Easy; Night Covers up)	1947	*vocal*	4	MS.
Saturday and Sunday (G. Barker)	1949	*vocal*	4	MS.
Beside One Dead (A. J. M. Smith)	1950	*vocal*	1½	MS.
Take, O Take Those Lips Away	1949	*vocal*	2	MS.
Know not Surprise	1947	*vocal*	2	MS.

Incidental Music to *Hassan* (J. E. Fletcher), *Will Shakespeare* (C. Dane), *Coriolanus* (Shakespeare)' *The Ascent of F 6* (Auden and Isherwood), *For the Time Being* (Auden).

Eaton, Richard Stephen

Pianist, organist, choirmaster, lecturer and composer. Born in Victoria, B.C., January 16th, 1914.

Musical education at McGill Conservatorium in Montreal with Claude Champagne, Walter Hungerford and John Reymes-King (theory, piano and organ). Degree: Mus.Bac. (McGill). Diploma: Licentiate (McGill).

Was choirmaster at Christ Church Cathedral, Victoria, B.C. and music master at Upper Canada College, Preparatory School, Toronto. In 1944 was appointed teacher of instrumental music at Ottawa Technical High School and organist in Ottawa. In 1947 was appointed lecturer and in 1948 assistant professor and head of the Music Division, University of Alberta and director of the Western Board of Music for Alberta.

Address: c/o Music Division, Dept. of Fine Arts, University of Alberta, Edmonton, Alta.

COMPOSITIONS

TITLE	DATE	TYPE	TIME (MIN.)	PUBLISHER
Passacaglia in A minor		*organ*	7½	MS.
Blessed Are the Pure in Heart		*choral*	6	Oxford U.P.
Land of My Soul's True Health		*choral*	5	MS.
Love Is Come Again		*choral*	4	MS.

Edwards, Eric Vernon

Piano teacher, conductor, organist and composer. Born in Woking, England, October 10th, 1913.

Obtained L.R.S.M. diploma (piano) under Miss E. Barfoot, A.R.C.T. diploma (organ) under Frederick Chubb. Studied composition with J. T. Flitcroft.

Came to Canada in 1920. Began teaching piano in Victoria, B.C. at the age of 18. Piano recitals on radio, 1936-37. Organist and choirmaster since 1936. During war, arranger for Army Show Headquarters. In 1939 conducted Victoria Male Choir and Elgar Choir of Sidney, B.C. Now conducts North Sasnick Musical Society, Sidney, B.C.

Address: 112 Linden Avenue, Victoria, B.C.

COMPOSITIONS

TITLE	DATE	TYPE	TIME (MIN.)	PUBLISHER
Artaban (cantata)	1949	children and adult voices	90	MS.
Star of Wonder (cantata)	1948	children and adult voices	60	MS.
Mexican Rhapsody	1938	piano and orch.	4½	MS.
		or: piano solo	4½	MS.
Arioso (style of Handel)	1941	string orchestra	3	MS.
Festal March	1947	organ	4	MS.
Sonata in C	1937	piano	10	MS.
Pastoral	1936	piano		MS.
Hunting Song	1939	piano		MS.
Mavis Waltz	1940	piano		MS.
Sonata in E flat	1941	piano duet	4	MS.
Song of Remembrance	1945	vocal	3½	G. V. Thompson

Egener, Dr. Frederic Tristram

Organist and composer. Born in Hamilton, Ont., 1886.

Musical education at University of Toronto and Potomac University, Washington, D.C. Teachers: T. J. Palmer, Goss Custard, H. A. Wheeldon (organ), Frederick Keel (singing). Degrees: Mus.Bac., Mus.Doc. Diploma: F.C.C.M.

Has held positions as organist and choirmaster in Ontario towns and as concert organist in American theatres. Up until 1949 had given 2,318 organ recitals in Ontario, the United States, England and Switzerland.

Address: 609 Wellington Street, London, Ont.

COMPOSITIONS

TITLE	DATE	TYPE	TIME (MIN.)	PUBLISHER
Canadian Scenes (8 pieces)		organ	ea. 4-5	Waterloo Music
Happy Song		organ		Waterloo Music
Toccata on a Bell Theme		organ		Waterloo Music
Valse—con amore		piano		Waterloo Music
The Lord's Prayer		choral		Waterloo Music
Clouds and Sunshine		vocal		Breitkopf & Härtel
If Love Were Always Laughter		vocal		Breitkopf & Härtel
For We Came Out From Canada		vocal		F. Egener

Egerton, Dr. Arthur Henry

Organist, composer and lecturer. Born in Montreal in 1891.

Musical education at McGill Conservatorium, Montreal; Strathcona Scholar at Royal College of Music, London, England. Degrees: Mus.Bac. (McGill), Mus.Doc. (Toronto, 1936). Diplomas: honorary A.R.C.M., F.R.C.O. Was professor of music at Wells College, Aurora, N.Y. Is supervisor of music in Outremont (P.Q.) Schools, organ recitalist and lecturer. Chairman of Canadian College of Organists and Casavant Society. Formerly organist at Christ Church Cathedral, now at Trinity Memorial Church, Montreal.

Address: 1546 Crescent Street, Montreal, P.Q.

COMPOSITIONS

TITLE	DATE	TYPE	TIME (MIN.)	PUBLISHER
A Sailor's Wedding (Bliss Carman)		*solo, choir, orch.*		MS.
Veni Emmanuel		*organ*	5	Oxford U.P.
O Filii et Filiae		*organ*	4	Oxford U.P.
Prelude and Fugue on Iste Confessor		*organ*	7	H. W. Gray & Co.
An Easter Prelude		*organ*		MS.
Te Deum in C sharp minor		*choir and organ*		Western Music
Blessed Art Thou, O Lord		*choir and organ*		Western Music
Psalm 67		*choir and organ*		MS.
Psalm 100		*choir and organ*		H. W. Gray & Co.
The Frost Is Here		*choral (unison)*		MS.
Immortal Love Forever Full		*vocal*		Western Music

Arrangements for women's voices (Purcell, Tallis, Gibbons, Wesley) published by Carl Fischer.

Evans, Gladstone

Architect, pianist and composer. Born in England, April 23rd, 1894.

Musical education in England with Dr. E. T. Sweeting (piano) and in Toronto with W. K. Vincent (piano). Architect in practice in Toronto. Music is a hobby. For several years served as organist at St. Peter's Church, Toronto. Won first prize in Ont. Mus. Association festival in 1923 (Piano Sonata). Won Lord Willingdon prize in 1931 for vocal setting of *Wanderlied*. Elected to membership of the Arts & Letters Club of Toronto, 1950.

Address: 19 Donwoods Drive, Toronto, Ont.

COMPOSITIONS

TITLE	DATE	TYPE	TIME (MIN.)	PUBLISHER
String Quartet		*string quartet*	10	MS.
Lullaby		*vln and piano*	5½	Oxford U.P.
Sonata		*piano*		MS.
Album Leaf		*piano*	3	MS.
Crossing the Bar		*choral*	3	MS.
Te Deum		*choral*	7	MS.
Algonquin		*vocal*	3	MS.
Wanderlied (M. Pickthall)		*vocal*	3	MS.
Cheerio, Thumbs Up!		*vocal*	2½	MS.
Land of the Maple	1949	*vocal*	2	MS.

Faith, Percy

Pianist, conductor, arranger and composer. Born in Toronto, April 7th, 1908.

Musical education at Royal Conservatory, Toronto with L. Waizman (harmony and composition) and Frank S. Welsman (conducting).

From the age of 11 to 20 gained piano experience in concert halls, theatres, hotels and orchestras. Entered radio in 1927 as pianist, later made orchestral arrangements. Arranger and conductor for CBC in 1933, later for United States network programs. At present is musical director for Columbia Records, Inc.

Address: 35 Pond Park Road, Great Neck, New York, U.S.A.

TITLE	DATE	COMPOSITIONS TYPE	TIME (MIN.)	PUBLISHER
The Gandy Dancer		*operetta*		MS.
This Is My America		*solo, choir, orch.*	10	MS.
Radio		*solo, choir, orch.*	10-13	MS.
The Snow Goose	1947	*orch. or piano*	5	Harms, Inc.
Brazilian Sleigh Bells	1950	*orch. or piano*	3	Mutual Music Soc.
Aphrodite		*piano*		Harms, Inc.
Noche Caribe (Carribean Night)		*piano*		Harms, Inc.
Perpetual Notion		*piano*		Harms, Inc.
Nervous Gavotte		*piano*		Harms, Inc.
Contrasts		*vocal*	3	Th. Presser
Manon	1950	*vocal*		Harms, Inc.

Several choral and orchestral arrangements published by Th. Presser.
Various popular songs.

Farmer, Ernest Jones

Pianist, writer and composer. Born in Woodstock, Ont., March 18th, 1883.

Musical education at Royal Conservatory, Toronto with Lena M. Hayes and A. S. Vogt, at Royal Conservatory of Music in Leipzig with Gustav Schreck, Richard Hoffmann, Max Reger and Carl Wendling, at Hambourg Conservatory, Toronto with Michael Hambourg. Teacher and member of examination board, Royal Conservatory, Toronto. Writer of editorials on economics.

Address: 48 Fulton Avenue, Toronto, Ont.

TITLE	DATE	COMPOSITIONS TYPE	TIME (MIN.)	PUBLISHER
Intermezzo		*organ*	4½	MS.
Quasi tempo di Valse		*piano, vln, vc*	8	MS.
Alla Polacca		*piano, vln, vc*	4½	MS.
Three Piano Sketches		*piano*	ea. 2½	MS.
Island Nights (4 nocturnes)		*piano*	ea. 4	MS.
The Long Waves		*piano*	2	MS.
The Whitethroat		*vocal*	2½	MS.
Sally Anne		*vocal*	1	MS.
The Doughman		*vocal*	1	MS.
The Toys That Are Left Out Nights		*vocal*	1	MS.

Farnon, Robert Joseph

Composer, violinist and pianist. Born in Toronto, July 24th, 1917.

Began to study music at the age of nine. Studied with Louis Waizman (theory) and with other private teachers (violin and piano). Worked professionally in music since the age of thirteen. During World War II was with Army Show. Now lives in London, England. Music director for films *Maytime in Mayfair, Spring in Park Lane, Elizabeth and Lady Mead.*

Address: c/o British Broadcasting Corporation, London, W.1., England.

Affiliation: CAPAC.

		COMPOSITIONS		
TITLE	DATE	TYPE	TIME (MIN.)	PUBLISHER
Symphony No. 1 in D flat major		orchestra	27	MS.
Ottawa Symphony		orchestra	30	MS.
Cascades to the Sea		orchestra	18	Boosey & Hawkes
Hornblower Suite		orchestra	12	Feldman
Witch of Endor		orchestra	3	Feldman
Babes in the Wood (suite)		orchestra	15	MS.
Dressmaker's Ballet (suite)		orchestra	8	MS.
Symphonette		small orchestra	9	MS.
Three Etudes		piano	7	MS.
Mad Genius		piano	3	MS.
Tinker, Tailor, Soldier, Sailor (suite)		piano	11	MS.
Wedding Gown		vocal	3	Fields
H'ya, Mom		vocal	3½	G. V. Thompson

Shorter orchestral works in manuscript (2-9 minutes each):

Nightingale Song; Valse; Mobile Horse; Circus Parade; Maypole and Roundabout; Harlequin and Columbine; White Heather; Just William; The Three Bears; The Valiant Tailor; The Princess and the Ugly Frog; The Duel; Tortoise and the Hare; Three Little Pigs; The Bird Ballet; District Nurse (comedy overture).

Songs in manuscript:

Town Crier; Marion; The Baron; March Along; Joe Soldier; Leave Your Name and Number; Gorgeous Gal; Thanks.

Over 30 pieces (1-4 min. each) published and recorded by Chappell & Co.

Fassio, Angelo

Violinist, conductor, publisher and composer. Born in St. Etienne, France, January 14th, 1888.

Musical education in France, Germany and Italy (violin and theory). Has played violin and viola professionally since 1909 and conducted operettas and variety shows. Arranged and wrote music for pantomimes and movies.

Address: P.O. Box 208, Lachute, P.Q.

		COMPOSITIONS		
TITLE	DATE	TYPE	TIME (MIN.)	PUBLISHER
Overture Militaire		orchestra or band	12	MS.
Thumbs Up (march)		orchestra or band	4	MS.
Fanfare-Introduction		orchestra	1	Waterson
Serenade-Pizzicato		strings	3½	MS.
Solitude (reverie)		vln and piano	3	E. B. Marks
Pomp and Pageantry (march)		organ or piano	2½	Parnasse Musical
Daughters of Canada (march)		piano	2½	Parnasse Musical
		or: band	2½	MS.

A few other military marches for band or orchestra in manuscript and a number of chansonettes.

Finch, Robert Duer Claydon

French professor, pianist, composer and poet. Born in Long Island, N.Y., 1900.

Music teachers included Alberto Guerrero and Wanda Landowska. Musical amateur. Has given many public piano recitals and lectured on medieval and English music. Associate professor of French, University of Toronto.

Address: c/o University College, Toronto, Ont.

COMPOSITIONS

TITLE	DATE	TYPE	TIME (MIN.)	PUBLISHER
Six Inventions	1930-40	*piano*	5	MS.
Antigone (incidental music for Hart House production)	1949	*flute solo*	5	MS.
The Leaves Descend	1925	*vocal*	1½	MS.
Weisser Flieder	1930	*vocal*	2	MS.
Le Vent d'automne	1932	*vocal*	2	MS.

Fisher, Charlotte E. (Carlotta)

Violinist, pianist and composer. Born in London, England.

Musical education in Vienna, London, Leipzig and Toronto, studying with Leschetizky, Lutz (piano), Toeving (violin), Heynsen, Dr. Ettore Mazzoleni (harmony and composition) and Lindner (singing). Served in censorship and British Intelligence in France, 1916-18. Was editor, Toronto Symphony Orchestra News.

Address: 96 Glen Road, Toronto, Ont.

Affiliation: CAPAC.

COMPOSITIONS

TITLE	DATE	TYPE	TIME (MIN.)	PUBLISHER
Baroque	1941	*piano*	2	Bosworth & Co.
Invitation to Quebec	1941	*vocal*	2	Bosworth & Co.
One Perfect Rose	1942	*vocal*	2	Bosworth & Co.
Christmas Chant		*vocal*	4	Bosworth & Co.
By the Deep Blue Saguenay	1944	*vocal*	3	Bosworth & Co.
Bells of Montreal	1948	*vocal*	5	MS.
Canada—My Home (folk song)	1949	*vocal*	4	MS.

Fleming, Gordon Charles James

Organist, pianist, composer and arranger. Born in Goderich, Ont., May 27th, 1903.

Musical education at Royal Conservatory, Toronto with Alberto Guerrero (piano) and in Detroit with Mischa Kottler (piano and composition). Has played professionally since 1918 in theatres, churches, in concerts and on radio. For past 19 years has been organist, pianist, composer and arranger for radio station CKLW of Windsor, Ont. Has composed music for Canadian films and CBC radio programs. Works have been performed by Chicago Philharmonic and Detroit Symphony.

Address: 1082 Dawson Road, Windsor, Ont.

COMPOSITIONS

TITLE	DATE	TYPE	TIME (MIN.)	PUBLISHER
Symphony No. 1 (3 mvmts)	1942	orchestra	28	MS.
La Journée (symphonic poem)	1940	orchestra	18	MS..
Louis des Jardins and the Devil (symph. poem)	1949	orchestra	20	MS.
Piano Concerto in A minor	1948	piano and orch.	15	MS.
Serenade	1945	strgs, wwd, hns	4	MS.
Allegro in D minor	1945	string quartet	6	MS.
Nocturne in F sharp minor	1947	2 pianos	4½	MS.
Nocturne in B flat major	1948	organ	3½	MS.
Choral-Festal Communion Service	1946	choral	18	MS.
Two Motets on "Bread of Life"	1946	choral	ea. 1½	MS.

Fleming, Robert James Berkeley

Pianist and composer. Born in Prince Albert, Sask., November 12th, 1921.

Musical education at Royal College of Music, London, 1937-39 with Arthur Benjamin (piano) and Herbert Howells (composition). In Saskatoon studied with Lyell Gustin and at Royal Conservatory, Toronto with Healey Willan (composition), Frederick Silvester and John Weatherseed (organ), Ettore Mazzoleni (conducting). Diploma: L.R.S.M. (1941, piano). Won Council Exhibition prize in England and two CAPAC scholarships.

Since 1946 has been composer, conductor and music editor with National Film Board. Compositions have been performed throughout Canada, in Europe, U.S.A., Australia, Central and South America.

Address: 589 Highland Avenue, Ottawa, Ont.

Affiliation: CAPAC.

COMPOSITIONS

TITLE	DATE	TYPE	TIME (MIN.)	PUBLISHER
Instrumental works:				
Around the House (Nursery Suite)	1942	orchestra	20	MS.
Kaleidoscope	1949	orchestra	8	MS.
Rondo	1946	orchestra	6	MS.
Chapter 13 (ballet, concert version in preparation)	1948	orchestra or 2 pianos	25	MS.
Country Fair	1950	orchestra	6	MS.
Seaboard Sketches	1950	small orch.	12	MS.
Suite for Strings	1942	string orch.	10	MS.
Six Improvisations on a Liturgical Theme	1946	string orch.	8	MS.
Hymn to War (J. Coulter)	1950	tenor and strgs	7	MS.
Skip Caprice	1941	vln and piano	4	MS.
Sonata ("Bella Bella")	1944	vln and piano	16	MS.
Juguette	1947	vln and piano	5	MS.
Sonatina	1940-41	piano	8	Oxford U.P.
Spanish Banks	1943	piano	3	MS.

COMPOSITIONS

TITLE	DATE	TYPE	TIME (MIN.)	PUBLISHER
Humoresque	1942	*piano*	3	MS.
Three Preludes of the Mediums	1939-41	*piano*	7	MS.
Rhythmpromptu No. 1	1946	*piano*	3	MS.
Rhythmpromptu No. 2	1948	*piano*	4	MS.
Five Modernistics	1946	*piano*	7	MS.
Waltz and Siesta	1949	*piano*	9½	MS.
Post Script	1950	*piano*	1¼	MS.
Five Short Duets for Children	1940	*piano duet*	5	MS.
Caprice	1940	*two pianos*	4	MS.
The Winter's Tale	1941	*two pianos*	6	MS.
Rondo	1942	*two pianos*	6	MS.

Choral and vocal works:

TITLE	DATE	TYPE	TIME (MIN.)	PUBLISHER
Song of the Women	1940	*choral*	6	MS.
Dusk Lights	1940	*choral*	4	MS.
Lynn Valley	1940	*choral*	4	MS.
Nunc Dimittis	1943	*choral*	3	MS.
150th Psalm	1942	*choral*	4	MS.
Missa Brevis	1942	*choral*	12	MS.
Would That I Were There	1942	*choral*	4	Oxford U.P.
Shepherd's Song	1936	*choral*	3	MS.
The Night	1948	*vocal duet*	4	MS.
The Moon Is Dead	1948	*vocal duet*	4	MS.
Secrets (cycle of 3 songs)	1942	*vocal*	10	Oxford U.P.
The Oxen	1942	*vocal*	4	Oxford U.P.

Songs in manuscript:

Mystic; Midnight; Starfall; Immortal Sails; Away; Courage; The Trusting Heart; Absent; February Morning; The Night; Auvergnat; The Little Serving Maid; Summer Thunder; Grave in the Quiet Glen; Summer Song; Song for June; Furrows; Summer Song; Why Do Ye Call the Poet Lonely; Music; Love Wonder; Song of Quoodles; Cradle Song; Fantasy; Song at Dusk; Dance My Dearies; The Voice; Quack; The Shepherd's Song. **Three Irish folk songs** arranged.

Fogg, Howard

Violinist, conductor and composer. Born in Lewiston, Maine, April 27th, 1892.

Musical education with Gustav Haanka and other teachers. Veteran of the First World War, having served as instructor in march-singing and small instruments. Has acted as composer, arranger and conductor for Canadian Victor Talking Machine Company, The Associated Screen News. For five years was conductor of the Dumbells' Revue. Musical director of 17th Duke of York's Royal Canadian Hussars. Conducted and prepared many series of programs for the CBC.

Address: 1166 Irvine Avenue, Montreal, P.Q.

Affiliation: BMI.

COMPOSITIONS

TITLE	DATE	TYPE	TIME (MIN.)	PUBLISHER
Land of Beautiful Waters (symphonic suite, 5 parts)		*orchestra*	35	MS.
Remembrance Day (symph. poem)		*orchestra*	7	MS.
Laurentian Suite		*orchestra*	19	MS.

	COMPOSITIONS			
TITLE	DATE	TYPE	TIME (MIN.)	PUBLISHER
Symphonic Suite		*orchestra*	17	MS.
Third Battle of Ypres		*orchestra*	8	MS.
Spanish Silhouette		*small orch.*	2	MS.
La Pensée		*small orch.*	3½	MS.
A Simple Song of Thanks		*small orch.*	1	MS.
French Canadian Medley		*small orch.*	4	MS.
Minuetto		*string orch.*	3	MS.
The Duke of York's Forever		*band*		MS.
Thoughts at Eventide		*piano*	2	G. Schirmer
Wanatea "Indian Intermezzo"		*piano*	3	W. Rolfe
A Babbling Brook		*piano*	4	MS.
Valse Sybil		*piano*		Turcot
Ashes		*vln and piano*	4	MS.
Darling I Love You		*vocal*	3	G. V. Thompson
Melodies of Yesterday		*vocal*	3	Sprague-Coleman
My Dearest Own		*vocal*	2	Turcot
May Prayer		*vocal*	3	MS.
Beloved		*vocal*	4	MS.

Background music for picture *Rhapsody in Two Languages*, orchestra, 11 min.
Many other short compositions.

Foot, Phyllis Margaret

Composer and music teacher. Born in London, England, October 15th, 1914.

Musical education at Royal Academy of Music, London, 1931-34. Diplomas: G.R.S.M., L.R.A.M. Taught music in English schools, 1934-47 and in Canada at St. Helen's, Quebec and Rupertsland, Winnipeg. Accompanied Winnipeg Ballet at Banff School of Fine Arts. Played own works over CKUA, Edmonton.

Address: 39 Mark Avenue, Apt. 9, Ottawa, Ont.

	COMPOSITIONS			
TITLE	DATE	TYPE	TIME (MIN.)	PUBLISHER
Dover Beach (inspired by M. Arnold's poem)	1933	*piano*	2	MS.
Holiday Suite (descriptive suite)	1949	*piano*	3	Western Music
Book of Ancient Classical Dances (original; 25)	1950	*piano*	35	MS.
Moment Musical (4 mvmts)	1950	*piano*	6	MS.
Our Forest Friends (for children)	1950	*piano*	12	MS.
Tziganka (a Russian fantasy)	1949	*piano*	3	MS.
Birds in the Cherry Orchard	1950	*piano*	3	MS.
The Little Dutch Boy (dance for children)	1950	*piano*	1	MS.
Canadian Cities (descriptive suite)	1950	*piano*		MS.
Jolly Beginners' Book (piano method)	1950	*piano*		Waterloo Music

Forsyth, Wesley Octavius

Pianist, composer, music teacher and critic. Born in Aurora, Ont., January 26th, 1863. Died in Toronto, May 1937.

Musical education in Toronto, in Leipzig with Jadassohn, Krause and Zwintscher and in Vienna with Epstein. Since 1892 taught piano and contributed articles to periodicals; was music critic of *The Week*. For some time directed Metropolitan School of Music in Toronto and later taught at Canadian Academy of Music.

His *Romanza* was first played under Jarrow in Leipzig, 1889 where the two orchestral suites were also heard. An all-Forsyth recital was given at the Toronto College of Music in 1889. Forsyth was the first Canadian-born Anglo-Saxon composer of any importance.

COMPOSITIONS

TITLE	DATE	TYPE	TIME (MIN.)	PUBLISHER
Two orchestral suites		*orchestra*		
Romanza		*orchestra*		
String Quartet		*string quartet*		
Prelude and Fugue in C minor, Op. 18		*organ*		Nordheimer

About 50 songs and 50 piano pieces with descriptive titles have been published by Heintzman, Whaley Royce, Nordheimer, Gordon V. Thompson, Empire Music and Travel Club in Toronto and by Frederick Harris, Theodore Presser, Carl Fischer, Jost & Sander (Leipzig) and others. Works have opus numbers from 1 to approximately 70.

Fortier, Achille

Choirmaster and music teacher. Born in St. Clet, P.Q., October 23rd, 1864. Died c. 1939.

Musical education with Guillaume Couture and Dominique Ducharme in Montreal and 1885-90 at Paris Conservatoire with Th. Dubois, R. Bussine and Ernest Guiraud. The first Canadian to enrol in the regular composition course of the Conservatoire.

After 1890 taught music in Montreal and later became government translator in Ottawa. A concert devoted to his works was given in Montreal in the 1890's. Before his death many manuscripts were destroyed in a fire.

COMPOSITIONS

TITLE	DATE	TYPE	TIME (MIN.)	PUBLISHER
Mass		*choir and orch.*		performed 1896
Haec Dies		*choral*		
March solennell		*orchestra*		
Valse		*orchestra*		
Meditation		*'cello, piano*		
Mon Bouquet (L. Fréchette)		*vocal*		
Philosophie (A. Sylvestre)		*vocal*		
20 Chansons populaires du Canada		*vocal*		Ed. Hardy, Montreal

Piano pieces, motets, songs and many other works.

See:
Léo-Pol Morin, *Papiers de Musique*, 1930.

Fortin, J. Louis-de-Gonzague

Organist, composer and agronomist. Born in St. Fabien, Rimouski, P.Q., March 4th, 1894.

Professor of agronomy at Ecole Supérieure d'Agriculture, Ste-Anne de la Pocatière. Composes music as a hobby.

Address: Ste-Anne de la Pocatière, P.Q.

COMPOSITIONS

TITLE	DATE	TYPE	TIME (MIN.)	PUBLISHER
Marche de l'école		orchestra	4	MS.
Chant de l'école		choral	4	MS.
Berceuse in F		piano	3-5	MS.
Cantate		vocal	20	MS.
Ave Maria		vocal	3-4	MS.
Chante mon gars		vocal	4	MS.
La Maison condamnée		vocal	3	MS.
Je veux revoir la maison		vocal	3	MS.

`No recent information obtained.

France, William Edward

Pianist, organist, writer and composer. Born in Milberta, Ont., April 21st, 1912.

Musical education with Thomas Martin, Gertrude Huntley (piano), Charles Peaker, Frederick Horwood, Eugene Hill, Healey Willan (composition). Degree: Mus.Bac. (Toronto). Diploma: F.C.C.O. Has held position of organist in many Ontario churches and is now organist and choirmaster of Chalmers United Church, Ottawa.

Address: c/o Chalmers Church, 357 Cooper Street, Ottawa, Ont.

Affiliation: BMI.

COMPOSITIONS

TITLE	DATE	TYPE	TIME (MIN.)	PUBLISHER
Four Miniatures	1948	small orchestra	6	MS.
Discourse	1950	fl, clar, bn	5	MS.
Sonatina	1946	vln, vc, piano	3½	MS.
Lament	1944	vc, piano	3	MS.
Solemn March	1945	piano	1½	MS.
Jig	1945	piano	1	BMI Canada
Story Hour (7 short pieces)	1946	piano	8	MS.
Minuet "Beauty and the Beast"	1946	piano	1	F. Harris
Elegie	1947	piano	1½	MS.
Four Chorale Preludes	1942	organ	6	MS.
Morning Song	1946	organ	1¼	Th. Presser
Introduction and Toccata	1947	organ	6	MS.
Miniature Suite	1947	organ	5	O. Ditson
Suite in A minor	1950	organ	7	MS.

Choral works:

The Fairy Frolic; O Mistress Mine	Oxford U.P.
O Trinity of Blessed Light; Christ Hath a Garden; Bread of the World	H. W. Gray & Co.

COMPOSITIONS

TITLE	DATE	TYPE	TIME (MIN.)	PUBLISHER
Unto Thee O Lord; Under the Greenwood Tree; It Was a Lover; My Sweet Sweeting; Light at Evening Time; When I Survey A Cradle Hymn				Galaxy Music Corp.
Lord of all Power; O Lord Support Us; Child's Prayer				F. Harris
Jesus, Tender Shepherd; An Easter Song; From All That Dwell				Th. Presser
The World's Desire; Soldiers of Christ, Arise				MS.
Vocal works:				
Compensation; My Light Thou Art; A Christmas Lullaby; My Sweet Sweeting; I Loved a Lass				Galaxy Music Corp.
With Rue My Heart Is Laden; The Wanderer; Song (1938); Mary's Lullaby; Winter; O Sleep; Magic; The Shepherdess; My Lady's Praise				MS.

Franchère-DesRosiers, Rose de Lima

Pianist, music teacher and composer. Born in Montreal, January 6th, 1863.

Musical education with Paul Letondal, R. O. Pelletier (piano), Alcibiade Béique and M. Dussault (harmony). Career has been spent in teaching piano and singing in girls' colleges. Acted as organist in many churches in and around Montreal. Is now retired.

Address: Hôpital St. Eusèbe, Boulevard Manseau, Chambre 417 Joliette, P.Q.

COMPOSITIONS

TITLE	DATE	TYPE	TIME (MIN.)	PUBLISHER
Pièce pour orgue	1940	*organ*	4	MS.
Pièce pour orgue	1945	*organ*	4	MS.
Bric-à-Brac	1941	*piano*	4	printed in Boston
La Brise (fantasy)	1939	*piano*	4	MS.
Le Dodo du Rossignol	1897	*piano*	3	MS.
Chorale	1941	*piano*	4	MS.
Promenade	1940	*piano*	3	MS.
Petite Pastorale	1940	*piano*	3	MS.
Etudiants et Copains	1940	*choral*	4	MS.
Ave Maria	1898	*vocal*	4	printed in Boston
Cantique de mariage	1898	*vocal*	4	printed in Boston
Les Oiseaux ont des coeurs d'enfants	1897	*vocal*	4	MS.

COMPOSITIONS

TITLE	DATE	TYPE	TIME (MIN.)	PUBLISHER
Tantum Ergo	1898	*vocal*	5	MS.
Souvenir	1920	*vocal*	4	MS.
Matinée d'octobre	1942	*vocal*	3	MS.
Souvenez vous	1893	*vocal*	3	MS.
Si tu voulais	1898	*vocal*	3	MS.
Les Roses de Saadi	1949	*vocal*	3	MS.
Prière	1950	*vocal*	3	MS.
Marie Reine des Coeurs	1944	*vocal*	3	MS.
Jésus vivant en Marie	1946	*vocal*	4	MS.
Illusion	1942	*vocal*	3	MS.

Fraser, Jean

Pianist, organist and composer. Born in Almonte, Ont., January 3rd, 1920.

Musical education at Royal Conservatory, Toronto with Healey Willan, John Reymes-King and Margaret Parsons Poole. Won CAPAC scholarship, 1941. Was organist at First Unitarian Church, Toronto. Degree: Mus.Bac. (Mount Allison University).

Address: New York City.

COMPOSITIONS

TITLE	DATE	TYPE	TIME (MIN.)	PUBLISHER
Theme and variations		*piano*		MS.
Four Burlesques		*piano*		MS.
Scherzo		*2 pianos*		MS.
Passacaglia		*organ*		MS.
Four Choral Preludes		*organ*		MS.
Elegy of Kremlin Bells		*choral*	3½	MS.

Songs in manuscript:

Madrigal; Canzonet; While in the Moon; The Legend of the Dove; Apology; Blue Squills; There Will Come Soft Rains; Alone; The Mystery; Exiled From the Nightingales; Praise of Women; Nocturne in a Deserted Brickyard; The Ship from Rio; Now that Soft April; A Song of Praise; The Swan.
No recent information obtained.

Frayn, Clarence Vernon

Pianist, violoncellist, organist, choirmaster and composer. Born in England, September 18th, 1888.

Musical education with Kathleen Frayn, Arthur Swaine and H. W. J. Cousen (piano, theory, organ, etc.). Was assistant organist at Richmont Terrace Church, Bradford, England. Has been organist and choirmaster at Westmount Methodist Church, Westmount, P.Q., St. Mathias Church, Westmount, Knox Crescent Presbyterian Church (for 27 years), Trinity Memorial Church (for 4 years). Had many years of orchestral experience in England.

Address: 488 Lansdowne Avenue, Westmount, P.Q.

COMPOSITIONS

TITLE	DATE	TYPE	TIME (MIN.)	PUBLISHER
The Regent of Bali		*comic opera*		MS.
Cash and Carry		*comic opera*		MS.

COMPOSITIONS

TITLE	DATE	TYPE	TIME (MIN.)	PUBLISHER
The Holy Nativity		*choral*	50	MS.
Weary Chilluns (spiritual)		*vocal*	5	P. Derek
Protection (sacred)		*vocal*	5	F. Harris

Songs in manuscript:

Going Gay; 12 children's songs from *Saucy and All; The Blind Jockey; October; The Plowman; The Whispering Poplars; In Flanders' Fields;* approximately 30 songs, mostly set to words by Canadian authors, and other secular and sacred songs.

Freedman, Harry

English horn and oboe player, composer. Born in Lodz, Poland, April 5th, 1922.

Musical education in Winnipeg with Arthur Hart (clarinet), in Toronto at Royal Conservatory with Perry Bauman (oboe) and John Weinzweig (composition). In 1949 won Tanglewood scholarship to study under Messiaen and Copland. Came to Canada in 1925. Since 1946 has been English horn player with Toronto Symphony Orchestra.

Address: 24 High Park Gardens, Toronto, Ont.

Affiliation: CAPAC.

COMPOSITIONS

TITLE	DATE	TYPE	TIME (MIN.)	PUBLISHER
Symphonic Suite	1948	*orchestra*	15	MS.
Serenade	1950	*orchestra*	20	MS.
Scherzo "Caricature"	1950	*small orchestra*	3½	MS.
Divertimento	1947	*oboe and strings*	15	MS.
Five Pieces	1949	*string quartet*	14	MS.
Trio	1948	*2 oboes, Eng. hn*	10	MS.
March; Pastoral	1951	*woodwinds*	4	MS.
Dark Cry (ballet)	1948	*piano*	8	MS.
Piano Suite	1950	*piano*	8	MS.
Six French Canadian folk songs arr.	1950	*vln and piano*	5	MS.

Frère Barnabé

(see: Lemieux, Dr. Joseph-Léopold)

Frère Placide

(see: Vermandere, Joseph)

Fricker, Dr. Herbert Austin

Choral conductor, organist and composer. Born in Canterbury, England, February 12th, 1868. Died in Toronto, November 11th, 1943.

Musical education in England with Dr. W. H. Longhurst of Canterbury Cathedral, Sir F. Bridge of Westminster Abbey and Edwin Lamare (organ). Degrees: Mus.Bac. (Durham), M.A. (Leeds) and hon. Mus.Doc. (Toronto, 1923). Diploma: F.R.C.O.

Became deputy organist of Canterbury Cathedral in 1884; associate organist and choirmaster of Holy Trinity Church, Folkestone, Kent, England in 1891. Appointed organist at Leeds City Hall, 1898. Organist and choirmaster of Leeds Music Festival; founder and conductor of Leeds Symphony Orchestra and conductor of choral societies. Left Leeds in 1917 and came to Canada as conductor of the Toronto Mendelssohn Choir (1917-42). Was president of Canadian College of Organists, 1925-26 and on faculty of music, Univ. of Toronto.

Affiliation (estate): CAPAC.

COMPOSITIONS

TITLE	DATE	TYPE	TIME (MIN.)	PUBLISHER
Concert Overture in C minor		*organ*	9	Novello
Fantaisie-Overture in G minor		*organ*		G. Schirmer
Suite		*organ*		H. W. Gray & Co.
Adagio in A flat major		*organ*		Chester
Romance in G flat major		*organ*		G. Schirmer
Scherzo Symphonique		*organ*		Beal, Stuttard & Co.
Cantilene Nuptiale		*organ*		Beal, Stuttard & Co.
Three Organ Pieces		*organ*		J. Broadbent
The Fairies		*choral*		Whaley Royce
The Shield of Faith		*choral*		
A Song of Thanksgiving		*choral*		Mendelssohn Choir
The Hermit		*choral*		
Magnificat		*choral*		Novello
Nunc Dimittis in G		*choral*		Novello
Seven Anthems		*choral*		Anglo-Canadian
The Faithless Swallow		*solo voice and trio*		O. Ditson

Many other compositions. Many arrangements for voices and organ have been published by various firms in England, New York and Toronto.

Gagnier, Dr. Josephat Jean

Clarinetist, bassoonist, pianist, conductor, adjudicator, lecturer and composer. Born in Montreal, December 2nd, 1885. Died in Montreal, September 16th, 1949.

Musical education with J. van Poock, L. van Loocke, L. Médard, O. Arnold (clarinet), E. Barbot, C. Westermeier (bassoon), A. Contant, R. O. Pelletier (piano), R. Pelletier, V. Tanguy, A. Contant, O. Deveaux (theory). Degree: Mus.Doc. (Montreal) Started musical studies at a very early age and when 14 became principal clarinetist in local theatres, bassoonist with the Montreal Symphony and Opera. Began conducting when 18 (military bands, orchestral and choral groups). Musical director at Parc Sohmer, Montreal, 1916-19. Captain and director of His Majesty's Canadian Grenadier Guards Band, 1913-1949. Founder and conductor of new Montreal Symphony and Montreal Little Symphony. Appeared as guest conductor, adjudicator, lecturer and conducting coach in Canada and the U.S. Was musical director for CBC French network. Compiled first edition of CBC Catalogue of Canadian Composers.

Affiliation (estate): CAPAC.

COMPOSITIONS

TITLE	DATE	TYPE	TIME (MIN.)	PUBLISHER
Works for orchestra:				
In the Shade of the Maples (suite)		*orchestra*	10	MS.
Mélodie brève		*orchestra* (*arr. piano*)	2½	MS.

COMPOSITIONS

TITLE	DATE	TYPE	TIME (MIN.)	PUBLISHER
Suite for harp (5 mvmts)		orchestra	13	S. Fox
Three Preludes		orchestra	3½	MS.
Reflets (prelude)		strings		Parnasse Musical
Têtes d'enfants (prelude)		strings		Parnasse Musical

Works for orchestra or band:

The Wind in the Leafless Maples		orch. or band	8	MS.
The Goatfooted Pan		orch. or band	12	MS.
Suite in the Olden Style		str. quintet or orch. or band	16½	MS.
Currente Calamo (prelude)		orch. or band	4	MS.
Queen of Hearts (overture)		orch. or band	8	Carl Fischer (band)
Toronto Bay (valse scherzo)		orch. or band	5	Carl Fischer (band)
Victoire (march)		orch. or band	3½	MS.

Works for band:

Skip Along (march)		band	2½	Carl Fischer
Hands Across the Border		band	2¾	Remick Music Corp.

The Joker; Ace of Spades; King of Clubs; Jack of Diamonds (overtures); Flaming Youth (waltz); Safety First (galop); Four Suites of Fanfares; The Draftee; The Corporal; The Sergeant; The Lieutenant; The Captain; The Adjutant; The Major; The Colonel; In the Air; Ca-Na-Ex; Les Mont-Régiens; Trompettes; Le Voyageur; Tank March; Kiwanis March; Here's to Tommy March; Maple Leaves March (marches)   MS.

Incidental music:

Dans le marais		orchestra	7½	MS.
Panache sur la neige		oboe and bn	8	MS.
Le Bandit		Eng. hn, bn, tymp.	11	MS.
Coucher de soleil		3 Fr. hn, Eng. hn, bn	11½	MS.
La Paix soit avec vous		harp	7¾	MS.
Le Faux Rossignol		fl, ob, cl, bn	10	MS.
Le Rival		orchestra	10	MS.
Cinq petits lapins		3 ob, Eng. hn	8	MS.

Works for piano, oboe and organ:

Petite Suite		oboe and piano	7	MS.
Ten Studies in Concert Form		piano		Archambault
Trois Esquisses Musicales		piano		Parnasse Musical
Soliloque		piano		MS.
Prelude (L'Eternelle Comédie)		organ		Parnasse Musical

Choral works:

Tritons et sirènes		fem. ch. and orch.	9	MS.
Pyrame et Thisbée		choir and orch.	13	Parnasse Musical
Hamac dans les voiles		choral	8½	Parnasse Musical

COMPOSITIONS

TITLE	DATE	TYPE	TIME (MIN.)	PUBLISHER
Le Chant de L'A.C.J.C.		solo and choir	3	A.C.J.C.
Hommage au seminaire (cantata)		choral	10	MS.

Published vocal works:

Ressemblance (romance)		vocal	3	Parnasse Musical
Le Canada		vocal	3½	Fr. des E.C.
Hymne à la Patrie		vocal	3	Passe-Temps
Kyrie		vocal	2	Fr. des E.C.
Quicumque		vocal	2½	Fr. des E.C.

Unpublished vocal works:

Hymne à mon collège; Le Sage; Regrets; O toi; Cor Jesu; Danses Maléchites (Indian song); *Danse de la Découverte* (Indian song); *Pisik* (Eskimo song); *Weather Incantation* (Eskimo song); *Sante Joseph; Adeste Fidelis; Filez, filez, o mon navire; Jesous Ahontania.*

Gagnier, René

Violinist, conductor and composer. Born in Montreal, May 30th, 1892.

Musical education with Albert Chamberland, Alfred De Sève and Saul Brant (violin), J. J. Gagnier (harmony and allied subjects). Was assistant conductor at Loew's Theatre, Montreal, 1918-29. Has been violinist with Montreal Orchestra, La Société des Concerts Symphoniques and the Montreal Little Symphony. Was member of Canadian Grenadier Guards Band for over 25 years as solo euphonium and assistant conductor; music teacher at the Quebec Provincial Conservatory; conductor of Union Musicale de Trois-Rivières (Three Rivers) for 11 years. Is now professor at the Nicolet Seminary and Académie de la Salle of Trois-Rivières.

Address: 454 Laurier, Trois Rivières, P.Q.

COMPOSITIONS

TITLE	DATE	TYPE	TIME (MIN.)	PUBLISHER
L'Union Musicale (march)		band	2½	MS.
Franc et sans dol (march)		band	2½	MS.
Maurice (march)		band	2½	MS.
Albert (march)		band	2½	MS.
Anniversaire (march)		band	2½	MS.
Perce-Neige (waltz)		band	4	MS.
Dorita (waltz)		band	3	MS.
Valse Intermezzo (waltz)		band	5	MS.
Petit Clairon (cornet solo)		band	3	MS.
Excentrique (baritone solo)		band	5	MS.
They'll Tramp Till Victory		vocal	3	MS.
Pourquoi fermes-tu les yeux		vocal	3	MS.

Gagnon, Gustave

Organist, composer and teacher. Born in Rivière-du-Loup (Louiseville), P.Q. November 6th, 1842. Died in Quebec, November 19th, 1930.

Musical education after 1860 in Montreal with Paul Letondal and between 1870-73 in Paris, Belgium, Italy and Leipzig. Around 1864 became organist at St.Jean-Baptiste, Quebec and from 1876-1915 was organist at Quebec Cathedral. For many years taught music at Ecole Normale Laval and at Séminaire de Québec. One of the founders of Académie de Musique de Québec in 1867 and at one time its president. Was the first director of Ecole de Musique, Université Laval, opened in 1922.

		COMPOSITIONS		
TITLE	DATE	TYPE	TIME (MIN.)	PUBLISHER
March pontificale				
(for Cardinal Taschereau)	1886	organ		
		arr. for orchestra		
		by J. Vézina		
Marche nocturne	1873	piano		
Gavotte in F	1890	piano		
Reflets du passé (valse de				
salon)		piano		Brainard
Souvenir de Leipzig		piano		

Many other compositions.

Gagnon, Henri (Charles Edouard Gustave Henri)

Organist, music teacher and composer. Born in Quebec, March 6th, 1887.

Musical education with Gustave Gagnon (solfeggio and piano), Joseph Vézina (solfeggio and harmony), William Reed, R. O. Pelletier and Romain Pelletier (organ) Arthur Letondal (piano), and Guillaume Couture (harmony and counterpoint). In Paris studied with Ch.M. Widor, Eugène Gigout, Joseph Bonnet and Isidore Philipp.

Has held positions as organist since 1903. Assistant organist since 1910 and organist since 1915 at Quebec Cathedral. Between 1910-16 appeared as piano and organ soloist. Since 1916 has taught piano and solfeggio at Quebec Normal Schools and piano and organ at Petit Séminaire de Québec. Since 1922 has been professor of piano and organ at Ecole de Musique, Université Laval. Since 1942 has been teacher at, and since 1946 director of, Quebec Provincial Conservatory, Quebec City section.

Son of Gustave Gagnon.

Address: 8 rue St. Flavien, Quebec, P.Q.

		COMPOSITIONS		
TITLE	DATE	TYPE	TIME (MIN.)	PUBLISHER
Deux pièces de genre	1904	piano	5	Lavigueur & Hutchison, Quebec
Mazurka	1907	piano	5	MS.
Deux Antiennes d'orgue	1920	organ	5	Passe-Temps, 1945
Prélude d'orgue	1949	organ	4	La Revue de St. Grégoire, Quebec
Rondel de Thibaut de Champagne	1916	vocal	4	MS.
Cantique au Sacré Coeur	1904	voice and organ	5 ⎫	Manuel de morceaux réligieux, Abbé Rancourt, Quebec
Ave Maria		voice and organ	4 ⎬	
Chant à Marie	1937	solo, choir, organ	5 ⎭	

See:
Léo-Pol Morin, Papiers de Musique, 1930.

Gamache, Gérard

Pianist and composer. Born in Trois Rivières, P.Q., January 25th, 1903.

Musical education with own mother, Charles E. A. Houde and Alfred Laliberté (piano), Oscar O'Brien and Louis Michiels (harmony). Has played in concerts and teaches piano. Founded Club Musical et Littéraire de Montréal, 1933.

Address: 10801 rue Saint Denis, Montreal, P.Q.

COMPOSITIONS

TITLE	DATE	TYPE	TIME (MIN.)	PUBLISHER
Pour Toi (waltz)		piano		MS.
Grande Valse in E flat		piano		MS.
Menuet		piano		MS.
Pièce brève		piano		MS.
Cor Jesus		choral		MS.
Hymne des chevaliers de Colomb		vocal		MS.

Garant, Albert Antonio Serge

Pianist, composer and clarinetist. Born in Quebec, September 22nd, 1929.

Musical education with Sylvio Lacharité and Yvonne Hubert (piano), P. Robicloux (harmony) and Claude Champagne (composition). Has appeared as piano soloist with bands in Sherbrooke. In 1950 won composition prize in Youth Festival of Sherbrooke. Plays dance music for a living and studies piano and composition in Montreal.

Address: 13 2nd Avenue, Sherbrooke, P.Q.

COMPOSITIONS

TITLE	DATE	TYPE	TIME (MIN.)	PUBLISHER
Ta forme monte comme la blessure du sang (A. Grandbois)	1950	string orchestra	6	MS.
Fantasie	1950	clarinet, piano	5½	MS.
Sonatine	1950	piano	8½	MS.
Un grand sommeil noir (Verlaine)	1949	vocal	1½	MS.
Music for saxophone, alto and band	1950	transcr. for symph. orchestra	6	MS.

Gayfer, Dr. James McDonald

Composer, conductor and music teacher. Born in Toronto, March 26th, 1916.

Musical education at Royal Conservatory, Toronto and University of Toronto. Degrees: Mus.Bac. (Toronto, 1941), Mus.Doc. (Toronto, 1950). Diplomas: L.R.A.M., A.R.C.M. (1946). Graduate of Royal Military School of Music, Kneller Hall, England.

Is director of music for Central Command of Canadian Army and associate conductor of Toronto Harmony Symphony Orchestra. Contest adjudicator. Won CAPAC prize in 1944 for String Quartet and in 1947 for Song Cycle.

Address: 484 Plains Road, Toronto, Ont.

Affiliation: CAPAC.

COMPOSITIONS

TITLE	DATE	TYPE	TIME (MIN.)	PUBLISHER
Symphony in B flat	1947	*orchestra*	20	MS.
Symphony in E flat	1950	*orchestra*	45	MS.
Pastorale	1944	*clar and orch.*	8	MS.
Canada Overseas (quick march)	1946	*military band*	3	MS.
Canadian Thistle (quick march)	1946	*brass band*	3	MS.
Suite for Wind Quintet	1947	*fl, ob, cl, Fr. hn, bn*	19	Boosey & Hawkes
Quartet in A minor	1943	*string quartet*	15	MS.
Six Translations from the Chinese (song cycle)	1946	*tenor and small orch.*	20	MS.

George, Dr. Graham

Composer, conductor, lecturer, organist and choirmaster. Born in Norwich, England, April 11th, 1912.

Musical education with Dr. Alfred Whitehead. Degree: Mus.Doc. (Toronto, 1939). Diplomas: F.C.C.O., A.R.C.O.

Was organist and choirmaster in several Montreal churches; master of music, St. Peter's, Sherbrooke, 1937-40; on active service 1941-45. Now is professor of music at Queen's University, Kingston and organist and choirmaster at Sydenham Street United Church, Kingston.

Won Prix Lallemand in 1938 (Variations for Orchestra), CAPAC awards in 1943 (Variations for Strings) and 1947 (Jabberwocky).

Address: 164 College Street, Kingston, Ont.

Affiliation: BMI.

COMPOSITIONS

TITLE	DATE	TYPE	TIME (MIN.)	PUBLISHER
Evangeline	1948	*opera*	90	MS.
King Lear	1946	*stage music*		MS.
The Tempest	1948	*stage music*		MS.
Peter Pan (4 acts)	1948	*ballet, orchestra*	90	MS.
Jabberwocky	1947	*bullet, small orch.*	15	MS.
The King, the Pigeon and the Hawk	1949	*ballet, small orch.*	14	MS.
The Queen's Jig	1950	*ballet, small orch.*	13	MS.
Tone-Poem on Song of Agincourt	1939	*orchestra, chorus*	30	MS.
Symphony	1951	*orchestra*	28	MS.
Prelude for Orchestra	1949	*orchestra*	20	MS.
Kingston Suite	1940 rev. 1950	*small orchestra*	10	MS.
Concerto for Chamber Orchestra	1950	*small orchestra*	20	MS.
Dorian Fugue	1942	*string orchestra*	20	MS.
Variations for String Quartet	1949	*string quartet*	3	MS.

COMPOSITIONS

TITLE	DATE	TYPE	TIME (MIN.)	PUBLISHER
String Quartet	1951	*string quartet*	25	MS.
Trio	1950	*flute, vln, va*	6	MS.
Duo	1950	*vln, 'cello*	8	MS.
Sonata	1950	*oboe, piano*	10	MS.
Prelude on "The King's Majesty"	1946	*organ*	5	MS.
Three Fugues	1950	*organ*	ea. 2	MS.
If Ye Love Me	1937	*choral*	2	H. W. Gray & Co.
Benedictus es, Domine	1938	*choral*	2	H. W. Gray & Co.
Lord of all Power	1939	*choral*	2	H. W. Gray & Co.
Ride on!	1940	*choral*	1½	H. W. Gray & Co.
O Worship the King	1940	*choral*	2	H. W. Gray & Co.
Unto Us a Son is Given	1942	*choral*	1½	Oxford U.P.
Tread Softly, Shepherds	1950	*choral*	1½	MS.
She Comes Not When Noon	1939	*choral*	1½	MS.
O Green Grow Now the Hedgerow	1949	*sop, ob, str. quart*	1½	MS.
A Lady Rode Down	1940	*vocal*	1½	MS.
The Heavenly Scarp	1949	*vocal*	2	MS.

Gillis, Ivan M.

Composer and organist. Born in Charlottetown, P.E.I., December 5th, 1918. Died January 6th, 1946.

Musical education at Halifax School for the Blind, Royal College of Music, London and Royal Conservatory, Toronto. Diplomas: F.T.C.L., A.R.C.O., L.T.C.M. Winner of gold medal in organ playing, Royal Conservatory, Toronto. Time was divided between composition and performance of classical music.

COMPOSITIONS

TITLE	DATE	TYPE	TIME (MIN.)	PUBLISHER
Sonata in A minor	1945	*piano*	15	MS. (Braille)
Four Preludes	1944	*piano*	ea. 3-4	MS.
Fantasia in D major		*organ*		MS.
Passacaglia in E minor		*organ*		MS.
Prelude on "St. Bernard"		*organ*		MS.
Four Choral Preludes		*organ*		MS. (Braille)
Reverie, Scherzo, Pastorale		*organ*		MS.
Evening Song		*vln and piano*		MS.
When I Set Out For Lyonesse		*male chorus*		MS.
Peace		*vocal*		MS.

Gingras, Dr. Rolland G.

Pianist, organist, pedagogue and composer. Born in Quebec, April 21st, 1899.

Musical education started at the age of twelve (piano, organ, Gregorian chant, harmony, composition, orchestration, conducting and, as minor subjects, voice, violin, 'cello and wind instruments). Degree: Ph.D. in musical pedagogy and musicography (Montreal, 1945).

Has been organist in churches in and near Quebec. Since 1925 has been organist at St. François-d'Assise, Quebec. Former musical director of Chanteurs de St. François and of Société Chorale St. Gérard.

Commander of the Order *Honneur et Mérite* (Haiti), *Chevalier de l'Ordre Latin* (France), member of jury of *Prix d'Europe* of Quebec Province. President of Syndicat National Catholique des Musiciens de Québec and of Comité Canada-Haiti de Québec. Member of many musical and other organizations.

Has accompanied on CBC, acted as impresario and lecturer and has contributed to many periodicals and newspapers.

Address: 24 rue St.-Jean, Quebec, P.Q.

COMPOSITIONS

TITLE	DATE	TYPE	TIME (MIN.)	PUBLISHER
L'Appel du Missionaire	1925	*operetta*		MS.
Quatre chansons populaires		*soli, choir, orch*		MS.
Douze chansons de France (harmonized)		*vocal*		printed
Official Song of the Feminine Catholic League		*vocal*		printed
Le Vieux Missel		*voice, str, qua*		MS.

Many religious pieces and songs, harmonizations, arrangements and orchestrations.

Books:
Les Hymnes nationaux (out of print).
Questionnaire de Théorie Musicale.

Girard, Joseph Auguste Fernand

Civil engineer, singer and composer. Born in Drummondville, P.Q., December 30th, 1907.

Musical education with Eugène Lapierre (harmony and composition), Roger Larivière (singing) and Oscar Arnold (clarinet and saxophone). Received honor diploma at Quebec Festival competition, 1937 (1st prize Tenor, B).

Address: 3469 Henri-Julien, Montreal, P.Q.

COMPOSITIONS

TITLE	DATE	TYPE	TIME (MIN.)	PUBLISHER
Dehors, il fait si froid	1949	*vocal*	2	multilith
Reine, permettrais-tu?	1949	*vocal*	2	multilith
La Flamme et le papillon	1949	*vocal*	3	multilith

Songs in manuscript (words by Oscar Le Myre):
Petite Violette; Pour toi seul; Renouveau; Les Larmes; Le Mendiant; Lorsque nous serons deux; Fleur jolie; Baisers; Joyeux Noël (Gerard Delage).

Glackemeyer, Frederic Henri

Bandmaster, instrumentalist and music teacher. Born in Hanover, Germany, 1751. Died in Quebec, January 12th, 1836.

Showed remarkable musical talent as a small child and took up the violin. In 1776 was bandleader of one of the Brunswick regiments in Canada but may have come to Canada before that date. Organist of Quebec Cathedral, 1816-18. The leading musician in the Quebec of his time, perhaps the first professionally equipped musician in Canada. Taught music, imported instruments and music. A collection of the latter is now in the hands of Laval University. In 1820 founded Société Harmonique de Québec, probably Canada's first musical society, and became its first president.

Compositions

March in honor of the arrival of Prince Edward Augustus, 1791. Manuscript.
(Now the slow march of the Royal Fusilier Regiment, with minor changes).
March in honor of the battle of Chateauguay, dedicated to Colonel Salaberry, c. 1813.

See:
J. M. Gibbon, *Canadian Mosaic.*
La Musique (periodical), 1919.

Goodwill, Lawrence William

Pianist and composer. Born in Sunderland, England, June 5th, 1920.

Musical education in Vancouver with Jean Coulthard (piano, composition), in Toronto with A. Guerrero (piano) and Healey Willan (composition). Degree: Mus.Bac. (Toronto, 1949). Diplomas: A.T.C.M., L.R.S.M. Studied with Darius Milhaud, summer 1949. Won several scholarships and composition prizes (CAPAC, 1940, 41, 42). Member of faculty, Royal Conservatory, Toronto.

Address: 63 Roehampton Avenue, Apt. 12, Toronto, Ont.

COMPOSITIONS				
TITLE	DATE	TYPE	TIME (MIN.)	PUBLISHER
String Quartet	1949	*string quartet*	15	MS.
Suite for Trio	1950	*vln, clar, 'cello*		MS.
Canon for String Trio (3 in 1)	1950	*vln, va, 'cello*	2	MS.
Theme and Variations in E minor		*piano*	10	MS.
Variations and Fugue on "God rest you merry, Gentlemen"		*piano*	12	MS.
March	1939	*piano*	10	MS.
Ballerina		*piano*	3	MS.
Fugue on two expositions	1950	*piano*	5	MS.
Introduction, Fugue and Postlude	1950	*organ*	3	MS.
Poème		*violin*	6	MS.
Shall I Go Bound and You Go Free		*vocal*	3	MS.
Lullaby		*vocal*	2	MS.
Trans Canada		*piano*	3	MS.
War Widow		*vocal*	1½	MS.
Under the Pines		*vocal*	1	MS.

Gratton, J. J. Hector

Pianist, conductor and composer. Born in Hull, P.Q., August 13th, 1900.

Musical education with Alphonse Martin and Alfred Laliberté (piano), Albertine Morin-Labrecque, Oscar O'Brien, Dr. Alfred Whitehead (harmony, counterpoint and form). Toured as accompanist to the famous French Canadian bard Charles Marchand.

Won Prix Lallemand for symphonic poem *Légende*. Since 1937 has written scores for radio feature programs.

Address: 4725 Fabre Street, Montreal, P.Q.

Affiliation: BMI.

COMPOSITIONS

TITLE	DATE	TYPE	TIME (MIN.)	PUBLISHER
Instrumental:				
Légende (symphonic poem)		*orchestra*	13½	MS.
Fantasia on 2 Can. folk tunes		*orchestra*	3½	MS.
A la Veillée		*accordion (violin or harmonica) and orchestra*	3¾	MS.
Nocturne de Maria Chapdelaine		*orchestra or strings*	3¾	MS.
Sous les Erables (Fant. on "O Canada")		*small orchestra*	4½	MS.
Suite Pastorale (3 mvmts)		*strings*	6½	MS.
Près de la fontaine		*strings*	1½	MS.
La Joie de vivre		*small orch. or strings or piano*	1¾	Passe-Temps
La Joie de vivre		*small orch. or strings or piano*	1½	MS.
Tendresse		*small orch. or strings or piano*	1½	MS.
Inquietude		*small orch. or strings or piano*	1¾	MS.
Première Danse Canadienne		*violin and piano*	3¼	F. Harris
Deuxième Danse Canadienne		*vln and piano or strings*	2¾	F. Harris
Troisième Danse Canadienne		*dto. or small orchestra*	1½	MS.
Quatrième Danse Canadienne (in G)		*vln and piano or strings*	2¾	BMI Canada
Cinquième Danse Canadienne (in A)		*str. quartet or strings*	2¾	MS.
Reminiscence		*vln and piano or strings*	2¾	F. Harris
Chanson Enfantine		*vln and piano or strings*	1¼	MS.
L'Ecossaise (clog dance)		*dto. or orchestra*	3¾	MS.
Chanson Pastorale		*piano or strings*	3¼	MS.
Chanson Intime		*piano or strings*	3½	MS.
Berceuse Sauvage		*piano or strings*	3½	MS.
Danse Rustique		*piano or strings*	2¾	MS.
Chanson Ecossaise		*piano or strings*	2½	MS.
Coucher de Soleil (suite of 4 mvmts)		*piano or strings*	12	MS.
Rondo		*str. qui. and piano or strings*	3¾	MS.
Légende		*'cello and piano*	3	MS.
Papillon tu es volage		*'cello and piano*	2¾	MS.
Serenade		*'cello and piano*	2½	MS.
Etude sur le mvmt perpétuel de Weber		*piano*		
Sonata (3 mvmts)		*piano*	17	MS.
Vocal:				
L'Imagerie (Christmas carol for radio presentation; Cec. Chobot)		*comedians, soloists, choir, small orch.*	60	MS.

COMPOSITIONS

TITLE	DATE	TYPE	TIME (MIN.)	PUBLISHER
O Canada (Lavallée, new setting)		*choir and orchestra*		
Complainte de Père Buteux		*male choir and strings*	3	MS.
Pique à la Pointe		*male choir and strings*	3	MS.
Ola Glomstula (Norwegian folk tune)		*choir and piano*	4	MS.
A St. Malo (Canadian folk tune)		*choir and piano*	3	MS.
La Croix et le drapeau		*choir and piano*		Archambault
Vocero		*choral (a capella)*	4	MS.
Nocturne		*voice and piano or orch.*	1¾	MS.
Le Violoneur (Marcel Gagnon)		*voice and piano or orch.*		MS.
Les Sucres (Marcel Gagnon)		*voice and piano or orch.*		MS.
L'Epluchette (Marcel Gagnon)		*voice and piano or orch.*		MS.
D'ou viens-tu bergère		*voice or choir and strings*	2¾	MS.
Dollard t'appelle (wartime song)		*vocal*		Archambault
Blondinette (Pallascio Morin)		*vocal*		MS.
Marianne s'en va-t-au moulin		*duet and orchestra*		MS.
Le Roi Dagobert		*voice and orchestra*		MS.
19 French Canadian folk songs, arr.		*voice and orchestra*		MS.
180 Canadian folk songs, harmonized		*3 male voices*		MS.

Gray, Ronald James

Composer, arranger and clarinetist. Born in Hamiota, Man., December 24th, 1920.

Musical education self-taught till 1946. From 1946-50 studied composition at Royal Conservatory, Toronto with Barbara Pentland and John Weinzweig, and clarinet. From 1938-40 toured Western Canada with dance-band; from 1940-46 toured in RCAF with concert bands and entertainment units; also arranged. At present studies and plays in and arranges for dance bands and radio.

Address: 6 Gertrude Place, Toronto, Ont.

COMPOSITIONS

TITLE	DATE	TYPE	TIME (MIN.)	PUBLISHER
String Quartet	1948-49	*string quartet*	12	MS.
Movement for Orchestra	1949-50	*orchestra*	6	MS.

Grossmith, Dr. Leslie

Pianist, composer, conductor, music teacher and violinist. Born in Birmingham, England, May 19th, 1870.

Has made concert tours throughout the British Empire. Lived in Australia for a number of years and came to Canada in 1918. Teaches music in Victoria, B.C. Has toured Canada from coast to coast twice. Degree: Mus.Doc. (Melbourne). *Air de Ballet* won first prize in contest sponsored by Musical Canada periodical.

Address: 608 Harbinger Avenue, Victoria, B.C.

		COMPOSITIONS		
TITLE	DATE	TYPE	TIME (MIN.)	PUBLISHER
The Immortal Slave		opera (3 acts)	180	MS.
Zip Van Twinkle of the Canadian Rockies		musical comedy (3 acts)	150	MS.
Jubilee Symphony in D	1951	orchestra		MS.
The Vision of Terpsichore (ballet suite)		orchestra		MS.
Almighty Gold (vaudeville song-scene)		bar and orch.		MS.
Air de Ballet		piano		Musical Canada
Chinese Romance		piano		Musical Canada
The Little French Soldier		piano		P. Derek
Kopski's March		piano		Francis, Day & Hunter
Cappricio in A flat		piano		MS.
Mademoiselle Frou-Frou		piano		MS.
Tranquilité (nocturne)		piano		MS.

Guillemette, Louis Auguste

Organist, pianist and composer. Born in Isle Verte, P.Q., December 9th, 1908.

Musical education at Conservatoire National de Musique, Montreal, at Pius X Institute in New York and in Paris with Motte-Lacroix (piano) and Marcel Dupré (organ).

Address: 5260 Clark, Montreal, P.Q.

Songs in manuscript:
O Salutaris; Cor Jesu; Kyrie; Ave Verum; Alma Redemptoris; Souvenir; Mon Amour; L'Hirondelle.
No recent information obtained.

Gummer, Phyllis Mary

Composer and instrumentalist. Born in Kingston, Ont., March 12th, 1919.

Musical education at Queen's University, Kingston, Royal Conservatory, Toronto and Juilliard School, New York. Degrees: B.A. (Queen's), Mus.Bac. (Toronto). Won CAPAC scholarship in 1940. Has worked for National Film Board.

Address: c/o Mrs. C. F. Gummer, 149 Collingwood Street, Kingston, Ont.

		COMPOSITIONS		
TITLE	DATE	TYPE	TIME (MIN.)	PUBLISHER
Four String Quartets		string quartet		MS.
Trio		vln, vc, piano		MS.
Trio "Non gravius"		fl, clar, va		MS.
Sonata		'cello and piano		MS.
Sonata		flute and piano		MS.
Sonata in A major (CAPAC prize)		piano		MS.
Sonata in C major		piano		MS.
38 songs		vocal		MS.

Many pieces for flute, clarinet, piano, organ and choir.

Haehnel, William Frederick

Lecturer in engineering drawing and composer. Born in Waterloo, Ont., April 30th, 1908.

Musical education at Royal Conservatory, Toronto. Degree: Mus.Bac. (Toronto, 1936). Was on theory staff of Royal Conservatory, Toronto from 1935-41. Is now lecturer in engineering drawing at Univ. of Toronto and composes as a hobby.

Address: 24 Prince Arthur Avenue, Toronto, Ont.

COMPOSITIONS

TITLE	DATE	TYPE	TIME (MIN.)	PUBLISHER
Fantasy	1937	*small orchestra*	5-6	MS.
Allegro	1938	*string orchestra*	8	MS.
Prelude	1940	*piano*	2	MS.
Nocturne	1940	*piano*	3	MS.
`Prelude in C minor	1947	*piano*	2	MS.
Little March	1948	*piano*	2	MS.

Songs in manuscript:
An Autumn Song; Loveliest of Trees; The Lonely Land; The Life in August; An Angel.

Ham, Dr. Albert

Organist, choirmaster, lecturer and composer. Born in Bath, England, June 7th, 1858. Died in Brighton, England, March, 1940.

Was musical director at St. James Cathedral, Toronto from 1897. Founder and conductor of the National Chorus, Toronto, 1903-28. One of founders and the first president of Canadian College of Organists, 1909. Lecturer and examiner, University of Toronto. Dean of faculty of music, University of Bishop's College, Lennoxville, P.Q. Degrees: Mus.Doc. (Dublin, 1894), hon. Mus.Doc. (Toronto, 1906), hon. D.C.L. (Bishop's).

COMPOSITIONS

TITLE	DATE	TYPE	TIME (MIN.)	PUBLISHER
The Solitudes of the Passion		*cantata*		Novello, 1917
Advent Cantata		*soli, choir, orch.*		
The Hope of the Ages		*choir and orch.*		
Suite for Orchestra		*orchestra*		
Minuet and Trio from Suite		*arr. organ*		published 1926
Imperium et Unitas (march)		*orchestra*		
The Queen's Own (march)		*orchestra*		
Heroes of Canada (march)	1925	*band*		

Many choral works, anthems, hymns, songs and offertory sentences, published by Novello, O. Ditson and H. W. Gray & Co.
Many marches for piano or band.

Books:
A Manual on the Boy's Voice and its Culture.
Graces and Embellishments of the Bach-Handel Period.

Hamer, Harold

Organist, lecturer, choirmaster and composer. Born in Leeds, England, March 9th, 1900.

Musical education at Durham Cathedral Chorister's School and with Dr. Alban Hamer (Cape Town, S.A.) and Dr. A. C. Tysoe (St. Albans, England). Diploma:

F.R.C.O. Came to Canada in 1927. Until 1949 was director of music, Mount Allison University, N.B. Since 1949 has been lecturer in music and director of student musical activities, Dalhousie University, N.S.; registrar and professor of organ and theory, Halifax Conservatory; lecturer in music, Pine Hill Divinity Hall; organist and choirmaster, St. David's Church. Prize winner, CBC International Service song contest, 1950.

Address: 438 Chebucto Road, Halifax, N.S.

COMPOSITIONS

TITLE	DATE	TYPE	TIME (MIN.)	PUBLISHER
God, That Madest Earth and Heaven	1949	*choir, organ*	7	Boston Music Co.
Saviour Breathe an Evening Blessing	1949	*choir, organ*	7	Boston Music Co.
Lord of Our Life	1950	*choir, organ*	10	Boston Music Co.
O Brother Man		*choir, organ*	7	to be published
Look, ye Saints		*choir, organ*	6	Boston Music Co.

Several songs and organ works in manuscript.

Hamilton, Henry Cooke

Music critic, pianist, organist and composer. Born in England, January 24th, 1881.

Musical education at Royal Conservatory, Toronto with Dr. A. S. Vogt and J. D. A. Tripp (piano, organ, composition etc.). Was organist in many Ontario churches. Was associate director, critic and interviewer for Musical Canada magazine. Contributor to the Etude, Choir Herald, Onward, Canadian Countryman and Musical Courier magazines. Was member of teaching staff of the Hambourg Conservatory, Toronto.

Address: 194 Wellesley Street East, Toronto, Ont.

COMPOSITIONS

TITLE	DATE	TYPE	TIME (MIN.)	PUBLISHER
Nocturne in F		*piano*	3	MS.
Variations on "Rule Britannia," "Hearts of Oak" and "God Save the King"		*piano*		printed
Variations on "O Canada" and "The Maple Leaf"		*piano*		MS.
Variations on 20 hymn tunes		*organ*	ea. 1-5	MS.
Christmas Hymns		*choral*		MS.
Christians, Awake; Vesper Hymn; Communion Hymn; Gloria in Excelsis		*choral*	ea. 1	Waterloo Music
Saviour Like a Shepherd Lead Us		*vocal*		MS.
Blue Eyes		*vocal*		MS.
Arrangements:				
Familiar Melodies		*organ*	15-20	F. Harris
Trio in G (Mozart)		*organ*		Etude

Hanson, Dr. Frank
(Franklin Keith Hanson)

Lecturer and composer. Born in Lynn, Mass., August 8th, 1899.

Musical education at McGill University and at Cincinnati and Toronto Conservatories and Eastman and Juilliard Schools of Music. Degrees: Mus.Bac., Mus.Doc.

(McGill, 1947). Won L. G. bronze medal. Came to Canada in 1914. Is lecturer in harmony, counterpoint and school music at McGill University Conservatorium of Music; assistant professor of education, School for Teachers, Macdonald College (McGill Univ.).

Address: P.O. Box 264, Macdonald College, P.Q.

COMPOSITIONS

TITLE	DATE	TYPE	TIME (MIN.)	PUBLISHER
Symphony of Canada	1947	*orchestra*	40	MS.
Hornpipe	1934	*orchestra*	6	MS.

Several smaller works (songs, piano pieces, string quartet etc.).

Hardiman, Ellena G.

Pianist and composer. Born in Canada, 1890. Died in 1949.

Musical education at Toronto College of Music and in Winnipeg with Cyril R. Hogg (piano) and W. E. Fairclough (theory). Diploma: A.T.C.M., 1918.

COMPOSITIONS

TITLE	DATE	TYPE	TIME (MIN.)	PUBLISHER
Isti and Beau Vingt	1945	*opera*	120	MS.
Symphonic Poem of Global War		*orchestra*	20	MS.
Sonata of the Sea		*orchestra*	20	MS.
The Rushing Wind		*string quartet*	5	MS.
Coronation March Suite		*piano*	20	A. H. Stockwell
Our Memorial in France	1937	*vocal*		A. H. Stockwell
That's That		*vocal*		A. H. Stockwell
Go to It		*vocal*		A. H. Stockwell
Distaff		*vocal*		A. H. Stockwell

Songs in manuscript:
Bless Our Country; This Is Why Canada Is Here, etc., 24 songs.

Harmer, Daniel Jevon

Composer, arranger, pianist and organist. Born in Qu'Appelle, Sask., 1911.

Musical education at Regina and Toronto Conservatories. Diplomas: A.T.C.M., L.S.C.M. Teachers included Leo Smith, Healey Willan and John Weinzweig. Has arranged for King Edward Hotel Orchestra (Toronto) for six years.

Address: P.O. Box 19, Meyronne, Sask.

Affiliation: BMI.

COMPOSITIONS

TITLE	DATE	TYPE	TIME (MIN.)	PUBLISHER
Trio in D major	1951	*vln, vc, piano*	30	MS.
Three Prairie Sketches (Morning; On a Summer's Day; Evening)	1948	*vln and piano*	15	BMI Canada
Set of 34 original Canadian folk dances, primarily of Western origin	1949	*vln and piano*		MS.

Harris, Neil Foster

Pianist, arranger, composer and free lance writer. Born in Young, Sask., April 21st, 1925.

Musical studies with Mrs. Josephine Stableford in Saskatoon. Degree: B.A. (Saskatchewan, 1947). Graduate of Academy of Radio Arts, Toronto. Directed and wrote musical productions at Univ. of Saskatchewan. Worked for National Film Board, 1949. Now is dance orchestra pianist, arranger and free lance writer.

Address: 39 Sweetland Avenue, Ottawa, Ont.

COMPOSITIONS

TITLE	DATE	TYPE	TIME (MIN.)	PUBLISHER
Prairie Cantata	1949	*soli, choir, orch.*	15	MS.
Prairie Postcard	1950	*string orchestra*	5	MS.
Oedipus Rex (incidental music)	1950	*orchestra*	10	MS.
Three Songs	1951	*strgs, wwds*	15	MS.

Harriss, Dr. Charles Albert Edwin

Composer, organist, choral conductor and impresario. Born in London, England, December 15th, 1862. Died in Ottawa, August 1st, 1929.

Musical education in England. Was chorister at St. Mark's, Wrexham at the age of eight and later was organist in England. Came to Canada in 1882 (Ottawa) and in 1883 settled in Montreal, first as organist and *regens chori* at Christ Church Cathedral, later at St. James the Apostle Church. Founder and director, 1904-08, of McGill Conservatorium of Music. Founded choral societies. In 1903 organized the series of British-American festivals conducted by Sir Alexander Mackenzie throughout Canada. In June 1906 led a Canadian Music Festival in London, England. Organized music festivals and tours throughout the British Empire. Degree: Mus.Doc. (Cantuar.). *Torquil* was performed in Montreal, 1900.

COMPOSITIONS

TITLE	DATE	TYPE	TIME (MIN.)	PUBLISHER
Torquil		*opera*		Whaley Royce, 1896
The Pipes of Pan (a choric idyl)		*soli, choir, orch.*		Novello, 1904
Daniel Before the King	1890	*cantata*		G. Schirmer
The Sands of Dee (ballad)	perf. 1907	*choir and orch.*		Novello
Coronation Mass for Edward VII	1902	*choir and orch.*		(same work as next?)
The Crowning of the King		*choir and orch.*		Novello
Alma Patrol		*band*		O. Ditson
Fantasia on Church Chimes		*organ*		G. Schirmer
Romanza in B flat		*organ*		G. Schirmer
Allegro Pomposo		*organ*		G. Schirmer
Empire and Motherland	1913	*choral*		
As Pants the Hart		*choral or vocal*		G. Schirmer
When Shades of Night		*choral*		G. Schirmer
Wilt Thou Relent		*choral*		G. Schirmer

Songs:

Sing, Britain's Sons (Novello).

A Brigand Bold; Ebb and Flow; Sleep Lady Fair; Under the Standard (Ascherberg).

Dreams, Only Dreams; Abbey Portals; Gay Gitana; I Heard the Voice of Jesus; Like a Dream; Love's Old Story; Sun of My Soul; Throne of Grace; When the Shades of Night Around Us Close; While Shepherds Watched Their Flocks (G. Schirmer)

O Salutaris; Old Tubal Cain (O. Ditson)

My Land of Spain (Boosey & Hawkes)

Other compositions.

Hayward, Richard B.

Conductor and composer. Born in London, England, 1874.

Musical education at Westminster School of Music and at Royal Military School of Music, Kneller Hall, England. In British Army, 1887-1914. Bandmaster of Royal Irish Rifles, Queen's Own Rifles of Canada and Toronto Concert Band.

Address: 289 Manor Road East, Toronto 12, Ont.

Affiliation: CAPAC.

COMPOSITIONS

TITLE	DATE	TYPE	TIME (MIN.)	PUBLISHER
In a Spanish City (suite)		band	14	Carl Fischer
Three Characteristic Dances (suite)		band	12	Carl Fischer
The Corsair's Bride (overture)		band	7	Carl Fischer
Anita (cornet solo)		band	6	Carl Fischer
Three Jolly Trumpeters		band	3	Carl Fischer
Eventide (reverie)		band	4	Carl Fischer
The Band that Jack Built		band	5½	Carl Fischer
Fraternity Parade (novelty)		band	5	Carl Fischer
A Barnyard Competition (novelty)		band	6	Carl Fischer
The Troubadour (trombone solo)		band	5	Boosey & Hawkes
Oriental Rhapsody		band	6½	Boosey & Hawkes
Zingaree (overture)		band	7	Boosey & Hawkes
Norsemen (overture)		band	7	G. Schirmer
Liberation Overture		band	6	MS.
Mountain Valleys (overture)		band	6½	MS.
Kasr el Nil (overture)		band	8½	MS.
Copenhagen Overture		band	7	MS.
Lauda Park March		band	3	MS.

Several other works in manuscript.

Heins, Francis Donaldson (Donald)

Violinist, violist, organist, conductor and composer. Born in Hereford, England, February 19th, 1878. Died in Toronto, January 1st, 1949.

Musical education at Leipzig Conservatory (1892-97) with H. Sitt (violin) and G. Schreck (harmony), in London with A. Wilhelmj (violin) and in U.S. with L. Auer. Came to Canada in 1902, resided in Ottawa till 1927 and later in Toronto. Organist in Ottawa and Toronto. Founded and conducted for over 20 years the Ottawa Symphony Orchestra. From 1927 until his death was associated with the Toronto Symphony Orchestra as violist and one-time concertmaster and assistant conductor.

COMPOSITIONS

TITLE	DATE	TYPE	TIME (MIN.)	PUBLISHER
Concertino		*vln and orchestra*		MS.
Variations in D minor		*orchestra*		MS.
An Old Tortugas	1936	*short operetta*		MS. (CBC)
Yellow Back	1939	*short operetta*		MS. (CBC)
17th Century Sketches		*quartet and string orchestra*		MS.
Mass St. Ursula		*female choir, small orchestra*		MS.
Office of Holy Communion (Anglican)		*choir and organ*		MS.

Several published anthems and pieces for violin, piano and 'cello.

Heintzman, Cornelia
(see: Richardson, Cornelia Heintzman)

Henry, John

Vocal teacher, choral conductor and composer. Born in Swansea, Wales, 1872. Died in Regina, Sask.

Musical education in Swansea with Dr. A. Hay (theory). Came to Canada in 1907 and became active as choral conductor. Directed the Classic Choir and The Plainsmen from 1919-36.

COMPOSITIONS

TITLE	DATE	TYPE	TIME (MIN.)	PUBLISHER
The Canadian Hunter		*piano*		Delmar
In Heavenly Love Abiding		*choral*		Gamble Hinged
Praise the Lord		*choral*		MS.
God Is Our Refuge		*choir and orch.*		MS.

Songs in manuscript:
Romany Song; The Little Inns of England; Love; Bow Down Thine Ear; Thy Ways Not Mine, O Lord.
Ballads and other music arranged for educational film *That They Live* (cancer) sponsored by Government of Saskatchewan.

Hewlett, Dr. William Henry

Organist, choral conductor, teacher and composer. Born in Bath, England, 1873. Died in Hamilton, Ont., June 13th, 1950.

Musical education in Toronto with Augustus Vogt, Albert Ham and others, in Berlin and London. Degrees: Mus.Bac. (Trinity, Toronto), hon. Mus.Doc. (Toronto, 1926). Was organist in Hamilton for about 50 years; principal of the Hamilton Conservatory, 1919-38 and conductor of the Hamilton Elgar Choir, 1922-36. President of Canadian College of Organists, 1928-29.

COMPOSITIONS

TITLE	DATE	TYPE	TIME (MIN.)	PUBLISHER
Jappy Chappy		*musical play*		Novello
Doris (valse caprice)		*piano*		Ashdown
Fierce Was the Wild Billow (anthem)		*choral*		G. Schirmer
Three-fold Amen		*choral*		F. Harris
Three Songs from the Pastoral of "Pan and the Young Shepherd"		*vocal*		Metzler, London

Many other compositions.

Higgin, Clifford

Organist, choirmaster, singer, conductor and composer. Born in Bacup, Lancashire, England, June 28th, 1873.

Musical education with Charles Nuttall and Hamilton Harris (voice). Organist and choirmaster in Blackpool, 1896; organist and conductor of Orpheus (*a capella*) Glee Society. Winner of trophy at Paris Concours International in 1912 in competition with choirs from all over Europe. Was invited by Dr. Vogt to come to Canada. Was organist and choirmaster in Brantford and since 1920 at Knox Church in Calgary. Conductor of Calgary Light Opera Society.

Address: 3239 Elbow Drive, Calgary, Alta.

COMPOSITIONS

TITLE	DATE	TYPE	TIME (MIN.)	PUBLISHER
Calvary		*oratorio*	75	Breitkopf & Härtel
The Queen of Romance		*light opera*	120	MS.
The Elfman and the Frogs		*children's operetta*	25	MS.
Freedom		*orchestra*	25	MS.
A Lake in the Clouds (Lake Agnes)	1948	*orchestra*	10	MS.
Lake Minnewanka (with choral finale)	1949	*choir and orch.*	23	MS.
Rocky Mountain		*strings*	15	MS.
Canadian Sketches		*strings*	15	MS.
Butterfly's Ball		*piano and orch.*	5	Cary
Trio in A major		*flute, clar, piano*	10	MS.
Andante Cantabile		*vln and piano*	5	MS.
Meditation		*vln and piano*	5	MS.
Romance		*vln and piano*	5	MS.
Day Dreams		*piano*	4	Stuttard
Four 3-part songs		*female choir*	10	Whaley Royce
Forest Fire		*choral*	10	MS.
Spring Is Here		*vocal*	4	Boosey & Hawkes
Undaunted		*vocal*	4	Waterloo Music
To a Faded Violet		*vocal*	5	Ashdowns

Songs in manuscript:

Repentance; Angel's Requiem; To Mary; Remembrance; Range Fever; The Skylark; Big Bill and Little Bill; The Four Winds.

Hill, Dr. Lewis Eugene

Organist, choirmaster and composer. Born in Toronto, April 8th, 1909.

Musical education at Royal Conservatory, Toronto with Dr. Charles Peaker (organ), Dr. Healey Willan (composition), at Royal Academy of Music, London with Dr. G. D. Cunningham (organ), Dr. Eric Thiman (composition). Degrees: Mus.Bac., Mus.Doc. (Toronto, 1946). Diplomas: A.R.C.O., F.C.C.O., L.R.S.M. Was organist and choirmaster at St. Alban-the Martyr's, Toronto and taught at Royal Conservatory, Toronto. Is now professor at Miami University, Ohio.

Address: c/o Miami University, Oxford, Ohio, U.S.A.

Affiliation: BMI.

COMPOSITIONS

TITLE	DATE	TYPE	TIME (MIN.)	PUBLISHERS
Two Sketches (Legend, Scherzetto)		*small orchestra*	10	MS.
Serenade Québecoise		*string orchestra*	6	MS.
Serenade		*tenor, strgs, piano*	9	MS.
Sonata in D minor		*vln and piano*	11	MS.
Three Pieces for Piano		*piano*	8	Waterloo Music
Four Dances for Piano		*piano*		MS.
Three Short Pieces		*organ*	3	J. Fischer & Bro
Four Chorale Preludes		*organ*	3	Waterloo Music
Sonatina		*organ*	7	BMI Canada
Epilogue		*organ*	4	MS.
The Whole Bright World Rejoices		*choral*	2	H. W. Gray & Co.
Sion's Daughter		*choral*	2	Oxford U.P.
Weep You No More		*choral*	3	Oxford U.P.
When All Thy Mercies		*choral*	3	Oxford U.P.
A Christmas Carol		*choral*	2	Oxford U.P.
Rejoice, Ye Christians!		*choral*	2	F. Harris
Hail the Day That Sees Him Rise!		*choral*	2	MS.
Be Present Holy Trinity		*choral*	2	MS.
Jesu, the Very Thought of Thee		*vocal*	2	Waterloo Music
Come Thou Long Expected Jesus		*vocal*	2	Waterloo Music
Two Wordsworth Sonnets		*vocal*	5	MS.
A Song for Christmas		*vocal*	2	MS.
When Molly Smiles		*vocal*	2	MS.

Hinchey, Edward Reginald

Bandmaster and composer. Born in Belleville, Ont., February 18th, 1886.

Musical education with J. M. Denmark, Edward Barrett and Albert Cooke. Made extensive tours with the Canadian Kilties Band, playing in 21 countries. Was bandmaster of I.O.O.F. Band; the Argyll Light Infantry Band; the G.W.V.A. Band and the Belleville Municipal Band, all of Belleville (totalling 25 years of service). During World War II was attached to U.S. Quartermaster Corps and wrote their official march *With Sword and Key.*

Address: P.O. Box 129, Belleville, Ont.

Affiliation: CAPAC.

COMPOSITIONS

TITLE	DATE	TYPE	TIME (MIN.)	PUBLISHER
Athene (C.W.A.C. regimental march)		*band*		Waterloo Music
International Patrol		*band*		Waterloo Music
Men of O.V.C. (march arrangements)		*band*		BMI Canada
My Land (tone poem)		*band*		MS.
Come to Me, Sweetheart (waltz)		*band*		MS.
Sagonaska (suite in 4 parts)		*band*		MS.

Band compositions in manuscript:

Marches: *Pubicon; Thurlow; Our Country's Finest; Argyll Light Infantry; The Commando; The Paratrooper; Convoy, Ahoy!; The Canadian Legion; Eyes Front; Knights of the Air; Bugles and Drums; Imperial City; Kibocema; With Sword and Key; The P. B. I.*

Piano and band overtures: *Primo. Riggsonia; Dramatique.*

Humoresques: *Three Blind Mice; Chinatown; The Busy Drummer.*
Xylophone Solos: *W. G. Special; Jigade Jig; Quinte Polka.*
Selections: *Nonsense for Band; Radio Theme Song.*
Many arrangements and paraphrases.

Hone, Jules

Violinist, conductor, teacher and composer. Born in Liège, Belgium, April 7th, 1833. Died in Montreal, September 15th, 1913.

Musical education in Belgium. Conductor in New York for several years. Then settled in Montreal (before 1865) as teacher in various convents and conductor of an amateur orchestra.

COMPOSITIONS

TITLE	DATE	TYPE	TIME (MIN.)	PUBLISHER
The Grandee		*opera*		performed 1899, Montreal
Mass		*choral*		performed in Montreal
Marche Militaire (to Dr. Sun-Yat-Sen)		*band*		
Souvenir d'Arthabaska (ronde canadienne)		*vln and piano*		
Fantaisie écossaise		*vln and piano*		
Sweet Spirit, Hear My Prayer		*vln and piano*		Carl Fischer

Pieces for violin and piano were published by Schott (Brussels) and O. Ditson. Harmonizations of Canadian and Irish songs.

Textbook:
Méthode (violin), published by Schott (Brussels).

Horner, Dr. Ralph Joseph

Conductor, composer and music teacher. Born in Newport, England, April 28th, 1848. Died in Winnipeg, April 7th, 1926.

Musical education in Leipzig, 1864-67. Choral and operatic conductor in England. Went to New York in 1906 and to Winnipeg in 1909 as director of Imperial Academy of Music and Arts and conductor of the Oratorio Society (1909-12). Also directed and conducted own opera troupe in Winnipeg. Bandmaster in the army, 1916-17. Degree: Mus.Doc. (Durham, 1898).

COMPOSITIONS

TITLE	DATE	TYPE	TIME (MIN.)	PUBLISHER
Confucius	1888	*opera*		
Amy Rosbart		*opera*		
The Belles of Barcelona	1911	*comic opera*		MS., performed 1911
Six operettas		*operetta*		
St. Peter		*oratorio*		
David's First Victory		*oratorio*		
Suite for Orchestra in D minor		*orchestra*		
Torch-Dance (Earl Grey Prize)	1911	*orchestra*		

Sacred cantatas, anthems, piano pieces, approximately 100 songs and other works. Some vocal pieces were published by Reeder, Weekes and Ashdown. Many of these works were written before Dr. Horner came to Canada.

Hurst, George

Conductor, pianist and composer. Born in Edinburgh, May 20th, 1926.

Musical education at Royal Conservatory, Toronto with Boris Berlin (piano), Ettore Mazzoleni (conducting), Leo Smith and Godfrey Ridout (composition). Was conductor of Royal Conservatory Little Symphony Orchestra. Appointed teacher of composition, orchestration and conducting at Peabody Conservatory, Baltimore in 1947 and conductor of York Symphony Orchestra, Pennsylvania, in 1950.

Address: 2213 Callow Avenue, Baltimore 17, Md., U.S.A.

Affiliation: BMI.

COMPOSITIONS

TITLE	DATE	TYPE	TIME (MIN.)	PUBLISHER
Symphonic Movement	1946	*orchestra*	12	MS.
Three Canadian Pastorals		*orchestra*	11	MS.
Scherzo		*orchestra*	3	MS.
Rounds	1948	*orchestra*	14	MS.
Overture (19th century style)		*string orchestra*	8	MS.
Ode		*string orchestra*	5	MS.
Inhumanitas Inquieta (poème)		*string orchestra*	5	MS.
Symphonietta		*string orchestra*	15	MS.
Sinfonia	1949	*string orchestra*	15	MS.
Concertino		*piano and strgs*	8	MS.
Quartet (2 mvmts)	1947	*string quartet*	10	MS.
Duo	1948	*vln and 'cello*	12	MS.
Choral Prelude		*organ*	4	MS.
Two Preludes		*piano*	4	MS.
Suite		*piano*	15	MS.
Christmas Music		*piano*	5	MS.
Fantasy	1948	*piano*	10	MS.
Masque	1945	*piano*	5	BMI Canada
Toccata	1948	*piano*	4	BMI Canada
Music When Soft Voices Die	1946	*vocal*	5	BMI Canada
Two Chinese Love Songs	1949	*vocal*	8	BMI Canada

Songs in manuscript:
Rain Song (Rio Grande); Ring Out Wild Bells; To Night; Murder.

Jehin-Prume, Frantz

Violinist, conductor and composer. Born in Spa, Belgium, April 18th, 1839. Died in Montreal, May 29th, 1899.

Musical education with his uncle, François Prume and de Bériot, Léonard, Fétis, Vieuxtemps and Wieniawski. Child prodigy. Started his first concert tour (Germany and Russia) at the age of 16. Became violinist to the Belgian King and received many high distinctions. Concertized in France, Holland, Scandinavia, Mexico, U.S. and in Canada first in 1865. In 1866 married the Canadian singer Rosita del Vecchio (1848-81) and settled in Montreal, but made many American and European concert tours and travels. From 1875 on appeared in many concerts with Calixa Lavallée. Founded Association Artistique in Montreal (1891-1896) to present chamber music concerts. One of the presidents of Académie de Musique de Québec. A pioneer of classical instrumental music in Montreal.

COMPOSITIONS

TITLE	DATE	TYPE	TIME (MIN.)	PUBLISHER
Concerto No. 1, Op. 14	1860	*vln and orchestra*		
Concerto No. 2, Op. 31	1874	*vln and orchestra*		
Fantaisie Caprice, Op. 45	1879	*vln and orchestra*		
Oratorio (à Léon XIII), Op. 42	1886	*oratorio*		

About 30 pieces for violin and piano, 12 works for violin and orchestra, 4 sacred choral pieces, 25 songs, 7 transcriptions for violin, Grande Valse de Concert for orchestra, cadenzas for the violin concertos of Viotti, de Bériot and Beethoven. Several works were published by Schott.

See:

Jehin-Prume, *Une Vie d'artiste*, Montreal, publ. Constantineau.
(This book contains a list of works, numbering from Opus 1 to 88).

Jodoin, Laurent

Pianist, composer, writer and radio producer. Born in Montreal, May 20th, 1911.

Musical education with Auguste Descarries (piano, harmony and composition). Most time spent in writing songs and original scripts for feature radio programs.

Address: 10 340 St. Urbain Street, Montreal, P.Q.

Affiliation: BMI.

COMPOSITIONS

TITLE	DATE	TYPE	TIME (MIN.)	PUBLISHER
Chant		*orchestra*	9	MS.
Symphonic Poem		*orchestra*	8	MS.
Absence		*piano*	2¾	MS.
Prelude		*piano*	4	MS.
Piece for Violin		*violin*	3	MS.
Berceuse Indienne		*piano*	4	MS.
Si je meurs (for Giraudoux's Tessa)		*vocal*		Parnasse Musical
Reine du Rosaire		*vocal*		BMI Canada

Songs in manuscript (2½-4 minutes each):

Grisailles; Joies Ephémères; Obsession; Vision; Au coin du feu; Sonnet amoureux; Plaintive; Le Passant; Regrets; Chemin Perdu; The Quest; Berceuses 1, 2, 3; Depart; Solitude; Jardin delaisse; Se fondre à la nuit; Incertitude; Huis Clos (for J-P Sartre's play).
Background music for *Tessa* (Jean Giraudoux) with recitatives, including the songs: *La Charade; L'Air des Borgia;.La Chanson du pourceau; Si je meurs* (see above).
Several choral pieces. About 200 little French and English songs.

Johnston, Dr. Albert Richard

Composer and lecturer. Born in Chicago, May 7th, 1917.

Musical education at Northwestern University (Mus.Bac.) and at Eastman School of Music, University of Rochester (M.Mus., Ph.D., 1951). Private study with Nadia Boulanger.

Was professor of harmony and piano at Luther College, Wahoo, Nebraska and member of teaching staff in harmony and piano, Eastman School of Music. Came to Canada in 1947 and is professor of harmony, counterpoint, ear-training and composition, University of Toronto and Royal Conservatory, Toronto. Conductor and commentator, CBC.

Address: 335 Windermere Avenue, Toronto, Ont.

COMPOSITIONS

TITLE	DATE	TYPE	TIME (MIN.)	PUBLISHER
Symphony in F major	1950	*orchestra*	25	MS.
102 Kenilworth Terrace (suite)	1950	*chamber orch.*	15	MS.
Suite for Bassoon	1946	*bn and piano or chamber orch.*	8	MS.
Sonatina	1945	*vln and piano*	7	MS.
Brian the Sea Lion (children's story)	1949	*wwd quintet and narrator*	10	MS.
O Mistress Mine		*vocal*	3	MS.
Love for Sale		*vocal*	3	MS.

Jones, Trevor Morgan

Pianist and composer. Born in Springhill, N.S., June 13th, 1899.

Musical education with Healey Willan (harmony) and with Clement Gale in New York (harmony and composition). Mostly self-taught in orchestration. From 1923-38 was pianist in vaudeville, dance band and radio in U.S.A. with exception of engagements in Havana, Cuba and Helsinki, Finland. In 1938 returned to Canada and because of ill health discontinued music as a profession but composes in spare time.

Address: 9 Liverpool Street, Halifax, N.S.

Affiliation: BMI.

COMPOSITIONS

TITLE	DATE	TYPE	TIME (MIN.)	PUBLISHER
Symphony to Halifax (written for Bicentennial Celebration, 1949)	1949	*choir, orchestra*	9½	MS.
This Holy Day of Days (anthem)	1946	*choir and organ*		Harold Flammer
A Mother's-Day Prayer (anthem)	1947	*choir and organ*		Boston Music Co.
Lord, Have Mercy Upon Us (anthem)	1949	*choir and organ*		Boston Music Co.
June Night (arr. Finnish folk song)	1946	*choral*		Boston Music Co.
Sandy, the Bell Ringer in Story and Songs (children's book)	1950	*vocal*		Boston Music Co.

Kalnins, Janis (John)

Conductor, composer and organist. Born in Pernava, Latvia, November 3rd, 1904.

Graduate of Latvian State Conservatory of Music. Former conductor of Latvian National Theatre and Latvian National Opera. Guest conductor in Sweden, Poland and Germany. Received decorations in Sweden and Latvia. Came to Canada in 1948. Is organist and choirmaster of St. Paul's United Church, Fredericton, N.B. Winne in 1950 CBC International Service song contest (*The Bird's Lullaby*). Operas, ballets etc. have been performed in public. Most compositions were written prior to arrival in Canada.

Address: 321 Regent Street, Fredericton, N.B.

Affiliation: CAPAC.

COMPOSITIONS

TITLE	DATE	TYPE	TIME (MIN.)	PUBLISHER
Symphony in C minor		*orchestra*	40	MS.
Violin Concerto in F sharp minor		*vln and orch.*	26	MS.
Two Latvian Dances		*orchestra*	7	Universal Edition
String Quartet		*string quartet*	32	MS.
Lolita's Magic Bird		*opera*	150	MS. in Latvia
Hamlet		*opera*	150	MS. in Latvia
In the Fire		*opera*	180	MS. in Latvia
Two Ballets				MS. in Latvia
The Bird's Lullaby (P. Johnson)		*vocal*		MS.

Other compositions.

Kane, John Jack

Arranger, composer and clarinetist. Born in London, England, November 29th, 1924.

Musical education at University of Toronto (Mus.Bac., 1950) and at Royal Conservatory, Toronto with John Weinzweig (composition). Instrumental work for CBC since 1946 and assistant arranger-conductor to Howard Cable since 1949. From 1942-46 was unit director, Canadian Army Show. In 1951 won the Maurice Rosenfeld Prize as a "promising newcomer to Canadian radio".

Address: 170 Grace Street, Toronto, Ont.

COMPOSITIONS

TITLE	DATE	TYPE	TIME (MIN.)	PUBLISHER
Suite for Orchestra	1950	*orchestra*	20	MS.
Concerto for Saxophone	1951	*sax, strings, hp and celeste*	20	MS.
String Quartet	1948-49	*string quartet*	12	MS.
Three Sketches	1948	*ob, clar, bn*	10	MS.
Interludes	1947	*flute and clar*	3½	MS.
Interludes	1947	*bn and clar*	3	MS.
Waltz	1947	*piano*	3	MS.

Karam, Frederick

Organist, trombonist, singer and composer. Born in Ottawa, March 26th, 1926.

Musical education at University and Royal Conservatory of Toronto with Gerald Bales, Dr. Drummond Wolff and Dr. Healey Willan. Degree: Mus.Bac. (Toronto). Diploma: A.R.C.T. in organ. Is organist and choirmaster of St. Elijah's Syrian Orthodox Church in Ottawa and musical director of Toronto Opera Lover's Group.

Address: 519 Sussex Street, Ottawa, Ont.

Affiliation: BMI.

COMPOSITIONS

TITLE	DATE	TYPE	TIME (MIN.)	PUBLISHER
Symphonic Sketch	1951	*orchestra*		MS.
Poem for Strings		*string orchestra*	4	Associated Music Publishers
Passacaglia in F minor		*organ*		MS.
Ceremonial Music		*organ*		MS.
Jubilate		*organ*		MS.
Folk Tune		*organ*		MS.
Modal Trumpet		*organ*	3¾	BMI Canada
Gigue		*organ*		MS.
Magnificat and Nunc Dimittis		*choir and orch.*		MS.
Praise to the Lord (anthem)		*choral*		BMI Canada
Dear Lord and Father of Mankind		*choral*		BMI Canada
O, For a Closer Walk with God		*choral*		MS.
Jesus, Thou Joy of Loving Hearts		*choral*		MS.
Shepherd to His Love (C. Marlowe)		*choral*		MS.

Kaufmann, Walter

Conductor and composer. Born in Karlevy Vary, Czechoslovakia, April 1st, 1907. Musical education at State College of Music in Berlin (pupil of Franz Schreker) and at Prague University (musicology, graduate in philosophy). Conducted in various opera houses in Europe, in Komoedienhaus, Berlin, as guest in Prague, on radio etc.

From 1934-46 lived in Bombay, India; till 1938 was film composer, from 1938-46 was director of music, All India Radio. In 1946 arranged and conducted for BBC in London and composed music for two short films (Rank: *This Modern Age*); was assistant to music director, Rank Films.

Came to Canada in 1947. Until 1948 was head of piano department, Halifax Conservatory. In 1948 was appointed permanent conductor of Winnipeg Symphony Orchestra. Works have been performed on CBC, BBC, NBC, by Toronto and Winnipeg symphony orchestras etc.

Address: 431 Oxford Street, Winnipeg, Man.

Affiliation: CAPAC.

COMPOSITIONS

TITLE	DATE	TYPE	TIME (MIN.)	PUBLISHER
Bashmackin		*opera*	120	MS.
Symphony No. 6	1950	*orchestra*	25	MS.
Sinfonietta		*orchestra*	10	MS.
Two Slavonic Dances		*orchestra*	15	Arcadia Music
Dirge		*orchestra*	8	MS.
Strange Town at Night (variations)		*orchestra*	12	MS.
Faces in the Dark	1949	*orchestra*	12	MS.
Picturebook for Katherine		*orchestra*	15	MS.
Chivaree (overture)	1950	*orchestra*	3	MS.
Six Indian Miniatures		*orchestra*	15	Arcadia Music

COMPOSITIONS

TITLE	DATE	TYPE	TIME (MIN.)	PUBLISHER
Fleet Street Overture		orchestra	10	Arcadia Music
Visages (ballet)		small orchestra	20	MS.
Rose and the Ring		small orchestra	55	MS.
Caprice	1950	small orchestra	5	MS.
Kalif Stork (fairy tale)		narrator and orch.	25	MS.
Concerto		piano and orch. or strings	30	Arcadia Music
Andhera		piano and orch.	20	MS.
Fantasy	1949	piano and orch.	30	MS.
Concerto		'cello and orch.	25	MS.
Symphony No. 1		string orchestra	15	MS.
Variations for Strings		string orchestra	15	MS.
Divertimento		string orchestra	10	MS.
Four Skies		string orchestra	15	MS.
Suite		string quartet	15	MS.
Sonata	1950	piano	30	MS.
Sonatina	1948	piano	10	MS.
Lullaby	1951	male choir	3	MS.

Kent, Ada Twohy (Mrs. W. G.)

Pianist, organist and composer. Born in Denver, Col., February 8th, 1888.

Musical education in Hamilton with J. E. P. Aldous and at Royal Conservatory Toronto with Dr. Vogt. Degree: Mus.Bac. (Toronto). Diploma: L.R.A.M. Has served as organist in various churches in Hamilton and Toronto. Was accompanist with Mendelssohn Choir for the last nine years of Dr. Vogt's and the first year of Dr. Fricker's conductorship. Was on teaching staff of Royal Conservatory, Toronto.

Address: 51 Oriole Gardens, Toronto 12, Ont.

COMPOSITIONS

TITLE	DATE	TYPE	TIME (MIN.)	PUBLISHER
Dominion Hymn		solo and choir	4	Waterloo Music
Peace Hymn		solo and choir	4	Waterloo Music
When Love's Afar		vocal	3	F. Harris
Petunia (Negro Serenade)		vocal	2	Stainer & Bell
Twilight Town (lullaby)		vocal	3	Stainer & Bell
Dorothea		vocal	3	Stainer & Bell
Hey Ho for Open Road		vocal	3	Stainer & Bell
I Travel East		vocal	2	Stainer & Bell
Long Ago		vocal	4	Waterloo Music
At Christmastide		vocal	4	Waterloo Music
How Near to God (Wedding song)		vocal	5	Waterloo Music
Two Songs of Autumn		vocal	ea. 3	G. V. Thompson
No Flower So Fair		choral	4	Carl Fischer
Sing a Song of Canada (27 children's songs)				Thos. Nelson, Toronto
119 short children's songs		vocal		MS.
Let's Pretend (volume of children's songs)		vocal		Gage, Toronto

Kerr, Bessie Maude

Pianist and composer. Born in Toronto, June 4th, 1888.

Musical education at Toronto College of Music, in London, Ont. with Willgoose (harmony, counterpoint and composition) and at Royal Conservatory, Toronto with Dr. Horwood (composition). Is teacher of piano and theory in St. Thomas, Ont.

Address: 46 White Street, St. Thomas, Ont.

COMPOSITIONS

TITLE	DATE	TYPE	TIME (MIN.)	PUBLISHER
Two Movements (Night Clouds; Morning Reflections)		string quartet		MS.
Group of Songs (Riding; Dream River; Wanderlied)		vocal		MS.
Lake of Bays Suite (The New Moon; The Moon-bridge; On Waves of Rose and Gold)		vocal	10	MS.
Miniatures for Young Pianists		piano	5	G. V. Thompson

Piano pieces in manuscript:
Minute Rhapsody; Two Short Preludes; *Fantasy;* Capriccio in F minor; *Mirage; Pastorale;* Prelude; Nocturne.

Kilby, Muriel Laura

Pianist, marimbist and composer. Born in Toronto, November 5th, 1929.

Musical education at Royal Conservatory, Toronto with Hayunga Carman (piano) and Oscar Morawetz (composition). Won CAPAC prizes for composition in 1949 and 1950. Has been engaged frequently as marimbist with Toronto Symphony Orchestra. In 1951 won full scholarship of National Federation of Music Clubs to attend Chautauqua Institute, N.Y., studying piano with James Friskin.

Address: 115 Gough Avenue, Toronto, Ont.

Affiliation: CAPAC.

COMPOSITIONS

TITLE	DATE	TYPE	TIME (MIN.)	PUBLISHER
Fantasy	1951	vln and piano		MS.
Piano Suite	1949	piano	10-15	MS.
Ballet Suite	1950	piano	10	MS.
First song from "Songs of the Sea-children"	1949	vocal	1½	MS.
No. 40 from "A Shropshire Lad"	1949	vocal	2	MS.
The Scarecrow	1950	vocal	3	MS.
Young Sea	1950	vocal	3	MS.

Kruspe, Dr. Glenn Clarence

Organist, conductor and composer. Born in Tavistock, Ont., January 25th, 1909.

Musical education at Royal Conservatory and University of Toronto and in London, England. Degrees: Mus.Bac. (Toronto, 1940), Mus.Doc. (Toronto, 1949). Diplomas: A.T.C.M., A.R.C.O., A.R.C.M.

Is organist at Zion Evangelical Church in Kitchener; teacher; conductor Kitchener-Waterloo Symphony Orchestra and Philharmonic Choir.

Address: 74 St. George Street, Kitchener, Ont.

COMPOSITIONS

TITLE	DATE	TYPE	TIME (MIN.)	PUBLISHER
Symphony in C sharp minor	1947	*orchestra*	30	MS.
String Quartet in F major	1940	*string quartet*	15	MS.
Songs, carols, anthems				MS.

von Kunits, Dr. Luigi

Conductor, violinist and composer. Born in Vienna, July 20th, 1870. Died in Toronto, October 8th, 1931.

Musical education in Vienna with Bruckner and Jacksch (composition), Hanslick (music history), Kral, Gruen, Sevcik (violin); student at Vienna Conservatory. Degrees: Dr. phil. (Vienna), hon. Mus.Doc. (Toronto, 1926).

Came to America in 1893. From 1897-1910 was concertmaster of Pittsburgh Symphony Orchestra, founder of own music school. From 1910-12 lived in Europe. Came to Toronto in 1912 as violin teacher at Can. Academy of Music and leader of Academy String Quartet. In 1915 founded the Canadian Journal of Music (1915-19). Was conductor of Toronto Symphony Band and 1923-31 of New Symphony Orchestra (1927 renamed Toronto Symphony Orchestra).

COMPOSITIONS

TITLE	DATE	TYPE	TIME (MIN.)	PUBLISHER
Violin Concerto in E minor	1891	*vln and orchestra*		MS.
Violin Concerto		*vln and orchestra*		MS.
Der Fruehling (overture)		*orchestra*		MS.
String Quartet in D minor	1890	*string quartet*		MS.
Viola Sonata	1917	*viola and piano*		MS.
Suite		*4 violins*		MS.
Legend	1895	*vln and piano*		Detmer
Romanza	1911	*vln and piano*		Carl Fischer
Four Pieces	1928	*vln and piano*		F. Harris
Three Etudes	1894	*vln and piano*		G. Schirmer
Scotch Lullaby		*vln and piano or vocal or piano solo*		Carl Fischer
Song of the Maple		*vocal*		Musical Canada 1931
La Cabine d'or		*vocal*		Musical Canada 1931
Heart's Delight		*vocal*		Musical Canada 1931

Minor orchestral works, quartets, sonatas, violin pieces and etudes; some published by G. Schirmer, Carl Fischer and Frederick Harris.

Some manuscripts are in the hands of Mrs. Wilfred Campbell, Toronto and the Frederick Harris Co., Oakville, Ont.

Book:

The Hero as Musician (Beethoven), 1913.

Kunz, Alfred

Composer and pianist. Born in Neudorf, Sask., May 26th, 1929.

Musical education with Keith Rogers, Oscar Morawetz, John Weinzweig and Reginald Godden.

Address: 6 Ongiara, Centre Island, Toronto, Ont.

COMPOSITIONS

TITLE	DATE	TYPE	TIME (MIN.)	PUBLISHER
Canadian Cantata	1951	narrator, soli, choir, orchestra	30	MS.
Student Concerto	1950	piano and small orchestra	10	MS.
String Quartet	1950	string quartet	40	MS.
Three Short Pieces	1950	string or wind trio	10	MS.
Sonata	1950	violin and piano	15	MS.
Two Piano Sonatas	1950	piano	15-25	MS.
Two Songs of Autumn	1950	vocal	10	MS.
Monologue	1950	vocal	45	MS.

Other songs and piano pieces.

Kurth, Burton Lowell

Organist, choral conductor and composer. Born in Buffalo, N.Y., April 27th, 1890.

Musical education with private teachers in New York City, Chicago and Minneapolis. Came to Canada in 1909. Was vocal teacher, organist and choral conductor in Winnipeg for 20 years. In Vancouver since 1929. Is chief supervisor of music in the Vancouver schools, organist and choirmaster at Chown Memorial Church, conductor of the CBR Singers for seven years. On staff of the Victoria Summer School since 1938.

Address: 2526 Wallace Crescent, Vancouver, B.C.

Compositions:

Songs published by Western Music Company:
Christmas Lullaby; Elegy for Summer; The Road to Rainy River; Daffodil; White Dreams; Freckles; The Circus Clown and many others.
Compiled, edited and arranged school and choral volumes: *Little Songs for Little People* (1941), *The Music Makers* (1944), *Sing Hey Ho* (1949, with Kinley and McManus).

Labelle, Charles

Choirmaster, singer and composer. Born in Champlain, N.Y., August 15th, 1849. Died in Montreal, May 21st, 1902 or 1903.

Musical education in Montreal and in Paris (1880) with Bussini (voice). From 1884-91 was musical director at Notre-Dame Cathedral in Montreal and later choirmaster at St. Louis-de-France Church, Montreal. Was made a member of Institut Populaire de France.

Compositions:

Messe funèbre
Dies Irae
Two Ave Maria
Pie Jesu

O Salutaris
Songs
Romance for 'cello
Piano Pieces

Labelle, Jean-Baptiste

Organist, teacher and composer. Born in Plattsburgh, N.Y., September 8th, 1828. Died in Montreal, September 9th, 1898.

Teachers included L. von Meyer and in Paris S. Thalberg (piano). Organist in Canada since 1843; at Notre-Dame Cathedral in Montreal from 1849-91. In 1857 made a concert tour through U.S. and to South America. Taught in various colleges and convents in and around Montreal.

COMPOSITIONS

TITLE	DATE	TYPE	TIME (MIN.)	PUBLISHER
Cantate à la Confédération				
Cantate aux Zouaves pontificaux				
Several operettas				
O Canada, mon pays, mes amours (Gge-Etienne Cartier, 1834)		vocal		Passe-Temps; La Bonne Chanson; G. V. Thompson
Les Echos de Notre-Dame (series of sacred pieces)				
Le Repertoire de l'Organiste (collection of Gregorian Chant)				publ. in many editions

Lachapelle, Abbé Paul

Pianist and composer. Born in St. Paul L'Ermite, P.Q., June 23rd, 1897.

Musical education with Rodolphe Mathieu (harmony and composition), Rodolphe Plamondon (voice) and in Paris with Lucien Muratore (interpretation). Music is a hobby.

Address: 2900 St. Catherine Road, Montreal, P.Q.

COMPOSITIONS

TITLE	DATE	TYPE	TIME (MIN.)	PUBLISHER
Prélude		vln and piano	3	MS.
Colloque		piano	2	MS.
Au Fil de l'eau		piano	2	MS.
Pastiche		piano	2	MS.
Spleen		piano	2	MS.
Premier Prélude		piano	1	MS.
Romance		voice, vln, piano	3	MS.
Oculus Non Vidit		choral	2	MS.
Tantum Ergo		choral	4	MS.

Songs in manuscript:
Tantum Ergo; Sanctus; L'Amitié; Beau soir; Le Pardon; La Vierge à midi.

Lacharité, Sylvio

Conductor and composer. Born in Sherbrooke, P.Q.

Musical education with Germaine Malépart, Paul-Marcel Robidoux and Pierre Monteux (conducting). In 1939 founded Sherbrooke Symphony Orchestra and became its conductor. Since 1945 has been director of Sherbrooke Band. Is studying music in France under Milhaud.

Address: 94 Gillespie Street, Sherbrooke, P.Q.

COMPOSITIONS

TITLE	DATE	TYPE	TIME (MIN.)	PUBLISHER
Vision of Ezekiel (overture)		orchestra		MS.
The Ship of Gold (tone poem)		orchestra		MS.
Portraits in Miniature		orchestra		MS.

Other compositions and orchestral transcriptions and settings of folk songs.

Lafleur, Lucienne
(Soeur M.-Thérèse-de-la-Sainte-Face, S.S.A.)

Pianist, organist, composer and music teacher. Born in Ste. Agathe-des-Monts, P.Q., February 8th, 1904.

Studied piano, organ, voice and composition with Claude Champagne, Alfred Lamoureaux, Jean Charbonneau and Auguste Descarries. Degrees: Lauréat de l'Institut Musical, Bachelor and Licentiate of Montreal University. Now teaches at Ecole Supérieure de Musique d'Outremont.

Address: 1250 rue St.-Joseph, Lachine, P.Q.

COMPOSITIONS

TITLE	DATE	TYPE	TIME (MIN.)	PUBLISHER
Six Cantatas				
Gloire à ton Institut	1946	choir and piano	10	Archambault
Hymne à Sainte-Anne	1946	choir and organ	10	Archambault
Mai	1948	choir and piano	5	MS.
Jubilé d'argent	1947	choir and piano	7	MS.
Pais mes Agneaux!	1948	choir and piano	7	MS.
Les Cloches du pays natal	1948	choir and piano	7	MS.
Mon offertoire	1947	choir and organ	4	Archambault
Offertoire in D	1947	choir and organ	4	MS.
A Sainte-Anne	1949	choir and organ		MS.
Au Coeur Immaculé de M.	1949	choir and organ		MS.
A nos Saints Martyrs Canadiens	1948	choir and organ		MS.
Par Lui, avec Lui, en Lui	1949	choir and organ		MS.
O ma céleste Mère	1949	choir and organ		MS.
Par la main d'une femme une lampe s'allume!	1949	choir and piano	25	MS.
Chant de ralliement	1947	choir and piano	3	MS.
Le Matin	1944	vocal	3	MS.
Berceuse	1944	vocal	5	Archambault
Le Rouet du bonheur	1945	vocal	2	MS.
Pinson chanteur	1945	vocal	3	MS.
A ma mère- A mon père	1945	vocal	3	MS.
Bonjour Noël	1946	vocal	3	Archambault
Petits Oiseaux	1949	vocal	2	MS.
Bluette (noël)	1949	vocal	2	MS.
Trois Saluts du T.S. Sacrement				No. 1: Archambault
About 15 piano pieces		piano		MS.

Lajeunesse, Emma (Mme Albani)

(Marie Louise Cecilia Emma Lajeunesse)

Singer, pianist, and in her youth, composer. Born in Chambly, P.Q., November 1st, 1847. Died in London, England, April 3rd, 1930.

The famous prima donna received all her early training in Canada which she did not leave till 1866. Her operatic debut took place in Messina in 1870 (La Sonnambula). Her operatic career took her to France, Italy, England (Covent Garden), Germany, Russia and North America.

COMPOSITIONS

TITLE	DATE	TYPE	TIME (MIN.)	PUBLISHER
Grand Duett (on themes from Sabatier's Cantata; see Sabatier)	c. 1860	2 pianos		MS. (25 pages)
Grande marche triomphale	c. 1860	piano		MS.
Grand Fantasia on "When this Cruel War is Over"	before 1864	piano (?)		MS.
Variations on " 'Tis the Last Rose of Summer"	c. 1864	harp		MS.
Hymn to Pius IX	c. 1860	vocal and choral		MS.
And Must These States Now Sever	c. 1864	vocal		MS.
Les Martyrs	c. 1860	vocal		MS.
Travail de Reconnaissance	c. 1860	vocal (?)		MS.
O Salutaris	c. 1867	vocal		Hallenson, N.Y.

See:
Emma Albani, Forty Years of Song, London, 1911.
Hélène Charbonneau, L'Albani, Montreal, 1938.
Any musical dictionary.

Laliberté, Joseph François Alfred

Pianist and composer. Born in St. Jean, P.Q., February 10th, 1882.

Musical education in Berlin, 1900-05, at Stern Conservatorium (scholarships) with Dr. Paul Lutzenko (piano), Ernest Baeker (harmony) and Dr. Wilhelm Klatte (counterpoint and composition). Further studies with Teresa Carreno (piano) and Alexandre Scriabine (piano and composition).

Gave recitals in Berlin, Brussels, London and Paris. Returned to Montreal in 1911 as piano teacher and has been an exponent of the works of Scriabine.

Address: 72 Columbia Street, Montreal, P.Q.

COMPOSITIONS

TITLE	DATE	TYPE	TIME (MIN.)	PUBLISHER
Soeur Béatrice		opera	360	MS.
Passacaglia and Choral Finale		choir, organ, orch.	45	MS.
Chant du Rossignol		string quartet		MS.
Deux chansons indiennes		string quartet		MS.
Refrain Lyrique		violin and piano		Belgo-Canadienne
Danse		piano or vln and piano		MS.

COMPOSITIONS

TITLE	DATE	TYPE	TIME (MIN.)	PUBLISHER
Choral Prelude (arr. for organ by M. Dupré)		*piano*		MS.
Page d'album		*piano*		MS.
Refrain lyrique		*piano*		MS.
Variations sur un chant de voyageur canadien		*piano*		MS.
La Chanson Canadienne		*voice and string quartet*		MS.
Trois chansons d'Eve		*vocal*		Eschig
Duo d'Ame		*vocal*		Eschig
Amour Androgyne		*vocal*		Eschig
Le Soleil et la montagne		*vocal*		Eschig
St. Marguerite		*vocal*		Eschig
Cantique		*vocal*		Eschig
Quatre chants de la fatalité		*vocal*	25	MS.
Vers les étoiles		*vocal*		MS.
Heures claires (4 melodies)		*vocal*		MS.
24 Indian songs (harmonized)		*vocal*		MS.
17 Eskimo songs (harmonized)		*vocal*		MS.
2 Czechoslovakian songs (harmonized)		*vocal*		MS.
3 Scottish songs (harmonized)		*vocal*		MS.
1 English song (harmonized)		*vocal*		MS.
800 Canadian songs (harmonized)		*vocal*		approx. 20: Passe-Temps

Lamoureux, Dr. Alfred

Pianist, organist, composer and lecturer. Born in Montreal, December 29th, 1876.

Musical education with Achille Fortier (voice), R. O. Pelletier (piano and organ) and Jéhin-Prume (violin). Doctor degree (Montreal University).

Address: 10845 St. Hubert, Montreal, P.Q.

COMPOSITIONS

TITLE	DATE	TYPE	TIME (MIN.)	PUBLISHER
Tragédie d'Esther		*choral*	60	MS.
Messe du St. Nom de Marie		*choral*		printed
Four Cor Jesu		*choral*		Whaley Royce
Les Lilas		*vocal*		Whaley Royce
Canadiens toujours		*vocal*		printed
Messe sur vieux noëls		*choral*		printed

Choral works in manuscript:

Les Voix du pensionnat; La Fileuse; Pour la Patrie; Le Vent d'ouest; Pour les compagnons de Dollard; Chants des voyageurs; Deux épées; Rondel; La Fontaine; Messe à la Vierge Marie; Messe à St-Joseph; Salve Regina; Tantum Ergo; Ecce Fidelis; Ave Maria; Laetantur Coeli and several hymns.

Songs in manuscript:

La Jeunesse qu'il nous faut; Madeleine de Verchères; Le Lien; Les Choses ailées; Nos aieux; Chant de la patrie; Conseils; Sur des roses, sous la neige.

Lapierre, Dr. Joseph-Eugène

Pianist, organist, writer and composer. Born in Montreal, June 8th, 1899.

Musical education at Institut Grégorien and Schola Cantorum in Paris with Vincent d'Indy (composition), Marcel Dupré (organ), Georges Caussade (harmony) and P. S. Hérard (piano). Degree: Mus.Doc. (Montreal, 1930).

Director of Conservatoire National de Musique since 1927. Secretary, Faculty of Musical Arts, Montreal Univ. since 1950. Member of faculty, Gregorian Institute of America (Toledo, Ohio). In 1937 won *Prix David* in literature for biographical work on Calixa Lavallée.

Address: 275 Sherbrooke East, Montreal, P.Q.

Affiliation: CAPAC.

COMPOSITIONS

TITLE	DATE	TYPE	TIME (MIN.)	PUBLISHER
Le Père des Amours (on life of J. Quesnel)	1942	*opera*	180	MS.
Menuet (from above opera)	1942	*small orchestra*	3½	MS.
Trio	1950	*fl, ob, bn*	5	MS.
Passacaille	1929	*organ*	14	MS.
Adeste (berceuse)	1944	*organ*	5	A. J. Boucher
Alma (postlude)	1937	*organ*	2	MS.
Pastorale	1945	*organ*	5	A. J. Boucher
Marche solennelle	1951	*organ*	4	MS.
Gavotte et Musette		*piano*	2½	Archambault
Gavotte in A	1941	*piano*	3	MS.
Les Clochers Canadiens		*cantata*	14	MS.
Canadien, souviens-toi		*choral*	3	E. Lapierre
Alma Mater	1943	*choral*	3	Montreal University
Tantum Ergo	1944	*choral*	2	MS.
Minuet	1942	*choral*	4	MS.
St.-Jean de Dieu (hymn)	1935	*choral*	3	A. J. Boucher
Ecce Fidelis	1926	*motet*	3	Herelle, Paris
Qui ad justitiam	1950	*motet*	4	MS.
Ave Admirabile	1948	*motet*	2	La Bonne Chanson
Prière Nuptiale	1947	*vocal*	3	La Bonne Chanson
Wedding Prayer (separate)		*vocal*	3	La Bonne Chanson
Le Tinton	1941	*vocal*	3	La Bonne Chanson
Villanelle	1942	*vocal*	2¼	La Bonne Chanson
Le Viel Arbre	1940	*vocal*	3	Fassio, Lachute
Romance du soir	1942	*vocal*	3	Fassio, Lachute
Noël canadien	1943	*vocal*	3	MS.
Chanson de Charlemagne		*vocal*	2	MS.
La Luciole (Firefly)	1946	*vocal*	5	MS.
Dis-moi, Lina	1946	*vocal*	4	MS.

Translations into French or adaptations:

Sans toi ma vie (Down
through the years)   G. V. Thompson

Nous nous verrons (We'll
meet again)   G. V. Thompson

Cuban Breezes (Baldomero)   Parnasse
Musical

Books:

Calixa Lavallée, musicien national du Canada, Granger, rev. ed., 1950.
Pourquoi la Musique, 1933.
La Musique au Sanctuaire, 1932.
Gregorian Chant Accompaniment, 1949.

Lapp, Horace

Organist, pianist, conductor and composer. Born in Uxbridge, Ont., 1904.

Musical education at Royal Conservatory, Toronto with Alberto Guerrero (piano) and others. Has been active as church and theatre organist; radio work for over 15 years.

Address: 641 Lakeshore Road, Mimico, Ont.

COMPOSITIONS

TITLE	DATE	TYPE	TIME (MIN.)	PUBLISHER
Poem	1951	*piano and orch.*	15	MS.
Overture	1951	*small orchestra*	5	MS.
Oriental Suite	1950	*piano*	12	MS.
Recitative and Scena	1948	*sop and orch.*	10	MS.
Hymn to Canada	1949	*choral*	2½	MS.
Childrens Songs (The Spider and the Fly; The Snow; Fairy's Ride)	1938	*vocal*	11	MS.
Dear Love	1948	*vocal*	3	MS.
Norwegian Song	1948	*vocal*	4	MS.
Flirting Song	1934	*vocal*	3	MS.

Other songs; radio background music.

Lavallée, Calixa

Composer, pianist, conductor and music teacher. Born in Verchères, P.Q., December 28th, 1842. Died in Boston, January 21st, 1891.

Grew up in a musical home and took first lessons in Montreal with Paul Letondal and C. W. Sabatier (piano and organ). Also became a proficient cornet and violin player. Said to have given first recital in Montreal when 13. A few years later left for U.S. and won a prize for performance in New Orleans. Accompanied Spanish violinist Olivera on tour to South America, West Indies and Southern U.S. (1860).

From 1861-62, enlisted as musician in 4th Rhode Island Regiment with the Northern forces in the American Civil War. In 1864 settled as music teacher in Montreal. In 1867 lived in Lowell, Mass. From 1870-72 conductor and artistic director at New York Grand Opera House.

From 1873-75 studied in Paris at Conservatoire National under Bazin, Boieldieu fils and Marmontel (piano and composition); at this time he was already called "Canada's national composer". From 1875-80 lived in Montreal and Quebec, teaching and concertizing in association with Frantz and Mrs. Jehin-Prume. Staged Gounod's *Jeanne d'Arc* (1877) and Boieldieu's *Dame Blanche* (1878), conducted choirs etc. His ultimote aim of establishing a national conservatory in Canada was not realized.

In 1880 left for U.S. Accompanied Etelka Gerster, soprano on tour in 1883 (1881?). Settled in Boston and became teacher of piano and composition at Petersilea Conservatory and reportedly New England Conservatory and musical director at Catholic Cathedral. Elected to program committee of Music Teacher's National Association in 1881, elected president 1886-87. In 1884 presented one of the first concerts of American compositions (Cleveland). M.T.N.A. delegate to Conference of the National Society of Professional Musicians, London, England, 1888. Honoured with a banquet by the mayor of London.

In 1933 his remains were transferred from Boston to Montreal.

COMPOSITIONS

TITLE	DATE	TYPE	TIME (MIN.)	PUBLISHER

O Canada, terre de nos aïeux (national song)

Composed in 1880. Words by Judge Adolphe B. Routhier (1880). Accepteα English version by Dr. Robert Stanley Weir (1908). First performance June 24th, 1880.

Available in various arrangements and keys from many Canadian music publishers.

Stage works:

Lou-Lou	1872	*opéra-bouffe (3 acts)*	
La Veuve (The Widow)		*opéra-comique (3 acts)*	J. M. Russell, Boston, c. 1882
Tiq (Settled at last)		*melodramatic musical satire (2 acts)*	J. M. Russell, Bostou, 1883
Le Jugement de Salomon			2 scenes performed 1886

Choral works with orchestra:

Tu es Petrus		*oratorio*	published (?)
Offertory		*soli, choir, orch.*	performed in N.Y., 1885
Hymne à la paix dédié à toutes les nations du monde		*choir and orchestra*	MS. (Gagnier collection)
Cantate en l'honneur du Marquis de Lorne et de la Princesse Louise	1879	*choir and orchestra*	lost
Symphony dedicated to Boston city		*choir and orchestra*	lost

Orchestral and band works:

Symphony		*orchestra*	lost (perf. in Paris 1874)
Two Suites		*orchestra*	lost
Bridal Rose Overture (Rose nuptiale)		*orchestra and various arrangements*	Cundy Music Co., Boston; now: Cundy-Bettoney
King of Diamonds Overture (Le Roi de Carreau)		*orchestra and various arrangements*	Cundy Music Cc., Boston; now: Cundy-Bettoney

		COMPOSITIONS		
TITLE	DATE	TYPE	TIME (MIN.)	PUBLISHER
Golden Fleece Overture		*orchestra and various arrangements*		Cundy Music Co., Boston; now: Cundy-Bettoney
Rhapsodie des airs irlandais		*band*		
Andalouse (bolero)		*band*		White (U.S.)
Harmonie (for a band contest)		*band*		

Works for small ensemble:

'Cello Concerto		*'cello and piano*		perf. Detroit 1887 (the piano part was never written down)
Two String Quartets		*string quartet*		lost
Piano Trio		*vln, vc, piano*		lost
Suite		*vc and piano*		lost
Sonata		*vln and piano*		lost
Grande Fantasie, Op. 75		*cornet and piano*		Carl Fischer
Meditation		*cornet and piano*		Carl Fischer

Piano works:

30 etudes for piano, including: "Papillons" Op. 18 (Op. 10?)		*piano*		Eveillard, Paris, c. 1875 (c. 10 other publishers)
Sonata		*piano*		lost
War Fever (grand galop), Op. 4		*piano*		H. S. Gordon, N.Y.
Grande Valse de Concert, Op. 6		*piano*		H. S. Gordon, N.Y.
Fleur de Mai (polka de salon)		*piano*		H. S. Gordon, N.Y.
L'Oiseau mouche (Humming Bird)		*piano*		A. J. Boucher (c. 1866), O. Ditson
Mouvement à la Pavane		*piano*		White
Valse de Salon, Op. 39		*piano*		White
Souvenir de Tolède, Op. 17		*piano*		Eveillard, Paris
Grande Marche de Concert, Op. 14		*piano*		Eveillard, Paris
Pas redoublé sur des airs canadiens		*piano*		La Presse (newspaper) 1912
Vole au vent (galop)		*piano*		Le Minerve (newspaper)

Choral works:

O Canada (see above)				
The Rock and the Hills		*choral*		J. Curwen
With Pleasure In Each Glance		*choral*		J. Curwen
Beautiful Girl of Kildare		*solo and choir*		O. Ditson

Vocal works:

Spring Flowers		*vocal*		White
Trois chansons		*vocal*		published
Restons Français		*vocal*		Le Passe-Temps, 1933

COMPOSITIONS

TITLE	DATE	TYPE	TIME (MIN.)	PUBLISHER
Violette		vocal		Le Passe-Temps, 1933
L'Absence		vocal		Le Passe-Temps, 1933
Nuit d'Eté		vocal		MS.
La Mansarde		vocal		MS.
Chant de ralliement		vocal		published
16 Melodies (with Premio-Réal)		vocal		published

Various works (instrumentation not known):

Berceuse				
Marche funèbre à Pie IX, dedicated to Mgr Bourget				
Marche Indienne (from Tiq?)				
Marche Americaine (for London city)	1887			published
La Couronne des lauriers				published c. 1866
Bon Voyage (galop)				

Many other compositions have been lost or have not been traced yet.

See:
Dr. E. Lapierre, *Calixa Lavallée, Notre musicien national*, revised edition, Granger, 1950.
Le Passe-Temps (periodical), August 1933.

Lavallée-Smith, Alphonse

Organist, music teacher and composer. Born in Berthierville, P.Q., 1873. Died in Ste.-Agathe, P.Q., July, 1912.

Musical education in Nicolet, P.Q. and 1896-97 in Paris with Widor and Guilmant (organ). Organist and music teacher in Montreal. In 1905 founded Conservatoire National de Musique in Montreal.

COMPOSITIONS

TITLE	DATE	TYPE	TIME (MIN.)	PUBLISHER
Gisèle		operetta		
Toccata		organ		performed 1917
Prelude and Cantata (L. Frechette)		choir and soli		performed 1903
O Salutaris		choral		performed 1905
La Mère et l'enfant		vocal		Passe-Temps
Lévis dans l'Ile Ste-Hélène		vocal		Passe-Temps
Oubli		vocal		Archambault
Brunette		vocal		performed 1903

Many other works, including some published sacred compositions.

Lavigne, Ernest

Cornet virtuoso, conductor and composer. Born in Montreal, December 17th, 1851. Died in Montreal, January 18th, 1909.

In 1868 went to Rome with the fourth detachment of the Papal Zouaves and studied in Europe for several years. Excelled as cornet virtuoso and organized many open-air concerts, especially the Parc Sohmer concerts in Montreal (1889-1919, later conducted by others).

	COMPOSITIONS			
TITLE	DATE	TYPE	TIME (MIN.)	PUBLISHER
25 Melodies	1901	*vocal*		Archambault
Vive la France		*vocal*		La Bonne Chanson
Dieu Sauve la France		*vocal*		in Chants Acadiens
Le Retour		*vocal*		Archambault

About 45 other songs.

Lavigueur, Célestin

Violinist, music teacher and composer. Born in Quebec, January 19th, 1830. Died in Lowell, Mass., December 11th, 1885.

Musical education in Quebec. Was music teacher at Quebec Seminary for 30 years.

	COMPOSITIONS			
TITLE	DATE	TYPE	TIME (MIN.)	PUBLISHER
Les Enfants du Manoir (own libretto)		*opera (3 acts)*		MS., almost completed
Un Mariage improvisé		*opera*		
La Fiancée des bois (P. Lemay)		*operetta (3 acts)*		
La Huronne		*vocal*		L. Brousseau, Quebec (see: Vézina, Mosaïque)
Le Nom de ma soeur (romance)		*vocal*		
O Canada (patriotic song)		• *vocal*		
Donnez (invitation to charity)		*vocal*		
Soyez la bienvenue (to Princess Louise)		*vocal*		
Thérèse la blonde		*vocal*		
Amour		*vocal*		
Le Petit Ramoneur		*vocal*		

Lavoie, Claude

Pianist, organist and composer. Born in Rivière-du-Loup, P.Q., July 19th, 1918.

Musical education in Canada with Rev. A. Tardif (piano, organ and harmony), and at Longy School of Music in Boston with Nadia Boulanger (organ and theory), E. Power Biggs (organ) and Melville Smith (theory). At New England Conservatory, Boston, studied with Francis Findlay (choral conducting). Won Quebec Province *Prix d'Europe* in 1942. Organist in Beauport, P.Q. At present in Paris, France.

	COMPOSITIONS			
TITLE	DATE	TYPE	TIME (MIN.)	PUBLISHER
10 Variations on "Ave Maris Stella"		*organ*	12	MS.
Variations on "Ah! vous dirai-je maman"		*piano*	12	MS.
Tantum Ergo		*choral*	5	MS.
Le Brayage		*vocal*	5	Lavoie

COMPOSITIONS

TITLE	DATE	TYPE	TIME (MIN.)	PUBLISHER
Profil de vieux moulin		vocal	5	Lavoie
Les Chants de la patrie		vocal	5	La Bonne Chanson
Le Canada		vocal	12	MS.

French-Canadian folk songs harmonized.
No recent information obtained.

Leacock, Leonard Henry

Pianist and composer. Born in England, May 28th, 1904.

Musical education in Everett, Mass. with Mrs. Holbrook, in Banff with W. E. Round, at Royal Conservatory, Toronto with F. A. Oliver, T. J. Crawford and in Calgary with G. Egbert, P. L. Newcombe, J. Cotten. Diplomas: A.T.C.M., L.R.S.M. Has ʾbeen teaching at Mount Royal College for 25 years.

Address: c/o Mount Royal College, Calgary, Alta.

COMPOSITIONS

TITLE	DATE	TYPE	TIME (MIN.)	PUBLISHER
Western Prelude		orchestra	9	MS.
Homage to Old Masters	1948	string orchestra	7	MS.
A Negro Melody	1949	vln and piano	4	MS.
The Lonely Lake	1949	vln and piano	5	MS.
Etude Caprice	1948	vln and piano	2½	MS.
Monkey-March—A Jungle Lullaby	1946	vc and piano	3	MS.
Midnight in Minneapolis		piano quartet	7	MS.
Sea Fancies (five pieces)		piano	8	MS.
Prelude, Sarabande and Fugue	1947	violin solo	7	MS.
The Widow Bird		vocal	2	MS.
In France 1917		vocal	4	MS.
Carol (Woodcarver's Wife)		vocal	4	MS.
Chinese Love Song		vocal	2	MS.

Lefebvre, Françoise
(Soeur Paul du Crucifix; Pseudonym: Paduci)

Composer and teacher of piano, organ, voice and theory. Born in Valleyfield, P.Q., February 17th, 1912.

Musical education at Ecole Supérieure de Musique d'Outremont. Teachers: Claude Champagne, Jean Beaudet, Raoul Pâquet. Degree: Mus.Bac. In 1947 won CAPAC award for Symphony. Teaches at Ecole Supérieure de Musique d'Outremont.

Address: 1410 Mount Royal Boulevard, Outremont, P.Q.

COMPOSITIONS

TITLE	DATE	TYPE	TIME (MIN.)	PUBLISHER
Symphony No. 1	1946	organ	23	Ecole Supérieure de Musique d'Outremont

	COMPOSITIONS			
TITLE	DATE	TYPE	TIME (MIN.)	PUBLISHER
Symphony No. 2	1950	*organ*	20	MS.
Fugue in C minor	1941	*organ*	7	MS.
Poèmes évangéliques	1950	*organ*		MS.
Sonata	1949	*2 pianos*	28	MS.
Theme and Variations	1950	*piano*		MS.
Messe brève à l'unisson	1944	*choral*	8	MS.
Cantate	1944	*choral*	8	MS.
Salut du Saint-Sacrement (6 pieces)	1950	*choral*	15	MS.
Several motets		*choral*		MS.

LeLacheur, Rex

Singer and composer. Born in Guernsey, Channel Islands, January 5th, 1910.

Musical education in London with J. H. Howell (voice), in Toronto with Dr. H. A. Fricker (harmony and counterpoint).

Address: 99 Marlborough Avenue, Ottawa, Ont.

Affiliation: CAPAC.

	COMPOSITIONS			
TITLE	DATE	TYPE	TIME (MIN.)	PUBLISHER
Forever England		*choral*	3	Can. Music Sales
Mothers of the World		*choral*	3	Can. Music Sales
Seek Ye the Lord		*choral*		Can. Music Sales
Bow Down Thine Ear		*choral*		Can. Music Sales
Nunc Dimittis		*choral*		Can. Music Sales
All Suddenly the Wind Comes Soft		*vocal*	3	Can. Music Sales
Ave Maria		*vocal*	2½	Can. Music Sales
Men of the Merchant Marine		*vocal*	4	Can. Music Sales

Lemieux, Dr. Joseph-Léopold

(Rev. Frère Barnabé, s.c.)

Organist and composer. Born in Montreal, June 30th, 1908.

Musical education at Conservatoire National in Montreal with Eugène Lapierre (theory) and Alice Raymond (singing), in St. Benoît du Lac with D. Mercure (Gregorian Chant), in Arthabaska with Dr. Arthur Charlebois (organ, harmony and allied subjects). Now teaches music and is organist and choirmaster at Ecole Normale d'Arthabaska, P.Q. Degree: Mus. Doc. (Montreal, 1948).

Address: Scolasticat des Frères du Sacré-Coeur, Arthabaska, P.Q.

COMPOSITIONS

TITLE	DATE	TYPE	TIME (MIN.)	PUBLISHER
Les Premices (or) Les Saints Martyrs Canadiens		*oratorio*	150-180	MS.
La Visite de M. l'Inspecteur		*operetta*	90	MS.
Three Masses		*mixed voices*		MS.
Requiem Mass		*male voices*		MS.
Motets		*mixed voices*		MS.
Many songs for 1, 2, or 3 voices				
Album of about 80 songs				Les Editions Sainte-Cécile, Arthabaska

Le Sieur, Léo

Organist, pianist and composer. Born in Lowell, Mass., May 21st, 1897.

Musical studies in piano, organ, theory, voice and Gregorian chant with various private teachers. As boy sang as soprano soloist. Was in Canada from 1922-24 and has been since 1928. Has been cinema organist in New England and Montreal. Director in vaudeville shows and dance band leader. Produced and participated in many radio programs.

Address: 4472 rue St. Denis, Montreal, P.Q.

Affiliation: CAPAC.

COMPOSITIONS

TITLE	DATE	TYPE	TIME (MIN.)	PUBLISHER
Canadien pour toujours (Canadian I'll Always Be); Chère Amie; Faut pas faire; I Went to the Market; Maman; Pourquoi; Pour toi mon amour; Quand je danse avec toi; Si tu savais; Souvenirs du passé; Tango d'amour; Tou-di-la-di-tou		*vocal*		Edition Prima
Je t'aime; C'est un charme qui nous grise; Hantise; Qui?; Charms; Goodnight, dear		*vocal*		MS.
Chant d'amour; Romanesque; Badinage; Au matin		*instrumental*		La Lyre
Trois Turlutaines; Valse Caprice; Improvisation		*instrumental*		Edition Prima
Tango Morose		*instrumental*		MS.

Numerous popular songs, instrumental pieces and some radio music, published by Editions Prima, La Lyre, Maurice Baron and Leo Feist.

Commercial recordings made by various record companies.

Letondal, Arthur

Pianist, organist and composer. Born in Montreal, April 30th, 1869.

Musical education in Paris with Marmontel and Taudou (piano, organ, harmony etc.), in Brussels with Mailly and Jufferath. Has served as organist in principal churches in Montreal and at Montreal Cathedral since 1923; has taught music.

Address: 418 West Pine Avenue, Montreal, P.Q.

COMPOSITIONS

TITLE	DATE	TYPE	TIME (MIN.)	PUBLISHER
Troise pièces de genre		*piano arr. for orchestra by J. J. Gagnier*		Ed. Hardy, Montreal
Danse Moyen-Age	c. 1898	*piano*		Lavigueur & Hutchison, Quebec
Sarabande		*piano*		O. Ditson
Berceuse		*piano*		Edition Musica, Paris
Toccata		*organ*		Fischer
Prélude grave		*organ*		Belgo-Canadienne
Offertoire		*organ*		Belgo-Canadienne
Ave Maria		*vocal*		Fischer
Ave Maria		*vocal*		MS.
Cors Jesu		*vocal*		Ed. Hardy, Montreal
Tantum Ergo		*vocal*		Schola Cantorum
O Salutaris		*vocal*		Bélair, Montreal

Létourneau, Omer

Pianist, organist and composer. Born in Quebec, March 13th, 1891.

Musical education at Académie de Musique de Québec (piano and organ). Winner of Quebec Province *Prix d'Europe* in 1913. Studied in Paris with Louis Vierne, Félix Fourdrain and at the Schola Cantorum. Has been organist at St. Sauveur Church, Quebec ,since 1915. Professor at Laval University, Quebec. Member of Société des Auteurs et Compositeurs de Paris.

Address: 99 De Callières Street, Quebec, P.Q.

COMPOSITIONS

TITLE	DATE	TYPE	TIME (MIN.)	PUBLISHER
Coup d'soleil		*operetta*		MS.
Vive la Canadienne		*operetta*		MS.
Mam'zell Bébé		*operetta*		MS.
Intermezzo		*organ*	2½	Procure générale
Air de ballet		*piano*	4	Procure générale
Petite gavotte		*piano*	3	Procure générale
Air de ballet (sur "Vive la Canadienne")		*piano*	3	La Lyre
O Canada (variations)		*piano duet*		Procure générale
Danse rustique		*vln and piano*	2½	Procure générale
		or orchestra	2½	MS.

Choral works published by Procure générale:

Ave Maria, Op. 100; *Ave Maria*, Op. 101; *Ego Sum; In Manus Tuas; O Salutaris; Panis Angelicus; Deux messes faciles* (C and D major); *Benedicte; Dieu te garde mon Canada; La Voix de ma mère; L'Agnelet; Le Ruisseau et la lavandière; Prière des oiseaux; Quand il neige sur mon pays; Marianne s'en va-t-au moulin; Veni Electa Mea; Vierge, bénissez notre Père; Silence, ciel; Cloches Sonnez;* Six cantiques de Noel (harmonizations).

Songs published by Procure générale:

A ma petite fille; Berceuse; Berceuse de l'enfant-Jésus; Chanson grise; Courage et labeur; Isabeau s'y promène; Gavotte Mam'zelle Bébé; La Chanson de l'Alouette; La Croix du chemin; La Vie est vaine; La Voix de ma mère;

Le Semeur; L'Extase; Loin de l'amant; Maison paternelle; Marianne s'en va-t-au moulin; Madrigal; Obstination; Les Papillons; Pour une blonde; Pour toi; Près d'un berceau; Reste petite; Si l'amour est un doux servage; Tais toi mon coeur; Souvenir; Rêves d'enfant; O Saint-Laurent.

Theoretical works:

Théorie Musicale complète, publ. Procure générale.
Questionnaire de la théorie, publ. Procure générale.
Ecole de la Dictée Musicale, 2 vol., pub. Procure générale.

Lord, Frederick

Choral conductor, organist and composer. Born in Bradford, England, November 15th, 1886. Died in Brantford, Ont., August, 1945.

Musical education with Eaglefield Hull (composition), other private teachers and at Conservatory in Montreux, Switzerland. Came to Canada in 1923. In 1928 founded the Canadian Choir of Brantford which he conducted till his death. The choir toured Great Britain in 1930 and twice visited New York. Was director of music at Ontario School for the Blind.

Inquiries: Mrs. F. Lord, 159 Brant Avenue, Brantford, Ont.

COMPOSITIONS

TITLE	DATE	TYPE	TIME (MIN.)	PUBLISHER
Symphony		*orchestra*		MS.
Piano Concerto		*orchestra*	35	MS.
The Battle of Morgarten (cantata)		*choir, orchestra*	45	MS.
Psalm XC (symphonic poem)		*bar, choir, orch.*	25	MS.
The Evening Cloud		*female choir, strings*	6	MS.
Sonata		*vln and piano*		MS.
Ballade No. 2		*piano*		J. & W. Chester
Three Preludes		*piano*		J. & W. Chester
Various piano pieces		*piano*		J. & W. Chester
Windy Nights		*male chorus*	3	G. Schirmer
Ye Fond Kiss		*choral*		Novello
God Be in My Head (anthem)		*choral*		Anglo-Canadian
In Peace I Will Lay Me Down (anthem)		*choral*		Anglo-Canadian

Many piano pieces, vocal solos and part songs in manuscript are in the hands of Mrs. F. Lord.

Lowe, John Maurice

Pianist and composer. Born in Sheffield, England, October 8th, 1902.

Came to Canada before 1910. Musical studies in Winnipeg with Leonard Heaton (mostly self-taught). Has appeared as composer-pianist in Western Canada and in Seattle.

Address: White Rock, B.C.

Affiliation: CAPAC.

COMPOSITIONS

TITLE	DATE	TYPE	TIME (MIN.)	PUBLISHER
Thalaba		*orchestra*	12	MS.
Irish Rhapsody		*piano and orchestra*	15	MS.
Eastern Fantasy		*piano and strings*	10	MS.

COMPOSITIONS

TITLE	DATE	TYPE	TIME (MIN.)	PUBLISHER
Pan's Dance		*piano and strings*	4	MS.
To the Children		*strings*	5	MS.
Fugue for Four Strings		*strings*	5	MS.
Berceuse		*organ*	2	MS.
Litany		*organ*	4	MS.
Fairy Tale of Slieve Bloom		*two pianos*	8	MS.
Sonata		*two pianos*		
Irish Rhapsody		*two pianos*		
Tread Softly Here		*choral*	3	MS.
Two Songs for Young Listeners		*choral*	3	MS.
To Mercy		*choral*	3	MS.

Piano pieces in manuscript:

Scottish Etude; Barcarolle; The River Legend; Arabesque; Two Toccatas; Yule 1932; Lethe; Huckleberry Finn; Domestic Counterpoints (6 miniatures); *Good King Wenceslas* (variations); *Fantasy Sonata; Flossie's Wedding.*

Songs in manuscript:

To Spring; Workers' Marching Song; Beware!; Love's Prisoner; Lullaby; Five Nature Songs; Remember Me; Rain on Rahoon; Stray Birds (12 songs); *To Canada; The Dancer's Dress; Love's Nearness; At Parting; Dawn; The Wildflower's Song.*
No recent information obtained.

Lucas, Clarence

Composer, conductor, critic and music editor. Born in Niagara, Ont., October 9th, 1866. Died in Paris, France, July 1st, 1947.

Musical education in Montreal and from 1886-89 in Paris with Gounod, Massenet, G. Marty, Th. Dubois and others. Degree: Mus.Bac. (Toronto, 1893). From 1889-91 was theory teacher at Toronto College of Music; also conducted Hamilton Philharmonic Society. In 1891 taught at Uticah, N.Y., Conservatory. Since 1893 lived in London, New York and Paris. Was correspondent and later associate editor of Musical Courier. Did editorial work for Chappell & Co. Although Lucas left Canada as a young man he was for many decades considered the most outstanding Anglo-Canadian composer of his time.

COMPOSITIONS

TITLE	DATE	TYPE	TIME (MIN.)	PUBLISHER
Seven operas including:				
The Money Spider		*opera*		performed in London, 1897
Peggy Machree		*opera*		perf. in England, 1904, U.S., 1907
Orchestral works:				
Symphony		*orchestra*		
Two symphonic poems		*orchestra*		
Othello (overture)		*orchestra*		
As You Like It (overture Op. 35)		*orchestra*		Chappell & Co. 1899
Macbeth (overture Op. 39)		*orchestra*		Chappell & Co., c. 1900
Four oratorios and cantatas including:				
The Birth of Christ		*oratorio*		perf. in Chicago, 1902

COMPOSITIONS

TITLE	DATE	TYPE	TIME (MIN.)	PUBLISHER
Choral works:				
Requiem Mass in C minor	1936-37	*choral, orchestra*		MS.
The Bells		*choral, orchestra*		Boosey & Hawkes
Organ works				
including:				
Seven Short Pieces		*organ*		Ascherberg
Two Compositions		*organ*		Ascherberg
Canadian Wedding March, Op. 66		*organ*		
Deux Pièces, Op. 27		*organ*		Schott
Piano pieces				
including:				
Fantasy and Fugue, Op. 22		*piano*		Simrock
Prelude and Fugue, Op. 32		*piano*		
Prelude and Fugue, F minor, Op. 38		*piano*		G. Schirmer
Saga, Ein islaendisches Maerchen, Op. 25		*piano*		Breitkopf & Hartel
Epithalamium (Impromptu), Op. 54		*piano*		G. Schirmer
Ariel (scherzo), Op. 55		*piano*		G. Schirmer
Holiday Sketches, Op. 61		*piano*		Boosey & Hawkes, 1915
About 70 songs				
including:				
Album of Six Baritone Songs, Op. 29		*vocal*		Chappell & Co., c. 1894
When the Stars Arise		*vocal*		G. Schirmer
The Royal Red Rose		*vocal*		G. Schirmer
When Comes the Spring		*vocal*		O. Ditson, 1891

Many other compositions. Other publishers include Edwin Ashdown, Augener, Theodore Presser, Forsyth Bro.

Book:

The Story of Musical Form, London, 1908. (The music-story series).

MacConnell, Howard Bruce

Architect, pianist and composer. Born in Springbrook, Ont., August 14th, 1886.

Musical education at Albert College, Belleville with Prof. Cameron and at Royal Conservatory, Toronto with H. Anger (theory). Studied architecture, engineering and was engaged in building construction, estimating and designing from 1919-43. Music is a hobby.

Address: 212 South Vickers Street, Fort William, Ont.

COMPOSITIONS

TITLE	DATE	TYPE	TIME (MIN.)	PUBLISHER
In Memoriam (string symphony)	1949	*string orchestra*	25	MS.
String Quartet		*string quartet*	30	MS.

COMPOSITIONS

TITLE	DATE	TYPE	TIME (MIN.)	PUBLISHER
New Year's Eve Suite	1945	*2 pianos*	15	MS.
Easter Suite	1948	*2 pianos*	14	MS.
Polonaise	1946	*2 pianos*	10	MS.
Ave Maria		*voice, piano, small orch.*	3	MS.

Works for piano in manuscript:

Theme and 24 Variations (15 min.); *Carnival* (15 min.); *Berceuse* (10 min.); Three Etudes; Four Preludes; *Nocturne; Three Fantasies; Lament; Valse humoresque;* Waltz; *Humoresque; Nocturne; Romantic Fantasy.*

Vocal works in manuscript:

But Know I Know; Once More a Music; Out of the Night; Sweet Is My Love.

Children's pieces in manuscript:

Lullaby; Waltz; Romance; A Summer Day (piano); Andante (violin and piano).

MacDermid, James Gardiner

Pianist, vocalist, accompanist and composer. Born in Utica, Ont., June 10th, 1875.

Musical education in London, Ont. with B. Saunders (piano), in Minnesota with F. E. Woodward and G. Tyler (singing), in Chicago with A. Williams and G. Hamlin. Has lived in the U.S. since 1893. Has been engaged in church and concert work in U.S. and has toured as accompanist for his wife Sybil Sammis MacDermid in song recitals for many years.

Address: Hotel Riverside Plaza, 253 West 73rd Street, New York City, U.S.A.

Affiliation: ASCAP.

Compositions:

About 75 sacred and secular songs published by Forster Music Publishers Inc., Chicago and Horace J. Carver, Boston.

See:

ASCAP *Biographical Dictionary.*

Macdonald, Fraser Pringle

Composer and writer. Born in Toronto, April 3rd, 1912.

Musical education with Mme J. LeSaunier in Edmonton (piano) and with John Weinzweig in Toronto (composition). Degree: B.A. (Alberta). Musical continuity writer for CBC.

Address: c/o Canadian Broadcasting Corporation, Toronto, Ont.

COMPOSITIONS

TITLE	DATE	TYPE	TIME (MIN.)	PUBLISHER
Concerto on French Can. themes	1933-37	*piano and orchestra*		MS.
Capriccio	1935-36	*piano and orchestra*		MS.
Adventures of a Piano (a fairy tale)	1941-48	*piano and orchestra*	18	MS.
Earth (ballet)	1941	*orchestra*	40	MS.
Things for Strings (5 short pieces)	1948	*string orchestra*	8	MS.
		or string quartet	8	MS.
Quartet in E minor	1950	*string quartet*		MS.

COMPOSITIONS

TITLE	DATE	TYPE	TIME (MIN.)	PUBLISHER
Andante	1943	*vln and piano*		MS.
		or string quartet		MS.
Dance	1944	*vln and piano*		MS.
Suite for Four Hands	1938	*piano duet*		MS.
Five Nocturnes (parodies of well-known styles)	1938-40	*piano duet*		MS.
Tarantella	1948-49	*piano duet*		MS.
Divertimento	1948-49	*piano duet*		MS.
Thumb-nail Sketches (An expanding collection of short short pieces)	1944-	*piano*		MS.
Siciliano	1947	*piano*		MS.
Fantasia	1949	*piano*		MS.
Three Pictures	1934-35	*piano*		MS.
Two Short Songs (Credo; Triolet)	1935	*vocal*		MS.
The Dole of the King's Daughter	1938	*vocal*		MS.
The Route March	1941	*vocal*		MS.
Five Shakespeare Songs	1950	*voice and str qua.*		MS.
A Midsummer Night's Dream	1945	*incidental music (songs)*		MS.
Tobias and the Angel	1945	*incidental music (songs)*		MS.
As You Like It	1949	*incidental music (songs)*		MS.
Much Ado About Nothing	1949	*incidental music (songs)*		MS.
Two Noble Kinsmen	1949	*incidental music (songs)*		MS.
The Taming of the Shrew	1950	*incidental music (songs)*		MS.
The Tempest	1950	*incidental music (songs)*		MS.

MacIntosh, G. A. (widow Dr. M.)

(Pen-name Claire Harris MacIntosh)

Nurse, writer and composer. Born in Londonderry, N.S., 1882.

Musical education at Edgehill School, Windsor, N.S. and with Fred Clark at Halifax Conservatory. Has done extensive work for Red Cross, St. John Ambulance Association, Women's Canadian Club, Victorian Order of Nurses (executive work for 36 years).

Address: 4 Roy Apts., Bedford, N.S.

COMPOSITIONS

TITLE	DATE	TYPE	TIME (MIN.)	PUBLISHER
(words by composer)				
A Song of Nova Scotia	1935	*vocal*		Mrs. MacIntosh
Five Bird Songs (in story-book "Attune with Spring in Acadie")	1931	*vocal*		Putnam's Sons; Copp Clark

Songs in manuscript:
Lullaby: Abegweit or *The Garden of the Gulf* (P.E.I.); *Their Wedding Bells; Just a Black-capped Chickadee;* Hymn: *O God of Light; Our Babies* (1932-1944).
Several poems have been set to music by Trevor Jones.

Maclean, Quentin Stuart Morvaren

Organist and composer. Born in London, England, May 14th, 1896.

Musical education at Conservatory of Music, Leipzig with Karl Straube (organ) and Max Reger (composition). Soloist at Leipzig Bach Festival 1914. Interned at Ruhleben near Berlin from 1914-18. Assistant organist at Westminster Cathedral, London, 1919. Theatre organist at Regal Marble Arch and Trocadero, London. Regular broadcasting for BBC. Opened BBC theatre organ in 1935. Gave first performance of Hindemith Organ Concerto for BBC.

Now lives in Toronto. Has been organist at Shea's and Victoria theatres and is organist at Holy Rosary Church and teacher at Royal Conservatory, Toronto, and formerly at St. Michael's Schola Cantorum. Has appeared in recitals for Toronto Casavant Society.

Address: 37 Southvale Drive, Toronto, Ont.

COMPOSITIONS

TITLE	DATE	TYPE	TIME (MIN.)	PUBLISHER
Stabat Mater	1941	*tenor, choir, orch.*	45	MS.
Variations on "The Carman's Whistle"	1943	*orchestra*	15	MS.
Babbling		*orchestra*	3½	K. Prowse
Rondelet		*orchestra*	3	K. Prowse
Rhapsody on two English folk tunes	1938	*harp and orchestral*		MS.
Parade of the Sunbeams		*orch. or band*	2½	K. Prowse
Concerto for Electric Organ	1945	*organ, dance orch.*	15-20	MS.
String Quartet	1936	*string quartet*	25	MS.
Trio	1937	*vln, vc, piano*	20	MS.
Trio	1937	*guitar, fl, va*	12	MS.
Algonquin Legend	1942	*vln and piano or strings*	6	MS.
Sonata	1932	*organ*	20	MS.
Concerto for Organ	1935	*organ*	30	MS.
Postlude on Victimae Paschali	1944	*organ*	4	MS.
Mass for Four Voices	1946	*choir and organ*	20	MS.
Mass on Easter Themes	1947	*choir and organ*	20	MS.
Mass "Jesu Redemptor Omnium"	1949	*choir and organ*	15	MS.
Offertory-Motet "Terra Tremuit"	1948	*choir and organ*	3½	MS.
The Three Rivers	1949	*vocal*	3	MS.

MacLeod, Philip Arnold

Pianist and composer. Born in Calgary, Alta., 1908.

Music teachers included Hutcheson, Ernest Consolo, Tobias Matthay, York Bowen (piano), B. J. Dale (composition). Studied at Royal Academy of Music, London and University of Toronto. Degrees: Mus.Bac. (Toronto, 1948), B.A. (Univ. of British

Columbia). Professional pianist. Has given recitals in London and New York Town Hall, over BBC and CBC.

Address: 6135 MacDonald Street, Vancouver, B.C.

COMPOSITIONS

TITLE	DATE	TYPE	TIME (MIN.)	PUBLISHER
Variations on a Scottish Ballad		*orchestra*		MS.
Quartet for Strings	1949	*string quartet*	23-24	MS.
Sonata	1950	*vln and piano*		MS.
Sarabande (style of early 18th century)		*piano or strgs*		MS.
Two Fugues		*piano or strgs*		MS.
Cradle Song (A. MacLeod)	1950	*vocal*	1-1½	MS.

MacMillan, Sir Ernest Campbell

Conductor, organist, pianist, lecturer and composer. Born in Mimico, Ont., August 18th, 1893.

Musical education in Edinburgh with F. Niecks, A. Hollins, Dr. W. B. Ross and in Paris. Made his debut as concert organist at the age of ten. When 13 received A.R.C.O. diploma and in 1911 F.R.C.O. diploma. When 14 was appointed organist of Knox Church, Toronto. When 18 received Mus.Bac. degree from Oxford University. While visiting Bayreuth in 1914 war broke out and he was interned in Ruhleben near Berlin for four years. On his return to Canada toured extensively as organist.

Principal of the Toronto Conservatory of Music, 1926-42 and dean, faculty of music, Univ. of Toronto since 1926. In 1931 was appointed conductor of the Toronto Symphony Orchestra and in 1942 conductor of Toronto Mendelssohn Choir. Chairman, Canadian Music Council; President, CAPAC.

Has been guest conductor with symphony orchestras in London, Edinburgh, New York, Hollywood Bowl, Chicago, Philadelphia, Washington, Detroit, Rio de Janeiro, Australia and in many cities of Canada. Was knighted in 1935 by His late Majesty King George V.

Degrees: B.A. (Modern History, Toronto), Mus.Doc. (Oxon.), LL.D. (U. of B.C.), LL.D. (Queen's), Mus.Doc. (Laval), Litt.D. (McMaster). Diplomas: F.R.C.O. (Lafontaine prize), F.R.C.M. (elected 1931), Hon. R.A.M. (1938).

Address: 135 College Street, Toronto, Ont.

Affiliation: CAPAC.

COMPOSITIONS

TITLE	DATE	TYPE	TIME (MIN.)	PUBLISHER
England (Ode by Swinburne)		*soli, choir, orch.*	40	Novello
Te Deum		*chorus and orchestra*	8	MS.
A Song of Deliverance		*chorus and orchestra*		Oxford U.P.
Concert Overture in A		*orchestra*	12	MS.
Two Sketches: "Notre Seigneur en pauvre", "A Saint Malo"		*string orchestra or string quartet*	7½ 7½	rental Oxford U.P.
String Quartet in C minor		*string quartet*	25	MS.
Six Bergerettes du Bas Canada (arr.)		*3-5 voices, ob, va, vc, hp*	18	Oxford U.P.
Two Carols		*voice, strg trio or piano*	6	F. Harris

COMPOSITIONS

TITLE	DATE	TYPE	TIME (MIN.)	PUBLISHER
Four Chansons of French Canada (arr.)		*male chorus*		Boston Music
Three Indian Songs of the West Coast		*vocal*		F. Harris
21 Songs of French Canada		*vocal*		F. Harris

Arrangements for orchestra (all in manuscript):

Adagio from Beethoven's *Pathetique Sonata; Nocturne in E flat* by Chopin; Adagio from Mendelssohn's first Organ Sonata; *Scottish Songs, A St. Andrew's Day Medley; A Medley of Carols.*

Song books:

Northland Songs (G. V. Thompson); *A Canadian Song Book* (Dent).

Educational works (all published by Frederick Harris):

On the Preparation of Ear Tests; Graded Piano Sight Reading Exercises (with H. Willan); with Boris Berlin: *The Modern Piano Student; Our Piano Class; Twenty Lessons in Ear Training*, grades 1 to 6.

Recording:

Two Sketches for String Orchestra (CBC Canadian Album No. 2).

MacNutt, Walter Louis

Organist and composer. Born in Charlottetown, P.E.I., June 2nd, 1910.

Musical education at Royal Conservatory, Toronto with Healey Willan (organ and composition) and Reginald Godden (piano). Organist at Church of the Holy Trinity, Toronto until 1942. After serving in the army was organist at All Saints' Church, Winnipeg (1946-49) and since 1949 has been at All Saints' Church, Windsor.

Address: c/o All Saints' Church, Windsor, Ont.

Affiliation: BMI.

COMPOSITIONS

TITLE	DATE	TYPE	TIME (MIN.)	PUBLISHER
Island of the Fay		*orchestra*	18	MS.
String Suite		*strings*	10	MS.
Violin Sonata		*vln and piano*	20	MS.
Piano Suite		*piano*	10	F. Harris
Ride on in Majesty		*choral*	5	Carl Fischer
Missa Sancti Aidani		*choral*	10	Faith
Two Songs		*vocal*	3-5	F. Harris
Two Songs	1936-37	*vocal*	ea. 2	Western Music
Two Songs of Wm. Blake	1934	*vocal*	ea. 3	BMI Canada
Wedding Hymn (arr. from Handel)	1950	*vocal*	4	BMI Canada
Atque Vale	1934	*vocal*	4½	BMI Canada

Mann, Frederic George

Organist, choirmaster, music teacher and composer. Born in Norwich, England, December 11th, 1889.

Started musical career as boy chorister. Teachers included Dr. E. Bunnett, Dr. J. P. Illsley, Dr. H. Sanders. Came to Canada in 1906. Has been organist and choirmaster in Ottawa and for 27 years at St. John's Church, Peterborough. Hon. local secretary of faculty of music, McGill University since 1923. Member, Canadian College of Organists since 1916. Conductor of Scottish Rite Choir (Octette) of Peterborough.

Address: 199 London Street, Peterborough, Ont.

COMPOSITIONS

TITLE	DATE	TYPE	TIME (MIN.)	PUBLISHER
Grand Choeur in G	1936	*organ*	5	Novello
I Will Give Thanks	1927	*choral*	5	Novello
I Know My Redeemer Lives	1932	*choral*	4	Novello
Crossing the Bar	1928	*choral*	3	Novello
Lead Kindly Light	1929	*choral*	4	Novello
O Great First Cause	1928	*choral*	3	Novello
Introit for Christmas	1928	*choral*	2	Anglo-Canadian
Communion Office in A flat	1922	*choral*		Ashmall
Communion Office in F	1950	*choral*		to be published
Intercession Hymn (for war)	1939	*choral*	3	to be published
Call Yo'Chillun Home	1938	*choral*	3	photostat
The Wondrous Birth (words and music)	1936	*vocal*	3	Novello

Manson, Robert Graham

Violinist, violist, pianist and composer. Born in London, England, June 11th, 1883. Died in Toronto, February 14th, 1950.

Musical education at Royal College of Music, London. Teachers included Arthur Somervell, Sir Frederick Bridge and Sir Charles Stanford. Was violinist in many London orchestras, violist in the Scottish and Cleveland orchestras. For 20 years played with Toronto Symphony Orchestra. Was on staff of the Hambourg Conservatory of Music, Toronto.

COMPOSITIONS

TITLE	DATE	TYPE	TIME (MIN.)	PUBLISHER
Symphony in C minor		*orchestra*	25	MS.
An Atlantean Episode (tone poem)		*orchestra*	12	MS.
Niagara		*orchestra*	8	MS.
Canadian Fantasy		*orchestra or band*	12	MS.
Ukrainian Fantasy		*orchestra or band*	13	MS.
Quintet in F major		*wind instruments*	18	MS.
Quartet in D major		*string quartet*	15	MS.
Alouette		*string quartet*	3	MS.

Many arrangements of folk songs for flute, oboe, clarinet and strings.

Margolian, Samuel

Violinist and composer. Born in Yarmouth, N.S., July 27th, 1922.

Musical education at Dalhousie University and Halifax Conservatory with Ifan Williams and H. L. Burchell, at University of Toronto and Royal Conservatory, Toronto with Kathleen Parlow, Leo Smith and Arnold Walter. Degree: Mus.Bac. (1941). In 1940 was awarded scholarship to study for three years at Royal Academy, London. In 1943, '44 won CAPAC prizes for composition. Since 1946 has given recitals throughout England and Wales. Won Royal Philharmonic Prize for Violin Concerto No. 2 (1948) and Royal Academy Prize for Piano Variations (1949). Studied with Howard Ferguson and returned to Canada in 1949.

Address: 270 George Street, Fredericton, N.B.

COMPOSITIONS

TITLE	DATE	TYPE	TIME (MIN.)	PUBLISHER
Alice in Wonderland (ballet)	1945	*orchestra*	21	MS.
Fugue		*orchestra*	3½	MS.
Violin Concerto No. 1		*vln and orchestra*	23	MS.
Violin Concerto No. 2	1947	*vln and orchestra*	18	MS.
Viola Concerto	1949	*va, string quartet*	13	MS.
Viola Sonata	1948	*va, string quartet*	12	MS.
String Suite		*string orchestra*	16	MS.
Fugue-Waltz		*string orchestra*	5	MS.
String Quartet in G		*string quartet*	18	MS.
String Quartet in E		*string quartet*	23	MS.
String Quartet in F		*string quartet*	17	MS.
Trio for Woodwind	1949	*ob, clar, bn*	8	MS.
Sonata		*vc and piano*	15	MS.
Sonata		*vln and piano*	10	MS.
Sonatina		*vln and piano*	10	MS.
Theme and Variations	1948	*piano*	8	MS.
Sonatina		*piano*	12	MS.
Psalm 107		*choir and organ*	15	MS.
Psalm 150		*choir and organ*	8½	MS.
With Rue My Heart is Laden		*vocal*	4	MS.
Daisies		*vocal*	3	MS.
The Fly		*vocal*	2½	MS.

Martin, Abbé Charles-Amador

Priest and musician. Born in Quebec, March 7th, 1648. Died in Sainte-Foy near Quebec, June 19th, 1711.

Classical education at Jesuit College and theological studies at Seminary in Quebec. The second Canadian to be ordained priest (1671). Parish priest in Beauport, Sainte-Famille, Chateau-Richer and Sainte-Foy; canon of Quebec cathedral. Singer and composer of merit. The prose *Sainte-Famille* is the oldest composition in Canada of which the manuscript has been preserved. It was written for the celebration of the Sainte-Famille (2nd Sunday after Epiphany). The words were written by Abbé de Santeuil of Paris.

COMPOSITION

TITLE	DATE	TYPE	TIME (MIN.)	PUBLISHER
Prose "Sainte-Famille"	1670	*plain chant*		MS. at Hôtel-Dieu, Quebec

See:

Le Jeune, *Dictionnaire Général du Canada*, Ottawa, 1931.

Gosselin, *Mgr De Laval*, vol. I.

Masella, Raffaele

Clarinetist, pianist and composer. Born in Montreal, P.Q., October 1st, 1922.

Musical education at McGill Conservatorium with Jos. Moretti (clarinet), Henri Miro, Claude Champagne (harmony), at Juilliard School of Music, N.Y. and in Paris at Conservatoire, 1946-48. Was member of H.M. Canadian Grenadier Guards Band and plays clarinet with Montreal CBC orchestra, Les Concert Symphoniques and the Little Symphony. Placed second at Geneva International Competition among 23 clarinetists and won first prize at Paris Conservatoire.

Address: 6747 Drolet Street, Montreal, P.Q.

TITLE	DATE	COMPOSITIONS TYPE	TIME (MIN.)	PUBLISHER
The Navy on Parade		band	3	MS.
La Petite Canadienne		band or piano	3	MS.
Menuet (17th century)		strgs or piano	3½	MS.
Adagio		strings	3½	MS.
Elegie		Fr. hn, piano	2½	MS.
Sonata (2 mvmts)	1947	vln and piano	10	MS.
Fantasia		piano		MS.
Variations		piano		MS.
L'Entrée de mon amour		vocal	2	MS.
Till We Meet Again		vocal		MS.

Mathieu, André

Pianist and composer. Born in Montreal, February 18th, 1929.

Musical education in Montreal with Rodolphe Mathieu, in Paris with Alfred Cortot, Giraud Latarse, Jacques de la Presle, Jules Gentil and Simonne Féjard, in New York with Harold Morriss. Won two scholarships from the Province of Quebec to study in Europe. Gave first recital at the age of four and a half in Montreal. Recent concert tours to Europe (1946, 47) and through United States and Canada (1948,49). Son of Rodolphe Mathieu.

Address: 4519 Berri, Montreal, P.Q.

TITLE	DATE	COMPOSITIONS TYPE	TIME (MIN.)	PUBLISHER
Concerto No. 1		piano, orchestra	10	MS.
Concerto No. 2		piano, orchestra	15	MS.
Concerto No. 3 including "Quebec Concerto"	1944	piano, orchestra	30 10	MS. Southern Music
Concerto No. 4	1949	piano, orchestra	20	MS.
Trio	1947	vln, vc, piano	20	MS.
Sonata	1943	vln and piano	20	MS.
Fantaisie Brésilienne		vln and piano		Parnasse Musical
Trois études		piano	4	Southern Music
Trois pièces pittoresques (Danse sauvage; Procession d'elephants; Les Mouettes)		piano	9	Senart, Paris
Trois pièces pour les enfants (Tristesse; Hommage à Mozart; Berceuse)		piano	9	Senart, Paris
Dans la nuit		piano	2	Southern Music
Les Gros Chars		piano	2	Southern Music
Les Abeilles		piano	1½	Southern Music
Les Vagues		piano	5	MS.
Saisons		piano	15	MS.
Deux Laurentiennes	1942	piano	12	MS.
Cinq Bagatelles	1943	piano	15	MS.
Fantaisie	1948	piano	7	MS.
Quatre mélodies	1948	vocal	10	MS.

Recordings:

Quebec Concerto (from movie *Whispering City*, Parlophone); Trois études; *Les Abeilles; Dans la nuit; Danse sauvage* (performed by the composer, Boîte à musique).

Mathieu, Rodolphe

Pianist and composer. Born in Grondines, P.Q., July 10th, 1896.

Musical education at Schola Cantorum of Paris with Vincent d'Indy. Teacher of harmony, counterpoint and fugue at the Institute Pedagogique de Montréal and at Couvent des Soeurs de Ste.-Anne, Lachine, P.Q. Founder and director of the Canadian Institute of Music.

Address: 4519 Berri, Montreal, P.Q.

COMPOSITIONS

TITLE	DATE	TYPE	TIME (MIN.)	PUBLISHER
Trois Préludes		*orchestra*	10	Hérel, Paris
Chant Patriotique		*choir and orch.*	8	Musique Canadienne (R. Mathieu)
Melodies		*voice and orch.*	8	MS.
Quintet	1946	*piano, str. quart*	20	MS.
Quartet		*string quartet*	15	MS.
Deux Poèmes		*voice and str. qua.*	10	MS.
Sonate		*'cello and piano*	15	MS.
Sonate		*piano*	15	MS.
Chevauchée		*piano*	6	MS.
Saisons Canadiennes		*vocal*	20	MS.

Book:

Parlons Musique, Levesque, 1932.

See:

Léo-Pol Morin, *Papiers de Musique*, 1930.

Matton, Roger

Composer and pianist. Born in Granby, P.Q., May 18th, 1929.

Musical education at Quebec Provincial Conservatory in Montreal with Claude Champagne (composition), Arthur Letondal (piano) and Gabriel Cusson (musical dictation), in Paris at Conservatoire for one year with Olivier Messiaen (analysis) and Mme Arthur Honegger (counterpoint). Works have been performed in Norway under Alexander Brott and on CBC.

Address: 214 rue St.-Jacques, Granby, P.Q.

COMPOSITIONS

TITLE	DATE	TYPE	TIME (MIN.)	PUBLISHER
Pax (symphonic suite, 3 parts)	1950	*orchestra*	20	MS.
Danse Brésilienne	1946	*orchestra (arr. 2 pianos)*	8	MS.
Danse Lente (Gymnopédie)	1947	*orchestra*	4	MS.
Concerto for Saxophone	1948	*strings and percussion*	14	MS.
String Quartet	1949	*string quartet*	15	MS.
Etude	1946	*clar and piano*	5	MS.

COMPOSITIONS

TITLE	DATE	TYPE	TIME (MIN.)	PUBLISHER
Three Préludes	1946, 48, 50	*piano*	11	MS.
Berceuse	1945	*piano*	3½	MS.
Suite sur thèmes grégoriens (Ite missa est; prière; choral)	1950	*organ*	14	MS.

McCaughan, Abbé Dr. Paul Emile

Priest, organist and composer. Born in Montreal, May 18th, 1911.

Musical education with Frédéric Payette, Jean-Julien Clossey, Etienne Guillet and Georges-Emile Tanguay. Degrees: B.A. (1932), Licentiate in Theology (1936), Mus.Doc. (Montreal, 1945). Diploma of teacher of Gregorian chant (1933), Diplôme de Maître de Chapelle et Titre de Lauréat de la Schola Cantorum (1934). Ordained as priest in 1936. Teacher at College André-Grasset from 1936-39 and 1941-50.

Address: 54 Bellingham Road, Outremont, P.Q.

COMPOSITIONS

TITLE	DATE	TYPE	TIME (MIN.)	PUBLISHER
Messe solennelle, G minor	1938	*choir and organ*		McCaughan
Messe solennelle	1943	*choir and organ*		McCaughan
Hodie Christus Natus Est	1949	*choir and organ*		Blé d'or
Messe Cathédrale	1944	*choir and organ*		MS.
Tantum Ergo (motet)	1950	*choir and organ*		MS.
Panis Angelicus (motet)	1950	*choir and organ*		MS.
O Salutaris (motet)	1938	*choral*		MS.
Laetantur Coeli (motet)	1940	*choral*		MS.
Hymne à la Musique	1950	*choral*		MS.
Plaisir d'amour (by Martini, arranged)	1950	*choral*		MS.
Alleluia	1939	*voice and piano*		McCaughan
Notre Père	1940	*voice and piano*		McCaughan
La Valse du Souvenir	1944	*voice and piano*		C-H. Grignon, depository
La Valse du Muguet	1946	*voice and piano*		McCaughan
Pourquoi m'as-tu-quitté?	1949	*voice and piano*		Blé d'or
Les Trottoirs de bois	1949	*voice and piano*		Blé d'or
O Douce Providence	1941	*voice and piano*		MS.
Grand Air de Nadya	1943	*voice and piano*		MS.
Regrets	1943	*voice and piano*		MS.
L'Oraison dominicale	1949	*voice and organ*		Blé d'or
Agnus Dei (motet)	1949	*voice and organ*		MS.
Ecce Panis (motet)	1950	*voice and organ*		MS.

In preparation: Symphony in C minor

Book:

La Philosophie de la Musique, Essai de Synthèse (doctor thesis), publ. 1946, Les Editions du Blé d'or, 54 Bellingham Road, Outremont, P.Q.

McCauley, William Alexander

Trombonist, pianist, arranger and composer. Born in Tofield, Alta., February 14th, 1917.

Musical education with Margaret Parsons (piano), Harry Hawe and Rudolph Baumler (trombone). Degree and diploma: Mus.Bac. (Toronto, 1947), A.T.C.M. Has played with various popular orchestras. In 1942 was made assistant bandmaster. RCAF (later became pilot). In 1947 was appointed director of music and teacher of instrumental music at Ottawa Technical High School. In 1949 joined Crawley Films as director of music. Since 1947 has been first trombone player with National Film Board and Ottawa Philharmonic Orchestra. *Day Dreams* was performed by CBC Symphony Band, 1942.

Address: 306 Oakdale Avenue, Ottawa, Ont.

Affiliation: CAPAC.

COMPOSITIONS

TITLE	DATE	TYPE	TIME (MIN.)	PUBLISHER
To-morrow To-day (movie background)	1950	*orchestra*	15	MS.
Pierre and Marie (movie background) (based on Fr.-Can. folk songs)	1950	*orchestra*	12	MS.
Newfoundland (movie background)	1951	*orchestra*	30	MS.
Day Dreams (tone poem)	1940	*band*	10	MS.
Canadian Ski Trail (rondo)	1948	*band*	10	MS.
String Quartet No. 1	1947	*string quartet*	15	MS.

McIntyre, Margaret

Violinist and composer. Born in England.

Studied music at Royal Manchester College of Music and at Cornish School of Music, Seattle, U.S. Started musical career as a concert violinist. Came to Canada in 1930 and started to teach music. Has done radio and concert work, trained small orchestras and vocal groups. *Lost Lagoon* won prize in CBC International Service song writing contest.

Address: Roberts Creek, B.C.

COMPOSITIONS

TITLE	DATE	TYPE	TIME (MIN.)	PUBLISHER
Valse in E minor	1930	*orchestra*	10	MS.
Three Nocturnes	1949	*orchestra*	20	MS.
Song of Autumn	1935	*orchestra*	20	MS.
Songs of the North	1950	*sop, female choir, orchestra*		MS.
Chinese Songs	1949	*vocal*		MS.
Four Songs	1930-40	*vocal*		MS.
Lost Lagoon	1949	*vocal*	5	MS.

McIntyre, Paul Poirier

Composer and pianist. Born in Peterborough, Ont., October 7th, 1931.

Musical education at Senior School, Royal Conservatory, Toronto and faculty of music, University of Toronto. Teachers: Dr. Arnold Walter and Oscar Morawetz (composition), Béla Böszörményi-Nagy (piano). Degree: Mus.Bac. (Toronto, 1951). Awarded CAPAC scholarship in 1949, 1950 and 1951.

Address: 40 Vanderhoof Avenue, Toronto, Ont.

Affiliation: CAPAC.

COMPOSITIONS

TITLE	DATE	TYPE	TIME (MIN.)	PUBLISHER
String Quartet	1951	*string quartet*	16	MS.
Trio-Serenade in E	1949	*vln, vc, piano*	6-7	MS.
Scherzo	1949	*flute and piano*	5	MS.
Theme and Variations	1950	*piano*	10	MS.
Sonatina	1950	*piano*	10	MS.
Sonata	1951	*piano*	10	MS.
Four Songs (De La Mare)	1950	*vocal*	7	MS.

McIver, Allan

Pianist, conductor and composer. Born in Thetford Mines, P.Q., January 17th, 1904.

Musical studies on flute, violin and piano. Has worked in theatres and concert halls. At present arranges and conducts CBC radio programs.

Address: 4855 Maplewood Avenue, Montreal, P.Q.

COMPOSITIONS

TITLE	DATE	TYPE	TIME (MIN.)	PUBLISHER
Francesca		*orchestra*	4	Southern Music
2½ Dominic Court		*orchestra*	4	MS.
Fiddler's Frolic	1951	*orchestra*	3	MS.
Les Lumières de ma ville (movie)	1950	*orchestra*		MS.
Timpani		*band*	4	MS.

Many scores for dramatic broadcasts.

McNichol, Frederick William

Conductor and composer. Born in Saint John, N.B., January 5th, 1884.

Musical education at New England Conservatory of Music, Boston with Benjamin Cutter. Bandmaster with 3rd Regt. Canadian Artillery 1905-14; Temple Band, Saint John, N.B., 1910-14; 95th Batt. Queen's Own Rifles, Toronto, overseas 1915-17; 2nd Canadian Garrison Regt., Toronto, 1918. Not engaged in musical activities at present.

Address: 366 Main Street, Saint John, N.B.

COMPOSITIONS

TITLE	DATE	TYPE	TIME (MIN.)	PUBLISHER
Sons of Britain		*band or orchestra*		Carl Fischer
Flanders		*band*		Carl Fischer
Castle Hall		*band*		Carl Fischer
Nearer My God to Thee		*band*		Carl Fischer
L'Argonne		*band*		Fillmore
Dakar		*band*		MS.

McTaggart, John

Organist, conductor, piano and voice teacher and composer. Born in Great Britain.

Musical education with Sir Charles Stanford, Dr. W. H. Hunt, Dr. A. W. Marchant, Dr. A. J. Greenish (theory of composition), A. Visetti, Dr. Hunt (singing), W. H. Jude (organ), John Evans (piano). Diplomas: L.R.A.M., A.R.C.M., L.T.C.M., Fellow of the Tonic Solfa College, Member, Royal Society of Teachers (London, England).

Was teacher at Sutton (Surrey) Conservatoire and sometime lecturer in public speaking at St. John's College, Winnipeg. Was choirmaster and organist in various churches in Scotland. Conductor of orchestras, amateur opera and choral societies in Scotland and in Winnipeg, including CBC *Zephyr Strings*.

Address: 23 Whittier Apts., Winnipeg, Man.

COMPOSITIONS

TITLE	DATE	TYPE	TIME (MIN.)	PUBLISHER
A Ruler in Israel (Christmas cantata)		*cantata*		J. Curwen
Peridot and Mirami (operetta for schools, libretto by Effie McTaggart)		*operetta*		MS.
Five Short Pieces for Young Piano Students		*piano*		MS.
Idyll		*vln and piano*		MS.
Seven Scots Songs		*choral (S.S.A.)*		J. Curwen
Seven Scots Songs (second series)		*choral (S.S.A.)*		MS.
Thine Am I, My Faithful Fair		*choral*		MS.
To Daisies		*choral*		MS.
A Lullaby		*choral*		Paterson
Search Me O God (anthem)		*choral*		Beal, Studdard
The Song of Selma (song cycle, Ossianic)		*vocal*		MS.

Songs in manuscript:

A Lullaby; An Easter Song; Phantom; Invictus; The Last Invocation; A Lover's Greeting; The Song of the Shulamite (orchestra or piano); In Leinster; Exiled; The Music of the Sea; Du hast Diamanten und Perlen; Golden Bridges; Sunday Up the River; O Stars that Tremble; The Tortoise-shell Cat; etc.

Sacred works:

Evening Service (Magnificat and Nunc Dimittis); Three Short Introductory Sentences; Bread of the World; Eight Hymn Tunes; Two Vespers.

Meek, Kenneth

Organist, virginalist and composer. Born in England, May 21st, 1908.

Musical education with Dr. Herbert Sanders. Degree: Mus.Bac. (Toronto). Has been church organist since the age of 16. On faculty of McGill Conservatorium, Montreal.

Address: 1104 Elgin Terrace, Montreal, P.Q.

COMPOSITIONS

TITLE	DATE	TYPE	TIME (MIN.)	PUBLISHER
The Consolation of Israel		*cantata*	25	MS.
Green Bushes		*small orchestra*	10	MS.
Darby and Joan		*strings*	9	MS.
Brother Arbeau's Pavane (variations)		*2 pianos*		MS.
Eleven Friends		*piano*		MS.

Mercure, Pierre

Composer, basson and violoncello player, pianist and conductor. Born in Montreal, February 21st, 1927.

Studied piano, bassoon and 'cello at Quebec Provincial Conservatory. Since September 1949 has studied music in Paris on a bursary of the Province of Quebec. Teachers: Leon Barzin (conducting), Claude Champagne Nadia Boulanger,, Darius Milhaud, Arthur Hoérée (composition) and Jean Fournet (conducting).

Has played second bassoon in Les Concerts Symphoniques de Montréal and in other Montreal orchestras.

Address: 3849 Kent Avenue, Montreal, P.Q.

Affiliation: BMI.

COMPOSITIONS

TITLE	DATE	TYPE	TIME (MIN.)	PUBLISHER
`Alice in Wonderland (incidental music)	1946	4 sopranos, chamber orch.	25	MS.
Kaleidoscope (symphonic fantasy)	1947-48	orchestra	12	MS.
Pantomime	1949	14 winds, tymp	5¼	MS.
Lucrèce Borgia	1949	tpt, hpchd, perc.	4	MS.
Emprise	1950	clar, bn, vc, piano	8	MS.
Ils ont détruit la ville	1950	choir, 18 instr.	5	MS.
Colloque	1947	vocal	3	BMI Canada
Duality (ballet music)	1948	tpt and piano	5	MS.

Mignault, Alfred J. E.

Pianist, organist and composer. Born in St. Augustin, Deux Montagnes, P.Q., December 8th, 1895.

Musical education with Eugène Lapierre and Emile Lambert (organ), Alfred Laliberté, Léo-Pol Morin (piano), J. Harbour (harmony). Organist in many churches in and around Montreal. For two years was director of the radio presentation l'Heure Provinçiale. Is on teaching staff of Quebec Provincial Conservatory. Director of vocal instruction for the catholic schools of Montreal.

Address: 87 West St. Joseph Boulevard, Montreal, P.Q.

COMPOSITIONS

TITLE	DATE	TYPE	TIME (MIN.)	PUBLISHER
Divertissement		piano and orchestra	12	MS.
Petite Suite		orchestra	11	MS.
Minstrels		small orchestra	2	MS.
Intermezzo		string quintet	3	MS.
Ronde Canadienne		vln, vc, piano	1½	MS.
Meditation		violin	1¾	MS.
Chant Russe		'cello	2	MS.
Andalouse		'cello	3	MS.
Legende		'cello	3	MS.
Suite in Olden Style		'cello	14¾	MS.
Petite Pastorale en re		organ		A. J. Boucher
Pastorale en fa		organ		MS.
Rhapsodie sur les "Noël"		organ		MS.

Works for piano in manuscript (1-7 minutes each):
Crepuscule (nocturne); *Page d'Album; Rossignol sauvage; Theme et Variations; Flutes de Pan; Piano d'Italie; Le Grillon; Prelude Romantique; Minstrels; Scherzo.*

COMPOSITIONS

TITLE	DATE	TYPE	TIME (MIN.)	PUBLISHER
Cor Jesu		*choral*	1¾	A. Mignault
Ecce Fidelis		*choral*	¾	A. Mignault
Homo Quidam		*choral*	2½	A. J. Boucher
O Salutaris		*choral*	2½	A. J. Boucher
Messe de Requiem		*choral*	35	MS.

Choral works in manuscript (1-4 minutes each):
Mimi pinson; La Violette double; Justus ut palma; Cor Jesu; Laudate.

Les Cloches du soir		*vocal*	3	Ed. du Conservatoire
Souvenez-vous, Vierge Marie		*vocal*	2	A. Mignault
Ave Maria		*vocal*	2	A. J. Boucher
Je vous salue, Marie		*vocal*	2	Archambault
Notre Père		*vocal*	3	A. Mignault

Songs in manuscript (1½-3 minutes each):
Rondel; Je veux dire; Melodie; Chiens; Allegorie pastorale; Cantique Profane; Mes vers fuiraient; Chanson de mer; J'ai grand' peur des loups; Ave Verum. Several folk song settings.

Miles, William Maurice

Violoncellist, pianist and composer. Born in Erith, Kent, England, 1883.

Musical education at Royal Academy of Music, London with Alessandro Pezzi ('cello) and F. W. Davenport (composition). Came to Winnipeg in 1905. Resided there until 1923, teaching and playing the 'cello. Moved to Vancouver in 1923.

Address: 3575 West 37th Avenue, Vancouver, B.C.

Affiliation: CAPAC.

COMPOSITIONS

TITLE	DATE	TYPE	TIME (MIN.)	PUBLISHER
The Two Swans (tone poem after T. Hood)	1948	*orchestra*	4½	MS.
Andante and Scherzo		*string orchestra*	6½	MS.
Novelette		*string orchestra*	5	MS.
Four Pastels		*string orchestra*	13½	MS.
Symphonic Suite		*string orchestra*	25	MS.
Leaves from an old sketch book (suite)		*string orchestra*	8½	MS.
Threnody and Dance		*small orchestra*	6½	MS.
Quintet in D		*piano and str. qua.*		MS.
Quartet		*string quartet*	25	MS.
Quartet		*4 'cellos*	20	MS.
Sonate		*violin*	20½	MS.
Sonate		*'cello*	22	MS.
Sonate		*hn and piano*	17	MS.
Three Elizabethan Lyrics		*vocal*	17	MS.

Milette, Dr. Juliette
(Soeur M.-Henri de la Croix)

Teacher of organ and Gregorian chant, composer. Born in Montreal, June 17th, 1900.

Musical education at Ecole Supérieure de Musique d'Outremont with Alfred Laliberté (piano), Raoul Pâquet (organ), Claude Champagne (composition). Degree: Mus.Doc. (Montreal, "magna cum laude", 1949).

Teacher at Ecole Supérieure.

Address: 1410 Mount Royal Boulevard, Outremont, P.Q.

COMPOSITIONS

TITLE	DATE	TYPE	TIME (MIN.)	PUBLISHER
Leur Maison	1945	*oratorio (organ acc.)*	60	MS.
Prélude et fugue	1938	*organ*	10	MS.
Chorals variés 1. G major	1936	*organ*	5	MS.
2 B minor	1937	*organ*	8½	MS.
Aurore printanière	1935	*choral*	2	MS.
Notre Père	1936	*choral*	2	MS.
Aubade	1937	*choral*	2	MS.
O Mère, ton étoile	1940	*duet*	1½	MS.
Marie, o douce Souveraine	1940	*duet*	3	MS.
Notre-Dame du Canada	1950	*duet*	4	MS.
Les Cloches d'argent (cantata)	1950	*2 children's voices*	5	MS.

Miró, Henri (Enrique)

Pianist, conductor and composer. Born in Tarrega, Spain, November 13th, 1879. Died in Montreal, July 19th, 1950.

Musical education in Spain at Montserrat Music School and at Barcelona Conservatory of Music. For three years toured in France with opera companies. In 1902 settled in Montreal where he was engaged for over 40 years in conducting, arranging and composing. For four years was musical director for the Berliner Talking Machine Company. Conducted feature radio programs. Winner of the *Prix Lallemand* for composition in 1936.

Affiliation (estate): CAPAC.

COMPOSITIONS

TITLE	DATE	TYPE	TIME (MIN.)	PUBLISHER
Roman de Suzon		*operetta*	60	MS.
Lolita		*operetta*	60	MS.
Messe solennelle		*choir, soli, orch.*	90	MS. performed 1904
Vox Populi		*choir, soli, orch.*	30	MS.
Two Concertos		*'cello and orch.*	45	MS.
Symphonic Canadienne		*orchestra*	25	MS.
Luxor (symphonic suite)		*orchestra*	25	MS.
Scènes Mauresques		*orchestra*	8	MS.
Deux Préludes Symphoniques		*orchestra*	12	MS.
Dans le jardin du rêve		*orchestra*	12	MS.

COMPOSITIONS

TITLE	DATE	TYPE	TIME (MIN.)	PUBLISHER
Entr'acte Symphonique		*orchestra*	4	MS.
Mercedès (valse)		*orchestra*	3	G. Schirmer
Chanson Mauresque		*orchestra*	3-4	MS.
A los Toros (paso-doble)		*orchestra*	3	MS.
Paquita (tango-habanera)		*small orchestra*	3	MS.
A donde vas? (tango-argentino)		*small orchestra*	3	MS.
Confidencia (tango-argentino)		*small orchestra*	3	MS.
Serenade		*vln and orch.*	10	MS.
Romance		*violin*		La Lyre
Water, Love, Dream, Star, Moon and Cigarette Symphonies		*soli and choir*	ea. 30	MS.
Tota pulchra es Maria		*choral*		La Lyre
Nuit d'amour (chanson valse)		*voice, piano or orchestra*		published
Enchantement (romance)		*voice, piano or orchestra*		published

Piano works published by La Lyre:

O Canada mon pays, mes amours (arranged); *Douce pensée; Pompadour; Nocturne; Danse des patins; Abeille et Papillon; Silhouette; Danse infernale; Etude en octavas; Prière; Gondoliera; Constellation* (manuscript).

Vocal works published by La Lyre:

La Rose du Boulevard; Au Pays d'Allah; La Conquête; Je veux sécher tes yeux; A qui mon coeur; Si tu reviens; L'Auberge du coeur; Puisque l'amour nous rassemble; Prière pour un baiser; Méditation; Les Minutes; Je veux t'aimer; Couplets des moutons; Puisque tu reviens; Cantique à Ste Thérèse; Ne pleure plus, Lili! (published by Le Passe-Temps).

Various other compositions, published and unpublished.

Moisse, Séverin Joseph

Pianist, teacher and composer. Born in Chastre, Belgium, June 8th, 1895.

Musical education at Conservatoire Royale de Bruxelles (piano, solfeggio and theory). Has done much teaching at various schools in Belgium. Came to Canada in 1926. For several years was head of piano classes at McGill Conservatorium, Montreal. At present lives in Belgium.

COMPOSITIONS

TITLE	DATE	TYPE	TIME (MIN.)	PUBLISHER
Menuet dans le style ancien		*violin and piano*		Passe-Temps
Variations sur un thème de Paganini		*piano*		Parnasse Musical
Etude in C minor		*piano*		Parnasse Musical
Six petites études symétriques		*piano*		Parnasse Musical
Consolation		*vocal*		Parnasse Musical
You'll Find Canada There		*vocal*		Moisse
We Will Win the War		*vocal*		Moisse
Péché de Femme (popular)		*vocal*		Parnasse Musical

No recent information obtained.

Molt, Theodore F.

Music teacher, organist and pianist. Born in Germany c. 1796. Died in Burlington, Vermont, November 19th, 1856.

Came to Canada as a young man, settling in Quebec. From 1825-26 revisited Europe where he met Beethoven and other great musicians. After his return to Quebec taught music and was organist at the Cathedral, 1841-49. Later was professor of music at Burlington Female Seminary. The first writer of musical instruction books in Canada.

Compositions:

Sol Canadien, terre chérie (patriotic song)
  (Words by Isidore Bedard, publ. Jan. 1st, 1829)   Passe-Temps

T. F. Molt, the composer of the following piano works, published by Brainard is probably the Theodore F. Molt mentioned above.

June Training (slow march); *Lucy Long* (variations); *O Susanna* (variations); *Quickstep* (gallopade); *Swiss Boy* (variations).

Books:

Traité élémentaire de Musique, Quebec, 1828.
Traité élémentaire de Musique Vocale, Quebec, 1845.
Lyre Sainte, Quebec, 1844.
New and Original Method for the Pianoforte, Burlington.
The Pupil's Guide and Young Teacher's Manual, Burlington, 1854.

Montgomery, William Augustus

Organist, choirmaster and composer. Born in Hawick, Scotland, November 25th, 1872. Died in Halifax, N.S., December 18th, 1948.

Musical education with Dr. E. L. Allum, Dr. W. A. Marchant and Dr. Eaglefield Hull. Degree: Mus.Bac. (Durham, 1897). Diplomas: L.T.C.L., 1894, L.R.A.M., 1905, F.R.C.O., 1910.

Came to Canada in 1913 and held positions as organist in Sherbrooke, Calgary and since 1921 at Cathedral of All Saints in Halifax. In 1942 was made organist emeritus.

Inquiries: D. Hector Montgomery, 20 Henry Street, Halifax, N.S.

COMPOSITIONS

TITLE	DATE	TYPE	TIME (MIN.)	PUBLISHER
Grand Choeur in E flat		*organ*	4	Ashdown
Grand Choeur in D		*organ*		Novello
Andante Con Moto		*organ*	3	W. Reeves
In His Name	1935	*organ*	1½	Lorenz, N.Y.
Twilight Thoughts	1893	*organ*	3	Church Choir Guild
Ecclesiae Organum		*organ*		Patterson, London
Chant de repos		*vln and piano*	3	Mozart Allan, Glasgow
Summer Eve		*vln and piano*	2½	Mozart Allan, Glasgow
Gigue in D major		*piano*	2	Mozart Allan, Glasgow
Six Characteristic Sketches		*piano*		Joseph Williams
Carrissima		*piano*		Duff
Valse de salon	1898	*piano*	3½	Joseph Williams
In the Lord Put I My Trust	1929	*anthem*	2	Banks & Son, London

COMPOSITIONS

TITLE	DATE	TYPE	TIME (MIN.)	PUBLISHER
King of Love	1931	*anthem*	2½	Waterloo Music
Through the Day	1930	*anthem*	3	Waterloo Music
Life Is But a Melancholy Flower	1931	*choral*	2	O. Ditson
Greeting to the Flag	1935	*choral*	2	G. Schirmer
Royal Bethlehem (Christmas)		*choral or vocal*		Novello
Down to the Sea in Ships	1931	*vocal*	2½	Peter Derek
Journey of Life		*vocal*	2½	Mozart Allan
When Love is True		*vocal*	2½	Mozart Allan

Many other works. Altogether there are about 100 published and many unpublished works.

Moore, Ernest Alwyn

Organist, choral conductor and composer. Born in Queensbury, Yorkshire, England, May 30th, 1899.

Musical education at Durham University. Degree: Mus.Bac. Diploma: F.R.C.O. Came to Canada in 1939. Is organist and choir-director, McDougall Church, Edmonton and director of music, Alberta College, Edmonton.

Address: c/o Alberta College, Edmonton, Alta.

COMPOSITIONS

TITLE	DATE	TYPE	TIME (MIN.)	PUBLISHER
White Heather	1928	*piano*	3	W. Paxton
Minuet and Trio	1918	*organ*	3	Bayley & Ferguson
Prelude and Fugue	1922	*organ*	7	Bayley & Ferguson
Festival Toccata	1936	*organ*	6	MS.
Woodland Idyll	1939	*organ*	3	MS.
A Fugal Improvisation	1950	*organ*	6	MS.
Still, Still With Thee	1945	*anthem*	2½	G. V. Thompson
Vesper and Choral Amen	1924	*choral*	2	Bayley & Ferguson
Praise Ye The Lord (fugue)	1941	*choral*	4	MS.
A Wet Sheet and a Flowing Sea	1940	*choral*	4	MS.
Christmas Joy (carol)	1944	*vocal*	3	MS.

Morawetz, Oscar

Pianist and composer. Born in Czechoslovakia, January 17th, 1917.

Musical education at Prague Conservatory with Hofmeister (piano) and J. Kricka (theory), in Vienna with Julius Isserlis (piano), in Paris with Lazare Levy (piano), in Toronto at Royal Conservatory with Alberto Guerrero (piano) and Leo Smith (theory). Degree: Mus.Bac. (Toronto, 1943).

Is teacher of orchestration, harmony, counterpoint, score reading and composition at Royal Conservatory, Toronto. Won CAPAC composition award twice. Has written scores for National Film Board and background music for first Canadian full length film *Forbidden Journey*. Works have been performed by many artists and conductors (Firkusny, Maynor, Sir Adrian Boult, Sir Bernard Heinze, Sir Ernest MacMillan etc.) in Europe, Australia, Israel and America. Has played on CBC shortwave broadcasts.

Address: 17 Dewbourne Avenue, Toronto, Ont.

Affiliation: CAPAC.

COMPOSITIONS

TITLE	DATE	TYPE	TIME (MIN.)	PUBLISHER
Ouverture solemne		*orchestra*	15	MS.
Carnival Ouverture	1945	*orchestra*	5½	MS.
Anthem to Canada	1951	*choir, orchestra*	5	MS.
Serenade	1947	*strings*	6	MS.
String Quartet in F minor		*string quartet*	32	MS.
Piano Trio		*vln, vc, piano*	21	MS.
Duo	1945	*vln and piano*	8	MS.
Sonata		*vln and piano*	15	MS.
Ballade for 'Cello		*vc and piano*	7	MS.
Two Sonatas		*piano*	ea. 20	MS.
Scherzo	1946	*piano*	5	MS.
Fantasie	1948	*piano*	13	MS.
Tarantella	1949	*piano*	6	MS.
Ballade	1951	*piano*	7½	MS.
Songs		*vocal*		MS.

Morel, François d'Assise

Pianist and composer. Born in Montreal, March 14th, 1926.

Musical education at Quebec Provincial Conservatory in Montreal with Edmond Trudel and Germaine Malépart (piano), Gabriel Cusson (ear training), Alfred Mignault and Ria Lenssens (solfeggio), Isabel Delorme (theory), Jean Papineau-Couture (advanced theory) and Claude Champagne (composition and orchestration). Diploma from Académie de Québec (piano teacher) and laureat diploma. Orchestral works have been performed by orchestras in Canada and Scandinavia, in concert and over CBC.

Address: 4391 Delanaudière, Montreal, P.Q.

COMPOSITIONS

TITLE	DATE	TYPE	TIME (MIN.)	PUBLISHER
Esquisse	1946-47	*orchestra*	6¼	MS.
Suite (2 pieces)	1948	*orchestra*	9	MS.
Quartet No. 1	1947-48	*string quartet*	15½	MS.
Trois Miniatures	1950	*flute and piano*	5	MS.
Ronde Enfantine	1949	*piano*	2½	MS.
	1949	*arr. for wwd. quintet*	2½	MS.
Quatre Chants Japonais	1949	*vocal*	10	MS.

Morin, Léo-Pol (Léopold)

Pianist, writer, critic and composer. Born in Cap St.-Ignace, P.Q., July 13th, 1892. Died in Montreal, May 29th, 1941.

Musical education in Montreal and Paris. Winner of Quebec Province *Prix d'Europe* in 1912. Lived in Montreal and Paris. Appeared in many recitals and contributed articles to many Canadian newspapers and periodicals. A pioneer of modern music in Canada.

COMPOSITIONS
(under pseudonym James Callihou)

TITLE	DATE	TYPE	TIME (MIN.)	PUBLISHER
Suite Canadienne				
(Rigaudon; Chanson; Gigue)		*piano*		Archambault
Three Eskimos				
(Weather Incantation; Dance Song;				
Incantation Dance)		*piano*		
Aquarium		*piano*		MS.
Promenade des Dauphins		*piano*		MS.
Sentimentale		*piano*		MS.

Eskimo and Indian songs:

Trois Chants de Sacrifice; Anetsu-Jete; Gidaranits' Song; Cayaga Sun Dance; Love Song of the Sikanais; Nadu, Nadudu; Berceuse pour un mort (arranged for choir and two pianos by Victor Brault).

French Canadian songs:

Sommeilles-tu Manon?; Voilà la récompense; Les deux pailles d'orge; Je me lève à l'aurore du jour; L'Herbe verdit tous les printemps; Oh' toi belle hirondelle; A la claire fontaine.

French songs:

Le soldat par chagrin; La petite Janneton (chanson bugyste); *Mademoiselle Lisette; Les époux de Berry; Chez le Bon Dieu; Le miracle du Nouveau-Né; Simone; Touro, Louro, Louro* (noël de Saboly).

Books:

Papiers de Musique, Montreal, 1930. (See in particular the chapter on James Callihou). *Musique*, Montreal, 1944.

Morin-Labrecque, Dr. Albertine

Pianist, teacher and composer. Born in Montreal, June 8th, 1896.

Musical education in Montreal with R. O. Pelletier (piano), in Paris with J. Macaire (harmony and composition). Made her debut as pianist at the age of seven. Concertized in the U.S., France and Belgium. Professor of pedagogy at Montreal University. Degree: Mus.Doc.

COMPOSITIONS

TITLE	DATE	TYPE	TIME (MIN.)	PUBLISHER
Pas-chu (Chinese opera)		*opera*		MS.
Madrini		*opera comique*		MS.
Francine		*opera comique*		MS.
Les Rives du Danube		*ballet*		MS.
Au Petit Trianon		*ballet*		MS.
Russe		*ballet*		MS.
Bohèmien		*ballet*		MS.
Jugement dernier (symphonic poem)		*orchestra*		MS.
Prélude tragique		*orchestra*		MS.
Valse de concert		*orchestra*		MS.
Marche funèbre		*orchestra*		MS.
Pantomime		*band*		MS.
Comme le dit un vieil adage		*band*		MS.
Quand on porte l'uniforme		*band*		MS.
Concerto (poème sur Jeanne d'Arc)		*2 pianos, strings*		MS.

COMPOSITIONS

TITLE	DATE	TYPE	TIME (MIN.)	PUBLISHER
Concerto in C minor		*2 pianos*		MS.
Grande Valse brillante de concert		*2 pianos*		MS.
Album de 10 études de concert		*piano*		Archambault
Album de 24 préludes		*piano*		Archambault
Album de Miniatures		*piano*		Zimmerman, Cincinnati
Grande Etude de Concert		*piano*		Leduc, Paris
Pastorale; Confidence; Berceuse		*piano*		Leduc, Paris
Album de six Pastels		*organ*		Archambault
Légende		*vln and piano*		Parnasse Musical
A toi, Sainte Vierge Marie		*choral*		Archambault
Farandole		*choral*		Archambault
`La Main Divine		*choral*		Archambault
Souvenez-vous		*choral*		Archambault

Many other piano pieces and songs published by Archambault.

Instruction books:
Méthode de Piano, 2 vol., Archambault.
Receuil de Modèles, Archambault.
L'Art d'étudier le Piano, J. E. Turcot.
No recent information obtained.

Morley, Glen

Composer, conductor and violoncellist. Born in Vancouver, B.C., September 17th, 1912.

Studied 'cello with Bruno Coletti in Portland, Oregon, Boris Hambourg in Toronto; conducting with Reginald Stewart and Ettore Mazzoleni in Toronto, Sir Henry Wood in London; composition with Allard de Ridder in Vancouver, John Weinzweig in Toronto, William Alwyn in London and Bernard Rogers in Rochester, N.Y.

Has been 'cellist in orchestras in Vancouver, Montreal and Toronto and, since 1947, 'cellist in Rochester Philharmonic and Rochester Civic Orchestras. Member of Bay View (Mich.) Association String Quartet since 1949.

Was musical director of Canadian Army Concert Parties, London 1941-45. Conducted BBC programs to Allied Services, 1941-43. Wrote and conducted score for motion picture *Playtime for Workers* in London, 1943. Is now on staff of Eastman School of Music, Rochester, N.Y.

Address: c/o Rochester Civic Music Association, Eastman Theatre Building, 60 Gibbs Street, Rochester, N.Y.

Affiliation: BMI.

COMPOSITIONS

TITLE	DATE	TYPE	TIME (MIN.)	PUBLISHER
A Christmas Overture	1950	*orchestra*	8½	MS.
Scherzo	1951	*piano and strgs*	9	MS.
Fantasy	1950	*string quartet or string orch.*	8	MS.
Five Pieces	1946 rev. 1951	*viola and piano*	18	MS.
Nocturne	1946	*piano*	3	MS.

Mosher, Frances Elizabeth

(Betty, née Jordan)

Composer, painter and writer. Born in Saint John, N.B., October 23rd, 1911.

Musical education with private teachers. Stood first in composition contest in New Brunswick Music Festival.

Address: 144 Douglas Avenue, Saint John, N.B.

Affiliation: CAPAC.

Compositions:
Written since 1949. All works are short and most are in manuscript.

Piano works:
The March of the Dolls; A Reverie; At Dawn; Chamber Music; Dance of Childhood.

Works for piano and voice:
Song of Saint John; Fundy Folk Song; A Salt and Pepper Shaker (children's music: published by F. Harris); *Gretchen's Lullaby; Fisherfolk Love Song; A Sea Song; Good-bye Little Lamb.*

Moss, Cyril

Organist and composer. Born in Strood, Kent, England, January 3rd, 1891.

Musical education at Royal Conservatory, Toronto with Dr. George Knight and Sir Ernest MacMillan and at Eastman School of Music, Rochester, N.Y. with Harold Gleason. Diplomas: F.C.C.O., L.T.C.M. Now is organist at Leamington (Ont.) United Church.

Address: 67 Mill Street East, Leamington, Ont.

COMPOSITIONS

TITLE	DATE	TYPE	TIME (MIN.)	PUBLISHER
Fantasie Brillante	1950	*piano and organ acc.*		MS.
Capriccio	1949	*piano and organ acc.*		MS.
Petit Concerto in G minor	1949	*piano*		MS.
Jesu, Soul of My Heart Desire		*choral*		Boosey, also F. Harris
Let Thy Merciful Ears		*choral*		Boosey, also F. Harris
Around 50 anthems		*choral*		MS.

Organ works in manuscript:
Harmonies du soir; Within a Cathedral; Prière; Offertoire; Larghetto; Symphonic Poem; Romance; Appassionata; Moonlight; Among the Pines; 6 Lynx Lake Impressions; 12 Chorales on Hymn tunes; Gigue; Arabian Bazaar; Minuet Antique; Toccata Brillante; Marche Festive; Postlude; Legend of Vimy; Westminster Suite; Concert Overture in B flat; Choral Fantasy.

Mull, Arthur

Composer, conductor and instrumentalist. Born in London, England, December 23rd, 1891.

Musical education at Exeter (Devon) Cathedral School under Dr. D. J. Wood. Chorister there for seven years. Came to Canada in 1909 where he has farmed, ranched etc. Plays the piano, 'cello and piccolo. Non-professional musician.

Address: Vulcan, Alta.

		COMPOSITIONS		
TITLE	DATE	TYPE	TIME (MIN.)	PUBLISHER
Cavatina		*2 vlns, vc, piano*	4	MS.
Reverie		*2 vlns, vc, piano*	4	MS.
Theme on "Who killed Cock Robin"		*violin or vc and piano*	5	MS.
String Trio		*2 vlns, 'cello*	4	MS.
Sonata		*vln and piano*	8	MS.
Gypsy Melody		*vln and piano*	4	MS.
Requiem		*vln and piano*	4	MS.
Crossing the Bar		*choral*	4	MS.
Awake, Awake (anthem)		*choral*	4	MS.
Thy Word is a Lantern (anthem)		*choral*	5	MS.
Who is Sylvia		*vocal*	3	MS.
Suddenly (semi-sacred)		*vocal*	4	MS.
When I Am Dead		*vocal*	3	MS.
The Blind Boy (boy's solo)		*vocal*	3	MS.

Neufeld, Kornelius H.

Singer, conductor and composer. Born in Russia, December 10th, 1892.

Musical education at Halbstadt, South Russia and in Berlin with Max Pohl. While studying at Moscow University also studied at Moscow Conservatory and in 1917 joined opera chorus of Simin Opera in Moscow. Settled in Winkler, Man. in 1924. In 1928 organized the Bergthaler Church Choir and since then has been organizer, conductor, teacher and coach of several choral societies in Canada.

Compositions:

Choral works, published by author:
The Chapel; Be Still; Patiently Waiting; Come Today; Our Schooldays; Springtime; The Finest Time; God's Love Without End; On the Way Home; Drop Your Sorrow; In the Light Above; Thy Life is like an Ocean; Thou Alone (solo).

Niermeier, Dr. Frans Cornelis

Violinist, violist, pianist, organist, clarinetist, oboist and composer. Born in Deventer, Holland, March 19th, 1903.

Musical education at Arnhem Conservatory of Music with H. Heytze, Van Beinum, G. Dekker, Mr. Doomernik (instruments and composition), at University of Toronto with Dr. Peaker and Dr. Horwood. Degrees: Mus.Bac., Mus.Doc. (Toronto, 1940). Diplomas: A.C.C.O., F.C.C.O. From 1924-44 was organist in principal cities of Western Canada. Is now teaching at Mennonite Bible College, Winnipeg. Examiner of music for University of Manitoba.

Address: 68 Polson Avenue, Winnipeg, Man.

		COMPOSITIONS		
TITLE	DATE	TYPE	TIME (MIN.)	PUBLISHER
Symphony in A minor		*orchestra*	35	MS.
Sextet in G		*strings*	10	MS.
Quartet in C minor		*strings*	8	MS.
Trio in D minor		*2 vlns and piano*	10	MS.
Sonata in A minor		*'cello*		MS.

COMPOSITIONS

TITLE	DATE	TYPE	TIME (MIN.)	PUBLISHER
Sonata in E minor		*violin*		MS.
Scherzino in B minor		*violin*		MS.
Air in B major		*violin*		MS.
Preludes and Fugues in C. D, E, F, G, A. B, minor, C and D major		*organ*		MS.
Prelude in E major		*organ*		MS.
Rondo in C major		*organ*		MS.
Novelette in A major		*organ*		MS.
Toccata in C flat		*piano*		MS.
Arabesque in E flat minor		*piano*		MS.
Nordic Legend in D		*piano*		MS.

Vocal works in manuscript (1-5 minutes each):

Have Mercy Upon Me, O God; Blessed Be the Pure in Heart; Deus Misereatur; Lord, Dismiss Us; Seven Easter Carols; Ave Maria; Darkness; A Prayer to Spirit; The Fisher's Widow; Devotion; Life's Epitome; Vestigia; Fragment; Pastorale; Just A Little Sunshine; Prayer; He Whistled as He Went; The Miller of the Dee.

Nimmons, Phillip Rista

Composer, arranger, clarinetist. Born in Kamloops, B.C., June 3rd, 1923.

Musical education at Juilliard School of Music (clarinet scholarship) and at Royal Conservatory, Toronto with Arnold Walter and John Weinzweig, Has written drama scores and musical arrangements for CBC. Degree: B.A. (U. of B.C., 1944).

Address: 65 Highland Avenue, Toronto, Ont.

Affiliation: BMI.

COMPOSITIONS

TITLE	DATE	TYPE	TIME (MIN.)	PUBLISHER
Scherzo	1950	*orchestra*	6	MS.
Suite for Spring	1951	*orchestra*	7	MS.
Sonatina	1948	*flute and str. quart.*	10	MS.
String Quartet	1950	*string quartet*	18	MS.
Interlude	1951	*viola and piano*	5	MS.
Piano Sonata	1949	*piano*	15	MS.
Toccata	1949	*piano*	5	MS.
Summer Rain	1948	*vocal*	2	MS.
Parting	1948	*vocal*	5	MS.
A Little Black Man	1948	*vocal*	3	MS.

Nizoff, Avenir Alexander

Pianist, writer and composer. Born in Moscow, June 6th, 1908.

Musical education with own father, a graduate of Moscow Conservatory and a former member of Moscow Opera (piano, theory, harmony and allied subjects). Writer of text books on harmony and music form. Concert soloist and recitalist. Diploma: A.T.C.M.

Address: 9844-103rd Street, Edmonton, Alta.

TITLE	DATE	TYPE	TIME (MIN.)	PUBLISHER
Sonata No. 1 in B minor		*piano*	15	MS.
Sonata No. 2 in E minor		*piano*	13	MS.
Sonata No. 3 in A minor		*piano*	14	MS.
Sonata No. 4 in D minor		*piano*		MS.
Theme and Variations in A minor		*piano*	24	MS.
Variations on a theme by Schubert		*piano*	10	MS.
Variations "Virtuoso"		*piano*	12	MS.
Variations on "Wandering" (Schubert)		*piano*	6	MS.
Variations on a Russian folk song		*piano*	5	MS.
Variations on a Cossack Dance		*piano*	5	MS.
Suite No. 1 "Woodland Pictures"		*piano*	14	MS.
Suite No. 2 "At the Fair"		*piano*	12	MS.
Suite No. 3 "Long Ago"		*piano*	10	MS.
Six Waltzes		*piano*	ea. 2-3½	MS.
Two Etudes in A and E minor		*piano*	ea. 3½	MS.
Elegy		*piano*	10	MS.

Shorter pieces for piano in manuscript:

March; *Capriccio; Scherzo; Toccata; Rondo; Tango;* two Serenades in D major and B minor; Gavotte in G minor; *Turkish March; Gypsy Rondo; Barcarolle; The Juggler No. 2; Jolly Blacksmith; Gypsy Air;* Minuet in F minor; Minuet in G major; *The Lark; Cradle Song; Cuckoo Miniatures;* 24 Fugues.

Pieces for two pianos in manuscript:

Grandfather's Clock; Waltz in B flat; *March of the Gnomes.*

Pieces for violin in manuscript:

Serenade; Nightingale; The Brook; Music When Soft Voices Die.
Many arrangements and transcriptions for piano.

Books:

Model Pupil in Harmony, published.
Model Piano Technic, published.
Model Pupil in Musical Form, published.
No recent information received.

Norbury, F. Ethel (née Fall)

Composer and music teacher. Born in Liverpool, April 20th, 1872.

Musical education with various teachers, history and theory with H. Wild in Canada. Came to Canada in 1920 and became teacher of piano and theory at Alberta College, Edmonton. Several children's operettas, songs and duets have been performed.

Address: 11610-122nd Street, Edmonton, Alta.

TITLE	DATE	TYPE	TIME (MIN.)	PUBLISHER
Will You Come Back Home	before 1920	*vocal*	5	Ryalls & Jones
Lullaby	before 1920	*vocal*		Liverpool Exchange Press
Two Operettas for children	before 1920	*voices and piano*		MS.
Two Operas	since 1920	*voices and piano*		MS.

COMPOSITIONS

TITLE	DATE	TYPE	TIME (MIN.)	PUBLISHER
Annabel Lee (tone poem)	since 1920	*voices and piano*		MS.
The South Wind and the Sun (tone poem)	since 1920	*voices and piano*		MS.

Many songs and choral pieces. The names of the operettas and operas are: *A Dream Fantasy; The Vendor of Amulets; Lalapaloo; Quenilda.*

O'Brien, Rev. Brother Oscar

Pianist, organist and composer. Born in Ottawa, September 7th, 1892.

Musical education with Amadée Tremblay (organ and piano). Was assistant organist at Ottawa Cathedral for 12 years and teacher of piano and harmony at University of Ottawa School of Music. Taught harmony in Montreal. After 1918 was active in the development of French Canadian folklore in collaboration with Charles Marchand and J. M. Gibbon. From 1927-29 participated in the Quebec Festivals organized by the C.P.R; in 1931 became director of the Alouette Quartet which toured Canada, Europe and the U.S. Now lives in Benedictine monastery.

Address: Benedictine Monastery, St. Benoit du Lac, Magog, P.Q.

Affiliation: CAPAC.

COMPOSITIONS

TITLE	DATE	TYPE	TIME (MIN.)	PUBLISHER
Philippino (C. Valois)		*light opera*		MS.
Gloire au sang		*cantata*		MS.
Sonata based on folk melodies		*'cello and piano*		MS. perf. 1927
Four Preludes		*piano*		MS.
Canadian Sketches (based on folk themes) (a) Isabeau s'u promène, (b) Tourne la navette, (c) Joli coeur de rose		*piano*		MS.
Requiem Mass		*male choir and capella*		MS.
Mass in B flat major		*male choir and capella*		MS.
Ave Maria		*male choir and capella*		MS.
Deus Abraham		*male choir and organ*		MS.
Ave Maria		*voice and organ*		MS.
La Fermière canadienne		*vocal*		La Bonne Chanson
La Marseillaise de l'Habitant		*vocal*		La Bonne Chanson
Hymne à Dollard des Ormeaux		*vocal*		La Bonne Chanson
La Terre de chez-nous		*vocal*		La Bonne Chanson
Le Réveil rural		*vocal*		La Bonne Chanson
La Grand'D'mande		*vocal*		La Bonne Chanson
Folklore:				
Forestiers et Voyageurs (1810)		*ballad opera*		MS. perf. 1928
Une Noce canadienne-française en 1830		*ballad opera*		MS. perf. 1930

COMPOSITIONS

TITLE	DATE	TYPE	TIME (MIN.)	PUBLISHER
A Saint-Malo (based on sailor songs)	*ballad opera*			MS. perf. 1930
Pastorale (based on shepherd songs)	*ballad opera*			MS. perf. 1930
200 French Canadian folk songs harmonized				MS. and published

About 25 songs in English and French.
Over 150 songs arranged for male quartet, over 50 songs arranged for mixed voices.

Song book:

Canadian Folk Songs (Old and New), J. M. Gibbon, G. O.'Hara and O. O'Brien, publ. Dent, 1927, 1949.
No recent information obtained.

O'Hara, Dr. Geoffrey

Composer, pianist and lecturer. Born in Chatham, Ont., February 2nd, 1882.

Musical education with private teachers. Went to U.S. and started in theatrical work in 1904. In 1913 became instructor in native Indian music for U.S. Department of Interior. 1936-37, instructor in community music and song writing, Teachers College, Columbia University, N.Y. Elected to ASCAP board in 1941, to SPA council in 1943. USO camp tours, 1942-43. Makes occasional visits to Canada. Degree: hon. Mus.Doc. (Huron College, S.D.)

Address: South Quaker Hill, Pawling, N.Y., U.S.A.

Affiliation: ASCAP.

COMPOSITIONS

TITLE	DATE	TYPE	TIME (MIN.)	PUBLISHER
Peggy and the Pirate	1927	*operetta*		Birchard
Riding Down the Sky	1928	*operetta*		Birchard
The Count and the Co-Ed	1929	*operetta*		Birchard
The Smiling Sixpence	1930	*operetta*		Willis
Rogues and Vagabonds	1931	*operetta*		
Lantern Land	1931	*operetta*		Birchard
Harmony Hall	1933	*operetta*		Samuel French
The Princess Runs Away	1934	*operetta*		Samuel French
Puddin'head the First	1936	*operetta*		Gamble-Hinged
Our America	1942	*operetta*		Robbins
The Christmas Thieves	1943	*operetta*		Gamble-Hinged
Little Women	1948	*operetta*		Samuel French

About 500 songs and choral pieces, many of them published (by over 30 different publishers).

Song book:

Canadian Folk Songs (Old and New), J. M. Gibbon, G. O'Hara and O. O'Brien, publ. Dent, 1927, 1949.

See:

ASCAP *Biographical Dictionary*.

O'Neill, Dr. Charles

Organist, conductor and composer. Born in Duntocher, Scotland, August 31st, 1882.

Musical education in England at Royal Military School, Kneller Hall, London (conducting, orchestration) and with A. L. Peace (organ), Archibald Evans (harmony, counterpoint etc.); in Ottawa with Dr. Herbert Sanders (composition); in Montreal at McGill Conservatorium. Degrees: Mus.Bac. (1914), Mus. Doc. (McGill, 1924).

Held positions as organist in Scotland and England. Came to Canada as solo cornet with the Royal Canadian Artillery Band, Kingston, Ont. Bandmaster and director of music to Royal Canadian Artillery, Quebec. Later was director of music to Royal 22nd Regiment, Quebec. Was co-conductor of CBC's Little Symphony Orchestra, Quebec. Was acting director, music department, Univ. of Wisconsin. For 10 years was professor of composition and conducting at State Teachers' College, Potsdam, N.Y. Returned to Canada in 1947. Now teaches theory and composition at Royal Conservatory, Toronto.

Address: 184 Dunvegan Road, Toronto 12, Ont.

Affiliation: CAPAC.

COMPOSITIONS

TITLE	DATE	TYPE	TIME (MIN.)	PUBLISHER
The Ancient Mariner		*cantata*	50	MS.
A Day in June (4 mvmts)		*orchestra*	16	MS.
Remembrance		*orchestra*	5	MS.
The Land of the Maple and Beaver		*orchestra*	4	Boosey & Hawkes
Suite of four numbers	1948	*orchestra*	15	MS.
Air de Ballet "La Ballerina"	1950	*orchestra*	4	MS.
Prelude and Fugue in G	1945-46	*orchestra or band*	8	MS.
Remembrance (symphonic serenade)		*band*	5	Carl Fischer
Souvenir de Quebec		*band*	7	Carl Fischer
Mademoiselle Coquette		*band*	4	Carl Fischer
Sunshine and Flowers		*band*	4½	MS.
Andalusia		*band*	4½	MS.
The Knight Errand		*band*	8	Waterloo Music
The Silver Cord		*band*	6½	G. Schirmer
Builders of Youth		*band*	7½	Carl Fischer
Aladdin's Lamp		*band*	6½	Carl Fischer
The Three Graces		*band*	6½	S. Fox
Festival		*band*	7	MS.
Prince Charming		*band*	6	MS.
Concert Overture in F minor		*band*	7	MS.
Mon Ami		*band*		Waterloo Music
Nulli Secundus		*band*		Waterloo Music
The Emblem		*band*		Waterloo Music
Royal 22nd Regiment		*band*		MS.
Autumn Glory		*band*		MS.
Greghmount		*band*		MS.
Nobility (overture)	1943	*band*	6	Remick, N.Y.
Majesty (overture)	1945	*band*	6¼	Remick, N.Y.
Fidelity (overture)	1947	*band*	6	Remick, N.Y.
Sovereignty (overture)	1949	*band*	6½	Remick, N.Y.
Trumpet rune in the old style		*4 tpts or cornets and band*		MS.
I Will Extol Thee (anthem)		*choral*	4½	C. Fischer
Say thou dost love me		*choral*	6	C. Fischer
Sweet Echo		*choral*	8	MS.
Nunc Dimittis		*choral*	4	MS.

Osborne, Rev. Dr. Stanley Llewellyn

Pastor, pedagogue and composer. Born in Clarke Twp., Durham County, Ont., January 6th, 1907.

Musical education at Royal Conservatory, Toronto with Viggo Kihl (piano), Dr. Horwood (theory) and Dr. Peaker (organ). Degrees: Mus.Doc. (Toronto, 1945), B.A., B.D. Is principal of Ontario Ladies' College, Whitby; United Church minister; student of church music.

Address: Box 675, Whitby, Ont.

COMPOSITIONS

TITLE	DATE	TYPE	TIME (MIN.)	PUBLISHER
Salvator Mundi (sacred cantata)	1945	*2 soli, choir, orch.*	36	MS.
String Quartet in F major	1936	*string quartet*	20	MS.
Prelude and Fugue in D minor	1942	*organ*		MS.
Chorale Prelude on "Intercessor"	1935	*organ*		MS.
Chorale Prelude on "Tallis Ordinal" and "Salzburg"	1936	*organ*		MS.
Still Do the Stars	1935	*choral (5-part song)*		MS.

Several hymn tunes in *Canadian Youth Hymnal*, publ. Ryerson, 1940.
Some anthems (*O Lamb of God*, etc.) for unison voices in *Music for Worship*, ed. by Dr. Osborne, publ. by Frederick Harris.

Packer, Harold Stanley

Music teacher and composer. Born in Kingston, Ont., January 13th, 1901.

Musical education at Royal Conservatory, Toronto with Ernest Seitz and Alberto Guerrero (piano), Leo Smith (theory and composition). Diploma: A.T.C.M., 1920.

In 1923 was admitted to faculty, Royal Conservatory, Toronto. In 1940 became member of faculty, Hamilton Conservatory. Now teaches in Kingston. Has contributed articles to Etude magazine.

Address: 105 Princess Street, Kingston, Ont.

COMPOSITIONS

TITLE	DATE	TYPE	TIME (MIN.)	PUBLISHER
Symphonic Chorale	1939	*solo, choir, orch.*	20	MS.
Grey Day (tone poem)	1948	*choir, orchestra*	2½	MS.
The Buried Poems of Birdland	1935	*choir, piano or strgs.*	4¾	Waterloo Music
Hymn to the Eternal Spirit	1949	*choir, organ or piano*	4	Waterloo Music
Sleep While Murmuring Breezes	1929	*choir and piano*	1½	Waterloo Music
A Day with the Gypsies	1950	*violin and piano*	2	Waterloo Music

Piano works:

City Square; Valse Romantique; Petite Valse; 11 Children's Pieces;	Waterloo Music
Valse Arabesque; Kaleidoscope; Woodland Impressions (6 parts)	M.S.

Songs:

Three Lyric Songs (Waterloo Music, by arr. with Frederick Harris); *Après la Guerre* (Waterloo Music); *Vagrant* (M.S); *Over Salève* (MS.).

Palmer, Charles

Organist, pianist, choirmaster and composer. Born in Ringwood, Hants, England, June 24th, 1916.

Musical education in England. Degrees: M.A. (Oxon. parts 1 and 2), B.Mus. (Oxon.). Diplomas: A.R.C.M., A.R.C.O. Lived in Canada from 1919-27 and since 1947. Organist of Royal Chapel, Windsor, 1938-39. Is now organist and piano teacher in Victoria, B.C.

Address: 534 Broughton, Victoria, B.C.

COMPOSITIONS

TITLE	DATE	TYPE	TIME (MIN.)	PUBLISHER
Psalm XXIII (paraphrase)	1948	*barit. and orch.*	4-5	MS.
Fancy's Knell	1948	*choral*	5	MS.
The Mirror		*vocal*	2½	MS.
Orpheus with His Lute		*vocal*	2½	MS.
Little Piece for the Pops		*flute and strings*	10	MS.

Palmer, George C.

Pianist, expert on tonic solfa and composer. Born in Bristol, England, July 6th, 1879.

Diplomas: L.R.A.M., Licentiate of Incorporated Society of Musicians (England). Was music teacher and examiner at Saskatchewan University.

Address: 650 University Drive, Saskatoon, Sask.

COMPOSITIONS

TITLE	DATE	TYPE	TIME (MIN.)	PUBLISHER
The More We Get Together (arr. as vocal fugue)		*choral*		O. Ditson
The Sun Descending		*female choir*		MS.
The Coventry Carol (arr.)		*female choir*		MS.
Three Miniatures		*piano*		Oxford U.P.

Several other choral pieces.

Papineau-Couture, Jean

Pianist and composer. Born in Outremont, P.Q., November 12th, 1916.

Musical education with Françoise d'Amour, Léo-Pol Morin (piano), Gabriel Cusson (theory), at New England Conservatory of Music and for two years at Longy School of Music, Boston with Nadia Boulanger. Degree: Mus.Bac. Teaches theory at Quebec Provincial Conservatory, Montreal and is Montreal secretary of Académie de Musique de Québec.

Address: 4932 Coolbrook Avenue, Montreal 29, P.Q.

Affiliation: BMI.

COMPOSITIONS

TITLE	DATE	TYPE	TIME (MIN.)	PUBLISHER
Symphony in D major	1947-48	*orchestra*	32	MS.
Coups de Langue (Tittle Tattle ballet)	1949	*orchestra*	35	MS.
Violin Concerto	1951	*vln and orchestra*	19	MS.

COMPOSITIONS

TITLE	DATE	TYPE	TIME (MIN.)	PUBLISHER
Concerto grosso	1943	chamber orch.	18	MS.
Suite	1947	fl, cl, hn, bn, piano	10	MS.
Sonata	1944	vln and piano	12	MS.
Suite	1945	flute and piano	18	MS.
Aria	1946	solo violin	4	MS.
Rondo	1945	piano duet	4½	MS.
Suite (5 mvmts)	1942	piano	15	MS.
Rondo (from Suite)	1942	piano	5	BMI Canada
Etude	1945	piano	5	MS.
Sonata	1942	piano	30	MS.
Mouvement Perpétuel	1944	piano	1½	BMI Canada
Deux valses	1944, 46	piano	2	MS.
Les Voleurs volés (puppet show)	1949	piano	15	MS.
Marianne s'en va-t-en moulin (puppet show)	1950	str. quintet and celesta	10	MS.
Sous la grande tente (puppet show)	1950	cl, tpt, perc, piano	8	MS.
Le Plus Rusé des hommes (puppet show)	1948	vocal	8	MS.
Quatrains	1947	vocal	8	MS.
Complainte Populaire	1948	vocal	1½	MS.
Offertoire	1949	vocal	3	MS.
Pater; Ave Maria	1944-45	vocal	5	MS.
Eglogues	1942	vocal	6	Amérique-Française periodical

Pâquet, Joseph-I.

French horn player, pianist and composer. Born in St. Remi, P.Q., September 6th, 1883.

Active in and around Montreal for the last 50 years, performing on the cornet, French horn, piano, conducting, arranging and composing. Ex-member of Les Concerts Symphoniques de Montreal and H.M. Canadian Grenadier Guards Band. Conducts band of La Garde Civile, Montreal.

Address: 1958 Avenue Laurier Est., Montreal, P.Q.

COMPOSITIONS

TITLE	DATE	TYPE	TIME (MIN.)	PUBLISHER
Un Baiser sur le front		operetta	60	MS.
Tristesse d'amour		orchestra	5	
Baptiste Canayen (folklore)		band and orch.	4	
Wake up Basses (march)		band and orch.	3	
Veillée Canadienne		band	15	
Un Jour dans le val		band	12	
Enfantillage		band	9	

Shorter works for band in manuscript (ea. 2-6 minutes):

Les Gars de Dieppe; Zing-Boum-Zing; On the Road to Victory; The Liberator; Mlle Jasette; Les Gais Lurons; Roaring Bomber; Pepmania; Superbia; Basso-forte; Moose March; La Joyeuse; To Arms; March Espagnole; Vivette; Poupée rieuse; Raymonde; Mirka; Marcelle; Le premier baiser; Douce Extase; Pourquoi *s'aimer; Cora; Arscilla; Espièglerie; Kalid; Antonoia; Cabrioles; Little Miss Nono; Folichonnerie; Semitone; Danse des Pantins; Au Fil de l'eau; Potpourri Canadien; Nora; Salut à la Garde; Métropole; Thunderhead; Helldiver; Les Maquisars.*

COMPOSITIONS

TITLE	DATE	TYPE	TIME (MIN.)	PUBLISHER
Paul Jones		*piano*	3	
About 75 songs		*vocal*		(some) Passe-Temps

Pâquet, Raoul

Pianist, organist and composer. Born in Lacolle, P.Q., December 2nd, 1892. Died in 1946.

Musical education in Montreal with Arthur Letondal (piano) and Rodolphe Mathieu (harmony), in Paris with Marie Abel Decaux (organ), Mme Filtan Duparc (piano), Gallon and Marc Delmas (composition).

Was professor of organ and harmony at Maison Mère des Soeurs de Lachine, P.Q., Collège St. Laurent, Cartierville, P.Q., Ecole Supérieure des S.S.N. de Jésus et de Marie, Outremont, P.Q. Was organist at St. Jean Baptiste Church, Montreal. Was director of Quebec Provincial solfeggio classes in the Catholic public schools of Montreal.

COMPOSITIONS

TITLE	DATE	TYPE	TIME (MIN.)	PUBLISHER
Messe des morts		*choral*		MS.
Messe solennelle		*choral*		MS.
Dieu des Pères		*choral*		MS.
Suite for piano		*piano*		MS.
Toccate		*organ*		MS.
La Croix douloureuse		*vocal*		MS.

Paquin, Joseph E.

Pianist, organist, conductor, choirmaster and composer. Born in St. Cuthbert, P.Q., May 19th, 1885.

Musical education with Lavallée-Smith (piano), R. O. Pelletier (theory) and Dom Mocquereau (Gregorian chant). Since 1902 has been organist, teacher, choirmaster and conductor in Province of Quebec.

Address: 167 Des Erables Street, St. Hyacinthe, P.Q.

Compositions (all in manuscript):

La Patro (march)	*band*	Mass in D major	*choral*
Andante	*organ*	Dollard (cantata)	*choral*
Les Jeunes (march)	*piano*	La J. E. C. Normalienne	*choral*
Chant Maternel	*piano*	Cinq cantiques à Ste.-Anne	*choral*
O Salutaris	*vocal*	Resurrexit	*choral*
Si nos anges gardiens	*vocal*		

No recent information obtained.

Peacock, Kenneth

Composer and pianist. Born in Toronto, April 7th, 1922.

Musical education at Royal Conservatory, Toronto and University of Toronto. Teachers: Alma Cockburn, Mona Bates, Reginald Godden, Healey Willan, Leo Smith,

John Weinzweig; in Montreal Michel Hirvy and in Boston F. J. Cooke. Degree: Mus.Bac. (Toronto, 1948). Diploma: A.T.C.M.

String Quartet won McGill Chamber Music Competition award 1949. Has played in several Canadian cities. Piano music performed in North and South America and Europe. Is now teaching and composing in Ottawa.

Address: 540 Brierwood Avenue, Ottawa, Ont.

Affiliation: BMI

COMPOSITIONS

TITLE	DATE	TYPE	TIME (MIN.)	PUBLISHER
Rituals of Earth, Darkness and Fire	1950	*orchestra*		MS.
Essay No. 1	1949	*clar. and strings*	9	MS.
Essay No. 2	1950	*strings*		MS.
String Quartet	1949	*string quartet*	17	MS.
Two Little Fugues	1946	*string trio*	6	MS.
Trio	1950	*vln, vc, piano*	10	MS.
Violin Sonata	1947	*vln and piano*	13	MS.
Bridal Suite	1947	*piano*	7	BMI Canada
Images in Pentagon	1948	*piano*	13	MS.
Postlude	1946	*piano*	5	MS.
Children's Suite (5 pieces)	1950	*piano*	8	MS.
Songs of the Cedar	1950	*2 voices, vc, cb, fl, piano*	15	MS.
The Baffled Knight	1950	*vocal*		MS.
Do You See That Bird?	1950	*vocal*		MS.
The Parrot	1950	*vocal*		MS.

Recording:
Bridal Suite (London Records, perf. by Reginald Godden).

Pears, James R.

Choral conductor and composer. Born in England, 1881.

Has worked with choirs for over 50 years as chorister and conductor. Came to Canada in 1908.

Address: 221 Glasgow Street, Guelph, Ont.

Compositions:
Over 80 published anthems, songs, carols, sacred choral pieces etc. Published by Anglo-Canadian Music Co., Lorenz Publ. (Dayton, Ohio), H. W. Gray & Co., Willis Music Co., G. Schirmer, Boosey & Hawkes, Harold Flammer, Hall & McCreary Co., Gordon V. Thompson, Canadian Music Sales, Waterloo Music Co.

Pelletier, Dr. Frédéric

Music critic, choirmaster, lecturer and composer. Born in Montreal, May 1st, 1870. Died May 30th, 1944.

Musical education with R. O. Pelletier (piano), Guillaume Couture (voice) and Achille Fortier (harmony). Degrees: M.D. (Laval), hon. Mus.Doc. (Montreal). Was choirmaster at St. James Church, Montreal until 1936. Music critic for Le Devoir since 1915. Correspondent of the French Ministery of Fine Arts since 1920. Professor of music history at the Ecole Supérieure de Musique d'Outremont since 1930. President of Académie de Musique de Québec, 1932-35. Created Knight of the Papal Order of St. Gregory for services to church music. Son of Romain Octave Pelletier.

COMPOSITIONS

TITLE	DATE	TYPE	TIME (MIN.)	PUBLISHER
La Rédemption (oratorio in 3 parts)		*choir, orchestra*		MS.
Triptique d'oraisons		*choir, orchestra*	15	Messager Canadienne
Stabat Mater		*choir, organ, orchestra*	40	MS.
Laudus puerillis		*organ and orch.*		MS.
Valse brillante		*orchestra*		MS.
Requiem		*choral*		MS.
La Toréva		*choral*		MS.
O Canada		*choral*		Passe-Temps
A la claire fontaine		*choral*		Hérelle
Tantum Ergo		*vocal*		Parnasse Musical
Short motets		*vocal*		MS.

Pelletier, Dr. Romain Octave

Organist, choirmaster, teacher and composer. Born in Montreal, September 10th, 1844. Died in Montreal, March 4th, 1927.

Musical education in England with William Best, J. B. Calkin, in Brussels with Lemmens, in Paris with Widor and in Germany. Degree: hon. Mus.Doc. (Montreal, 1919). Notary Public. Organist at St. James, Montreal, c. 1857-1867 and 1887- c. 1922. Taught solfeggio at Jacques-Cartier Normal School, 1857-1919 and music at various other institutions. Member of Quebec Academy of Music. Wrote many articles on music. One of Canada's great pioneer musicians.

COMPOSITIONS

TITLE	DATE	TYPE	TIME (MIN.)	PUBLISHER
Messe de Noël		*choral*		MS.
Tantum Ergo		*choral*		MS.
Cor Jesu		*choral*		MS.
Libera		*choral*		MS.
Suite of four Christmas Carols		*choral*		MS.
Six organ pieces		*organ*		G. Schirmer
Ite Missa Est (voluntary)		*organ*		MS.
Valse Caprice		*piano*		A. J. Boucher
Prince Arthur March		*piano, arr. band*		MS.
Song and piano pieces				A. J. Boucher
Organ pieces				

Books:

Le Toucher du Pianiste (Piano Touch), 1916.
Etude de la Littérature de Piano (How to Study the Piano Masters), 1920.
L'Art pianistique (The Pianist's Art), 1922.
Le Guide du Professeur de Piano (The Piano Teacher's Guide), 1925.

See:

Arthur Laurendeau, *Romain-Octave Pelletier*, L'Action Nationale, June 1950.

Pentland, Barbara

Composer, lecturer and pianist. Born in Winnipeg, January 2nd, 1912.

Musical education in Paris Cécile Gauthiez, at Juilliard School of Music, New York with Bernard Wagenaar and Frederick Jacobi, at Berkshire Music Centre with Aaron

Copland and Eve Clare (piano). Also studied organ, violin and conducting. Diplomas: A.T.C.M. and L.A.B.

Started composing at the age of nine. Was on staff of Royal Conservatory, Toronto and since 1949 has been on faculty of University of British Columbia, music department. Works have been performed on radio or in concerts in Canada, U.S. and Europe.

Address: 2608 Tennis Crescent, University Hill, Vancouver, B.C.

Affiliation: BMI.

COMPOSITIONS

TITLE	DATE	TYPE	TIME (MIN.)	PUBLISHER
Symphony No. 1	1945-48	*orchestra*	25	print
Symphony No. 2	1950	*orchestra*	16	MS.
Holiday Suite	1941	*orchestra*	9	print
Arioso and Rondo	1941	*orchestra*	10	print
Lament	1939	*orchestra*	8	MS.
Payload (score for radio drama)	1940	*orchestra*	7½	MS.
Variations on a Boccherini Tune	1948	*small orchestra*	12	print
Violin Concerto	1942	*small orchestra*	18	print
Organ Concerto	1949	*organ and strings*	15	print
Colony Music	1947	*piano and strings*	15	print
Octet for Winds	1948	*4 wwd, 4 brass*	8	print
Piano Quartet	1939	*piano, vln, va, vc*	20	print
String Quartet	1944-45	*string quartet*	15	print
Sonata	1943	*'cello, piano*	15	print
Sonata	1946	*vln and piano*	14	print
Vista	1945	*vln and piano*	9	BMI Canada
Sonata	1950	*solo violin*	17	print
Three Cadenzas for Mozart's Concerto K. 207	1950	*solo violin*		MS.
Studies in Line	1941	*piano*	5	BMI Canada
Five Preludes	1938	*piano*	8	print
Rhapsody	1939	*piano*	5	print
Variations	1942	*piano*	7	print
Sonata	1945	*piano*	14	print
Sonata Fantasy	1947	*piano*	15	print
Sonatina	1951	*piano*	8	MS.
Beauty and the Beast (ballet)	1940	*2 pianos*	30	MS.

Various choral pieces and songs.

Recording:
Studies in Line (London Records, performed by Reginald Godden).

Pepin, Clermont

Pianist and composer. Born in St.-Georges de Beauce, P.Q., May 15th, 1926.

Musical education in Quebec with Georgette Dionne (piano and harmony), in Montreal with Claude Champagne (harmony) and Arthur Letondal (piano), at Curtis Institute, Philadelphia with Rosario Scalero (composition) and Jeanne Behrend (piano), at Royal Conservatory, Toronto with Arnold Walter (composition) and Lubka Kolessa (piano) and from 1949-51 in Paris with A. Honegger (composition). Degree: Mus.Bac.

Diplomas: Piano, Académie de Musique de Québec, 1935; Laval University, 1938. Artist's Diploma, Senior School, Royal Conservatory, Toronto. Winner of CAPAC junior prize in composition, 1937, and frequently since. Winner of Quebec Province *Prix d'Europe* in 1949. In 1951, won Canadian Amateur Hockey Ass'n. Scholarship.

Has conducted or played own works with orchestras in Quebec, Montreal and Toronto.

Address: St. Georges de Beauce, P.Q.

Affiliation: CAPAC.

COMPOSITIONS

TITLE	DATE	TYPE	TIME (MIN.)	PUBLISHER
Symphony No. 1	1948	*orchestra*	25	MS.
Symphonic Variations	1947	*orchestra*	13	MS.
Piano Concerto No. 1	1945-46	*orchestra*	26	MS.
Piano Concerto No. 2	1949	*orchestra*	18	MS.
Variations (original theme)	1944	*string orchestra*	6	MS.
Variations (original theme)	1944	*string quartet*	8	MS.
Trois Menuets	1944	*string quartet*	6	MS.
String Quartet	1948	*string quartet*	18	MS.
String Quartet in C major		*string quartet*	12½	MS.
Passacaglia	1950	*organ*	7	MS.
Quatre Etudes		*piano*	19	MS.
Trois Petites Etudes	1946	*piano*	ea. 2	Western Music
Trois Etudes	1949	*piano*	ea. 4	MS.
Quatre Allegros		*piano*	9, 11, 12, 7	MS.
Prelude	1937	*piano*		F. Harris
Deux Préludes	1947	*piano*	ea. 2	MS.
Trois Fugues	1947	*piano*	ea. 2	MS.
Andante in E major		*piano*	8	MS.
Menuet	1944	*piano*	3	MS.
Toccata	1946	*piano*	4	MS.
Theme and Variations	1947	*piano*	12	MS.
Sonata	1947	*piano*	12	MS.
Petite Suite	1950	*piano*	8	MS.
Danse Frénétique		*piano*		MS.
Cantique des Cantiques		*choral*		MS.
Hymne de la Mort		*vocal*	4	MS.
La Feuille d'un saule		*vocal*	4	MS.
Un Peu de silence		*vocal*	4	MS.
Song Cycle (7 songs by P. Eluard)	1948	*vocal*	13	MS.
Song Cycle (3 songs by Nelligan)	1950	*vocal*	8	MS.

Perrault, Michel

Composer, conductor, arranger and tymbalist. Born in Montreal, July 20th, 1925.

Musical education at McGill Conservatorium and Quebec Provincial Conservatory, Montreal, and in Paris. Teachers include: Gabriel Cusson (harmony), Réal Gagnier (oboe), Louis Decair (tympani), Nadia Boulanger and A. Honegger (composition). Plays tympani in The Little Symphony, Montreal.

Address: 308 Boulevard des Prairies, Laval des Rapides, P.Q.

Affiliation: BMI.

COMPOSITIONS

TITLE	DATE	TYPE	TIME (MIN.)	PUBLISHER
La Belle et la bête (not complete)	1950	*opera*	30-45	MS.
La Belle au bois dormant	1946	*orchestra*	10	MS.
Les Fleurettes (symphonic suite)	1947	*orchestra* *also arr. piano*	10½	MS.
Les trois Cones (symphonic poem)	1949	*vc and orchestra*	13½	MS.
Diane (symphonic poem)	1948	*Fr. hn and strings*	10½	MS.
Les Aquarelles (suite)	1946	*small orchestra* *also arr. vln and piano*	9	MS.
Sonata	1946	*vln and piano*	8	MS.
Solitude		*vln and piano*	5	BMI Canada
Pièce triangulaire (from Sonata)		*cl, hp, str. quart*		MS.
Les Fées	1949	*choral*	7	MS.
Short orchestral works on 14 French Canadian folklore themes			ea. 2-3	MS.

Background music for plays:

La Farce du pendu dependu; La Belle au bois; Le Voyage de Thesée; Caligula; Le Voyageur sans bagage Huon de Bordeaux; Antigone.

Perreault, Joseph-Julien, p.s.s.

Priest, choirmaster and composer. Born in Montreal, 1826. Died in Varennes, P.Q., August 2nd, 1866.

Education in Montreal and after 1847 in France. Choirmaster at Notre-Dame Cathedral, Montreal, for several years.

COMPOSITIONS

TITLE	DATE	TYPE	TIME (MIN.)	PUBLISHER
Messe des morts		*choral*		A. J. Boucher
Messe de Noël (Deo infanti) (re-arranged by Dr. E. Lapierre)		*choir, organ and orchestra*		published 1870
Messe, St. Antoine de Padoue		*male choir*		
Salve Regina	Paris, 1849	*choral*		
Tantum Ergo	1864	*choir and orchestra*		

Other religious works include:*Stabat; Passion; Lumen Ad Revelationem; Beatus Vir; O Salutaris; Laudate Pueri; Nunc Dimittis.*

See:

Le Canada Musical, 1866.

Piché, Eudore

Organist, choirmaster and composer. Born in Montreal, February 9th, 1906.

Musical education with Georges Emile Tanguay (mostly self taught). Organist in many churches in and around Montreal. Degrees: B.A., Lic. in Philosophy.
Address: 4034 Delorimier Street, Montreal, P.Q.

COMPOSITIONS

TITLE	DATE	TYPE	TIME (MIN.)	PUBLISHER
Chansons du vieux Quebec (arr.)		*vocal and choral*		Beauchemin, 1939 .
Jésus-Christ s'habille en pauvre		*choral*	10	MS.
Chant du muezin		*choral*	3	MS.
12 Canadian songs (arr.)		*choral*		MS.
Spleen		*vocal*	1	MS.

Numerous arrangements for voice and piano, men's voices, mixed voices of French-Canadian folklore. No recent information obtained.

Piché, Paul Bernard

Pianist, organist and composer. Born in Montreal, April 10th, 1908.

Musical education with Hervé Cloutier (piano, organ and harmony). Laureat and gold medalist, Académie de Musique de Québec, 1929. Winner of Quebec Province *Prix d'Europe*, 1932. Spent two years at Conservatoire Royal, Brussels, studying with De Malingreau and Charles Hens. In Paris studied with Charles Tournemire (organ and composition). Was organist in Trois Rivieres after 1932 and is now organist in Lewiston, Maine.

Address: 27 Forest Street, Lewiston, Maine, U.S.A.

COMPOSITIONS

TITLE	DATE	TYPE	TIME (MIN.)	PUBLISHER
Fugue sur l'Ite missa est (Pascal)		*organ*	6	MS.
Rhapsodie sur 4 noëls		*organ*	8	H. W. Gray & Co.
Scherzo		*organ*	4	H. W. Gray & Co.
By the Sea		*organ*	3	MS.
Easter Rhapsody		*organ*	5	MS.
Messe de Requiem		*vocal*		MS.

Poirier, Benoît

Pianist, organist and composer. Born on Prince Edward Island, October 17th, 1882.

Degree: M.A. (Univ.of New Brunswick). Has performed and taught most of his life. Organist of Notre-Dame Church, Montreal since 1920. Former president of Conservatoire National de Musique, Montreal. At present president of Conservatoire Royal de Montreal.

Address: 3846 Parc- La Fontaine, Montreal, P.Q.

COMPOSITIONS

TITLE	DATE	TYPE	TIME (MIN.)	PUBLISHER
Rhapsodie Canadienne		*piano or orchestra*	12	Archambault
Basso Ostinato		*string quartet or organ*	7	Boston Music Co.

COMPOSITIONS

TITLE	DATE	TYPE	TIME (MIN.)	PUBLISHER
Introduction and Fugue (on a Laudate)		organ		MS.
Fantasie et Fugue (on a Te Deum)		organ		MS.
Au Pays d'Evangeline		organ or orch.	5	MS.
Berceuse		organ		MS.
Marche du Centenaire		organ		MS.
Rhapsodie pour Noël		organ		MS.
Variations Epiphanie		organ		MS.
Cloches de Pâques		organ		MS.
Hommage à Ste.-Cécile		organ		MS.
Hymne au Maréchal Foch		vocal		Daily News
Hymne Tricentenaire de Québec		vocal		pub. on post-cards
Hymne Mutualiste		vocal		Passe-Temps
Hymne Universitaire		vocal		Montréal Musical
Ecce Fidelis		choral		Archambault
Sanctus		choral		MS.
Carabin, Carabine		vocal		Montréal Musical
St. François et les oiseaux		vocal		Librairie Franciscaine
25 cantiques Grégoriens				Desclée
25 sacred motets				MS.
Pièce de concert sur l'Hymne Acadien				MS.
Organ compositions for the principal festivals of the liturgical year				MS.
25 songs				MS.

Pratt, Paul

Clarinetist, pianist, conductor and composer. Born in Longueuil, P.Q., November 25th, 1894.

Musical education with O. F. Devaux, Arthur Letondal, Romain Pelletier (piano and harmony), Céline Marier (vocal culture), Camille Couture (violin). Diploma: Lauréat, Conservatoire National de Musique, Montreal. Member of the Canadian Grenadier Guards Band, 1919-1939. Has played contra-bass clarinet with different symphonic organizations of Montreal. Is bandmaster of Metropolitan Concert Band of Montreal, musical director of a male quartet in Longueuil. Mayor of Longueuil for past 16 years.

Address: 198 St. Alexander Avenue, Longueuil, P.Q.

COMPOSITIONS

TITLE	DATE	TYPE	TIME (MIN.)	PUBLISHER
Marche Longueuilloise		orchestra	5	MS.
Marche des petits soldats		orchestra	4	MS.
Marche des roses		orchestra	5	MS.
Nini (valse caprice)		band	10	MS.
Fantaisie-Impromptue (fantasy)		band	8	MS.
Valse Canadienne		band	6	MS.
Sur le lac Champlain (barcarole)		piano	4	MS.
Valsons-nous		piano	5-6	MS.

Price, Gordon Chatham

Pianist, organist and composer. Born in Edmonton, December 31st, 1914.

Studied piano with Avenir Nizoff. First prize winner in University of Alberta Musical Club contest (Suite for Piano). Diploma: A.T.C.M.

Address: 11205-64th Street, Edmonton, Alta.

		COMPOSITIONS		
TITLE	DATE	TYPE	TIME (MIN.)	PUBLISHER
Two Preludes		*piano*	5	MS.
Prelude in E minor	1948	*piano*	1	MS.
A Suite of four "Minor Moments"		*piano*	15	MS.
Variations on original theme		*piano*	6-7	MS.
Tid Bits	1947-49	*piano*	4	MS.
11 miscellaneous piano pieces		*piano*		
Intermezzo		*violin*	5	MS.
Three Songs		*vocal*	7-8	MS.

Price, Percival Frank

Carillonneur, campanologist, writer and composer. Born in Toronto, October 7th, 1901.

Musical education in Toronto with Frank Burt (organ), E. Lois Wilson (theory), Dr. Fricker (orchestration), H. Carman (piano), in Belgium at Beiaardschool te Mechelen with Jos. Denyn and Jef Van Hoof (carillon), in Vienna with A. Willner (composition and analysis) and Dr. F. Nilius (conducting), in Basle at Hochschule with F. Weingartner (conducting), in New York with B. Grosbayne (conducting). Degree: Mus. Bac. (Toronto).

First non-European to receive Carillonneur Diploma. Has been carillonneur at Massey Memorial Carillon, Toronto, Rockefeller Memorial Carillon, N.Y. and Houses of Parliament, Ottawa. Is professor of campanology and university carillonneur at Univ. of Michigan, Ann Arbor.

Has given recitals on over 100 carillons in Europe, Canada and the U.S. Consultant on designing and installation of carillons. From 1942-43 prepared list of carillons in Europe and has given assistance on the restitution of bells to various Allied, Italian and German government commissions. *St. Lawrence Symphony* brought the Pulitzer Prize in music to a Canadian for the first time.

Address: c/o Burton Tower, University of Michigan, Ann Arbor, Mich., U.S.A.

		COMPOSITIONS		
TITLE	DATE	TYPE	TIME (MIN.)	PUBLISHER
The Saint Lawrence (romantic symphony)		*orchestra*		MS.
Concerto for Carillon and Brasses		*carillon and brasses*		MS.
Wedding Fanfare with Carillon		*carillon and brasses*		MS.
March for RCAF Band (Trenton)		*band*		MS.
Fanfare for the Peace Tower Battlements		*band*		MS.
Yamachiche Suite		*strings or piano trio*		MS.
The Merman		*choral*		MS.
Air for Carillon		*carillon*		Oxford U.P. & Carl Fischer

Carillon works in manuscript:

7 Preludes (4 min. ea.); 4 Fantaisies (7 min. ea.); 4 Carillon Studies; 7 Andantes (2-3 min. ea); 3 Rhapsodies for two carillonneurs (8 min. ea.); 2 Victory Rhapsodies (for small carillon 2 min.; for large carillon 8 min.); Sonata for 23 bells (4 move, 25 min.); Sonata for 30 bells (3 move, 25 min.); Sonata for 35 bells (4 move 25 min.); Sonata for 43 bells (3 move, 25 min.); Sonata for 45 bells (4 move, 25 min.); Fugue (2 min.); *Kellosvel* Variations (on theme for the bells of Berghall Church, Finland, by Sibelius, 10 min.);*Canadian Suite.*

Songs in manuscript:

The Merman; Song of the Bell; Urceus Exit; They Are Not Long; Reason for Living; Overtones; Time, you Old Gypsy Man; Prairie Sunset; Debout les Gas (French Can. song).
Over 500 arrangements for carillon.

Book:

The Carillon, Oxford U.P.

Prume, Frantz

(see: Jehin-Prume, Frantz)

Pruneau, Arthur

Violinist, vocalist and composer. Born in St. Maurice, P.Q., November 15th, 1875

Musical education at Ecole de Nazareth for the Blind. Teachers: Jules Hone, Thérèse Boucher, Jehin-Prume (violin), Amelie Wilscam, Achille Fortier (singing and harmony). Teacher of singing for over 45 years.

Address: 82 St. Joseph Boulevard West, Montreal, P.Q.

COMPOSITIONS

TITLE	DATE	TYPE	TIME (MIN.)	PUBLISHER
Prière à la Vierge (sacred)		*choral*		Whaley Royce
Cantique à Ste.-Famille		*choral*		MS.
Two Cor Jesu		*choral*		MS.
Ave Maria		*choral*		MS.
Invocations au Sacré-Coeur		*choral*		MS.
Salve Regina		*vocal*		Whaley Royce
Alma Redemptoris		*vocal*		MS.
Romance		*vocal*		MS.

Quesnel, Joseph

Playwright, poet and composer, ship's officer and merchant. Born in Saint-Malo, France, November 15th, 1749. Died in Montreal, July 3rd, 1809.

Finished his studies when 19 and went to sea, travelling to India, Africa and South America. Came to Canada in 1779 when his ship carrying munitions to the American revolutionary forces was captured by the English. Lived for many years in Boucherville, P.Q. as merchant and became a pioneer of the theatre in Montreal. Played the violin.

Compositions and stage works:

Colas et Colinette (or Le Bailli dupé), prose comedy in 3 acts, containing 7 vocal solos, 4 duets and vaudeville finale. Written 1788, performed 1790 in Montreal, 1808 in Quebec. MS. at Seminaire de Québec, text printed in *Répertoire National,* ed. Huston.

Lucas et Cécile	*operetta*	
Les Republicains Français	*comedy (prose)*	published in Paris
L'Anglomanie	*comedy (verse)*	published?

Quesnel wrote many poems and his musical output is said to have included motets, songs, duos, quartets and symphonies for grand orchestra.

Some literary works are printed in *Bibliothèque Canadienne*, Montreal, 1825-30, and in *Répertoire National* Montreal, 1848-50 and 1893, which also contains biographical material.

Eugène Lapierre's opera *Le Père des amours* is based on the life of Quesnel.

Rathburn, Eldon Davis

Pianist, organist and composer. Born in Queenstown, N.B., April 21st, 1916.

Musical education in Saint John, N.B. with Mrs. A. H. Campbell (piano) and Eric Rollinson (organ), at Royal Conservatory, Toronto with Healey Willan (composition), Charles Peaker (organ) and Reginald Godden (piano). Diploma: Licentiate of Music (McGill Univ.).

Was organist in Saint John, N.B. and is now on music staff of National Film Board, Ottawa. In 1938 won CAPAC scholarship for composition. In 1944 won Los Angeles Young Artists Competition Award in composition.

Address: 163 Genest Street, Eastview, Ottawa, Ont.

Affiliation: CAPAC.

COMPOSITIONS

TITLE	DATE	TYPE	TIME (MIN.)	PUBLISHER
Symphonette	1943	*orchestra*	15	MS.
Cartoon I	1944	*orchestra*	3½	MS.
Cartoon II	1944	*orchestra*	3½	MS.
Images of Childhood (suite from film "Hungry Minds")	1950	*orchestra*	10	MS.
Andante		*string quartet*	3¾	MS.
Twilight		*vocal*	2	MS.
A Ship, and Isle, a Sickle Moon		*vocal*	2	MS.
To a Wandering Cloud		*vocal*	1¾	MS.
Spring		*vocal*	2	MS.

Music for over 30 documentary films. Many scores arranged for radio programs.

Raymond, Madeleine

Pianist, composer and improvisator. Born in Donnaconna, P.Q., July 5th, 1919.

Musical education at Ecole Supérieure de Musique, Outremont, P.Q. Teachers: Claude Champagne, Jean Dansereau, Germaine Malépart, J. J. Gagnier. Has given numerous concerts as pianist and improvisator.

Address: 1410 Mount-Royal Boulevard, Outremont, P.Q.

COMPOSITIONS

TITLE	DATE	TYPE	TIME (MIN.)	PUBLISHER
Dans les brumes du Saint-Laurent		*orchestra*	MS.	
Amours villageoises		*harmonica and piano or small orch.*	6	MS.
Idylle	1949	*piano*		Passe-Temps
Theme and Variations		*piano*	8	MS.

TITLE	DATE	COMPOSITIONS TYPE	TIME (MIN.)	PUBLISHER
Printemps		*piano*		MS.
Ballade sur l'eau		*piano*		MS.
Danse marionette		*piano*		MS.
Donnacona (danse sauvage)		*piano*	5	MS. orchestrated by Maurice Dela
Scènes d'enfants		*piano*	4½	MS.
Three Etudes		*piano*		MS.
Two Pastorales		*piano*		MS.
Berceuse pour un noël d'enfant		*piano*		MS.
Variations sur l'automne		*piano*		MS.

Renaud, Emiliano

Pianist, organist and composer. Born in St.-Jean-de Matha, P.Q., June 26th, 1875. Died in Montreal, October 3rd, 1932.

Musical education with Paul Letondal and Dominique Ducharme in Montreal and after 1897 in Vienna and Berlin with Mme Stepanoff. Occupied various posts as organist, choirmaster and music teacher in Canada and the U.S. Gave numerous piano recitals in Canada, England and the U.S., also on radio. In 1930 a concert of his works was given in Montreal.

TITLE	DATE	COMPOSITIONS TYPE	TIME (MIN.)	PUBLISHER
Tantum Ergo		*organ*		Bornemann, Paris
Brise de mer, Op. 10		*piano*		Girod, Paris
Lancers de France (quadrille)		*piano*		Girod, Paris
Pauline (polka)		*piano*		Girod, Paris
Sur le lac (rêverie)		*piano*		New Music Publishing
Valse-Problème		*piano*		Musical Canada, 1922
Ave Maris Stella		*choral (with organ)*		Bornemann, Paris
Kyrie		*choral (with organ)*		Pérégally, Paris
Pater Noster		*vocal*		Costallat
Toinon		*vocal*		Musical Canada, 1922
Petits Chagrins		*vocal*		Musical Canada, 1922
Sans toi		*vocal*		performed 1903

Some 100 other works of similar type, including also a comic opera in English (libretto by composer) sonatas, chamber works and about 50 songs. Many of these pieces were published by the publishers mentioned above and by O. Ditson, White Smith (Boston) and Ed. Archambault.

Renshaw, Dr. Rosette

Linguist, composer, pianist and organist. Born in Montreal, May 4th, 1920.

Musical education with Dr. Alfred Whitehead and Dr. Claude Champagne. Degrees: B.A. (McGill), Mus.Doc. (Toronto, 1949). Is now attached to translation staff of House of Commons in Ottawa. Gives radio talks over CBC French network. Has done research in French Canadian folk music.

Won Governor General's gold medal for highest standing in modern languages (B.A.). *Madrigal for Strings* has been performed and broadcast by several orchestras.

Address: 148 Augusta Street, Ottawa, Ont.

Affiliation: BMI.

COMPOSITIONS

TITLE	DATE	TYPE	TIME (MIN.)	PUBLISHER
Symphony	1948	*orchestra*	30	MS.
Madrigal for Strings	1949	*strings*	6	MS.
Suite	1950	*piano or strings*	8	MS.
Sonatine	1950	*piano*	10	MS.
Six Sketches on Fr. Can. song "Rossignolet sauvage"	1950	*piano*	8	MS.
Lisette; Je me lève à l'aurore; Cette aimable tourterelle (harmonized folk songs)	1946	*vocal*	ea. 3	MS.

Rice, Charles Parker

Photographer, pianist, organist and composer. Born in Washington, D.C., July 26th, 1875.

Musical education with C. E. B. Price (organ), Charles Mullen and George Brewer (composition). Organist at First Baptist Church, Montreal. Is in photographic business; president of Rice Studios. Music is a hobby.

Address: 750 Sherbrooke Street West, Montreal, P.Q.

Affiliation: CAPAC.

COMPOSITIONS

TITLE	DATE	TYPE	TIME (MIN.)	PUBLISHER
Carency		*opera*		MS.
Yamakka		*opera*		MS.
Enidoroma		*piano*		La Lyre
Dis-moi des mots jolis		*vocal*		Schott Frères, Brussels
Oui		*vocal*		Schott Frères, Brussels
C'est le printemps		*vocal*		La Lyre
Votre rose		*vocal*		La Lyre
Riez		*vocal*		La Lyre
50 songs (recital type)		*vocal*		MS.

Richardson, Cornelia Heintzman

Song composer. Born in Waterloo, Ont., 1890.

Musical education at Royal Conservatory, Toronto and in Germany. Coached in piano by Josef Hofmann. Gave piano recitals with J. D. A. Tripp. A recital of own songs was given at Royal Conservatory, Toronto (with Mme Fahey and others). Musical amateur: piano, composition and whistling are chief musical activities.

Address: 75 Binscarth Road, Toronto, Ont.

Compositions:

Songs published by Nordheimer:
Daddy; Life and I; It Is Not Always May; Wind of the Sea; Lullaby; The Wind's Laughter; The Wind in a Frolic; Good Bye; To My First Love; Nuits de Juin; In the Willow Shade; A Rain Song.

Songs published by Whaley Royce:
Home Light; To Victory Arise; When Trees Are Green.

Ridout, Godfrey

Lecturer and composer. Born in Toronto, May 6th, 1918.

Musical education with Ettore Mazzoleni, Charles Peaker and Healey Willan (harmony and allied subjects). Appointed in 1939 to theory and composition faculty of Royal Conservatory, Toronto and in 1948 to faculty of Senior School and as special lecturer, faculty of music, University of Toronto. Has composed scores for National Film Board and for radio.

Address: 31 Sussex Avenue, Toronto, Ont.

Affiliation: CAPAC.

COMPOSITIONS

TITLE	DATE	TYPE	TIME (MIN.)	PUBLISHER
Esther (dramatic symphony)	1951	*soli, choir, orch.*	60	MS.
Comedy Overture	1941	*orchestra*	5	MS.
Dirge	1943	*orchestra*	7	MS.
Festal Overture	1939	*orchestra*	6½	MS.
Two Etudes	1946	*strings*	11	MS. (Chappell)
Ballade	1938	*viola and strgs*	7	MS.
Folk Song Fantasy	1951	*vln, vc, piano*	6	MS.
Two Songs	1939	*sop and oboe*	4	MS.
What Star Is This?	1941	*vocal*		Oxford U.P.

Ringuet, Léon

Organist, choirmaster, bandmaster, pianist, teacher and composer. Born in Louiseville, P.Q., January 3rd, 1858. Died in St.-Hyacinthe, 1933 (1932?).

Musical education with Paul Letondal (piano) and R. O. Pelletier (organ). Was organist at St.-Hyacinthe Cathedral after 1880. Directed St.-Hyacinthe Société Philharmonique for 52 years. From 1885-1928 was musical director of 84th Infantry Battalion. Contributor to *Etude* magazine.

Compositions:

Band works:

Collegian March; Gallant Seventh March; Major Oliver March; Philharmonic March; Patriotic March; Transvaal March.   H. Coleman, Philad.

Le Vaillant; Ma Belle; Fantaisie religieuse; Le Champion; Le Coursier; Le Prince Noir; La Citadelle; Marche triomphale; La Fillette; La Gamme; Aurélie; Tarentelle burlesque; Mésange; La Patineuse; Gloire au vainqueur; Georges Hamel; Drummondville; Le Syndicat; Pas redoublé; Belle Humeur; Marchons au pas; Yamaska; Allegro in C major; and many other pieces.

Organ works:

Toccata; Concerto; Prelude.

Piano works:

Valse Memento; Valse Etude; Valse Humoristique; Valse Aristocratique; Le Carillon (polka for piano duet); Lotus Flowers; Promenade polka; The Mill Song; Chatterer; Echoes of Poland etc.   Th. Presser

Chant du Moulin; A Toi (march); Valse Venetienne; Minuet etc.   Ed. Archambault
Many other pieces.

Religious works:

Messe à Saint Joseph; Messe des défunts; Reine des Cieux; Ave Maria; Prière pour le mariage; Vois tes enfants, Seigneur; etc.

See:

Le Passe-Temps, April 1947.

Robitaille, Gustave

Violinist, pianist, music teacher and composer. Born in Princeville, P.Q., August 31st, 1897.

Musical education with Benoît Verdickt (harmony, piano and allied subjects), Prof. Corentin, A. Salvetti (violin). Taught in New York for seven years, in Los Angeles for three years and since in Montreal.

Address: 6910 St. Hubert Street, Montreal, P.Q.

COMPOSITIONS

TITLE	DATE	TYPE	TIME (MIN.)	PUBLISHER
La Galiléenne		opera-trilogy		MS. (under revision)
Look Before You Leap		opera (2 acts)	75	MS.
Les Volatiles		operetta		MS.
Symphony in D		orchestra		MS.
Concerto for piano		piano and orch.		MS.
Concerto for Violin in D		vln and orch.		MS.
Concerto for Violin		vln and orch.	20	MS.
Fête Ibérique (19 Spanish pieces)		orchestra		MS.
Ballets Ethérés (24 pieces)		orchestra		MS.
La Rapsodie Fantaisiste		orchestra		MS.
Valse Caprice		piano	10	MS.
200 sacred songs in French		vocal		MS.

Roff, Dr. Joseph

Priest, composer and teacher. Born in Turin, Italy, December 26th, 1910.

Musical education at University of Toronto, mostly with Healey Willan and Leo Smith. Degrees (Univ. of Toronto): B.A. (honor music), M.A., Mus.Doc. (1948). Has a contract to write ecclesiastical music with the Gregorian Institute of America, Toledo, Ohio. Came to Canada in 1942.

Address: 15 Grace Street, Toronto, Ont.

Affiliation: BMI.

COMPOSITIONS

TITLE	DATE	TYPE	TIME (MIN.)	PUBLISHER
Ecclesiastical:				
Mass	1947	choir and organ	25	Gregorian Inst.
Mass	1946	choir and organ	20	MS.
Mass Alme Pater	1948	choir and organ	15	Gregorian Inst.
Requiem Mass	1949	choir and organ	35	Gregorian Inst.
Breath On Us Lord	1949	choir and organ	4	MS.
Ave Maria	1947	choir and organ	2½	J. Fischer & Bro
O Esca Viatorum	1947	choir and organ	2½	J. Fischer & Bro
Ave Maria	1947	choir and organ	2½	Th. Presser
Three 17th century chorales (arr.)	1947	choir and organ	2½	Th. Presser

COMPOSITIONS

TITLE	DATE	TYPE	TIME (MIN.)	PUBLISHER
Five Motets of the Church Year	1948	*choir and organ* ea.	2	Gregorian Inst.
Seven Eucharistic Motets	1948	*choir and organ* ea.	2	Gregorian Inst.
Tantum Ergo	1949	*choir and organ*	5	Voci Bianche
Sacerdos et Pontifex	1949	*choir and organ*	5	Voci Bianche
Propers of the Masses for the Year	1950	*choir and organ*		Gregorian Inst.
Requiem	1948	*choir and piano*	3	MS.
Panis Angelicus	1948	*solo and choir*	3½	MS.
Easter Anthem	1947	*solo and choir*	3	BMI Canada
Panis Angelicus	1948	*solo and choir*	2	Gregorian Inst.
Adoro Te Devote	1946	*choral*	2½	Parnasse Musical
Our Father	1948	*choral (also solo)*	2½	Parnasse Musical
De Profundis	1944	*voice and organ*	2½	Parnasse Musical
Ave Maria	1946	*voice and organ*	3	MS.
The Conversion of St. Paul	1949	*voice and piano*	4½	MS.

Secular:

Reverie	1950	*ob, strgs, harp*	4	MS.
Fragments for Strings (3)	1948	*strings*	4	MS.
Suite (5 mvmts)	1944	*vln and piano*	10	MS.
Minuet for Trumpet Stop	1948	*organ*	3	MS.
Pomp and Circumstance	1947	*organ*	8	MS.
Royal Cortege	1950	*organ*	4½	MS.
Five Short Improvisations	1949	*organ*	10	MS.
Seven Improvisations	1949	*organ*	15	Gregorian Inst.
Four Piano Pieces	1947	*piano*	10	MS.
In Flanders' Fields	1948	*choir and piano*	4	MS.
Prairie at Evening	1948	*choir and piano*	3½	MS.
Echo Song	1948	*choir and piano*	2½	MS.
Indian Summer	1950	*choir and piano*	3½	MS.
The Screech Owl	1950	*choir and piano*	3	MS.
The Snare	1948	*choir and piano*	2½	BMI Canada
Chesterton's Xmas Carol	1947	*solo and choir*	3	MS.
The Donkey (Chesterton)	1948	*solo and choir*	3	MS.
The Greatest Gift	1947	*voice and piano*	3	BMI Canada
My Cathedral	1948	*voice and piano*	3	H. W. Gray & Co.
To a Snow Flake	1945	*voice and piano*	4	MS.
Elegy	1945	*voice and piano*	3½	MS.
My Gun	1949	*voice and piano*	3½	MS.
God's Own Smile	1949	*voice and piano*	3	MS.
A Woman's Last Word	1947	*voice and piano*	4	MS.
Noël	1948	*voice and piano*	3	MS.
A Soldier's Prayer in France	1947	*voice and piano*	3½	MS.

Rogers, William Keith

Pianist and composer. Born in Charlottetown, P.E.I., March 16th, 1921.

Musical education at Juilliard School of Music with Arthur Newstead (piano), George A. Wedge (theory), Vittorio Giannini; fellowship in composition (1945) under Frederick Jacobi. Degree: M.Mus. (Juilliard, 1948). During 1948-50 taught at Hamilton Conservatory. At present is musical director for radio station CFCY, Charlottetown. Has won several composition awards.

Address: 3 Grafton Street, Charlottetown, P.E.I.

Affiliation: BMI.

COMPOSITIONS

TITLE	DATE	TYPE	TIME (MIN.)	PUBLISHER
Choral Episode from Antigone	1948	choir, orchestra	14	MS.
Concertino	1949	piano, small orch.	12	MS.
String Quartet	1947-48	string quartet	18	MS.
Fountains		piano	3	MS.
Ballade		piano	5	MS.
Valse Grotesque		piano	4	MS.
Pavane		piano	5	MS.
Suite for Piano		piano	7	MS.
Variations on Old Irish Air		piano	9	MS.
Sonatina	1946	piano	10	MS.
Sonata		vln and piano		MS.
Narration	1947	vln and piano	8	MS.
Fugue		woodwinds		MS.
Three Songs from Emily Dickenson	1948	choral	6	BMI Canada
Precocious		vocal		MS.
At the Aquarium		vocal		MS.
Clouds in Summer		vocal		MS.
Falling Snow		vocal		MS.

Ronan, Rt. Rev. Mgr. John Edward, D.P.

Composer and choral conductor. Born in Colgan, Ont., October 28th, 1894.

Early musical studies in theory in Toronto and at Pius Xth School, N.Y. In France studied with Dom. Macquereau at Solesmes Abbey (Gregorian chant), with Paul Fauchet and Louis Vierne (harmony and allied subjects). In Vienna studied with Dr. Richard Stohr (musical form); in Rome at Pontifical School of Sacred Music with Dom Ferretti, Casimiro, Refice and Dobici.

Is Diocesan director of music in Archdiocese of Toronto. Is professor of ecclesiastical chant at St. Augustine's Seminary since 1922. Founder and director of St. Michael's Schola Cantorum. Degrees: Magisterium in Gregorian chant; Licentiate in sacred composition.

Address: c/o St. Michael's Cathedral Schola Cantorum, 66 Bond Street, Toronto, Ont.

CHORAL COMPOSITIONS
(all in manuscript)

TITLE	TIME (MIN.)	TITLE	TIME (MIN.)
Ave Maria	2½	O Salutaris	3
De Profundis	3	Tantum Ergo	3
Ecce Sacerdos	4	Angels We Have Heard	5
Jubilate Deo	2½	Christmas Choral Overture	6
Kyrie Eleison	3	Sleep Holy Babe	3
Oremus Pro Pontifice	3	Benedictus-Canticle	
Tu Es Petrus (with organ)	2½	Regina Coeli	3
Vivat Pastor Bonus	2½	(S.A.A. and organ)	
Adoremus in Aeternum	3	Magnificat (2 choirs)	7

Jubilee Hymns, 2 books; *Jubilee Carols*.
Introits, Graduals, Offertories, Communions (S.A.T.B.) for the Sundays and principal feasts of the year.
Responsoria for Tenebrae (from the office of Holy Week): *Ecce Vidimus; In Monte Oliveti; Jerusalem Surge; Omnes Amici; Plange Quasi Virgo; Sicut Ovis; Tristis Est; Velum Templi; Vinea Mea Electa.*
Choral arrangements of *Adeste Fidelis; Panis Angelicus* (C. Frank); *Silent Night* (Gruber).

Ross, Dr. George

Organist, music teacher and composer. Born in Montrose, Scotland, April 9th, 1875.

Musical studies with own father and brother, with Dr. Iggulden of London and Dr. Healey Willan. Degree: Mus.Doc. (Toronto, 1931). Diploma: A.R.C.O. Organist and choirmaster in Scotland. Came to Canada in 1910. Organist at St. John's United Church, Moncton, N.B. and director of music in Moncton High School, private music teacher.

Address: 75 Archibald Street, Moncton, N.B.

COMPOSITIONS

TITLE	DATE	TYPE	TIME (MIN.)	PUBLISHER
The Voice of the Wind	1931	*soli, choir, orch.*	45	MS.
O Love Divine (anthem)	1932	*choral*	5	Carl Fischer
Give to Our God (anthem)	1932	*choral*	5	Carl Fischer
Our Goal Waiteth for the Lord (anthem)	1916	*choral*	5	O. Ditson
The Lord Is My Shepherd (anthem)		*choral*		MS.
In the Cross of Christ I Glory (anthem)		*choral (mixed or female)*		MS.
Aviator's Hymn (Lt. Gunn)		*choral (mixed or male)*		MS.
Four Scots Songs arranged		*choral*		MS.
Our Heritage		*unison*		MS.
Rise Up O Man of God	1948	*vocal*	5	Beacon, Toronto

Songs in manuscript:

Best of All; Legion Memorial Song; Beyond the Spanish Main; When June Is Come; Fain Would I Change That Note.

Roy, Joseph Alfred Léo

Pianist, organist, choirmaster, music critic and composer. Born in Quebec, November 27th, 1887.

Musical education with Philippe Roy (piano and organ) and in New York with Homer Bartlett (harmony and composition). Is engaged in teaching, performing and composing. Author of many articles on music.

Address: Quebec, P.Q.

COMPOSITIONS

TITLE	DATE	TYPE	TIME (MIN.)	PUBLISHER
Danse Canadienne, No. 1, 2, 3		orchestra		MS.
Hail to the Exhibition (overture)		band		MS.
Romance Québecoise		vln and piano		MS.
Sérénade		two pianos		published
Sérénade		piano		published
Prélude, Op. 49		piano		published
Prélude (prayer)		piano		published
Prélude romantique		piano		published
Canadienne		piano		published
Prélude in B minor		piano		published
Prélude Tragique		piano		published
Sérénade		piano		published
Marche Militaire		piano		published
30 Preludes		piano		MS.
Danse Sauvage		piano		MS.
34 Etudes		piano		MS.
Gavotte		organ		MS.
Prélude		organ		MS.
O Salutaris		choral		published
Tantum Ergo		choral		published
Hymne à Apollon		vocal		published
La Guignolée		vocal		published
Vive l'exposition		vocal		published
75 songs		vocal		MS.
600 folk songs harmonizations		vocal		MS.
42 noëls and hymns		vocal		MS.

Many other compositions.

Books:
Philosophie de l'Art Musical.
La Trilogie de l'Art Musical.
Histoire de la Musique.
No recent information received.

Sabatier, Charles Waugh

Pianist, composer and music teacher. Born in Germany or France in 1820 (of French origin). Died in Montreal, August 22nd, 1862.

Musical education in France. Came to Canada in 1848 as anti-Bonapartist emigrant. Until 1854 and after 1860 lived in Montreal, from 1854-58 in Quebec and then in Saint-Gervais and Chambly. Co-founder of l'Artiste, first musical periodical in Canada (1860, only 2 numbers appeared). One of the earliest piano virtuosi in Canada.

COMPOSITIONS

TITLE	DATE	TYPE	TIME (MIN.)	PUBLISHER
Cantata, to celebrate the visit of the Prince of Wales (E. Sempé)	perf. 1860	*choir, orchestra*		Boucher & Manseau, Montreal
Grande Marche militaire	perf. 1858	*band*		
Michel (quadrille caract.)	perf. 1858	*band*		
Marche aux flambeaux		*instrumental*		
Grande Marche Canadienne		*instrumental*		A. J. Boucher
Fantaisie sur "les Huguenots"		*instrumental*		
Fantaisie sur "La Traviata"		*instrumental*		
Fantaisie sur "la Favorite"	perf. 1858	*piano*		
Souvenirs de Jersey		*instrumental*		
Laura (schottische)		*instrumental*		J. Lovell, Montreal, 1858
Mes Derniers Quadrilles	1858	*instrumental*		published
Promenade sur le fleuve Saint-Laurent (mazurka-caprice)	perf. 1858	*instrumental*		
Le Papillon (mazurka)	perf. 1858	*piano*		
Galop de bravoure	perf. 1858	*piano*		
Souvenirs de bal	perf. 1858	*piano*		
La Voix humaine (andante)	perf. 1858	*piano*		
Fantaisie pour clarinette		*clarinet*		
Le Drapeau de Carillon (patriotic song)	1858	*vocal*		Passe-Temps; La Bonne Chanson
Sancta Maria		*vocal*		A. J. Boucher
Le Mendiant des Alpes (romance)		*vocal*		Sempé & Perrault, Montreal
Le Loup et l'agneau	perf. 1858	*vocal*		

Note:

The works designated as *instrumental* were probably written for band or for piano.

See:

Arthur Letondal, *Un musicien oublié*, L'Action Nationale, 1933.

Saucier, Marcel

Violinist, pianist, music teacher and composer. Born in Montreal, November 6th, 1912.

Musical education with Alfred De Sève, Raphael Kellert and Maurice Onderet (violin), Antonio Letourneau (piano) and at Conservatoire National, Montreal (harmony and composition). Degree: Laureat (Montreal). Professional diploma, piano and violin.

Has given violin recitals since February 9th, 1931, especially over radio. Since 1935 has specialized in teaching and has abandoned all concert and radio work. All listed works have been performed in concert and on radio.

Address: 7361 St. Denis, Montreal, P.Q.

COMPOSITIONS

TITLE	DATE	TYPE	TIME (MIN.)	PUBLISHER
Ballet for opera by A. Brassard	1936	*orchestra*	5	MS.
Fantasy in G minor (2 mvmts)	1930	*vln and piano*	8	MS.
Gavotte	1936	*violin solo*	3	Librairie des Clers St. Viateur
Chanson Orientale	1931	*violin solo*		MS.

Sauvageau, Charles

Instrumentalist, conductor and composer. Born in Quebec, 1809. Died in Quebec, June 19th, 1846.

In 1836 became bandmaster of Musique Canadienne, c. 1840 founded his own orchestra.

Compositions:
Chant Canadien (patriotic
    song, F. R. Angers)

Several compositions were published in *Le Ménestrel,* Quebec 1844-45. A concert conducted by Sauvageau in 1840 contained some violin solos of his own composition.

Pamphlet:
Notions Elémentaires, Quebec, 1844.

See:
Bulletins des Recherches Historiques, Lévis, 1937.

Savaria, Georges

Pianist, organist and composer. Born in Montreal, March 27th, 1916.

Musical education in Montreal with own father and Claude Champagne (piano, organ and harmony), in Paris with Lazare Lévy, Jules Gentil, Pierre Lucas and Marguerite Long (piano), with Daniel Lesur and Louis Aubert (theory and composition). Winner of Quebec Province *Prix d'Europe* in 1937. Active as recitalist and teacher.

Address: 4131 St. Hubert, Montreal, P.Q. (at present in Paris, France).

COMPOSITIONS

TITLE	DATE	TYPE	TIME (MIN.)	PUBLISHER
Piano Concerto	1951	*piano and orchestra*	25	MS.
Variations Canadiennes		*piano*	5	Laurentiennes
Hommage aux Romantiques		*piano*	6	MS.
Danse Villageoise		*piano*	7	Passe-Temps
Marionettes du Luxembourg		*piano*	3	MS.
Etudes poètiques		*piano*	4	MS.

COMPOSITIONS

TITLE	DATE	TYPE	TIME (MIN.)	PUBLISHER
Pavane de Michel		*piano*		Passe-Temps
Les Heures claires		*vocal*	1½	MS.
La Maison rose		*vocal*	2	MS.
A la claire fontaine		*vocal*	1	MS.

Sheppard, William Spurgeon

Cornetist, bandmaster, composer and arranger. Born in St. John, N.B., November 2nd, 1869.

Took harmony lessons by correspondence from Healey Willan. Was solo cornetist and assistant conductor of Waterloo Band. Was bandmaster of Cornwall Band, Galt Kilties Band and New Hambourg Band, trumpet player with the Kitchener-Waterloo Symphony Orchestra.

Address: 68 Albert Street, Waterloo, Ont.

COMPOSITIONS

TITLE	DATE	TYPE	TIME (MIN.)	PUBLISHER
Silver Trumpets		*band*	3	Waterloo Music
Pro Patria		*band*	3	Waterloo Music
March, Can. Bandmasters Association		*band*	3	Waterloo Music
Down the Line		*band*	3	Waterloo Music
Selection from "H.M.S. Pinafore"		*band*	9	Waterloo Music
Military Spirit		*band*	3	property of Waterloo Music

Band compositions in manuscript (approx. 3 minutes each):
Men of the North; Ever Forward; Woodside; Stepping Out; Jack Canuck; Pride of the Valley; the Optimist.

Shinn, Bonar Franklyn

Organist, music teacher and composer. Born in Barry Dock, S. Wales, July 7th, 1911.

Musical education with own father, W. H. Shinn, Herbert J. Sadler (organ), N. O'Neil and William Alwyn (composition). Diplomas: L.L.C.M., L.R.A.M. Studied at Royal Academy of Music, London, 1933-36. Came to Canada in 1914. At present is organist at St. John's United Church, Winnipeg, and teaches at Shinn Conservatory of Music.

Address: 356 Furby Street, Winnipeg, Man.

COMPOSITIONS

TITLE	DATE	TYPE	TIME (MIN.)	PUBLISHER
Prelude (tuba tune) and Toccata	1935	*organ*	12	MS.
Jesu Deliverer (arr. from Liszt, Ave Maria No. 2)	1938	*solo, choir, organ*	13	Th. Presser
The Risen Lord	1939	*solo, choir, organ*	35	MS.
Service Prelude and Introit-Anthem	1950	*solo, choir, organ*	12	MS.

Silvester, Frederick Caton

Organist, pianist, conductor and composer. Born in England, January 21st, 1901.

Musical education in England with C. Spencer Heap (organ) and in Canada with Lynnwood Farnam and Sir Ernest MacMillan (organ), Healey Willan (theory and composition). Since coming to Canada has acted as organist in Saskatoon and in various churches in Toronto. At present is organist and choirmaster at Bloor Street United Church, Toronto. Registrar, Royal Conservatory, Toronto.

Address: 152 Lascelles Boulevard, Toronto, Ont.

COMPOSITIONS

TITLE	DATE	TYPE	TIME (MIN.)	PUBLISHER
Be Merciful Unto Me, O Lord		*choral*	4	Frederick Harris
Blessed Are the Poor in Spirit		*choral*	4	Frederick Harris
Come, Ye Disconsolate		*choral*	3	Frederick Harris
He Who Would Valiant Be		*choral*	3½	Frederick Harris
I Will Give Thanks Unto the Lord		*choral*	4	Frederick Harris
Ride On, Ride On in Majesty		*choral*	4	Frederick Harris
Softly Now the Light of Day		*choral*	3½	Frederick Harris
Spirit of God (sacred)		*vocal*	4	Western Music
When I Survey the Wondrous Cross		*vocal*	4	MS.
O Perfect Love		*vocal*	3½	MS.
One Thing I of the Lord Desire		*vocal*	3½	MS.
Thee Will I Love		*vocal*	3	MS.
Thou Didst Leave Thy Throne		*vocal*	3½	MS.
Mine Eyes Have Seen the Glory		*vocal*	3½	Boosey & Hawkes
Song of Thanksgiving		*vocal*	3	Can. Music Sales
Father Eternal		*vocal*	3½	multigraph
And Didst Thou Love the Race		*vocal*	4	multigraph
Christ, Who Knows All His Sheep		*vocal*	2	multigraph
My Soul, There Is a Country		*vocal*	2	MS.
Fairest Lord Jesus		*vocal*	4	MS.
Wilt Thou Forgive That Sin		*vocal*	3½	MS.
Magnificat		*vocal*	3	MS.
My Soul Truly Waiteth Upon the Lord		*vocal*	2¾	MS.
Thou Shalt Know Him When He Comes		*vocal*	2	MS.
Strong Son of God		*vocal*	3½	MS.
The Trumpet Call		*vocal*	3¾	MS.
Eternal Father		*vocal*	3	MS.
Jesus, the Very Thought of Thee (sacred)		*vocal duet*	4	Western Music

Slatter, John (Captain)

Trombonist, bandmaster and composer. Born in London, England, February 21st, 1864.

Musical education at British Army Training School of Music. Was solo trombonist in British Army Band at the age of 14. Solo euphonium in H.M. First Life Guards,

London. Trombonist in Sousa's Band and Bellstedt's Band. First trombonist in Detroit Symphony Orchestra. Director of Music, 48th Highlanders, Toronto.

Address: 30 Harbord Street, Toronto, Ont.

Affiliation: CAPAC.

COMPOSITIONS

TITLE	DATE	TYPE	TIME (MIN.)	PUBLISHER
Canadian Patrol		*band*	5	Waterloo Music
The Road to the Isle		*pipes and band*	4	MS.

Band works in manuscript (3-7 minutes each):

The Maple Leaf Forever; Trombone Solo; Come into the Rye (troop march); *Salute to Quebec; Bonnie Brier Bush; Maple Leaf* (military marches); *Recessional* (arrangement).

Books:

Parade Band Books (3 volumes, 1: Toronto, 2: Halifax, 3: Regina, each containing 20 to 30 numbers), R. S. Williams Co., Ltd., later Waterloo Music Co.

Three sets of Scottish Bagpipe Tunes compiled for bands, each set about 12 minutes. Two books of Piston-Bugle Marches and various tunes for Piston-Bugle Bands, published by Whaley Royce, 1951.

Sloan, Thomas Reginald, K.C.

Lawyer, pianist and composer. Born in Hamilton, Ont., May 21st, 1889. Died in Hamilton, November 3rd, 1950.

Musical education at Hamilton Conservatory of Music. Was a lawyer in Hamilton; vice-chairman of Hamilton Parks Board of Management and chairman of Citizens Band Concert Committee. Initiated weekly band concerts in Hamilton parks. Music was a hobby.

Affiliation (estate): CAPAC.

COMPOSITIONS

TITLE	DATE	TYPE	TIME (MIN.)	PUBLISHER
The Old Thirteenth March		*band*	4	Shapiro, Bernstein
Out of the Night		*male, female or mixed choir or solo*	5	Mills Music Inc.
God Bless the Shore of England		*choral*	5	G. V. Thompson
Christmas Cavalcade		*voice and band*	4	Peer International

Also about 40 popular songs and instrumental pieces published by G. V. Thompson; Mills Music, N.Y.; Shapiro, Bernstein & Co., N.Y.; Primogram Inc., Hamilton, or in manuscript.

Smith, Joseph Leopold (Leo)

Violoncellist, lecturer and composer. Born in Birmingham, England, November 1881.

Musical education at Royal Manchester College of Music with Henry Hiles (theory). Carl Fuchs ('cello). Degree: Mus.Bac. (Manchester). Fellow of the Royal Manchester College of Music. Was 'cellist in Hallé's Orchestra for five years, 'cellist with Royal Opera, Covent Garden for five years. Came to Canada in 1908. Teacher and till 1950 lecturer and examiner, Royal Conservatory, Toronto. From 1938-50 professor of music, University of Toronto. For many years was co-editor of Toronto Conservatory Quarterly Review. At present is music editor, The Globe and Mail.

Address: 117 Park Road, Toronto, Ont.

Affiliation: CAPAC.

COMPOSITIONS

TITLE	DATE	TYPE	TIME (MIN.)	PUBLISHER
Divertissements in Waltz Time		*orchestra*	10	MS.
Elegy		*orchestra*		MS.
The Song Sparrow		*orchestra*	5	MS.
Three 'Cello Solos		*vc and orchestra*		MS.
A Summer Idyll		*small orchestra*	6	MS.
Henry VIII		*small orchestra*	6	MS.
String Quartet in D major		*string quartet*	30-35	MS.
Suite		*string quartet*	30-35	MS.
Trios		*vln, vc, piano*		MS.
Trios		*voice, vc, piano*		MS.
Quartet		*2 voices, vc, piano*		MS.
Sonata in E minor		*'cello and piano*	25	MS.
Four Pieces in an Old English Style		*'cello and piano*		Arthur P. Schmidt
Piano solos		*piano*	ea. 6	F. Harris
Piano solos		*piano*	1-5	G. V. Thompson
Many songs and part songs		*vocal, choral*		F. Harris, G. Schirmer
Transcriptions and paraphrases		*vlns and violas*		MS.
Chamber Music for viols and voices				MS.

Books:
Music in the Seventeenth and Eighteenth Centuries, Dent.
Musical Rudiments, Boston Music Co.
Elementary Part-writing, F. Harris.

Soeur Johane d'Arcie
(see: Decarie, Reine)

Soeur M.-Henri de la Croix
(see: Milette, Dr. Juliette)

Soeur Marie-Héloïse
(see: Villeneuve, Diane)

Soeur Marie-Jocelyne
(see: Vinette, Alice)

Soeur Marie-Stéphane
(see: Côte, Dr. Hélène)

Soeur Marie Thérèse
(see: Boucher, Lydia)

Soeur M.-Thérèse-de-la-Sainte-Face
(see: Lafleur, Lucienne)

Soeur Paul du Crucifix
(see: Lefebvre, Françoise)

Soeur St. Jean-du-Sacré-Coeur
(see: Cadoret, Charlotte)

Somers, Harry Stewart

Composer and pianist. Born September 11th, 1925 in Toronto.

Musical education with Dorothy Hornfelt and at Royal Conservatory, Toronto with Reginald Godden, Weldon Kilburn (piano) and John Weinzweig (composition). Won Royal Conservatory Jubilee Scholarship 1947-48 and 1948-49. Studied in Denver and San Francisco with Robert Schmitz (piano). In Paris studied composition with Darius Milhaud, 1949-50 as winner of the Canadian Amateur Hockey Association Scholarship.

Address: 36 Servington Crescent, Toronto, Ont.

Affiliation: BMI.

COMPOSITIONS

TITLE	DATE	TYPE	TIME (MIN.)	PUBLISHER
Sketches for Orchestra (3 pieces)	1946	*orchestra*	14	MS.
Piano Concerto	1947	*piano and orchestra*	20	MS.
Suite	1949	*harp and chamber orch.*	18	MS.
North Country (4 mvmts)	1948	*string orchestra*	12	MS.
Scherzo for Strings	1947	*string orchestra*	5	Associated Mus. Pub.
Slow Movement for Strings	1946	*string orchestra*	5	MS.
Quintet for Woodwinds	1948-49	*fl, ob, cl, hn, bn*	10	MS.
String Quartet No. 1	1943	*string quartet*	20	MS.
String Quartet No. 2	1950	*string quartet*	25	MS.
Rhapsody	1948	*vln and piano*	8	MS.
Mime	1949	*vln and piano*	5	MS.
Piano Sonata (Testament of Youth)	1945	*piano*	13	MS.
Piano Sonata No. 2	1946	*piano*	17	MS.
Piano Sonata No. 3	1950	*piano*	23	MS.
Piano Sonata No. 4	1950	*piano*	15	MS.
Strangeness of Heart	1942	*piano*	3½	BMI Canada
Two Etudes	1943	*piano*	5	MS.
Flights of Fancy (3 pieces)	1944	*piano*	7	MS.
Three Sonnets	1946	*piano*	10	BMI Canada
Solitudes (4 mvmts)	1947	*piano*	11	MS.
Four Songs (Walt Whitman)	1946	*vocal*	8	MS.
A Bunch of Rowan	1947	*vocal*	4	BMI Canada

Spence, William Ramsay

Pianist, organist, violoncellist and composer. Born in Montreal, February 27th, 1859. Died in Perth, Ont., July 26th, 1946.

Musical education with R. O. Pelletier (piano) and Vichtendahl in Montreal, with Stockbridge in Boston ('cello). Acted as organist in Montreal, Boston and Perth, Ont. for about 50 years.

COMPOSITIONS

TITLE	DATE	TYPE	TIME (MIN.)	PUBLISHER
The Story of Bethlehem		*cantata*	25	O. Ditson
Marche Militaire		*band*		MS.
Grand Chorus in D		*organ*		Arthur P. Schmidt
Song Without Words		*organ*		Arthur P. Schmidt
Valse Charmante		*piano*		Th. Presser
The Little Princess		*piano*		Th. Presser
In Flanders Fields		*choral*	10	O. Ditson
The Minuet		*vocal*	6	MS.

Over 100 anthems.

Spencer, Herbert

Violinist, pianist, conductor and composer. Born in Liverpool, England, February 28th, 1875. Died in Montreal, December 24th, 1945.

Musical education in England with Henry Lawson (violin), Helen Beer (piano) and W. J. Doran (harmony), in Canada with Horace Reyner (theory), Dr. Charles O'Neill (coaching). Diploma: Associate, Dominion College of Music, Montreal. Acted as theatre musical director in Montreal from 1891-1935. Founder of the Montreal Trio (1900-04). Was a member of Les Concerts Symphoniques de Montréal. Has arranged music for radio programs.

Affiliation (estate): CAPAC.

COMPOSITIONS

TITLE	DATE	TYPE	TIME (MIN.)	PUBLISHER
The Cavaliers		*operetta*		MS.
Imperial Grand March		*orchestra or band*	5	MS.
Laurentia (overture)		*orchestra or band*	11	MS.
O Carillon (paraphrase)		*orchestra or band*	5	MS.
Le Rossignol		*orchestra or band*	4	MS.
Bébé rose		*orchestra or band*	2	MS.
Sunset (entr'acte)		*orchestra or band*	3	MS.
Pensées distraites		*orchestra or band*	5	MS.
Nine Military Marches		*band*	4	MS.
Le Violoneux		*strgs, hp, celeste*	2½	MS.
Canzonetta		*vln, solo quintet*	4	MS.
Love Comes With the Dawning		*vocal*	4	MS.
The Clock Song		*vocal*	4	MS.

Spencer, Marguerita

Pianist, organist, violoncellist and composer. Born in Glace Bay, N.S., 1892.

Musical education in Glace Bay with Hilda Irwin, at Halifax Conservatory with Harry Dean, Romeo Corteri and Mrs. Pianconka, in Saskatoon with E. V. Morton, Mary Mitchener and Lyell Gustin, in Montreal with Clara Liechtenstein and in Madison with Conn. Diplomas: A.T.C.M., L.Mus. (McGill). Church organist, teacher of music, piano recitalist in Glace Bay, Sydney, N.S. and Saskatoon. Performed over CBC. Dominion network in 1947-48 with John Whelan.

Address: 915 Temperance Street, Saskatoon, Sask.

COMPOSITIONS

TITLE	DATE	TYPE	TIME (MIN.)	PUBLISHER
Trio		*vln, vc, piano*	10	MS.
String Quartet		*string quartet*	20	MS.
Prairie Suite		*piano*	10-15	MS.
By the River Saskatchewan (suite)		*piano*	20-25	MS.
Valse in D flat		*piano*	3-4	MS.
Early Morning Impression	1949	*piano*	2½	MS.
Song Without Words	1936	*piano*	3	MS.
Sunday Morning	1940	*pipe organ*	3½	MS.
Sunday Evening	1950	*pipe organ*	3	MS.
Spring Song	1950	*vocal*	3½	MS.

Recordings of many of these compositions are owned by the composer.

Spergel, Robert

Violoncellist, pianist and composer. Born in Toronto, December 9th, 1919.

Musical education at Royal Conservatory, Toronto, with Leo Smith and Viggo Kihl, at Juilliard Graduate School with Felix Salmond and Bernard Wagenaar. Taught at Royal Conservatory, Toronto for four years and since 1943 at Mount Royal College Calgary. Since 1949 is scholarship student in Budapest (composition).

Address: c/o 35 Evelyn Avenue, Toronto, Ont.

COMPOSITIONS

TITLE	DATE	TYPE	TIME (MIN.)	PUBLISHER
The Seasons		*string quartet*	35	MS.
Three Preludes		*piano*	5	MS.

Songs in manuscript:
The Dromedary; Soldier, Rest!; The Soldier; He Cometh Forth Into the Day; Two Psalms.

Standing, Russell Elmer

Pianist, singer and composer. Born in Belmont, Man., April 19th, 1893.

Musical education in Winnipeg with Leonard Heaton (piano), singing with James Isherwood. Teaches piano and theory in Winnipeg. Active in the Manitoba Registered Music Teachers Association.

Address: 368 Home Street, Winnipeg, Man.

Compositions:
(all in manuscript)

Piano works (1½–4 minutes each):
So They Say; Coon Song; Brandon Fair; Paraphrase on a Passacaglia by Handel.

Songs (2–4½ minutes each):
Once in Royal David's City; Winds Through the Olive Trees; Twilight; Music When Soft Voices Die; To You; Flower Rain; The Stars Are With the Voyageur.

Stone, Court

Pianist, teacher, critic and composer. Born in Renfrew, Ont., September 22nd. 1919.

Musical education with own mother, Louise Stone and Mona Bates (piano). Degrees: B.A., Mus.Bac. (Toronto). Has appeared on radio; contributed music reviews to the Toronto Globe and Mail; published poetry.

Address: 85 Glengrove Avenue West, Toronto, Ont.

		COMPOSITIONS		
TITLE	DATE	TYPE	TIME (MIN.)	PUBLISHER
Farmer in the Dell (musical comedy)	1951	*soli, choir, piano*	120	MS.
Morning Song	1946	*violin and piano*	3	MS.
Old Country Suite	1949	*piano*	7	Court Stone
Ten Easy Pieces	1951	*piano*		Court Stone
Ottawa Valley Legend (suite)	1951	*piano*	9	Court Stone
Four Canadian Songs	1950	*vocal*	11	MS

Sumner, Clare

Pianist, organist, music teacher and composer. Born in Birmingham, England, in 1886.

Musical education at Midland Institute, Birmingham with William Hartland and Mme Fromme (piano), W. Hoyle and W. Newey (organ). Diplomas: L.R.A.M., Licentiate Tonic Sol Fa. Taught in several schools in England. Came to Canada c. 1914. Has been engaged in teaching and for several years was supervisor of music in public schools in Point Grey, B.C.

Address: Vancouver, B.C.

		COMPOSITIONS		
TITLE	DATE	TYPE	TIME (MIN.)	PUBLISHER
Via Vancouver		*voice, orchestra*	3	published

Works for two pianos:
Flight; Valurka; Fantasia; Aspiration; April
MS.

Works for piano:
Study in F minor; Campanella Che Cantano
MS.

Choral works:
Apple Blossom; Easter Eve; Nunc Dimittis; My Lady Sleeps
MS.

COMPOSITIONS

TITLE	DATE	TYPE	TIME (MIN.)	PUBLISHER

Vocal works:

TITLE	DATE	TYPE	TIME (MIN.)	PUBLISHER
When I Am Dead; The Scented Hour; Sunset; Song of the Ace; Heart's Garden; There Are Fairies at the Bottom of Our Garden; Wanderlust				MS.
Birmingham over the Sea				published

No recent information obtained.

Surdin, Morris

Composer, arranger and conductor. Born in Toronto.

Musical education with Louis Gesensway in Philadelphia. Studied conducting with César Borré in Toronto. Musical work for radio and television dramas is main activity.

Address: 444 Glengrove Avenue, Toronto, Ont.

COMPOSITIONS

TITLE	DATE	TYPE	TIME (MIN.)	PUBLISHER
Credo		*orchestra*	13½	MS.
Two Symphonic Hoe Downs from the "Gallant Greenhorn"		*orchestra*	12	MS.
Softly as the Flute Blows		*flute, strings*	10	MS.
Spiritual		*Fr. hn, strings*	7	MS.
Nostalgia		*fl, 2 Fr. hns, strgs*	6	MS.
Inheritance		*strings, wwds*	6	MS.
Four by Strings		*strings, 4 wwds*	6	MS.
Largo and Dance		*strings*	10	MS.
Adagio and Danse Macabre		*strings*	8	MS.
Suite		*viola, piano or*	10	MS.
		va, strgs, piano	10	MS.
Bang Bang		*percussion, piano*	4	MS.
Free Fantasy for Assorted Brass		*brass*	5	MS.

Music for about 30 radio comedies and many other radio scores.

Swinburne, Dr. Thordur John William

Physician and composer. Born in Edinburgh, Scotland, 1891.

Graduate in medicine, Univ. of Edinburgh. Musical education with own father, Prof. Sv. Sveinbjörnsson and with Huxtable in Edinburgh. Amateur musician. Came to Canada in 1919. Several works have been performed since 1948.

Address: 514-1st Avenue West, Calgary, Alta.

Affiliation: CAPAC.

COMPOSITIONS

TITLE	DATE	TYPE	TIME (MIN.)	PUBLISHER
Sonata in A major	1947	*vln and piano*	15	MS.
Five Organ Pieces (fugues, preludes)	1946-50	*organ*	ea. 3-5	MS.
The Sleep	1937	*choir, organ*	5	MS.
Spring Song	1939	*vocal*	4	MS.
Only for Love	1948	*vocal*	3	MS.

Talbot, Dr. Jean Robert

Violinist, violist, author and composer. Born in Montmagny, P.Q., December 2nd 1893.

Musical education at Académie de Musique, Quebec and at Institute of Musical Art, New York with Stoessel, Kneisel and Svecenski. Degree: Mus.Doc. (Laval).

Secretary of Ecole de Musique, Université Laval, 1922-35 and director since 1932. Director of Société Symphonique de Québec, 1924-36. Member of Société Française de Musicologie (Paris), Internationale Gesellschaft fuer Musikwissenschaft (Basle), and Musical Association (London). Author of textbooks on musical theory, harmony, history etc. and of many articles on musical subjects for various periodicals.

Address: 255 Fraser Street, Quebec, P.Q.

COMPOSITIONS

TITLE	DATE	TYPE	TIME (MIN.)	PUBLISHER
Evangéline		*oratorio*		MS.
Celle qui voit		*lyrical drama*		MS.
Symphonie Classique		*orchestra*		MS.
Conte de Fées		*orchestra*		MS.
Une Journée à la campagne		*orchestra*		MS.
Poème		*vln and orch.*		MS.
Two String Quartets		*string quartet*		MS.
Adagio		*organ*		MS.
Avec le vent		*vocal*		MS.
A la chute des feuilles		*vocal*		MS.
Villanelle		*vocal*		MS.
Madrigal		*vocal*		MS.
L'Oiseau bleu		*vocal*		MS.
La Sainte Vierge		*vocal*		MS.

Tamblyn, Bertha Louise

Composer. Born in Oshawa, Ont.

Musical education at Whitby Ladies College and Royal Conservatory, Toronto with Dr. Vogt, Dr. Anger, D. D. Slater, Leo Smith and T. J. Crawford (piano, voice and composition).

Address: 19 Dunbar Road, Toronto, Ont.

COMPOSITIONS

TITLE	DATE	TYPE	TIME (MIN.)	PUBLISHER
In Holiday Mood	1945	*piano*		MS.
On the Lake	1950	*piano*		MS.
Valse in G	1950	*piano*		MS.
One Bright Morning (march)	1950	*piano*		MS.
Light and Shadow (Woodland Dance)	1946	*piano*		MS.
Glad Tidings (Christmas anthem)	1942	*choral*		Can. Music Sales
Three Anthems: Rest of the Weary; Praise the Lord; Light of Light Shine On	1949	*choral*		Can. Music Sales

COMPOSITIONS

TITLE	DATE	TYPE	TIME (MIN.)	PUBLISHER
Lord Give Us Peace (anthem)	1949	*choral*		F. Harris
Four Anthems: O Promise Blest; Wait Thou on God; O Little Town of Bethlehem; The Lord Is My Shepherd		*choral*		Lorenz, Dayton
Come in Lady Moon	1940	*women or children*		Hall & McCreary Co
Chloris in the Snow	1943	*women or children*		Can. Music Sales
Dear Little Christ Child	1943	*duet (S.A.)*		Can. Music Sales
We Are Seven (7 songs)	1928	*vocal*		G. V. Thompson
Holly Time Songs (15 Christmas songs)	1938	*vocal*		G. V. Thompson
·The Wasted Crust		*vocal*		Can. Music Sales
Mumps	1932	*vocal*		B. L. Tamblyn
Life's Lovely Things	1930	*vocal*		Waterloo Music
Such a Little Way Together	1950	*vocal*		Waterloo Music
God Is Near	1950	*vocal*		Waterloo Music
Grey Rocks and Greyer Sea	1943	*vocal*		B. L. Tamblyn
Good Night Good Morn	1943	*vocal*		B. L. Tamblyn
Flower Time and You	1943	*vocal*		B. L. Tamblun
Evensong	1932	*vocal*		Lorenz, Dayton
A Toast to Canada (patriotic song)	1933	*vocal*		G. V. Thompson
A Soldier's Socks (patriotic song)	1940	*vocal*		Waterloo Music
Life and Love (wedding song)	1943	*vocal*		B. L. Tamblyn

Several other songs and piano pieces.

Tanguay, Georges-Emile

Pianist, organist and composer. Born in Quebec, June 5th, 1893.

Musical education in Quebec with Dessane (piano) and J. A. Bernier (organ), in Paris with Caussade (harmony and counterpoint), Louis Vierne and Mignan (organ), Simone Plé (piano) and in New York with Pietro Yon. Diploma: Lauréat, Académie de Musique de Québec. Organist at L'Immaculée-Conception for over 20 years. Teacher of theory, organ and piano.

Address: 49 Princess Royale, Longueuil, P.Q.

COMPOSITIONS

TITLE	DATE	TYPE	TIME (MIN.)	PUBLISHER
Pavane		*orchestra*	8	MS.
		or piano	8	O. Ditson
Romance		*vln, hp, orchestra*	10	MS.
Lied		*string quintet*		
Souvenir		*'cello and piano*		· Durand, Paris
Air de Ballet		*piano*		Durand, Paris
Scherzo-Valse		*piano*		Durand, Paris
Menuet		*piano*		Durand, Paris

COMPOSITIONS

TITTE	DATE	TYPE	TIME (MIN.)	PUBLISHER
Three Short Pieces		*piano*	10	Roudanez, Paris
Sarabande		*piano*		Archambault
Causerie		*piano*		Passe-Temps
Gavotte et Musette		*piano*		Passe-Temps
O Salutaris		*choral*		Passe-Temps
Cor Jesu		*choral*		Passe-Temps
Cor Jesu		*choral*		L'Action Catholique

Recordings:

Pavane (CBC-Canadian Album No. 2); *Lied* (CBC-Canadian Album No. 3).

See:

Léo-Pol Morin, *Papiers de Musique*, 1930.
No recent information obtained.

Tardif, Rév. Père Hilaire-Marie, O.F.M.

Priest, organist, music teacher and composer. Born in Laconia, N.H., U.S.A., February 7th, 1903.

Musical education with J. Antonio Thompson and Benoît Poirier (piano), Raoul Pâquet (organ and harmony) and Rodolphe Plamondon (vocal culture). Diplomas: Lauréat du Conservatoire National de Montréal (piano), Lauréat de l'Académie de Musique de Québec, section Montréal (organ). Has given many organ recitals and teaches piano, organ and voice in Perth and Edmunston, N.B. and at Fort Fairfield, Maine, U.S. Is director of vocal department at Petit Conservatoire, Edmunston. Has played on radio. Compositions have been performed in Canada and U.S. and also broadcast in France.

Address: P.O. Box 280, Perth, N.B.

COMPOSITIONS

TITLE	DATE	TYPE	TIME (MIN.)	PUBLISHER
Triptyque Marial	1947	*organ*	10	A. Fassio
Berceuse (Lullaby)	1948	*organ*	4	Tardif
Liturgical Harmonies (10 pieces)	1951	*organ (or harmonium)*		H. W. Gray & Co.
Prelude and Fugue in E flat major	1950	*organ*	9	MS.
Fugue in D major	1950	*organ*	5	MS.
Offertoire mystique	1946	*organ (or harm.)*	2	to be published
Bel Astre que j'adore	1946	*choir and harm.*	1½	Librairie S. François, Montreal
Ave Verum	1950	*choir and organ*	3	to be published
L'Attente	1930	*vocal*	1½	Librairie S. François, Montreal
Avec des ailes	1932	*vocal*	2	Librairie S. François, Montreal
Quand l'oiseau (arr. from Martini)	1933	*vocal*	2	Librairie S. François, Montreal

COMPOSITIONS

TITLE	DATE	TYPE	TIME (MIN.)	PUBLISHER
Ave Maria	1950	*vocal duet*	5	MS.
Cantiques du Tiers-Ordre (collection ed. by R. P. Medoche)	1947	*vocal and some accompaniments*		Librairie S. François, Montreal

Several pieces for organ or harmonium in manuscript.

Note:

The two works "to be published" will appear in *La Revue musicale et liturgique* de Québec.

Thompson, Alan Dales

Radio producer, organist, lecturer and composer. Born in Middlesbrough, England' April 7th, 1901.

Musical education at London College of Music with Dr. C. Harris (organ), Sir Henry Wood (conducting) and Percy Pitt (conducting and theory). Diploma: L.L.C.M. Resided in Canada from 1912-16 and 1926-50. Career has included work as concert, church and theatre organist, radio work (for over 25 years) as organist, announcer, producer, conductor etc. On CBC staff from 1945-50. At present production director, radio station WEW, St. Louis, Mo. and part-time lecturer, faculty of music, St. Louis University.

Address: 3658-A Loghborough Avenue, St. Louis 16, Missouri, U.S.A.

Affiliation: BMI.

COMPOSITIONS

TITLE	DATE	TYPE	TIME (MIN.)	PUBLISHERS
Moses (partially completed)	1951	*cantata*	60-75	MS.
Dunkirk (ode)	1942	*bar, choir, orch.*	8	MS.
Per Ardua ad Astra	1942	*chorus and orch.*	9½	MS.
Three Preludes	1934	*organ*	ea. 4	MS.
Toccata on the hymn tune "Leoni"	1938	*organ*	6	MS.
O Father, Like a Child Asleep	1944	*choral*	3	BMI Canada
This Human Way	1947	*choral*	4½	BMI Canada
Reverie of a Soldier	1942	*vocal*	4	BMI Canada
Prayer for Easter Day	1942	*vocal*	3½	BMI Canada
Where He Sleeps	1946	*vocal*	3½	BMI Canada
The Oxen	1948	*vocal*	3½	BMI Canada
Night	1950	*vocal*	2	BMI Canada
Midsummer Fancy	1935	*vocal*	2½	MS.
Awake, O Heart, To Be Loved	1950	*vocal*	4½	MS.

Thompson, Gordon Vincent

Pianist, composer and music publisher. Born in Humberstone, Ont. in 1888.

Musical education with private teachers. Proprietor of Gordon V. Thompson Ltd. Has been writing and publishing music in Canada since 1909. One of active founders of Kiwanis Music Festivals. Is on board of directors of CAPAC. Director, Boys Clubs of Canada, Alma College, St. Thomas. Graduate of Toronto University.

Address: 45 Spadina Road, Apt. 14, Toronto, Ont.

Affiliation: CAPAC.

COMPOSITIONS

TITLE	DATE	TYPE	TIME (MIN.)	PUBLISHER
Life Songs (set of 10 sacred songs)		vocal		G. V. Thompson
Heart Songs (set of 5 sacred songs)		vocal		G. V. Thompson
My Heart's in Canada		vocal		G. V. Thompson
Look for the Dawn of the Morning		vocal		G. V. Thompson
Campfire Memories		vocal		G. V. Thompson
Li'l Black Sheep		vocal		Carl Fischer
Keep the Roses Blooming		vocal		Carl Fischer

Many popular songs.

Thompson, Dr. J. Antonio

Organist, choirmaster, bandmaster and composer. Born in Montreal, November 22nd, 1896.

Musical education in Montreal with J. N. Charbonneau and Elie Savaria (piano) and in Quebec with J. A. Bernier (organ). Degrees: Lauréat, Laval Univ. (organ, 1923); Mus.Doc. (magna cum laude, Montreal, 1950).

Organist since the age of 13. Since 1916 has been organist at Notre Dame des VII Allégresses, Trois Rivières. In 1930 was appointed professor of solfeggio and harmony for Provincial Government, Quebec. Since 1930 has been bandmaster of Philharmonie De La Salle. Has conducted choral and vocal groups.

Address: 928 Père Frédéric, Trois Rivières, P.Q.

COMPOSITIONS

TITLE	DATE	TYPE	TIME (MIN.)	PUBLISHER
Mon Pays (symphonic poem)	1936	orchestra	20	MS.
Voix de chez nous (Canadian songs)	1931	band	9	MS.
A la volette (military march)	1931	band	3	MS.
Le Gai Rosier (military march)	1932	band	3	MS.
Mélodie du Souvenir	1933	band	10	MS.
Valse des ordes	1935	band	6	MS.
Jour du Bonheur	1934	band and 2 solo cts	7	MS.
Fugue in A minor	1928	organ	5	MS.
Fugue, Regina Coeli	1950	organ		MS.
Nocturne E flat minor	1939	piano	5	MS.
Fantasie en forme d'étude	1940	piano	5	MS.
Elévation poétique	1942	piano	5	MS.
Five Preludes	1944-45	piano		MS.
Messe des Morts	1928	choral		MS.
Les sept paroles du Christ	1933	choral	25	MS. (mimeograph)
Messe de Noël	1935	choral		MS.
Messe de Pâques	1941	choral		MS.

COMPOSITIONS

TITLE	DATE	TYPE	TIME (MIN.)	PUBLISHER
Three chants	1928	*vocal*	4	MS.
Le Rossignol	1936	*vocal*	4	MS.
La Mort des Roses	1940	*vocal*	4	MS.
La Tombe et la Rose	1942	*vocal*	4	MS.
Fin de Jour	1935	*vocal*	4	MS.

Several military marches, about 100 folk songs harmonized, short piano pieces, etc.

Tremblay, Gilles Léonce

Composer and pianist. Born in Arvida (Saguenay), P.Q., September 6th, 1932.

Musical education at Quebec Provincial Conservatory in Montreal with Germaine Malépart (piano), Dr. C. Champagne (composition), Gabriel Cusson (ear training) and Mme Ria Lenssens (solfeggio).

Address: 5876 Côte-des-Neiges, Montreal, P.Q.

COMPOSITIONS

TITLE	DATE	TYPE	TIME (MIN.)	PUBLISHER
Double quintette	1950	*2 ea. fl, ob, cl, Fr. hn, bn*	8	MS.
Menuet	1950	*piano*	2½	MS.

Tremblay, Pierre-Joseph-Amadée

Organist and composer. Born in Montreal, April 14th, 1876. Died in Los Angeles, 1949.

Studied organ with Alcibiade Béique; mostly self-taught. Organist in Montreal till 1894; 1894-1920, at Basilica in Ottawa; 1920-23, at Madeleine Church, Salt-Lake-City, U.S.; 1923-49, at St. Vincent's Church in Los Angeles. *L'Intransigeant* was performed in Ottawa, c. 1906.

COMPOSITIONS INCLUDE:

TITLE	DATE	TYPE	TIME (MIN.)	PUBLISHER
L'Intransigeant		*operetta*		
Mass in D flat		*choral*		
Requiem		*choral*		
Ave Maria		*choral*		
O Jeanne d'Arc		*choral*		
Oraison dominicale		*choral*		
Motets		*choral*		
18 Chansons populaires du Canada (harmonized)		*4 male voices or piano*		J. L. Orme, Ottawa
Marche de la Victoire		*4 male voices or piano*		J. L. Orme, Ottawa
		piano		Passe-Temps
Suite (4 mvmts)		*organ*		J. Fischer & Bro
Je vous salue, Marie		*vocal*		
Ressemblances		*vocal*		Archambault
Pour la France		*vocal*		Passe-Temps
Le Canada		*vocal*		performed 1906

Turgeon, Joseph

Pianist, organist and composer. Born in Ste Claire, Dorchester Co., P.Q., March 31st, 1898.

Musical education with Mme Berthe Roy (piano), Henri Gagnon (organ), Robert Talbot and Leo Roy (harmony and composition). Organist at St. Roch, Quebec, since 1922. Professor of music at Laval University, Quebec. Teaches piano at Quebec Provincial Conservatory, Quebec Section.

Address: 157 rue des Franciscains, Quebec, P.Q

COMPOSITIONS

TITLE	DATE	TYPE	TIME (MIN.)	PUBLISHER
O Dieu Puissant	1938	*solo and choir*		L'Action Catholique
Marie modèle de l'épouse	1938	*solo and choir*		L'Action Catholique
Doux trésor de la terre	1938	*solo and choir*		L'Action Catholique
O Meritum Passionis	1939	*vocal*		L'Action Catholique
Pie Jesu	1939	*vocal*		L'Action Catholique
Ave Maria		*vocal*		Bulletin de la société des musiciens d'Eglises

Turner, Robert Comrie

Composer. Born in Montreal, June 6th, 1920.

Musical education at McGill University (Macdonald scholarship in composition) with Douglas Clarke and Claude Champagne; at Royal College of Music, London (composition scholarship, 1947-48) with Herbert Howells (composition) and Gordon Jacob (orchestration); at Berkshire Music Center, summer 1949 (composition department); with Roy Harris, Colorado, 1947 (composition); at Peabody College for Teachers, Nashville, Tenn., 1949-50 with Roy Harris (composition) and Egon Kenton (musicology). Degrees: Mus.Bac. (McGill, 1943), Master of Music (Peabody College). Is candidate for Ph.D (Eastman, Rochester, in composition).

Many works have been performed in concert and on radio in Canada, U.S. and England.

Address: 2668 Estevan Ave., Oak Bay, Victoria, B.C.

COMPOSITIONS

TITLE	DATE	TYPE	TIME (MIN.)	PUBLISHER
Symphonic Evocation	1946	*orchestra*		MS.
Variations in D	1948	*orchestra*		MS.
Canzone	1950	*orchestra*		MS.
Jig Overture	1947	*orchestra (medium)*		MS.
Concerto	1950	*chamber orch.*		MS.
Clarinet Concerto	1948	*clar and strgs*		MS.
Aria	1943	*flute and strgs*		MS.
Toccata Ostinato	1950	*15 brass and perc.*		MS.
Music for Band (3 mvmts)	1950	*symphonic band*		MS.
Scherzo	1946	*4 bassoons*		MS.
String Quartet No. 1	1946	*string quartet*		MS.
String Quartet No. 2	1949	*string quartet*		MS.
Passacaglia	1947	*string quartet*		MS.
Sonatina	1947	*trumpet and piano*		MS.

COMPOSITIONS

TITLE	DATE	TYPE	TIME (MIN.)	PUBLISHER
Sonatina	1951	*oboe and piano*		MS.
Prelude, Chorale and Dance	1948	*piano*		MS.
Libertad (Whitman)	1943	*choral (a capella)*		MS.
Groundswell (Pratt)	1947	*choral (a capella)*		MS.
Choral Cadences	1949	*choral (a capella)*		MS.
Chorale	1949	*choral (a capella)*		MS.
Various songs	1947-48	*vocal*		MS.

Twa, Andrew John

Violinist, violist and composer. Born in Ellisboro, Sask., December 13th, 1919.

Early musical training in Brandon, Man. Studied composition at Royal Conservatory, Toronto with John Weinzweig. Won McGill Chamber Music Society Award in 1949. Was on faculty of Royal Conservatory, Toronto. Works have been performed over CBC.

Address: 368A Bloor Street West, Toronto, Ont.

Affiliation: BMI.

COMPOSITIONS

TITLE	DATE	TYPE	TIME (MIN.)	PUBLISHER
Prairies	1947	*small orchestra*	12	MS.
Serenade No. 1	1948	*clar and strings*	6	MS.
Serenade No. 2	1950	*bn and strings*	8	MS.
String Quartet	1948	*string quartet*	15	MS.
Sonata	1951	*vln and piano*	7	MS.
Sonata	1948	*solo violin*	7	MS.
Sonata	1951	*viola and piano*	10	MS.

Vallerand, Jean

Music critic, composer, conductor and lecturer. Born in Montreal, December 24th 1915.

Musical education with Lucien Sicotte (violin) and Claude Champagne (harmony and allied subjects). Degrees and diploma: B.A., Lic. in Letters, Diploma in Journalism (Montreal Univ.). Music critic for seven years for Le Canada and also for Montréal-Matin. Conductor for Opera Guild of Montreal, CBC, Les Concerts Symphoniques. Lecturer and conductor for *Radio-Collège* for eight years. In 1942 was appointed general secretary for Quebec Provincial Conservatory. Teacher of music history and musicography, faculty of music, Montreal University. Winner of the Schumann trophy for composition in Quebec in 1940.

Address: 4292 Boyer Street, Montreal, P.Q.

Affiliation: CAPAC.

COMPOSITIONS

TITLE	DATE	TYPE	TIME (MIN.)	PUBLISHER
Symphony (3 mvmts)		*orchestra*		MS.
Symphony	1951	*orchestra*		MS.
Le Diable dans le beffroi		*orchestra*	14	MS.

COMPOSITIONS

TITLE	DATE	TYPE	TIME (MIN.)	PUBLISHER
Tryptique		*orchestra*		MS.
Prelude	1948	*orchestra*	13	MS.
Nocturne	1947	*orchestra*	28	MS.
Violin Concerto	1951	*vln and orch.*	26	MS.
Two Cantatas	1946	*ten, choir, orch.* ea.	6	MS.
Sonata	1950	*vln and piano*	15	MS.
Les Roses à la mer		*vocal*	3	MS.

Books:

La musique et les tout-petits, Montreal, 1950.
Introduction à la musique, Montreal, 1949.

Verdickt, Benoît

Organist, choirmaster and composer. Born in Wolverthem, Belgium, September 27th, 1884.

Musical education at Ecole Interdiocésaine de Musique Réligieuse with Edgar Tinel, Aloys Desmet and Oscar Depuydt. Organist in Victoriaville, P.Q., 1906-12, in Rochester, N.Y., 1912-13. Choirmaster in Lachine, P.Q. since 1913. Professor of solfeggio for Quebec Provincial Government for 26 years.

Address: 116 A-11th Avenue, Lachine, P.Q.

COMPOSITIONS

TITLE	DATE	TYPE	TIME (MIN.)	PUBLISHER
Missa pro defunctis		*choral*	35	Verdickt
Cantique de Mariage		*choral*		Verdickt
Ave Maria		*choral*		Verdickt

Vermandere, Dr. Joseph

(Rév. Frère Placide Vermandere, c.s.c.)

Organist and composer. Born in Heule, Belgium, January 18th, 1901.

Musical education with Benoît Poirier (organ) and Raoul Pâquet (organ and harmony), Alfred Laliberté (piano). Degree: Mus.Doc. (summa cum laude, Montreal, 1945). Has been organist of Oratoire St. Joseph for many years. *Te Deum* was performed over CBC on May 13th, 1945 to celebrate victory, and broadcast by transcription in Belgium in 1948.

Address: 46 Surrey Gardens, Westmount, Montreal, P.Q.

Affiliation: CAPAC.

COMPOSITIONS

TITLE	DATE	TYPE	TIME (MIN.)	PUBLISHER
Te Deum	1945	*soli, choir, orch, organ*	40-50	short score in ltd edition
Mass in E	1938	*choir and organ*		MS.
Hymne à Ville-Marie (Montreal tercentenary)	1942	*choral*		MS.
Ode à Jacques Cartier (Cartier quadricentennial)	1935	*soli, choir, organ*	15	Archambault

COMPOSITIONS

TITLE	DATE	TYPE	TIME (MIN.)	PUBLISHER
Les Ouvriers de Dieu	1925	*soli and chorus*		MS.
Salut à Québec	1939	*choral*		MS.
Choeur parlé de la J.O.C. (1)	1935	*band and speaking chorus*		MS.
Choeur parlé de la J.O.C. (2)	1936	*band and speaking chorus*		MS.
La Défaite de l'enfer (jeu choral)	1938	*soli and chorus*		MS.
Huon de Bordeaux (incidental music; Alex. Arnoux)	1947	*ballet, choir, orch.*	50	MS.
Polyeucte (incidental music; Corneille)	1934	*soli, choir, orch.*	60	MS.
Le Roi Cerf (incidental music; Pierre Barbier)	1948	*ballet, voice, orch.*	50	MS.
`Adeste Fidelis (harmon.)	1939	*choral*		MS.
La Légende de Sainte-Anne d'Auray (harmon.)	1941	*choral*		MS.
Dans tous les cantons (harmon.)	1935	*choral*		MS.
Marianne s'en va (harmon.)	1932	*choral*		MS.
Au Pied de la crèche (harmon.)	1943	*vocal*		Librairie St. François, Montreal
De Profundis (motet)	1938	*choral*		publ. in "Chants et motets pour les défunts," Quebec
Ecce Fidelis (motet)	1921	*choir and organ*		publ. in "Le Messager du T. S. Sacre-ment," March 1943
Quicumque Sanus (motet)	1922	*chora*		publ. in "Annales de St. Joseph du Mont-Royal" 1922

Many other motes, sacred and secular songs, incidental choruses, harmonisations and arrangements. Incidental music to *Canossa* (Lonhays), *Esther* (Racine), *Vercingétorix* (Bizeul and Jourand), *Les Matines de Saint Joseph* (Brochet) and other plays.

Vézina, Dr. Joseph

Conductor, bandmaster, instrumentalist, music teacher and composer. Born in Quebec, June 9th, 1849. Died in Quebec, October 5th, 1924.

Education at Quebec Seminary and Quebec Military School. Musical studies with own father, François Vézina and for six months with Calixa Lavallée (harmony); mostly self-taught. In 1867 joined the 9th Battalion band, and in 1869 became bandmaster. In 1875 founded Harmonie de Notre-Dame de Beauport. Founded and conducted many bands. In 1903 founded Société Symphonique de Québec and conducted it till 1924. Organist at St. Patrick's, Quebec, 1896-1912 and since 1912 choirmaster at Quebec Basilica. Conducted many festival concerts in Quebec. The *Mosaïque* contains *O Canada* and was first performed on June 24th, 1880. One of presidents of Académie de Musique, Québec. Degree: hon. Mus.Doc. (Laval, 1922). One of the great pioneers of music in Canada.

Inquiries: Raoul Vézina, Laval University, Quebec, P.Q.

COMPOSITIONS

TITLE	DATE	TYPE	TIME (MIN.)	PUBLISHER
Le Lauréat (hon. Marchand)	1906	*operetta*		MS.
Le Rajah (Ben. Michaud)	1910	*operette bouffe*		MS.
Le Fétiche (A. Langlais & A. Plante)	1912	*operette bouffe*		MS.
Mosaïque sur des airs populaires Canadiens	1880	*orchestra or band*		MS.
	1920-24	*arr. for piano*		Procure Générale
Ton Sourire (valse de concert)	1882	*orchestra or band*		MS.
Souffle Perfume (valse de concert)	1882	*orchestra or band*		MS.
La Brise (valse de concert)	1886	*orchestra or band*		MS.
Le Jubilé de la Reine Victoria (march)	1887	*orchestra or band*		MS.
Conversazione (gavotte)	1891	*orchestra or band*		MS.
Le Lys Blanc (mazurka)	1891	*orchestra or band*		MS.
Canadian Rifles (waltz)	1870	*band*		MS.
Le Voltigeur de Quebec (regim. march)	1879	*band*		MS.
Laetitia (polka)	1880	*band (cornet solo)*		MS.
Toujours aimée (waltz)	1881	*band*		MS.
Gallant Artilleur (overture)	1882	*band*		MS.
Mont Cenis (allegro militaire)	1883	*band*		MS.
Fantaisie Caractéristique	1883	*band*		MS.
Grand Valse de Concert	1883	*band (cornet solo)*		MS.
De Calgary à McLeod (march, souvenir of N.W. expeditions)	1889	*band*		MS.
Royal Rifles (regimental march)	1890	*band*		MS.
Paardeberg (march)	1900	*band*		MS.
Royal Grand March (Duke of York Visit)	1901	*band*		MS.
Friskarina (overture)	1905	*band*		Samuels, Boston
Les Roses d'or (waltz)	1876	*piano*		A. & J. Vézina
L'Oiseau mouche	1885	*flute*		MS.
En Avant (patriotic song)	1914	*vocal*		Passe-Temps

Other dance music:

Galops: *Frontenac* (1879); *Bucephale* (1876); *B.B. Battery Officers* (1880); *Presto* (1884); *Volcano* (1884); *Carneval de Québec* (1894).

Waltzes: *Une Pensée* (1886); *Alice* (1887); *Yeux Créoles* (1888); *Souvenir d'Amour* (1901); *Luciana* (1913); *Germania* (1913); *Pierrette* (1916); *Valse Chantée* (1880); *Fleur de Mai* (1877); *Estrella* (1881).
Polkas: *Cupid* (1884); *Noon Gun* (1883); *Ice Palace* (1894).

Marches for piano:

La Canadienne (1878); *Otto Lorne* (1879); *Goodbye Sweetheart* (1879); *Albany* (1879); *Glamorgan* (1894); *17th Regiment* (1895); *C. W. A. March* (1896); *Vive Champlain* (1898).

Miscellaneous works:

Pot-pourri sur des mélodies canadiennes (1877); *Chant de l'Union des Raquetteurs* (1886); *Quadrille de l'Union commerciale des Raquetteurs* (1886); *Hymne à l'Union Musicale* (1887); *Premier Neige* (cornet solo, 1889); *Je me souviens* (voice and choir, 1898); *Music Charms* (song with violin obl., 1907); *Antienne à St. François d'Assise* (1920); *Chant triomphal* (1923); *Duo de piston* (unfinished, 1924).
Manuscripts are in the hands of Mr. Raoul Vézina.

Villeneuve, Marie-Louise Diane

(Rév. Soeur Marie-Héloïse, S.S.A.)

Pianist, organist, choral conductor and composer. Born in Ste. Anne des Plaines, P.Q., August 15th, 1889.

Musical education with R. O. Pelletier, R. Pelletier, Raoul Pâquet, Rodolphe Mathieu, Auguste Descarries, Rev. Ethelbert Thibault, Fleurette Contant and Jean Charbonneau (theory, composition, singing, piano, organ, choral conducting). Degree: Mus.Bac. (Conservatoire National, Quebec). Diploma: Lauréat (Académie de Musique de Québec). Music teacher at convents of the Soeurs de Sainte-Anne.

Address: 1250 rue Saint-Joseph, Lachine, P.Q.

COMPOSITIONS

TITLE	DATE	TYPE	TIME (MIN.)	PUBLISHER
Prelude No. 1		*piano*	1	MS.
Prelude No. 2		*piano*	1	MS.
La Samaritaine		*vocal*	5	MS.
Le Semeur		*vocal*	15	MS.
Cor Jesu		*vocal*	2	MS.
O Salutaris		*vocal*	2	MS.
Adorate		*vocal*	2	MS.
Chemin faisant		*vocal*	2	MS.

Vinette, Alice

(Rév. Soeur Marie-Jocelyne, S.S.A.)

Pianist, organist and composer. Born in Saint-Urbain, P.Q., April 24th, 1894.

Musical education with R. O. Pelletier (piano), Raoul Pâquet (organ and harmony), Rodolphe Mathieu and Auguste Descarries (composition) and Fleurette Contant (singing). Degree: Mus.Bac. Teacher of harmony, counterpoint, voice, piano and organ at Institut Pédagogique des Soeurs de Sainte-Anne.

Address: 1250 rue Saint-Joseph, Lachine, P.Q.

COMPOSITIONS

TITLE	DATE	TYPE	TIME (MIN.)	PUBLISHER
Messe brève	1950	*3 equal voices*	35	Editions de la Violette
Prélude		*piano*	2	MS.
Si tu savais le don de Dieu (Poème evangélique)		*vocal*	13½	MS.

Shorter vocal works in manuscript:

Parce Domine; Regina Coeli; Cor Jesu; Sourire; Mes souhaits (pour le nouvel an); Voeux du coeur (fête de mères).

Vocelle, Lucien

Violinist, pianist and composer. Born in Quebec, July 2nd, 1910.

Musical education with Joseph Côté and J. Robert Talbot (violin), Rév. Frère Raymondien (theory), at Ecole de Musique, Université Laval with Omer Letourneau, J. R. Talbot, Emile Larochelle and Berthe Roy. Diploma: Lauréat (Académie de Musique de Québec, 1930). In the past few years has been adjudicator for Rotary Club competition "A la recherche des talents". Since 1949 has been member of Académie de Musique de Québec.

Address: 277 rue Richelieu, Quebec, P.Q.

COMPOSITIONS

TITLE	DATE	TYPE	TIME (MIN.)	PUBLISHER
Concerto for Violin	1946	*vln and orchestra*	37	MS.
Concerto for Piano	1936	*piano and orch.*	25	MS.
Edith Cavell (symphonic poem)	1942	*orchestra*	20	MS.
Manon (overture)	1935	*orchestra*	17	MS.
Trois Danses Canadiennes	1938	*orchestra*	18	MS.
Les Fonctionnaires (poème humoristique)	1949	*orchestra*	20	MS.
Ouverture pour une comédie	1950	*orchestra*	15	MS.
Les Ombres sur la neige	1948	*strings*	8	MS.
Poème	1943	*small orchestra*	8	MS.
Military Spirit	1945	*string quartet*	12	MS.
Minnewawa		*violin*	3	Parnasse Musical
Mélancolie		*piano*	2½	MS.
Mai; Berceuse		*piano*	5	MS.
Les Allées du Souvenir	1949	*vocal*		Parnasse Musical
Lilas; Complainte; Berceuse; La Lumière; Maison à louer		*vocal*		MS.

Vogt, Dr. Augustus Stephen

Choral conductor, organist, music teacher and composer. Born in Washington, Ont. (or Elmira, Ont.), August 14th, 1861. Died in Toronto, September 17th, 1926.

Musical education in Boston and from 1885-88 in Leipzig. Founded and conducted Mendelssohn Choir of Toronto, 1894-97, 1900-17. Principal of Toronto Conservatory of Music, 1913-26. Dean, faculty of music, University of Toronto, 1919-26. Degree: hon. Mus.Doc. (Toronto, 1906). One of Canada's great music pioneers.

COMPOSITIONS

TITLE	DATE	TYPE	TIME (MIN.)	PUBLISHER
The Sea		*choral*		G. Schirmer
Crossing the Bar		*choral*		Whaley Royce
An Indian Lullaby		*women's voices*		Whaley Royce
The Lord's Prayer, arr.		*choral*		Whaley Royce

Other choral works and arrangements.

Books:

Modern Pianoforte Technique, 1900.
Standard Anthem Book, 1894.

See:

Augustus Bridle, *Vogt, a great chorus master. The Year Book of Canadian Art,* 1913.
G. D. Atkinson, *Dr. Vogt and Church Music.* The New Outlook, Oct. 1926.

Waizman, Louis ·

Instrumentalist, librarian, composer and arranger. Born in Salzburg, Austria, November 6th, 1863. Died in Toronto, August 24th, 1951.

Musical education at Mozarteum School of Music in Salzburg. Graduated in 1884. Teachers: Dr. Hummel, Konrad, Charles Kunz, August Wild. Studied composition and counterpoint with J. Rheinberger. Came to Canada in 1893. Played trombone in band and for ten years viola in Toronto Symphony Orchestra, besides playing piano, viola and 'cello in theatres. For 23 years was librarian and later honorary librarian, Toronto Symphony Orchestra. Joined CBC in 1933 and was staff arranger until his death.

COMPOSITIONS

TITLE	DATE	TYPE	TIME (MIN.)	PUBLISHER
Ballet Suite		orchestra		MS., performed by T.S.O., 1930
Suite No. 3		orchestra		MS.
Happy Birthday Suite	1943	orchestra		MS.
Humoresque	1949	orchestra		MS.
Smiling Gypsy	1949	orchestra		MS.
Concert Caprice		piano and orch.		MS., performed 1906
Happy Family Suite	1943	strings		MS.
Berceuse	1946	strings		MS.
Smile! Smile!	1946	strings		MS.
The Witches Dance	1946	strings		MS.
Oh! It's You	1948	strings		MS.
Serenade	1948	strings		MS.
Humoresque	1948	strings		MS.
Song Without Words	1948	piano and strings		MS.
Impromptu	1950	piano and strings		MS.
Just You and Me	1948	ob, bn and strings		MS.
Suite	1948	Engl. hn and strings		MS.
Suite	1950	oboe and strings		MS.
Poème d'Amour	1928	piano or orchestra		Waterloo Music

Several piano pieces were printed in Musical Canada periodical, 1928-29. Many arrangements and other compositions. Many of the manuscripts listed above are in the CBC Toronto Music Library.

Walter, Dr. Arnold Maria

Composer, musicologist, lecturer, pianist and harpsichordist. Born in Hannsdorf, Moravia (formerly Austria), August 30th, 1902.

Education at University of Prague (Carolinum) and University of Berlin (under Hermann Abert, Johannes Wolf, Curt Sachs). Private teachers: R. M. Breithaupt and Frederic Lamond (piano) and Bruno Weigl (composition). Degree: Dr. iur. utr. (Prague, 1926).

Lecturer at Volkshochschule (Free University), Brno, Moravia, 1928-30. Musical editor of Vorwaerts and Weltbuehne, Berlin, 1930-33. Studies of Spanish and Catalan folklore—Palma de Mallorca, Barcelona, Madrid, 1933-36. Director of music at Upper Canada College, Toronto, 1937-43. Is director of Senior School and Opera School, Royal Conservatory, Toronto, and director of Royal Conservatory Opera Company. Vice-president, Canadian Music Council. Recipient of Christian Culture Gold Medal.

Address: 427 Roselawn Avenue, Toronto, Ont.

Affiliation: CAPAC.

COMPOSITIONS

TITLE	DATE	TYPE	TIME (MIN.)	PUBLISHER
Symphony in G minor	1944	*orchestra*	30	Assoc. Music Publ. (rental)
For the Fallen (cantata)	1949	*sop, choir, orch.*	16	MS.
Music for Harpischord and Strings		*hpchd and strgs*	10	MS.
Trio		*vln, vc, piano*	20	MS.
Sonata		*vln and piano*	20	MS.
Novelette		*vln and piano*	5	MS.
Sonatina		*vc and piano*	15	MS.
Praeludium, Notturno, Fuga (suite)	1945	*piano*	10	MS.
Six Studies	1946	*piano*	18	Oxford U.P.
Toccata	1947	*piano*	8	MS.
Sonata	1950	*piano*	15	G. V. Thompson
Sacred Songs (3)		*sop, strgs, piano*		MS.

Several scores of music for radio plays.

Waterman, Constance Dorothy

Pianist, accompanist and composer. Born in London, England.

Musical education in England with St. Quentin Downer and Miriam Genny, in Belgium at St. Ursule Convent with Mère Hélène Bartholdy, in Canada with Mme Borowski. At the age of 12 won honorable mention in an open English competition for setting of a "Grace". Winner of prizes for compositions.

Address: 1156 Burnaby Street, Vancouver, B.C.

COMPOSITIONS

TITLE	DATE	TYPE	TIME (MIN.)	PUBLISHER
I Will Lift Up Mine Eyes (anthem)	1939	*choral*	5	MS.
Dolly's Lullaby (grade II piece)	1949	*piano duet*	4	MS.

Songs:

The Lute; Ah! With the Grape				Western Music
Seasons; When I Am Dead; The Song My Paddle Sings; Okanagan Valley				MS.
The Great Big Bumble Bee (with orchestra)				published

Weatherseed, John Joseph

Pianist, organist, choirmaster, adjudicator, lecturer, conductor and composer. Born in Hastings, England, October 20th, 1900.

Musical education in Hastings with H. V. W. Batts and Reg. E. Groves (piano, organ, theory), in London with D. Harold Darke, Oscar Beringer and Walford Davies (organ, theory, piano and conducting). On staff of Royal Conservatory, Toronto.

Address: 111 Oriole Parkway, Toronto, Ont.

COMPOSITIONS

TITLE	DATE	TYPE	TIME (MIN.)	PUBLISHER
Prelude on a Plain Song		*organ*	4	MS.
An Easter Prelude	1950	*organ*	4	MS.
Thou O God Art Praised in Zion (anthem)		*choral*	3	Boston Music Co.
God Be Merciful Unto Us and Bless Us (anthem)		*choral*	4	Boston Music Co.
Lighten Our Darkness	1946	*choral*	3	Boston Music Co.
Prevent Us O Lord	1948	*choral*	3	Boston Music Co.
Descants for various hymns		*choral*		MS.

Weinzweig, John Jacob

Composer and music teacher. Born in Toronto, March 11th, 1913.

Musical education with Gertrude Anderson and George Boyce (piano), at University of Toronto with Leo Smith, Healey Willan, Sir Ernest MacMillan, Reginald Stewart (conducting), at Eastman School of Music, University of Rochester with Bernard Rogers (composition), Paul White (conducting), Nelson Watson (string bass). Degrees: Mus.Bac. (Toronto), M.Mus. (Rochester).

Founder and conductor of the University of Toronto Symphony Orchestra, 1934-37. Is now teacher of composition and orchestration at Royal Conservatory, Toronto. *Divertimento for Flute and Strings* won second prize (highest given) in Olympic Games musical competition, chamber-music class, 1948. A 1½-hour Trans-Canada broadcast of his works took place in May 1951. Is chairman of the Canadian League of Composers.

Address: 101 Belgravia Road, Toronto, Ont.

Affiliation: CAPAC.

COMPOSITIONS

TITLE	DATE	TYPE	TIME (MIN.)	PUBLISHER
Instrumental works:				
The Red Ear of Corn	1949	*ballet in 2 acts*	30	MS.
The Red Ear of Corn (suite)	1949	*orchestra*	15	MS.
Symphony No. 1	1940	*orchestra*	30	MS.
The Whirling Dwarf	1937	*orchestra*	3	MS.
Legend	1937	*orchestra*	5	MS.
The Enchanted Hill (tone poem)	1938	*orchestra*	10	MS.
Suite	1938	*orchestra*	7	MS.

COMPOSITIONS

TITLE	DATE	TYPE	TIME (MIN.)	PUBLISHER
A Tale of Tuamotu	1939	orchestra (solo bassoon)	23	MS.
Music for Radio No. 1 (Our Canada)	1943	orchestra	13	MS.
Prelude to a New Day	1944	orchestra	5	MS.
Music for Radio No. 2 (Edge of the World)	1946	orchestra	7	MS.
Round Dance	1950	orchestra	3	MS.
Violin Concerto	1951	vln and orch.	20	MS.
Spectre	1928	tymp and strings	7	MS.
Interlude in an Artist's Life	1943	strings	7	MS.
Divertimento No. 1	1946	flute and strings	10½	Boosey & Hawkes
Divertimento No. 2	1947	oboe and strings	14	Boosey & Hawkes
Fanfare for Brass Instruments	1943	brass	2¼	MS.
Band-Hut Sketches	1944	band	3	MS.
String Quartet No. 1	1937	string quartet	14	MS.
String Quartet No. 2	1946	string quartet	10	MS.
Intermissions	1943	flute and oboe	10	MS.
Sonata	1941	violin and piano	8	MS.
Sonata	1948-49	'cello and piano	15½	MS.
Improvisation on an Indian tune	1942	organ	5	MS.
Suite No. 1	1939	piano	10	MS.
Suite No. 2	1949-50	piano	10	MS.
Sonata	1950	piano	10	MS.

Vocal works:

To The Lands Over Yonder (Eskimo)	1945	choral	5	MS.
The Great Flood (Indian)	1948	choral and perc.		MS.
Of Time and the World (song cycle)	1947	vocal	6	MS.

Music for films (commissioned by the National Film Board) including *West-Wind* (Life and Art of Tom Thomson) 1942.
Music for radio (commissioned by CBC); over 100 scores for radio plays (1941-).

Recordings:
Interlude in an Artist's Life (CBC-Canadian Album No. 2)
String Quartet No. 1.
Music for Radio No. 1.

Whitehead, Dr. Alfred E.

Organist, lecturer and composer. Born in Peterborough, England, July 10th, 1887.

Musical education at Peterborough Cathedral with Dr. Haydn Keeton, in Huddersfield with Dr. Eaglefield Hull. Degree: Mus.Doc. (McGill, 1922). Diplomas: F.R.C.O., F.C.C.O. Organist and choirmaster in Peterborough, 1905-12. Came to Canada in 1912. Assistant director, Mount Allison Conservatory, Sackville, N.B., 1913-15. Organist of Christ Church Cathedral, Montreal, 1922-1947. President Canadian College of Organists, 1930-31, 1935-37. Since 1947 professor of organ and theoretical subjects and dean of the Conservatory, Mt. Allison University.

Address: c/o Mount Allison University, Sackville, N.B.

Affiliation: CAPAC.

COMPOSITIONS

TITLE	DATE	TYPE	TIME (MIN.)	PUBLISHER
Passacaglia		*organ*		H. W. Gray & Co.
Prelude on a theme by Gibbons		*organ*		H. W. Gray & Co.
Prelude on "Winchester Old"		*organ*		H. W. Gray & Co.

Anthems:

God, O Kinsman Loved; Grant Us Grace, Lord; Hast Thou Not Known; Heavens Declare the Glory; Lead Kindly Light; Now in This Holy Hour; Through the Night of Doubt and Sorrow   J. Curwen & Sons

If Ye Then Be Risen with Christ (Easter); Praise Him, Ye That Fear Him; Praise to the Lord; 'Tis the Spring of Souls Today   H. W. Gray & Co.

Jesu, Bread of Life, I Pray Thee; Saviour Breathe an Evening Blessing   Western Music

`Choral works for mixed voices:

The Jesus-Child My Joy Shall Be; In Songs of Rejoicing; Deck Thyself, My Soul; Alleluia; Chariots of the Lord Are Strong; Lord of Our Life; Whither, Shepherds; O Gladsome Light; Ye Choirs of Jerusalem   A. P. Schmidt

Whereas I View Thy Comely Grace; Lift Up Your Voices Now; Pioneers; Watch Thou, Dear Lord; Go, My Boat, and Bravely Sail   O. Ditson

Alleluia; Angels Holy; Come Sweet Evening Guest; Light Beyond Our Utmost Light; May the Strength of God; Watchman, From the Height Beholding   Boston Music Co.

Winter's End; As Bends the White Birch; The Hawthorne Tree   Galaxy Music Corp.

Carols:

All Mankind; All My Heart This Night Rejoices; Bell Carol   Boston Music Co.

In the Tomb the Dear Lord Lay (Easter); Whom of Old the Shepherds Praised; Unto Us Is Born   H. W. Gray & Co.

O Christ Child so Fair; See How Bright Is That Star; Prophets and Kings; I Have Seen Sweet Mary Go; Shout O Earth   J. Curwen & Sons

All You in This House; Sweet Baby, Sleep   O. Ditson

Come in, Dear Angels; Dear Nightingale, Awake!; O Jesus So Sweet; O Gay Is the Day We Sing; The Christ-Child Smiles   Western Music

The Seven Joys of Mary   A. P. Schmidt

Motets:

Almighty God, Whose Glory; Make Us Love Thee   A. P. Schmidt

O Lord Support Us; Jesu, Gentlest Saviour   G. V. Thompson

Jesu, the Very Thought of Thee   H. W. Gray & Co.

The King of Heaven (*6 part chorus*)   O. Ditson

Choral works for male voices:

The Dead Horse; Johnny, Come Down to Hilo; Tom's Gone to Hilo   H. W. Gray & Co.

Through a Long Cloister   Galaxy Music Corp.

Choral works for women's voices:

The Pedlar   O. Ditson

Circus Parade (*also for mixed choir*)   A. P. Schmidt

Songs:

The Milkman; Mister Fiddler, Play a Polka   O. Ditson

Woodlands in Spring (*soprano duet*); The Croon Carol   G. V. Thompson

Have You Seen a Lady   Novello

COMPOSITIONS

TITLE	DATE	TYPE	TIME (MIN.)	PUBLISHER

Other choral and vocal works:

TITLE	DATE	TYPE	TIME (MIN.)	PUBLISHER
Magnificat and Nunc Dimittis		*double choir and organ*		G. V. Thompson
Most Glorious Lord of Life (Easter motet)		*double choir and organ*		H. W. Gray & Co.
18 Fauxbourdons and Descants for well-known hymns				G. V. Thompson

Many other compositions, published and unpublished.
Arrangements of French Canadian folk songs.

Willan, Dr. Healey

Composer, organist, choral conductor and lecturer. Born near London, England, October 12th, 1880.

Musical education at St. Saviour's Choir School, Eastbourne and with Wm. Stevenson Hoyte. Degree: hon. Mus.Doc. (Toronto, 1920). Diploma: F.R.C.O. (1899).

Came to Canada in 1913 to become head of the theory department, Royal Conservatory, Toronto; vice-principal, 1920-36. In 1914 appointed lecturer and examiner, in 1932 university organist, in 1937 professor of music, University of Toronto. Retired except as university organist in 1950. From 1919-25 was musical director of Hart House Theatre, University of Toronto.

Organist and musical director of St. Mary Magdalen Church, Toronto, since 1921. Founder and conductor of Tudor Singers, 1934-39 (disbanded because of war). Their work has been taken over by the Choir of St. M.M. (in secular programs called St. M.M. Singers). Member, London Gregorian Society since 1910. President of Arts and Letters Club, Toronto, 1922. President of Canadian College of Organists, 1922-23 and 1933-35.

The dramatic works *Transit Through Fire, Deirdre,* and *Brebeuf* were commissioned and broadcast by the CBC.

Address: 139 Inglewood Drive, Toronto, Ont.

Affiliation: BMI.

COMPOSITIONS

TITLE	DATE	TYPE	TIME (MIN.)	PUBLISHER
Orchestral works:				
Symphony No. 1 in D minor	1936	*orchestra*		MS.
Symphony No. 2 in C minor	1950	*orchestra*		MS.
Coronation March	1937	*orchestra*		MS.
A Marching Tune	1942	*orchestra*		MS.
Concerto for Piano		*piano and orch.*		BMI Canada (rental)
Agincourt Song		*small orchestra*		Oxford U.P., 1929
Royce Hall Suite		*symphonic band*		Assoc. Music Publ., 1951
Chamber and piano works:				
Adagio in E		*string quartet*		MS.
Trio in B minor	1920	*vln, vc, piano*		MS.
Chorale Prelude No. 1		*arr. for str quartet*		MS.
Sonata No. 1 in E minor		*violin and piano*		F. Harris, 1928
Sonata No. 2 in E major	1923	*violin and piano*		Bosworth
Romance in E flat major		*violin and piano*		Augener

COMPOSITIONS

TITLE	DATE	TYPE	TIME (MIN.)	PUBLISHER
Theme and Variations	1916-43	*two pianos*		MS.
Three Sketches of Old London		*piano*		F. Harris, 1930
Three Short Pieces		*piano*		Cary
Peter's Book		*piano*		F. Harris, 1936
Valse in A major		*piano duet*		MS.
Suite in F major (3 mvmts)		*rhythm band*		F. Harris, 1938

Organ works:

Fantasia on "Ad coenam agni"		*organ*	4	Novello
Epilogue			5	Novello
Prelude and Fugue in B minor			6	Novello
Prelude and Fugue in C minor			8	Novello
Introduction, Passacaglia and Fugue			18	Oxford U.P., 1919
Chorale Prelude				
1. Puer nobis nascitur			4	Oxford U.P., 1926
2. Andernach			4	Oxford U.P.
Six Short Pieces: Prelude, Communion, Trio, Scherzo Intermezzo and Finale				Ascherberg, 1947
Barcarolle				Ascherberg, 1950
Elegy				H. W. Gray & Co.
Fugue in G minor	1947			MS.
Six Chorale Preludes (first set)				Concordia, 1950
Six Chorale Preludes (second set)				Concordia, 1951
Five Preludes on Plain song Melodies				Oxford U.P., 1951
Four pieces arranged for organ				Novello
Organ arrangements and albums				F. Harris

Dramatic works:

Transit Through Fire (J. Coulter)	1942	*radio opera (4 scenes)*		MS.
Deirdre (J. Coulter)	1946	*opera (3 acts)*		MS.
Brebeuf (prologue, incidental music, epilogue, E. J. Pratt)	1943			MS.
The Order of Good Cheer		*ballad opera*		F. Harris, 1928
Prince Charlie		*ballad opera*		MS.
Maureen		*ballad opera*		MS.
An Indian Christmas Play		*ballad opera*		MS.
The Ayrshire Ploughman		*ballad opera*		MS.
Castles in the Air (B. Forsyth)		*christmas play*		MS.
Chester Mysteries		*incidental music*		F. Harris, 1929
Indian Nativity Play (J. M. Gibbon)	1930	*incidental music*		MS.

COMPOSITIONS

TITLE	DATE	TYPE	TIME (MIN.)	PUBLISHER
The Beggar's Opera (with new symphonies and accompaniments, arr.)				F. Harris, 1928
Incidental music to many Hart House Productions				

Choral works with orchestra:

Te Deum (Coronation)		*double choir*	13	F. Harris, 1937
England, My England				H. W. Gray & Co., 1914
The Mystery of Bethlehem		*soli, brass and organ*		H. W. Gray, & Co., 1923
Coronation Ode		*with small orch.*		F. Harris, 1936
A Dirge for two Veterans				MS.
The Trumpet Call				Oxford, U.P., 1941

Carols and hymn tunes:

Here Are We in Bethlehem		*S.A.T.B.*		Oxford U.P., 1930
Regina Coeli Letare		*S.S.A.A.*		F. Harris, 1928
Tyrle Tyrlow		*S.S.A.A.*		F. Harris, 1928
Make We Merry		*S.A.T.B.*		BMI Canada, 1949
Welcome Yule		*T.T.B.B.*		BMI Canada, 1949
The Twelve Days of Christmas		*S.S.A.T.B.*		BMI Canada, 1949
A Christmas Lullaby		*S.S.A. and baritone*		BMI Canada, 1950
Recessional (Kipling)		*choir and organ*		F. Harris, 1928

Many arrangements of carols and hymn tunes, published by H. W. Gray & Co., Oxford U.P., F. Harris.

Hymns:

Ten Faux Bourdons on well-known hymns				Oxford U.P., 1927
Five Tunes				Oxford U.P., 1927
Four Processionals				H. W. Gray & Co., 1925
Book of Fauxbourdons				Western Music, 1950
Introits				Western Music, 1950

Services:

Te Deum in B flat (with antiphons for the coronation)		*choir and orchestra*		F. Harris, 1938
Te Deum in B flat				H. W. Gray & Co., 1909
Jubilate in B flat				H. W. Gray & Co., 1918
Benedictus in B flat				H. W. Gray & Co., 1917
Benedictus es, Domine				H. W. Gray & Co., 1935

COMPOSITIONS

TITLE	DATE	TYPE	TIME (MIN.)	PUBLISHER
Benedictus es, Domine (with fauxbourdon) (set to plain song tones)				H. W. Gray & Co., 1936
Benedicite in D				Novello, 1911
Two Magnificat and Nunc Dimittis (B flat, E flat)				Novello, 1906, 1912
Four Magnificat and Nunc Dimittis (set to plain song tones)				H. W. Gray & Co., 1909, 47, 48
Four Magnificat and Nunc Dimittis (set to plain song tones)				Faith Press, 1935, 37, 39
Six Magnificat and Nunc Dimittis (set to plain song tones)				Oxford U.P., 1928
Magnificat and Nunc Dimittis (set to plain song tones)				Oxford U.P., 1930,
Two Communion Services in G, and C and E flat				Novello, 1906, 1910
Communion Service in D (Unison; Missa de Sancta Maria Magdalena)				Oxford U.P., 1928
Communion Service in E flat (Missa de Sancti Albano)				Oxford U.P., 1929
Missa Brevis No. 1-6				Carl Fischer, 1932-35
Mass No. 7, "O Westron Wynde"				Faith Press, 1936
Mass of SS. Philip and James, No.8				Faith Press, 1939
Magnificat and Nunc Dimittis in D				H. W. Gray & Co., 1948
Missa Sancti Michaelis, No. 9				H. W. Gray & Co., 1947
Missa Brevis, No. 10				H. W. Gray & Co., 1948
Mass of St. Peter (Latin words, unison)				Cary, 1927
Mass of St. Teresa (Latin words, unison)				F. Harris, 1930
Mass of St. Hugh		*S.S.A. and organ*		Faith Press, 1935
Sanctus, Benedictus and Agnes Dei		*S.S.A. and organ*		C. Vincent, 1901
Arrangements of two Magnificat and Nunc Dimittis (8 and 1)				H.W. Gray & Co.
Arrangements of Mass John Merbecke				Oxford U.P.

Motets (mostly unaccompanied S.A.T.B.):

An Apostrophe to the Heavenly Hosts	*double and semi-chorus*	F. Harris, 1921
The Dead	*double chorus*	F. Harris, 1917
O Trinity, Most Blessed Light		Novello, 1925
The Reproaches		Novello, 1912

COMPOSITIONS

TITLE	DATE	TYPE	TIME (MIN.)	PUBLISHER
Six Motets (Hail Gladdening Light; O How Sweet; O How Glorious; Very Bread; O Sacred Feast; Let Us Worship)				F. Harris, 1924
Liturgical Motets (Preserve Us, O Lord; O King all Glorious; Fair in Face; I Beheld Her; Rise up My Love; O King of Glory; Lo, in the Time Appointed; O King, to Whom All Things Do Live; Behold, the Tabernacle of God; Hodie, Christus natus est; Who is She that Ascendeth)				Oxford U.P., 1928-37
Ave Verum Corpus (from "Brebeuf")				F. Harris, 1949
O Saving Victim (S.S.A.)				Faith Press, 1935
Look Down, O Lord				Faith Press, 1935
Five arrangements of motets				Flammer, 1938-39
Gloria Deo per immensa saecula (S.S.A.T.B.)				MS.

Anthems with organ accompaniment:

There were Shepherds				Novello, 1906
While all Things				Novello, 1907
Ave Verum (English and Latin words)				Novello, 1909
I Looked and Behold a White Cloud				Novello, 1907
O Strength and Stay				H. W. Gray & Co., 1918
O Perfect Love				H. W. Gray & Co., 1918
In the Name of Our God				H. W. Gray & Co., 1917
Before the Ending of the Day				Carl Fischer, 1937
Sing Alleluia Forth in Duteous Praise				F. Harris, 1940
Christ Hath a Garden Walled Around				F. Harris, 1940
Six Hymn-anthems				Concordia, 1950
Sing We Triumphant Songs of Praise				H. W. Gray & Co., 1951

Other unaccompanied choral works:

Come Shepherd Swains	*S.A.T.B.*			Novello, 1907.
My Little Pretty One	*S.A.T.B.*			Novello, 1907
We Must Not Part	*S.A.T.B.*			Novello, 1907
Gently Touch the Warbling Lyre	*S.A.T.B.*			Novello, 1908
To Chloe	*S.A.T.B.*			Novello, 1909
Had I a Cave	*S.A.T.B.*			Novello, 1909.
In Youth is Pleasure	*S.A.T.B.*			Novello, 1930
Sweet Echo	*S.A.T.B.*			Oxford U.P., 1931
Fain Would I Change That Note	*S.A.T.B.*			Stainer & Bell, 1911

COMPOSITIONS

TITLE	DATE	TYPE	TIME (MIN.)	PUBLISHER
Come, O Come My Life's Delight		S.S.A.T.B.		Stainer & Bell, 1911
The Three Kings		S.S.A.T.B.B.		Oxford U.P., 1928
A Clear Midnight		double chorus		Oxford U.P., 1930
Eternity		S.S.A.T.B.		Oxford U.P., 1931
Border Ballad		T.T.B.B.		Oxford U.P., 1931
Shule Agra		T.T.B.B. and solo		Oxford U.P., 1929
Sir Eglamore		T.T.B.B. and solo		Oxford U.P., 1929
Sigh No More, Ladies		S.S.A.A.		F. Harris, 1930

Secular choral works (accompanied):

Angel-spirits of Sleep		S.S.A.		Oxford U.P., 1927
Spring		S.A.		Oxford U.P., 1928
To Violets		S.S.A.		F. Harris 1931
When Belinda Plays		S.A.		F. Harris, 1931
Clown's Song		S.A.		F. Harris, 1931
Arrangements for male and mixed choir with piano accompaniment				Oxford U.P.
Arrangements of five French-Canadian songs		S.S.A.		F. Harris, 1937
On May Morning		S.S.A.		BMI Canada, 1950

Songs:

Dedication (Meredith)	Cary
Absence (Meredith)	Cary
Summer Night (Meredith)	Cary
Two Songs: O Mistress Mine; To Electra (R. Herrick)	Cary
At Dawn (E. W. Wilcox)	
To Blossoms (R. Herrick)	
Three Songs: Dimly Sinks the Summer Evening; Night Lies on the Silent Highways; O Death, Thou Art the Cooling Night	Cary
Cavalier Song	Novello
The Tourney	Cary
12 songs for medium voice (2 volumes)	F. Harris, 1925, 26
A Song of Canada	F. Harris, 1930
To Music	MS.
Three Songs of Devotion	F. Harris, 1939
Passing By	F. Harris, 1936

Vocal arrangements:

Chansons Canadiennes, 2 volumes, 24 songs	F. Harris, 1929

COMPOSITIONS

TITLE	DATE	TYPE	TIME (MIN.)	PUBLISHER
Songs of the British Isles, 2 volumes, 35 songs				F. Harris, 1928
Deux Chansons Canadiennes (Alouette, A la claire fontaine)				F. Harris
Brigg Fair				F. Harris, 1935

Manuals:

Graded Piano Sight Reading Tests, 2 vol., with Sir Ernest MacMillan, F. Harris.
A Standard Course of Graded Studies, 7 vol., F. Harris.

Recording:

Piano Concerto (CBC-Canadian Album No. 1).

See:

Christopher Wood, *Healey Willan, Canadian Review of Music and Art,* 1945.

Wilson, Charles Mills

Music student and composer. Born in Toronto, May 8th, 1931.

Student at faculty of music, University of Toronto in preparation for career as high school teacher. Won second prize in CAPAC competition for composition for two years. Winner CAPAC scholarship in 1951.

Address: 42 Hillhurst Boulevard, Toronto, Ont.

Affiliation: CAPAC.

COMPOSITIONS

TITLE	DATE	TYPE	TIME (MIN.)	PUBLISHER
Tone Poem	1950	*orchestra*	12	MS.
Theme and Variations	1951	*orchestra*		MS.
Divertimento	1951	*clar and strgs*	12	MS.
String Quartet	1950	*string quartet*	6	MS.
When I Set Out for Lyonesse	1949	*vocal*	5	MS.
The Flute-player	1950	*vocal (Eng. hn, fl)*	5	MS.
Six Songs (R. L. Stevenson)	1951	*vocal*	10	MS.

Wolff, Dr. S. Drummond

Organist, choirmaster, lecturer and composer. Born in London, England, February 4th, 1916.

Was Kent Scholar at the Royal College of Music, London. Degrees: Mus.Bac. (London Univ.), Mus.Doc. (Toronto, 1949). Diplomas: F.R.C.O., A.R.C.M. Won *Limpus* prize (1st prize) of Royal College of Organists, London. Started musical career as boy chorister at Hereford Cathedral. Was music director and conductor of the Clapham Operatic and Orchestral Society, organist of St. Martin's-in-the-Fields, London, 1938-46. Came to Canada in 1946. In 1946 was appointed to organ and theory staff, Royal Conservatory, Toronto. In 1948 was appointed lecturer and instructor, faculty of music, University of Toronto. Organist and choirmaster, Metropolitan United Church, Toronto. Conductor of Toronto Orpheus Choir.

Address: 486 St. Clements Avenue, Toronto, Ont.

COMPOSITIONS

TITLE	DATE	TYPE	TIME (MIN.)	PUBLISHER
12 Anthems	1946	*choir and organ*		G. V. Thompson
Festival Fanfare	1950	*organ*	4½	BMI Canada
Greensleeves Fantasy	1948	*organ*	3½	G. V. Thompson
Parish Eucharist	1939	*choral (unison)*	6	Novello
Missa Populi	1943	*choral*	5	Faith Press

Organ arrangements and transcriptions published by Cramer (London), Oxford UniversityPress and Gordon V. Thompson.

Zvankin, Peter

Businessman and composer. Born in Kherson, Russia, August 15th, 1879.

Amateur musician. Played second clarinet in Russian Army Orchestra, 1903-06. Came to Canada in 1906. Took piano lessons from Grisha Grutch in Winnipeg, 1913. Now engaged in textile business. Started to compose at the age of 55. *Poem for Orchestra* has been performed by Winnipeg Symphony over CBC network in 1951.

Address: Ste 22 Collegiate Apts., Winnipeg, Man.

Affiliation: CAPAC.

COMPOSITIONS

TITLE	DATE	TYPE	TIME (MIN.)	PUBLISHER
Poem for Orchestra	1942-50	*orchestra*	10	MS.
While Walking	1946	*piano*	2	MS.
Our School (Yiddish— for children)	1948	*choir and piano*	1½	MS.
Congratulations (Hebrew— for children)	1949	*vocal duet*	2	MS.

Songs with piano accompaniment (all in manuscript):

For children: *London Bridge is Falling Down;* in Yiddish: *The Young Teacher; Books.*

Prayers: *Rest in the Lord; Lord of the World* (Hebrew).

Anthems: *A Nation's Glory, No. 1* (also with violin, cello and piano); *A Nation's Glory, No. 2; God Guard Thee Newfoundland.*

Dramatic: *O Captain, My Captain,* in Yiddish; *I am a Jew; The Golden Goblet; Without a Country; These Candles; Day of Atonement; Restoration of the Second Temple;* in Hebrew: *Hero of Mitol Chai; My Brother; The Guard;* in Yiddish and Hebrew: *Yiddishe Sorrows; Faith; Our Land.*

Recitative: *The Day and the Work.*

Lyrics: *I Can't Tell You; We'll Meet Again; We'll Go No More A-Roving; June Night; The Lifer; You and I; Hail, Pacific; Jerusalem Delivered;* in Yiddish: *Return; Sing, My Heart; The Magic Plate; The Eternal Spark; While Dancing;* in Yiddish or English: *A Promise.*

Marching Songs: *Young Canada; Victory Song; We Won't Surrender* (Hebrew); *To a New Land* (Yiddish)

Humourous: *A Little Box;* in Yiddish: *The Gold Rush; Here and There; Where Lies the Secret; Star of David; The Sabbath.*

CROSS-INDEX OF FOLK SONG ARRANGEMENTS AND LARGE-SCALE WORKS

(Based on the Biographical Section only)

BALLET

ADASKIN
ANHALT
ASSALY
BECKWITH
BENOIST
BRABANT
COULTHARD

FARNON
FLEMING, R.
FREEDMAN
GEORGE
KAUFMANN
KILBY
MACDONALD

MARGOLIAN
MORIN-LABRECQUE
PAPINEAU-COUTURE
PENTLAND
ROBITAILLE
SAUCIER

VERMANDERE
WAIZMAN
WEINZWEIG

CONCERTO

AGOSTINI, L.
ANGUS
ANHALT
ARCHER
BALES
BELLEAU
BEVAN
BLACKBURN
BOREK
BROTT
BUTLER
CHAMPAGNE
COLLINS

DAVIS
DELA
DE MARKY
DE RIDDER
FLEMING, G.
GEORGE
HEINS
HURST
JEHIN-PRUME
KALNINS
KANE
KAUFMANN
VON KUNITS

LAVALLÉE
LORD
MACDONALD
MACLEAN
MARGOLIAN
MATHIEU, A.
MATTON
MIRÓ
MORIN-LABRECQUE
MOSS
PAPINEAU-COUTURE
PENTLAND
PEPIN

PRICE P.
RENAUD
RINGUET
ROBITAILLE
ROGERS
SAVARIA
SOMERS
TURNER
VALLERAND
VOCELLE
WEINZWEIG
WILLAN

FOLK SONG

(Arrangements of Canadian folk songs)

ANDERSON
APPLEBAUM
BÉDARD
BELL, L.
BERNIER, A.
BLACKBURN
BOUCHARD
BRASSARD
BROWN
CAMPBELL
CARON-LEGRIS
CHAMPAGNE

COOPER
CUSSON
D'ARAGON
DAUNAIS
DESCARRIES
FORTIER
FREEDMAN
GAGNIER, J. J.
GINGRAS
GRATTON
HARMER
HONE

LALIBERTÉ
LAVOIE
MCCAULEY
MACMILLAN
MANSON
MIGNAULT
MORIN
O'BRIEN
O'HARA
PELLETIER, F.
PERRAULT
PICHÉ, E.

RENSHAW
ROY
SAVARIA
SMITH
SPENCER, H.
THOMPSON, J. A.
TREMBLAY, P. J. A.
VERMANDERE
WILLAN

FOLK SONG

(Rhapsodies etc. on Canadian folk song)

CABLE
CHAMPAGNE
DESCARRIES

FOGG
GRATTON
MANSON

PÂQUET, J.
POIRIER
VÉZINA

MASS

BÉDARD	CRÉPAULT	LAMOUREUX	PELLETIER, R. O.
BERNIER, C.	D'ARAGON	LEFEBVRE	PERREAULT
BERNIER, J. A.	DÉCARIE	LEMIEUX	PICHÉ, P.B.
BLACKBURN	DELA	MCCAUGHAN	RINGUET
BOIVIN	DESCARRIES	MACLEAN	ROFF
BRAUNEIS, JR.	DESSANE	MCNUTT	THOMPSON, J. A.
BUTLER	FLEMING, R.	MIGNAULT	TREMBLAY, P. J. A.
CADORET	FORTIER	MIRÓ	VERDICKT
CARON, J. E.	HARRISS	O'BRIEN	VERMANDERE .
CHATILLON	HEINS	PÂQUET, R.	VINETTE
CONTANT	HONE	PAQUIN, J.	WILLAN
COUTURE	LABELLE, C.	PELLETIER, F.	WOLFF

OPERA AND OPERETTA

ACKLAND, JEANNE	GINGRAS	LAVALLÉE-SMITH	QUESNEL
ALDOUS	GROSSMITH	LAVIGUEUR	RENAUD
BENOIST	HARDIMAN	LEMIEUX	RICE
BISSELL	HARRISS	LÉTOURNEAU	ROBITAILLE
BLACKBURN	HIGGIN	LUCAS	SPENCER, H.
BORRÉ	HONE	MCTAGGART	STONE
BROOME	HORNER	MIRÓ	TREMBLAY, P. J. A.
BROWN	KALNINS	MORIN-LABRECQUE	VÉZINA
COOPER	KAUFMANN	NORBURY	WILLAN
DELAQUERRIÈRE	LABELLE, J. B.	O'BRIEN	
FAITH	LALIBERTÉ	O'HARA	
FRAYN	LAPIERRE	PÂQUET, J.	
GEORGE	LAVALLÉE	PERRAULT	

ORATORIO

BETTS	CRÉPAULT	LAMOUREUX	PELLETIER, F.
BOUCHER	CUSSON	LAVALLÉE	TALBOT
BRANSCOMBE	HIGGIN	LEMIEUX	VERMANDERE
CONTANT	HORNER	LUCAS	
COUTURE	JEHIN-PRUME	MILETTE	

RADIO AND FILM

ACKLAND, JEANNE	FAITH	KANE	PENTLAND
AGOSTINI, G.	FARNON	KAUFMANN	RATHBURN
AGOSTINI, L.	FLEMING, G.	LAPP	RIDOUT
APPLEBAUM	FLEMING, R.	LE SIEUR	SURDIN
BERTRAND	FOGG	MCCAULEY	WAIZMAN
BLACKBURN	GAGNIER, J. J.	MCIVER	WALTER
CABLE	GRATTON	MORAWETZ	WEINZWEIG
CHOTEM	HENRY	MORLEY	
DAVIS	JODOIN	NIMMONS	

SYMPHONY

ADASKIN	FARNON	LAVALLÉE	QUESNEL (?)
ARCHER	FLEMING, G.	LEFEBVRE	RENSHAW
BARCLAY	FOGG	LORD	RIDOUT
BERNIER, C.	GAYFER	LUCAS	ROBITAILLE
BLACKBURN	GEORGE	MCCAUGHAN	TALBOT
BORRÉ	GROSSMITH	MANSON	VALLERAND
BROTT	HANSON	MIRÓ	WALTER
BUTLER	JOHNSTON	NIERMEIER	WEINZWEIG
CARON, J. E.	JONES	PAPINEAU-COUTURE	WILLAN
CHAMPAGNE	KALNINS	PENTLAND	
COULTHARD	KAUFMANN	PEPIN	
DE RIDDER	KRUSPE	PRICE, P.	

SOME COMPOSITIONS INSPIRED BY CANADA

By non-Canadians:

BRITTEN, Benjamin, *Canadian Carnival*, Op. 19, for orchestra (Boosey & Hawkes)

EIGER, Walter, *Overture on Canadian Folk Tunes*, for orchestra (Southern Music)

GIGOUT, Eugène, *Rhapsodie sur des airs canadiens*, for organ (Durand, before 1898)

GILSON, Paul, *Fantasie canadienne*, for orchestra (Breitkopf, before 1898)

JACQUET, H. Maurice, *Suite canadienne*, for piano and violin or 'cello (C. C. Birchard, 1927)

MACKENZIE, Sir Alexander, *Canadian Rhapsody*, Op. 67, for orchestra (Breitkopf, c. 1905)

SULLIVAN, Sir Arthur, *Dominion Hymn*, (words: Marquis de Lorne), 1880

WYATT PARGETER, Maud, *String Quartet on Canadian Themes*, (O. Ditson, 1929)

By Canadians (not listed in the Biographical Section):

BOWLES, George, *Orchestral Suite on Canadian Themes*

BOWLES, George, *String Quartet on Canadian Airs* (Beatty Prize 1928)

GRANT-SCHAEFER, George Alfred, *Scènes canadiennes*, seven piano pieces

HOUDE, Charles, *Pot-pourri sur des airs canadiens*

LAURENDEAU, L. P., *Laurentian Echoes*, medley of Canadian airs for band or orchestra (C. Fischer)

LAURENDEAU, L. P., *The Shores of the St. Lawrence*, medley of Canadian airs for band (Cundy-Bettoney)

LLOYD, Arthur Cleland, *Suite canadienne* (Beatty Prize 1928)

MARTEL, Oscar, *Airs canadiens variés* for violin and piano (Gevaert)

There are some published patriotic songs by Canadians whose names do not appear in this catalogue. Some of these songs may be found in Toronto and McGill university song books.

A SUPPLEMENTARY LIST OF CANADIAN COMPOSERS

Where possible, the following particulars have been given: place of birth; year of birth and death; occupation; compositions; established residence.

ABRAHAMSEN, Dr. Julius, Norway, 1906; dentist; piano pieces; Toronto

ALBERT, Charles-Eugène, Province of Quebec, 1906; religious works

ALLAIRE, Uldéric, U.S., 1901; songs, marches (self-published); Victoriaville, P.Q.

ALLARD-DEMERS, Cécile, 1904-1949; songs; music teacher in Montreal

ANGER, Dr. Humphrey, England, 1862-1913; works published by Novello; Toronto

ARCHAMBAULT, J. D., Montreal, 1878; piano pieces, songs

AUSTEN, Thomas R., Saskatchewan, 1913; pianist; piano pieces

AVISON, John, Vancouver, 1915; pianist, conductor; radio music; Vancouver

BARFORD, Vernon, England, 1876; organist, conductor; songs and piano pieces (May Day Suite); music pioneer in Edmonton since 1900

BARIL, Jeanne (Soeur M. Louise-Andrée), Province of Quebec, 1913; music teacher; piano and choral works; Montreal

BARNES, Floyd, New York, 1926; orchestral and other works; Toronto

BARTMANOVICZ, Martin, Poland, 1898; farmer; chamber music; Manitoba

BEAUCHEMIN, Marie (Soeur Ste-Marie Cécile du Sacré-Coeur), Province of Quebec, 1892; music teacher; religious works; Montreal

BERRY, Margaret Mary Robinson, Alberta, 1918; piano, vocal, choral works; Calgary

BIRCH, J. Edgar, England, deceased; vocal works, dances (published); Ottawa

BIRON, Edouard, Quebec City, 1881; masses, motets; P.Q.

BLAIN DE ST-AUBIN, Emmanuel, France, 1833-1883; singer; songs, carols; Quebec

BOWLES, Ernest R., deceased; organist, anthems (published); Toronto

BOWLES, George, Quebec City; organist; suite and quartet on Canadian themes (1928); Winnipeg

CAREY, Dr. Bruce, Hamilton, 1876; choral conductor; choral works; U.S.

CHARBONNEAU, Jean, Montreal, 1912; singer; vocal works, Canadian folk songs

CHARLEBOIS, Père J. Antoine, Province of Quebec, 1853-1929; priest, musician; vocal works in MS.

CHUBB, Frederick, organist; published works; Victoria, B.C.

CLARKE, Phyllis Chapman, England; organist, teacher; various works; Calgary

COMPOSTEL, Jacques, Quebec City, 1904-1928; violinist; violin concertos

DAVELUY, Raymond, composer, organist; Prix d'Europe 1948; Montreal

DAVIS, Jean. No information obtained

DESAUTELS, Andrée, Montreal

DESJARDINS, Dr. L. Edouard, Province of Quebec, 1837-1919; physician, musician; Mass on Christmas Songs, published motets, Canadian folk songs; pseudonyms "Ancien Maitre de Chapelle", "Bon Vieux Temps"; Montreal

DONSON, William, choirmaster; Toronto

DORION, Lucien, Montreal, 1903; pianist; instrumental works; Montreal

FENWICK, Dr. Roy, Hamilton, 1889; Director of Music, Ontario Department of Education; choral works (published by Gordon V. Thompson); Toronto

FINN, (Caesar) George, deceased; string quartet, violin sonata etc.; Toronto

FISHER, Arthur E., deceased; works published by Novello; active in Toronto during 1890's

FOWLER, J. A., Montreal, 1845-1917; organist, some published church music; Montreal

GAGNON, Blanche, sacred pieces published by A. J. Boucher

GAUTHIER, Pierre, France, 1883; organist; sacred works, folk-song arrangements; Ottawa

GEROW, Russ, Ontario, 1904; radio background music; Toronto

GOLDBERG, Samuel, Toronto, 1924; songs, piano pieces, string quartet; Toronto

GOULD, Glenn, Toronto, 1932; pianist; piano works; Toronto

GRATON, Fernand, conductor and composer; Montreal

GREEN, Dorothy Haslam, Germany, 1887; music teacher; vocal works; Winnipeg

GUERRERO, Alberto, Chile, 1886; pianist; Tango for piano (F. Harris); Toronto

GUILLET, Joseph, Province of Quebec, 1887; organist; sacred vocal works: Montreal

GULBRANDSEN, Yvonne (Feuilletault Dion), Quebec, 1892; pianist, singer; songs; Montreal

GUTZEIT, Dr. W. H., deceased; physician, organist; published anthems; pseudonym "Bontemps"; Toronto

HAINS, S. B. (Whitey), songs; Moncton, N.B.

HAMBOURG, Boris, Russia, 1885; 'cellist; 'cello pieces and songs; Toronto

HAMPSHIRE, Cyril, choral conductor, director of music in Hamilton public schools; choral works published by Jarman Publications (*Patria, Yuletide Fantasy*); Hamilton

HARDY, Edmund, 1876; organist; piano pieces, songs; Toronto

HARRIS, Dr. C. L. M., deceased; published songs; active in Hamilton c. 1880-1915

HARRISON, Susie Frances, Toronto, 1859-1935; published songs, piano pieces and poetry; pseudonym "Seranus"; Toronto

HEATON, Leonard, published works (Western Music Co.); Winnipeg

HÉBERT, Georges, Province of Quebec, 1858-1931; organist; salon pieces

HORWOOD, Rev. Dr. Frederick, London, England, 1888; music teacher; various works; Toronto

HOUDE, Charles, Province of Quebec, 1861-1932; music teacher, instrumentalist; Montreal

HOULE, Charles Auguste, Montreal, 1899-1933; pianist, piano works; Montreal

HUGHES, A. E., salon pieces for piano, marches (Waterloo Music Co.); pseudonym Arthur Wellesley; active in Toronto c. 1910-1930

HUNTER, Basil, 1918; pianist; piano works; Vancouver

ILLSLEY, Dr. Percival, England, 1865-1924; organist; published anthems, songs, cantata *Ruth* (1896); Montreal

JORDAN, Dr. Henry K., Ontario, 1880-1949; choral conductor; songs, anthems; Brantford, Ont.

KEY, Harold Eustace, anthems, Canadian folk-song arrangements; Montreal

LABELLE, Gustave, Montreal, 1877-1929; 'cellist; 'cello and orchestral works; Montreal

LANDRY, Jean-Yves, composer and conductor; Trois Rivières, now in Paris

LANGLOIS, Ernest, Montreal, 1881-1924; pianist; mass, songs etc.; Montreal

LARIVIÈRE, Roméo C., Montreal, 1880; religious works, songs; P.Q.

LAURENDEAU, Louis Philippe, marches published by Carl Fischer and other publishers

LEFEVBRE, Père Charles, Province of Quebec, 1864; published church music; Quebec, Montreal.

LEMON, Laura, deceased; piano works; songs; Guelph, Ont.

LEVASSEUR, Nazaire, Quebec City, 1848-1927; organist; songs, instrumental works; Quebec

LLOYD, Arthur Cleland, Vancouver, 1908; orchestral suite (Beatty Prize 1928)

LUPTON, Harold Joseph, South Wales, 1882; organist, sacred songs, carols; Winnipeg

LYONNAIS, Roch, Quebec City, c. 1845-1915; instrument builder; some published songs, dances, piano pieces; Quebec

MacCaul, Rev. Dr. John, Dublin, 1807-1886; president, University College, Toronto, musical amateur and impresario; published anthems; Toronto

Macklem, Francis, England, 1888; harp concerto, instrumental pieces; Toronto

McMullin, Robert Wesley, U.S., 1921; band leader, arranger; *Sketches from the Rocky Mountains*, film and radio music; Edmonton

Maillet, Raynaldo, U.S., 1878-1947; trumpeter; radio arranger, band works; Montreal

Martel, Oscar, Province of Quebec, 1848-1924; violinist; violin pieces; Chicago

Martin, Lucien, Montreal, 1908-1950; violinist; songs; Montreal

Metcalfe, Bruce, organist; choral and piano teaching pieces published; Ontario

Muir, Alexander, Scotland, 1834-1906; teacher; *The Maple Leaf Forever* (words and music, 1867), other patriotic songs; Toronto

Myers, Russ, arranger; radio music; Toronto

Oliver, John, orchestral pieces, incidental music; Edmonton

Paquin, Anna, Province of Quebec, 1878-1923; religious works; P.Q.

Paquin, Dr. Louisa (Rev. Soeur Marie-Valentine), Province of Quebec, 1865-1950; music teacher; church music; Montreal

Parr, Patricia, Toronto, 1937; pianist; piano pieces; Toronto

Paul, Damis, Province of Quebec, 1827-1913; organist; various pieces; Quebec, U.S.

Paul, Georges, Province of Quebec, 1845-1876; priest; incidental music to *Tarare*, songs, band works; P.Q.

Rose, Clayton Crawford, Saskatchewan, 1927; various short pieces

Sanders, Dr. Herbert, England, 1879, deceased; organist; anthems, songs, organ works; Ottawa

Saunders, Florence Ward, songs; Vancouver

Schuller, Auguste (Frère Raymondien), Alsace, 1882; many masses and other church works; P.Q.

Seaberg, Erik, Sweden, 1892; Scandinavian dances; Vancouver

Seitz, Ernest, Hamilton, Ont., 1892; pianist; *The World Is Waiting for the Sunrise*, *Laddie Boy* and other published songs and piano pieces; Toronto

Slater, David Dick, died 1942; music teacher; published many vocal and piano pieces; Toronto

Smith, Mary Barber, England, 1878; vocal and organ works; Edmonton

Smith, Norman, Winnipeg

Soeur Ste. Cécile des Anges, Province of Quebec, 1889; music teacher; sacred and secular songs; Montreal

Spivak, Elie, Ukraine, 1902; violinist; violin pieces; Toronto

Strathy, Dr. George W., Scotland, c. 1825-1890; professor of music, Trinity University, Toronto; composer; Toronto

Tanguy, Charles. No information obtained

Torrington, Dr. Frederick Herbert, England, 1837-1917; organist, conductor; choral and organ pieces (published); Montreal, Toronto

Tripp, J. D. A., music teacher; active c. 1910; Toronto, Vancouver

Trudel, J. J. Edmond, Quebec City, 1892; religious and other works; U.S.

Vachon, Séraphin, Quebec City, 1842-1875; violinist; many unpublished pieces; Montreal

Vadeboncoeur, L. L. M., Province of Quebec, 1831-1886; vocal and sacred works; Joliette, P.Q.

Viau, Albert. No information obtained

Ward, Lela Hoover, Ontario; piano teacher; teaching material for piano published; Guelph, Ont.

Warren, W. H., pieces and arrangements in *Literary Garlands*, 1839, 1846 and later. Active as music teacher in Montreal during 1840's

Weil, Max, U.S.; conductor; string pieces, songs; active in Halifax and Calgary between 1892 and 1914

Wells, Paul, U.S., 1888-1927; pianist; piano pieces; Toronto

WHEELDON, H. A., organ and vocal pieces published by Novello; active c. 1914

WHEELER, Charles E., published anthems, songs, piano pieces (Schirmer etc.); active c. 1914; London, Ont., Winnipeg

WHYTE, Ernest, 1858-1922; about 30 published, 100 unpublished songs; Ottawa

WILD, Eric., conductor; radio music; Winnipeg

WILLIAMS, Rhyddid, Wales, 1894; organist; choral works; Sault Ste Marie, Ont.

AMERICAN COMPOSERS BORN IN CANADA

References:　(a)　*The International Cyclopedia of Music and Musicians,* ed. Thompson.
　　　　　　(b)　Baker's *Biographical Dictionary of Musicians.*
　　　　　　(c)　Grove's *Dictionary of Music and Musicians, American Supplement.*
　　　　　　(d)　Reis, *Composers in America.*
　　　　　　(e)　The *ASCAP Biographical Dictionary.*
　　　　　　(f)　*Dictionnaire biographique des musiciens canadiens.*

BRANT, Henry Dreyfus	Montreal 1913-	a, b, d
DETT, Robert Nathaniel	Drummondville, Ont. 1882—U.S. 1943	a, b, c, d, e
DUMOUCHEL, Arthur	Rigaud, P.Q. 1841—U.S. 1919	f
FAIRCLOUGH, George Herbert	Hamilton 1869-	a, b
FINLAY, Lorraine Noel	Montreal 1899-	e
FONTAINE, L. J. Oscar	St. Hyacinthe, P.Q., 1878-	f
GRANT-SCHAEFER, George Alfred	Williamstown, Ont. 1872—U.S. 1939	a, b
JONES, Charles	Tamsworth, Ont. 1910-	d
LEMONT, Cedric	Fredericton, N.B. 1879-	a, b
MANNING, Edward Betts	Saint John, N.B. 1874—U.S. 1948	a, b
MAZURETTE, Salomon	Montreal 1848—U.S. 1910	f
McPHEE, Colin	Montreal 1901-	a, b, d
STRANG, Gerald	Claresholm, Alta. 1908-	a, d
TREMBLAY, George Amadée	Ottawa 1911-	d
WARREN, Samuel Prowse	Montreal 1841- U.S. 1915	a, b, c

For the following emigrants consult the Biographical Section: AMBROSE, BOURDON, BRANSCOMBE, LUCAS, McDERMID, O'HARA.

COMPOSERS WHO RESIDED IN CANADA TEMPORARILY

(Country and year of birth; residence in Canada; present residence)

BANCROFT, Hugh	England, 1904; to Canada 1929; Australia
BENJAMIN, ARTHUR	Australia, 1893; Canada 1939-46; England
CLARKE, Herbert L.	U.S., 1867; left Canada 1923; died in U.S., 1945
HARRISON, Dr. Francis L.	Ireland, 1905; to Canada 1930; U.S.
KEVAN, Dr. George A.	England, 1908; to Canada 1927; U.S.
NAYLOR, Bernard	England, 1907; to Canada 1936; England
PERRIN, Dr. Harry C.	England, 1865; Canada 1908-30; England
REYMES KING, Dr. John	England, 1910; to Canada 1935; U.S.
SVEINBJORNSSON, Sveinbjorn	Iceland, 1847; left Canada 1922; died in Denmark, 1927

SOME CANADIAN COMPOSERS OF POPULAR MUSIC

Note: Composers of popular music who also appear as composers of serious music in the Biographical Section are excluded here. The following list, which should not be regarded as complete, contains some writers who have specialized in popular songs and others who, primarily, have written background music or arrangements.

BARNHAM-KAPPEY, Cecil
BELKNAP, John
BURT, John
CAMPBELL, Wishart
CARTER, Wilf
CHAFFE, Chester
CHARTERS, Clarence
COOK, George
COULTER, Jim
CROGHAN, James
D'AMOUR, Rolland
DOBSON, John
ECKSTEIN, Bill
EDWARDS, Lloyd
EVIS, Dr. Fred
FORTIER, Marcel

GRAHAM, Maud
GRAHAM, Violet
GRANT, Freddie
GROVES, Edith
HALLMAN, Arthur
HAMILL, Mel
HARRIS, Norman
HARRISON, Franklin
HARVEY, Al
HARVEY, Bob
HEYWOOD, Earl
HILLIAM, Bentley
HUBBS, George Clifford
KENNEY, Mart
L'HERBIER, Robert
LOWE, Ruth

McDONALD, Violet
McNUTT, Albert
MORROW, Arthur
MUNRO, Bill
NAMARO, Jimmy
NORRIS, Ray
O'CONNOR, Billy
PATTON, Stan
SNIDER, Lou
SNOW, Clarence
VADEBONCOEUR, André
WELLS, Deane (deceased)
WILLIAMS, Ozzie
WRIGHT, Don

Emigrants to the United States:

BAKER, Don
BROOKS, Shelton
CLARK, Amy Ashmore
CLINT, H. D. Reilly
CRAWFORD, Robert M.
HOLDEN, Sidney
KRAMER, Alex Charles

LOCKHART, Gene
LOMBARDO, Carmen
LOMBARDO, Guy
OSBORNE, William
REID, Don
RICE, Gitz (deceased)
YUFFY, Bernard